Who Needs Theatre

ALSO BY ROBERT BRUSTEIN

Robert Brustein

Who Needs Theatre

Dramatic Opinions

90-1935

THE ATLANTIC MONTHLY PRESS   New York

Some of the essays in *Who Needs Theatre* were first published in the *New York Review of Books* and the *New Republic*, and appear here through the courtesy of those magazines.

"The Century of Directors (Great Directors at Work; Grotowski and His Laboratory)" originally appeared in the *New York Times* as "Whose Stage Is It, Anyway?" Copyright © The New York Times Company. Reprinted by permission.

FIRST PAPERBACK EDITION

Library of Congress Cataloging-in-Publication Data

Brustein, Robert Sanford, 1927– . Who needs theatre.

  1. Drama. 2. Theater. I. Title.
PN1623.B78   1987   809.2   87-1310
ISBN 0-87113-206-0 (hc)
    0-87113-365-2 (pb)

Published simultaneously in Canada
Printed in the United States of America

First printing

*This book is dedicated
to all my friends in the theatre,
but especially to Judy Feiffer,
Rob and Pam Orchard,
Jan and Jeremy Geidt,
and Shirley Wilber.*

Acknowledgments

My thanks for the editorial help of Leon Wieseltier, Ann Hulbert, and Jennifer Krause at the *New Republic*, where most of these articles and reviews were published; Robert Silvers at the *New York Review*; Mike Levitas at the *New York Times*; and Gary Fisketjon and Ed Sedarbaum at Atlantic Monthly Press.

Table of Contents

The Auteur Director: The Avant-Garde and the Classics

The Broadway Musical

Preface

The essays and reviews gathered in this book were all written between 1980 and 1986, the same years the American Repertory Theatre began its association with Harvard. Having moved from New Haven, severing a thirteen-year-old relationship with the Yale School of Drama, my professional company took up residence in Cambridge, and I started writing drama criticism again for the *New Republic*. Most of these pieces are views of current theatre from a post I had held off and on since 1959.

I held it now with a difference. I was an engaged practitioner myself and not just a bemused observer of the passing scene. At Yale, my writing was desultory and occasional, limited largely to general theatrical subjects. In Cambridge, I was again writing once every two weeks (later once every three weeks) about specific theatre events and theatre artists. It was inevitable that I would occasionally be reviewing people I had worked with, possibly even covering productions I had originated. This obviously left me vulnerable to charges of partiality. Remarkably, such charges were not often made, at least within my hearing, though I was once accused of being a publicist for the avant-garde.

Recognizing that I was no longer a disinterested critic, if indeed I ever could have laid claim to such an exalted title, I tried to identify for the reader those occasions when my objectivity might be questionable. I revealed my relationships to actors or directors; I invented strategies to justify reviews of plays or productions in which I had had some involvement; I went into contortions to do my job with at least a semblance of detachment. Most of the time, I tried not to write about the work of friends. This was not always possible and sometimes I risked the friendship. More often, I was able to describe the artistic virtues that attracted me in the first place.

But the fact is that I was not—am not—impartial about the theatre. I believe the same passions that inflamed my early criticism informed the conduct of my company and my choice of theatrical associates. I have always been an advocate for a particular kind of dramatic art, and I have been fortunate in having the opportunity to help formulate that kind in my own theatre. In a sense, my criticism is an outgrowth of my practice, just as I have tried to make my practice an extension of my passions and ideas.

The kind of theatre I advocate is clear, I hope, in this book. It is theatre allied to a collective ideal, associated with training, organic in nature, continuous in operation, permanent in status. It is theatre that connects itself to the soul, mind, emotions of the audience, to the public and private life of the polity. It is a theatre that has as its goal not profits and deals but artistic fulfillment, not the advancement of careers but of talent, to be the springboard not for opportunism but of spiritual development and growth. It is a theatre of danger, dreams, surprise, adventure, a theatre of the unexpected and the unknown.

I believe that this kind of theatre is abundant in our country at the present time. With the (let us hope) temporary exclusion of many gifted actors, who are still succumbing to the lures of movies and TV, our stage is bursting with talented people in playwriting, directing, and design. I have referred to them more than once in these pages as constituting a theatrical renaissance. Up till now, advanced playwriting and advanced directing have followed parallel lines. The next step is the intersection of these two activities, the unification of heretofore independent artists toward a common goal.

So I admit my partiality, and I offer it without apology, as I submit this collection less to have my opinions endorsed regarding a specific play or production than to articulate a single, overriding concept of the theatre. For the theatre is my obsession, my daemon. I write and practice in the hope it will become yours.

Introduction: Who Needs Theatre?

Anyone in my position, writing about the American theatre these days, must wonder who his readers are; I certainly do. Critics for the daily papers and mass circulation magazines can be confident that their prose is being scanned by people curious to learn what to do with a night off in New York, but most of you, I suspect, don't descend into the theatre district very often, and even if you did, it is doubtful that your hesitant jaunts into Nighttown would be influenced much by my curmudgeonly mutterings. The liberal, educated, book- and magazine-reading public, once the solid nuclear core of intelligent theatregoers, seems to have surrendered its theatrical constituency in recent years, turned off by the various vexations of playgoing—the high price of tickets, the stronger pulls of books, movies, and television, and, most significant of all in my opinion, the increasing insularity of American life. With the new technology, we are told, our living rooms will have the capacity to transform into multiple entertainment parlors, wired to bring films, literature, games, sports events, even our banking and shopping transactions onto a gigantic home screen.

With such amenities, why leave the house at all except to go to the office? And why exchange one's pleasant and habitual surroundings for an unfamiliar environment where the seats are uncomfortable, the streets unsafe, and the restaurant selected for an unconscionably early meal doesn't have a free table? People who spend most of their day feeling hassled simply don't care to be hassled at night, and the theatre has come to represent the supreme example of avoidable discomfort and annoyance.

Hence the continuing saga of the socko smasheroo runaway Broadway hit. When you consider the trash we are willing to tolerate on the home screen and even in the movies, you wonder about the kind of demands we make on the stage. We are persuaded to see a play only by critical superlatives that would have been embarrassing enough applied to *The Oresteia* and *King Lear;* nothing less than the most inflated vocabulary of praise can mobilize our reluctant limbs to navigate the treacherous corridors of the Great White Way. We relax into our neighborhood movie house; we gird our loins and grit our teeth to go to the theatre.

I am talking, of course, primarily about Broadway, though similar conditions obtain in the commercial theatre districts of other American cities. The last two decades have seen the revival of a favored old relationship between crime, illicit sex, and the stage: hookers, pimps, porno shops, beggars, muggers—Elizabethan whores and Restoration bravos *redivivus*—have lately been crowding the thoroughfares of entertainment, so that the survival of the theatre is now largely tied to urban development. In Boston, this blighted area is known as the Combat Zone—an apt description for a group of alleyways where one walks safely only when armed with brass knuckles and a billy club, and an evening on the town earns one battle ribbons and a week of R & R.

It is true that a number of recently built resident theatres have been designed for both comfort and safety, and it is therefore still possible to go to a play, in such cities as San Francisco, Washington, Minneapolis, and Los Angeles, without a four-month training course in the Special Forces. It is in such places that the habit of theatregoing on a regular, rather than casual, basis has managed to survive, and it is in such places that the theatre itself is likely to be perpetuated. It is easy to argue against the concept of season subscriptions, and say that prepaid tickets inspire feelings of obligation rather than enthusiasm. But one thing in their favor is institutional support, and all that suggests about the value of theatre as an art form rather than a transient succession of conversation pieces.

If the American theatre is afflicted by its physical conditions, it is pulverized by its costs. Apart from such frills as computerized lighting boards, stereo sound, and advanced projection equipment, the theatre has benefited little from the ingenious technology now associated with its rival sister entertainments. The theatre remains what the economists call "labor intensive," which is to say it still takes the same number of people to perform the same number of tasks as when Thespis first left the chorus for a solo turn. As a result, a ticket that costs five dollars for a first-run movie now costs as much as forty-five dollars for a play, a consideration that may influence your decision to stay home. For a time, some producers used to muse about substituting holograms for actors as a way of cutting production expenses, maintaining a company of high quality over a long period, and guaranteeing consistent performances. But as long as muscle and bone are required to flesh out a costume, it is improbable that theatre tickets will cost substantially less.

It is, however, the muscle and bone of the theatre that are most often proposed as its reason for being. Along with the opera, the symphony, and the dance, the stage is our last chance to see animate human beings engaged in a collective creative act. One might question how important this is to audiences conditioned to watching people perform on two-dimensional screens, and whether it is worth the effort. The theatre is associated with sweat; in movies and television, the sweat is wiped away between takes. Which medium has the advantage? And how much advantage is there in being witness to the accidents of the theatre—the torn costume, the inoperative prop, the door that fails to open, the late entrance, the bungled lighting cues or act breaks, the understudy performance substituted without warning as a result of the illness of the star? The very nature of the theatre seems to be accidental, for it is a perchance activity, hostage to the whims and caprices of nature.

But human beings are nature's hostages, too, and in that sense the theatre best reflects our own condition, our fortuitous fate. "We are not free," wrote Antonin Artaud, "and the sky can still fall on our heads. And the theatre has been created to teach us that first of all." Artaud does not bother with the question—so pressing in an age when Chicken Little has become our prophet—as to whether we *want* to be instructed on such disturbing matters. Still, I can't believe that many of us are very enchanted with the plastic, antiseptic state of our daily lives, or the way this is now being reflected in the frozen images and isolating metaphors of our cultural technology. If the theatre has a single advantage over film and television it is its immediacy. Dramatic events exist in a continuum of present time, while celluloid and videotape, no matter how convincing or realistic the photography, are imprisoned in the past (so is narrative fiction, which declares its past condition with the author's "he saids" and "she saids"). The media are not happening; they have already happened. We are witnesses of history, remote, aloof, involuntarily disengaged.

It is for this reason, perhaps, that we want to be alone or in small groups when watching television or films, while we prefer to be with lots of people when seeing a play. A crowded movie house annoys us; an empty theatre leaves us feeling conspicuous, visible. Theatregoing is a communal act, moviegoing a solitary one, which may explain why the stage has proved less hospitable to the lures of pornography, that most private of practices, when the films and cable television are providing it with dark corners and empty rooms. Theatregoing, in short, is one of a dwindling group of activities that bring Americans into communication with each other; it is, therefore, an enterprise that preserves some vestige of belief in the possibilities of society, if not of communion. It may also be one of the last remaining shreds of evidence that we are a people, and not just an isolated mass of frightened fantasists, barricaded in our homes, seeking safety from a sinister and threatening external world.

To my question, "Who needs theatre?", then, I would reply, we all do—not for its superior aesthetic qualities, which it reveals so rarely, certainly not for its comfort or convenience, not even for its capacity to move forward in space and time in a culture of canned images, but because it represents social history in the making, both on the stage and in the audience. It signifies that community we have forsaken, the accidents and risks we would rather avoid, the sweat and gristle we prefer to disguise, the labor of humans working against odds. On the threshold of each new season no more promising than the last, the American theatre represents an act of confidence—banal and dangerous and inconvenient like life, and like life, still capable of inspiring hope.

Part I

Predecessors

STRINDBERG: NEW LIGHT ON A
DARK DRAMATIST

With the publication of two excellent books, Evert Sprinchorn's *Strindberg as Dramatist* and Harry G. Carlson's *Strindberg and the Poetry of Myth*, this tortured Swedish dramatist is at last becoming the subject of thoughtful, comprehensive inquiry. Encouraged by Strindberg himself, who called his work an exorcistic "poem of desperation," previous critics (myself included) have been more inclined to describe his fascinating pathology than to admire his art, as if the plays were important largely as chapters in a psychic biography. But if Strindberg is such an aberration, how do we explain his extensive impact on modern drama, which now exceeds even that of his archrival, Henrik Ibsen? He was the cherished literary father of Sean O'Casey and Eugene O'Neill. He has stamped his imprint on Tennessee Williams and Edward Albee. And he is commonly identified as crucial in the development of modern Expressionism and Symbolism, a seminal intellect who helped to nurture Artaud's theories of cruelty, Genet's extravagant fantasies, the surrealism of Cocteau, indeed the whole of postmodern experimental theatre.

7

Offering to explain why Strindberg, despite his acknowledged influence, has been misunderstood by criticism and neglected by the stage, Professor Sprinchorn cites both the dramatist's own deceptive self-image and his capacity to irritate his contemporaries. Sprinchorn, a leading authority on Scandinavian drama and one of Strindberg's best translators, offers to remove that wild-eyed portrait from Ibsen's wall ("I cannot write a line," Ibsen said, "without that madman staring at me with his mad eyes") and substitute a picture of a cantankerous but shrewd outsider who stubbornly resisted assimilation by the Swedish literary establishment, roasted his contemporaries in a series of eighty broadsides, and confounded them further by supporting a workers' strike after the conservative victory at the polls—thus managing to transform the "sedate Swedish cultural scene into a beerhouse brawl." (The Swedish Society retaliated by continually passing him over for the Nobel Prize, an honor also denied to Tolstoi, to whom Strindberg issued a public apology on behalf of all his benighted countrymen.)

Strindberg's combative nature was, of course, evident enough from his plays and memoirs, which throughout his career resulted in lawsuits, ostracism, even exile. But Sprinchorn also believes that Strindberg misrepresented his own methods, that far from being in the grip of his obsessions he was purposely experimenting with his life as he experimented with chemical matter and literary forms. Sprinchorn asserts, for example, that Strindberg deliberately inoculated himself with madness (through sleeplessness, alcohol, and drugs) in order to analyze his guilt, and that he consciously wrecked his three marriages for the express purpose of examining his reactions in extreme psychological states—this in preparation for his exploration of the war between the sexes. Sprinchorn's Strindberg seems like a character out of Pirandello—one who suffers and watches himself suffer, a self-conscious actor in a self-created drama, sacrificing himself and others in order to arrange the materials of his art.

I suspect that Sprinchorn is a little gulled by his subject's paranoid cunning, but one does not have to follow him this far to agree that Strindberg organized his work with considerably more forethought than has previously been acknowledged. Sprinchorn carefully extracts the philosophical and metaphysical references in Strindberg's plays, showing his indebtedness to nineteenth-century thought, particularly Swedenborg and Kierkegaard, his affinities with Jung, and his familiarity with the scientific method. If the breadth of his art has hitherto been minimized, it is because Strindberg preferred to emphasize his unconscious inspiration: "Everything comes so easily, half consciously, with just a little bit of planning," he said, adding that he was a "medium" through whom a mystery became manifest. It is more likely that, like his hero in *The Father*, who cited *The Odyssey*, the Bible, and Russian history to justify his doubts about paternity, Strindberg sought intellectual reinforcement for his paranoiac fears in an effort to master them through generalized references to literary sources.

Harry G. Carlson also testifies to Strindberg's vast reading and intellectual powers. His study concentrates entirely on Strindberg's mythopoesis in the conviction that virtually all of his work is indebted to biblical, Norse, Hindu, Buddhist, or Greek fables—particularly the myth of the Great Mother to which Strindberg was drawn for obvious psychological reasons. (His vacillating feelings toward maternal women also explains his fascination with the Hercules myth, and especially the story of Omphale, who unsexed Hercules by making him work at the distaff.) *Strindberg and the Poetry of Myth* is chiefly a scholarly source book, but together with Sprinchorn's research, it provides a valuable corrective to the popular image of a mad Romantic genius throwing lighted lamps at women or running through Paris pursued by witches determined to electrocute him. Despite their differing emphases and approaches, both scholars manage to find thick layers of thought even in Strindberg's most illogical plays, placing him in the tradition of Goethe and Dante (not to mention Eliot, Yeats, and Joyce) in the way he uses mythic imagery to establish a system of correspondences.

I am convinced they are right, but the odd thing is how this highly self-conscious spiritualist continued throughout his life to call himself a Naturalist. Strindberg's "Naturalism," of course, is highly unconventional, as Zola immediately perceived after Strindberg sent him *The Father*. But although he was incapable of writing kitchen dramas about oppressed classes in the grip of their heredity and environment, Strindberg never lost his passion for unconditioned, unreflective nature. What possessed him rather was what he called "the great Naturalism which seeks out the points where the great battles are fought . . . which delights in the struggle between natural forces"—a Naturalism, in short, of wills and minds in conflict. By insisting on the importance of these elements, he further confirmed the incorporeal nature of his art, for Strindberg's view of nature had as much to do with the invisible as with the visible, as much to say about the spirit as the flesh. "So let there be Naturalism," he wrote, "let there be rebirth of the harmony between matter and spirit."

Strindberg's divided attitudes toward matter, which he usually equated with the flesh, made it impossible for him to contemplate life without transcendence, but he was at the same time too honest to take refuge from material reality in a realm of absolute spirit. Strindberg built his castles not in the air but out of earth and muck—the flowering castle in *A Dream Play* is planted in a manure heap. Sprinchorn sees Freudian overtones in this blossoming edifice "with its ability to grow and raise itself, with its crown that resembles a flower bud, with the forest of hollyhocks that surround it," calling it "the optical equivalent of Strindberg's perception that the sex and excremental systems are joined." This perception obsessed Strindberg throughout his life, as it did Swift, Shaw, Brecht, Yeats, and all the other excremental visionaries. One wonders how he made love to his three wives when he could confess puzzlement over "what the higher love for the beautiful soul of a woman has to do with the not very nice reproductive system." But if Strindberg was repelled by the thought of love's mansion being pitched in the place of excrement, he was also disgusted by virtually every physical function, including sweating, spitting, even the sound of people eating soup—these things he identified with what he called "the dirt of life." Just as those who have visited his home can testify to his pathological neatness, so many of his plays (particularly *The Ghost Sonata*) bespeak his revulsion over the most trifling household inconvenience—a wobbly table, a smoky fireplace, even ink-stained fingers. Few in history have equaled his passion for domestic order, perhaps excepting Joan Crawford (who might have made a compatible mate).

It was inevitable that Strindberg would begin to seek solace in Eastern religions with their promise of release from the corruptible material world in Nirvana and other transcendent states. The purifying fire at the end of *A Dream Play* represents not just Death, but a left-luggage station for all earthly baggage; there the daughter of Indra deposits her shoes after having experienced the shame of being human. Strindberg's shame over being human made him a natural candidate for religious solutions. Significantly, in at least two of his plays—*Crimes and Crimes* and *To Damascus*—Strindberg's suffering characters find themselves at the door of the Church; more significantly, neither of them enter. For no matter how much he hates the flesh, Strindberg's castle remains embedded in the earth. This paradox supplies the basic tension of his work, even in a naturalistic play like *Miss Julie* where the characters' dreams concern climbing and falling and where an amorous boy can reach his childhood love only by squirming through a latrine.

He never, however, ceased in his efforts to transmute the physical into the spiritual, and one method was by experimenting with music in the theatre. Sprinchorn writes, "The young Strindberg would have been familiar with Schopenhauer's praise of music as the highest form of artistic expression, highest because it represents pure energy unadulterated by the phenomena of matter." This idea forms the basis for what is perhaps Sprinchorn's most original chapter—"Making Music"—where Strindberg's musical tastes are compared with those of his contemporaries, especially Ibsen, who is described as utterly indifferent to lyrical charms (not to mention flowers and children—Sprinchorn makes him sound like W. C. Fields), and who, in violation of stage custom, insisted that *Ghosts* be performed without overture or intermission music. This gave Strindberg further reason to fear and despite the Norwegian, and to try to surpass him. Following Nietzsche and Wagner, Strindberg made a conscious effort to recreate tragedy, in the manner of the Greeks, from the spirit of music.

Along with Nietzsche, however, Strindberg soon grew to despise Wagner, too, especially when he discovered that his music was not simply a reinforcement of the text, as he had once thought, but an ideological statement designed to exalt the German nation and celebrate paganism. Offended by the increasing complexity of Wagner's orchestration, Strindberg began to investigate more simplified modes that would dispense with floral harmony (Sprinchorn suggests he was anticipating Schoenberg here—in addition to being one of the first Action painters, Strindberg may have been an early atonalist). To Strindberg, Wagnerian opera was a contradiction. The text of the *Ring* cycle ridiculed ambition and conquest, while the score was "military music for the drill field."

In place of Wagner, Strindberg exalted Beethoven, with whose spirit and achievements he felt a strong affinity. At one point, Strindberg wrote:

I wanted to hear music, music of the greatest kind, music by that greatest of souls who suffered all his life—I wanted Beethoven, especially Beethoven, and I began to rouse to life in my inner ear the last movement of the "Moonlight Sonata," which has become for me the most sublime expression of mankind's yearning for liberation, of a sublimity beyond the reach of words.

This "sublimity beyond the reach of words" appealed to Strindberg because he had now become convinced that language was also an element of the dirt of life. "To put things into words is to degrade," he wrote, "to turn poetry into prose." Since true poetry could only be achieved through an alliance with music, he began to construct his plays on the pattern of symphonies *(A Dream Play)* and fugues *(To Damascus)*, while working rhythms and melodies into the web of the action.

Perhaps the most musical of Strindberg's works, however, as well as the one most heavily indebted to Beethoven, is *The Ghost Sonata*, whose very title comes from one of Beethoven's chamber pieces, and whose three scenes repeat the patterns of musical movements—allegro, largo, and andante—in classical sonata form. In constructing this play, Strindberg creates an unprecedented theatrical synaesthesia of visual and aural elements, transforming backgrounds into foregrounds, expositing, developing, and recapitulating themes from one episode to another, and gradually eliminating characters until only one is left at the end. *The Ghost Sonata* is the best in a series of "opuses" designed to revolutionize the theatre with a new sense of intimacy, simplicity, and affinity with other art forms, to which Strindberg gave a generic name also borrowed from music—Chamber Plays.

Considering the painstaking, original way in which Strindberg is now discovered to have created his drama, it is not surprising that large claims are being made for him that would have seemed excessive just a few years ago. Professor Sprinchorn argues passionately on behalf of a total reconsideration of Strindberg, asking that he be regarded not just as an influential literary predecessor but as one of the greatest innovators of modern times. Sprinchorn sees significance in the fact that Strindberg wrote *The Ghost Sonata* in the same year (1907) that Picasso painted *Les Demoiselles d'Avignon*, that Schoenberg wrote his Second String Quartet, and that Einstein conceived the happy thought that inspired his theory of relativity, for he believes that Strindberg's liberation of drama "from its long enslavement to character and motivation" is of equal weight with those achievements. Citing Einstein's observation that the "body and soul were not two different things but rather two different ways of perceiving the same thing," Sprinchorn proclaims Strindberg the first writer of the Einstein age in the sense that he was the first to see "the disintegration of the atom and the dissolution of the ego as parallel events auguring a new concept of the cosmos."

Strindberg would have enjoyed being included in such distinguished company, especially since he took his own scientific work so seriously (he valued his chemical experiments above his plays and professed to find more satisfaction in the publication of one of his scientific treatises than in the Berlin production of *Crimes and Crimes*). But even though Strindberg's experiments in alchemy and occultism were pretty harebrained, it is still possible to agree that science has finally caught up with his conviction regarding the forces behind life, not to mention his concept of continual change: "Everything is in flux, everything changes," he wrote toward the end of his life (after having changed his apartment in Stockholm alone at least twenty-two times). "How can one believe in the established order when nothing is established?" With the failure of materialistic science, as implicitly conceded in Heisenberg's indeterminacy theory, the kind of literature based on positivism and causality now seems quaint and archaic, while Strindberg's eccentric fantasies look like a relatively realistic way of describing the world.

"I don't hold any opinions," Strindberg wrote. "My views are impromptus. Life would be pretty monotonous if one thought and said the same things all the time. We've got to keep it new and fresh. One's whole life, after all, is a poem, and it is much more pleasant to float over the swamp than to stick one's feet in it to feel for solid ground where there isn't any." Elsewhere he said:

Do you know what makes life bearable to me? It is that every now and then I convince myself that life is only half real, a bad dream inflicted on us as a punishment, and that at the moment of death we awaken to the true reality, becoming aware that the other was only a dream. . . . That is redemption, salvation.

It is a perception he shares with Calderón in *Life Is a Dream* and with Shakespeare in *The Tempest*, not to mention a large number of Eastern and Western philosophers; but he held it with the passionate conviction of one who longs to escape his body, for whom death is the only true awakening. Suffering from inoperable cancer of the stomach, he wrote to his daughter, "Don't grieve for the old man for he only wants to go," and, dying, told his nurse, "Don't bother about me. I no longer exist."

When Yeats later came to Sweden to receive his Nobel Prize, he learned that, at least in the eyes of the literary establishment, Strindberg still did not exist. Although a few considered him the Shakespeare of Sweden, Strindberg had never been forgiven by the Swedish Academy for "his quarrels with his friends and his book about his first wife." Literary feuds die hard, this one harder than most, and Strindberg's reputation abroad had never been enough to compensate for his dismissal at home. With the publication of Sprinchorn and Carlson's books, however, Strindberg is at last beginning to exist—not for his influence on others but by virtue of his own achievements, not as a biographical curiosity but in recognition of his own unique gifts.

THE TWO AMERICAS OF BERTOLT BRECHT

Bertolt Brecht experienced at least two different Americas in his lifetime—the one provided him with images, the other fired his rage. As a young man in Berlin, writing his early poems and plays, Brecht used America as the chief stimulant of his urban imagination—a dream country, a phantom nation, a generous supply house of metaphors for a poetry of the city that, in savagery and terseness, remains virtually unequaled in the twentieth century. After the Nazis acknowledged the power of his poetry by forcing him to leave Germany in 1933, Brecht spent fourteen years in exile, six of them (1941 to 1947) in the America that had so intrigued him in his youth. His sojourn effectively dispelled any remaining illusions about the country he had once called the "New Atlantis."

Brecht's mythic America, featured in such works as *In the Jungle of Cities*, *Mahagonny*, *Arturo Ui*, and *The Rise and Fall of the City of Mahagonny*, was formed out of movies, novels, pulp fiction, news stories. It was a land of steel and concrete, of primitive emotions and primal innocence, embodying what Brecht called "the hostility of the big city, its malicious, stony consistency, its Babylonian confusion of language." To Brecht, America meant stockyards, Wall Street, Chicago gangsters, New Orleans jazz, Charlie Chaplin, boxing matches, hurricanes and typhoons. It had two kinds of landscape: Nature (the savannahs and prairies where one lives in lonely freedom) and the City (*Der Asphaltstadt* where one is mauled and lacerated by economic necessity), In *In the Jungle of Cities*, life is depicted as a wrestling match, where the motives are hidden, the stakes high, and the outcome fatal; the play is the perfect embodiment of Brecht's perception of America as a naked arena of social Darwinism. Before Brecht's conversion to Marxism in the late twenties, he was able to contemplate this concrete jungle with equanimity, even with a certain feverish excitement; the pulsing quality of those inflamed early plays owes much to his aloof and amoral yet self-hypnotized demeanor.

For Brecht, the American city was sometimes a disguised Berlin, but he had a genuine crush on the United States in his youth. "How this Germany bores me . . . ," he wrote in 1920. "There remains: America." In a poem of the same time, he described Germany as "a carrion land, anxiety hole" (*Aasland, Kummernisloch*), but, he added, "in the youth that you haven't corrupted awakes America!" Brecht's convictions about American incorruptibility were about as sound as his sense of American geography—in one play, Chicago is a port to the South Seas; in another, it is fourteen days' travel from Lake Michigan. But one suspects the confusions were deliberate. As James Joyce remarked about Shakespeare (another writer with a wayward grasp of geography), "A man of genius makes no mistakes—his errors are volitional and are the portals of discovery." In a book entitled *Brecht's America*, Patty Lee Parmalee examines the origins of Brecht's early fantasies about Americans—"this extraordinary unbiassed people," as he called us, "totally unspoiled by history"—by tracing his reading of such social novelists as Upton Sinclair, Jack London, Frank Norris, and Sherwood Anderson, not to mention the more exotic literature about America written by foreigners. This is useful—but what really attracted Brecht to America was not its literature; it was its haunted, unknown quality. As an undiscovered country, America had the capacity to stimulate the unconscious side of his art, to make the familiar strange.

It was historically inevitable that reality would retaliate by confronting Brecht with the *echt* America. Brecht had already changed his mind about our country, Ms. Parmalee tells us, when he began investigating Marxist politics, a study he undertook, according to legend, because he couldn't understand the complexities of the Chicago wheat exchange. When the stock market crashed in 1929, Brecht showed the dismay of a disenchanted lover. "What a bankruptcy! How great a fame has departed," he wrote in a poem significantly entitled "Late Lamented Fame of the Giant City of New York." The crash not only confirmed Brecht in his Marxism, it destroyed his belief that America was a source of any genuine strength. People were freezing and starving in the streets of Berlin as a result of an economic disaster thousands of miles away on Wall Street. Brecht's disillusionment resolved him to write a play, *St. Joan of the Stockyards*, which would be not only located in America, but actually *about* America— where he would look at the brutality, injustice, and exploitation of our country from a political-economic perspective. The archetypal American would now be named J. Piermont Mauler, not Shlink or Garga or Joe Fleischhacker; the asphalt American cities (in *Seven Deadly Sins*) would be exclusively identified with the struggle for money; and sardonic hosannas would be sung (in *Happy End*) to the Fords and Rockefellers.

Having lost his mythic America, Brecht was doomed to do penance in reality. The period of this American exile constitutes the subject of James K. Lyon's fascinating study, *Brecht in America*. Ms. Parmalee's book is a meandering, disjointed examination of the influences on Brecht's early views and the evolution of his Marxism that never seems to rise above the level of a senior research paper. Mr. Lyon's, on the other hand, is an impressively researched, cleanly written discourse on six important years in Brecht's life—his friends, his colleagues, his travels, his efforts to make a living in Hollywood, his failures on Broadway, and ultimately, his appearance before the House Un-American Activities Committee the day before his permanent departure for East Germany.

Although Brecht had once characterized Hollywood as "Tahiti in metropolitan form," his stay in this "mortuary of the easygoing" was far from pleasant. His early encounters here remind one of Charlie Chaplin in *The Immigrant*, an optimistic steerage passenger sailing into the port of New York who looks hopefully at the Statue of Liberty— then, having been roughly jostled by the ship's officers, throws it a second, more doubtful glance. As soon as Brecht arrived here from Europe, following eight years in Denmark and Finland, he was under suspicion as an enemy alien, made to register and forced to observe a curfew. Mr. Lyon, who has examined Brecht's FBI file (it runs to more than a thousand pages), tells us that the playwright was under surveillance from the moment of arrival, and that his phone was bugged for almost the entire period of his stay (Brecht's wife used to read Polish recipes over the phone to confuse the eavesdroppers and once invited his FBI tail into the house for a bite to eat). As for his efforts to support himself, these were pitifully unsuccessful. For Brecht, Hollywood was a marketplace "where lies are bought," but he was not effective in marketing his own. He was perfectly willing to sell out, but nobody was buying—at least in the beginning. Brecht had few qualms about exploiting his European friends—Peter Lorre, Oscar Homolka, Lion Feuchtwanger, and Erwin Piscator among them—but his work in Hollywood was a record of disappointment and piecemeal achievement, with the significant exception of his contribution to *Hangmen Also Die*, for which he failed to receive credit on the screenplay.

He was even less successful in impressing himself on the New York theatre. *The Threepenny Opera* had been produced on Broadway in 1933, closing after twelve performances, and the Theatre Union had produced *The Mother* in 1935—a production Brecht saw and hated. But until *Galileo* was performed in 1947, Brecht did not enjoy a major New York production of one of his plays. According to Mr. Lyon, he had set his mind on conquering Broadway, though he scorned it as "a branch of the world narcotics trade run by actors." But although he made some contribution to the Elizabeth Bergner *Duchess of Malfi* (it was Brecht's odd idea to have the black actor, Canada Lee, play Bosola in whiteface), and supervised the mangling of his *Private Life of the Master Race* by a group of German-accented actors, the greatest living dramatist of the time would have to wait at least two decades before his genius was acknowledged on the American stage.

Lyon attributes this to a combination of bad luck and bad temper; he provides more evidence of the latter. His book offers hair-raising documentation of Brecht's extraordinary capacity to alienate, insult, and repel just about everybody in America who might have been some help to him—with the single exception of his wife, Helene Weigel, who tolerated his curt behavior and relentless womanizing with a forgiving stoicism (Brecht's friends rewarded her saintliness by calling her a "kitchen slave"). Others were less tolerant. After Brecht had screamed at the actors of the Theatre Union that their work was "shit" and "crap," a pianist threatened to break every bone in his body. Albert Maltz complained of his "contentious arrogance" and of the smell emanating from his unwashed body, while George Sklar perceived in him "the same ranting and shrieking associated with the German dictator." Having written *The Caucasian Chalk Circle* with Luise Rainer in mind, Brecht became so abusive to her that she withdrew from the production. W. H. Auden found him a remarkable writer but "a most unpleasant man," "an odious person" whose behavior was justification for the death sentence ("In fact," he added ruefully, "I can imagine doing it to him myself"). Thomas Mann, whom Brecht loathed for his bourgeois leanings, called him "very gifted, unfortunately." Even Eric Bentley, who was to champion Brecht tirelessly throughout the postwar years as his translator, director, and chief publicist, wrote that "he has neither good manners nor elementary decency. . . . He is like Dubedat in *The Doctor's Dilemma*—a scoundrel but an artist."

The one Brecht play that did succeed in getting produced professionally during his stay in America—his *Life of Galileo*—was almost entirely managed through the good offices of Charles Laughton. Laughton was the kind of actor Brecht enjoyed; he was Epic not only in his acting but in his girth (Brecht once wrote a poem about his belly). The actor responded with a three-and-a-half-year collaboration, first as translator, later as star, on one of Brecht's most ambitious works. Brecht's behavior during this production was not very impressive either. For one thing, he bungled the opportunity to have Orson Welles produce and direct, though this would probably have assured its success. Brecht was perfectly aware of Welles's gifts; he had much admired his production of *Around the World*, which he considered a confirmation of his own Epic Theatre theories. Like most American theatre people, Welles was bored by Brecht's theories but he was enchanted with *Galileo*, and very eager to work on it. Brecht lost Welles—and what Welles characterized as potentially "one of the

greatest productions in contemporary theatre"—because he was looking for a better financial deal. After unsuccessful efforts to enlist Mike
Todd and Elia Kazan, Brecht settled for T. Edward Hambleton as
producer and Joseph Losey as director, two of the most mild-
mannered men in the American theatre. Even with these gentle
collaborators, Brecht could not control his nature. He refused to let
Hambleton have world rights to the play ("I've held out against
Hitler," he yelled at him, "and I'm not going to give in to you") and
abused Losey so much during rehearsals that he offered to resign from
the show.

Galileo was produced first in Hollywood and later (after Brecht had
left the country) in New York, delayed many times by Laughton's
crowded film schedule. Laughton, a timid man, was worried about
some of the political passages in the work, fearing that his association
with a subversive might jeopardize his application for American
citizenship. The production was also hampered by Laughton's mannerisms, particularly his nervous habit of playing with his genitals
whenever he was on the stage. (Brecht's wife, Helene Weigel—one of
the greatest actresses of the twentieth century reduced at this time to
working on costumes—momentarily solved the problem, with
Brecht's collusion, by sewing up the pockets of Laughton's pants.)
The critical response to the Hollywood production was pretty predictable. Some of the reviews were savage; others were obtuse. "Mr.
Brecht's corn is red," was the opinion of the critic for the *Los Angeles
Examiner*, while the recording angel of *Variety* announced that "the
overall impression is one of dullness" and that "the script" doesn't
"make the grade."

The "script" didn't make the "grade" when it was produced in New
York either. Mr. Lyon does not cover this opening, since by that time
Brecht had already left the United States—but I have a memory of
the *New York Times* comparing Brecht's masterpiece unfavorably with
Lamp at Midnight, another Galileo play of the time by Barry Stavis. It
was Stavis's play that entered the Samuel French catalogue, where it
was available for college performance while Brecht's was left to
languish in manuscript form for at least another fifteen years.

Brecht's greatest performance during his sojourn in the United
States was, by common consent, his appearance before the House
Un-American Activities Committee as one of the eleven "unfriendly"
Hollywood witnesses. Thanks to the FBI, the House investigators

had very precise information about Brecht's political activities and opinions. Nevertheless, two things saved him from the fate of the others: He had never joined the Communist party, either here or abroad, and he was an extremely sly human being. Determined to say or do nothing that might ruin his chances to leave the country safely, Brecht submitted to testimony before the committee for an hour in a manner Lyon characterizes as "a polite exercise in cunning and duplicity." He smoked cigars continually, under the impression that this would endear him to J. Parnell Thomas, the cigar-smoking committee chairman; he admitted to being "revolutionary" only in his desire to overthrow the Nazis; he characterized his frankly communist work *The Measures Taken* as "an old religious Japanese play" (cleverly confusing it with *The Yeasayer*); and generally persuaded everyone that he was a friendly and forthcoming witness. After hearing the committee praise him for his cooperativeness, he left the country forever, at the moment that his companions were being set up on contempt charges that would later land them in jail.

From the safety of East Berlin, Brecht wrote that the American investigators were better than the Nazis, since at least they had allowed him to smoke. That was about the only good thing he could find to say about his experience here. He believed that, for the most part, he had described America accurately in his plays: it was the most advanced form of capitalism and hence the most brutalized form of human existence. "No wonder," wrote Brecht, "that something ignoble, loathsome, undignified attends all associations between people and has been transferred to all objects, dwellings, tools, even the landscape itself." This was hardly a view of our country reflected in the Broadway of *Oklahoma* and *Carousel*, the Hollywood of *Journey for Margaret*, or the Madison Avenue of *Ozzie and Harriet*. But it would be articulated with increasing frequency in the sixties and seventies by Americans themselves, as the disillusionments associated with Vietnam began to stimulate perhaps the most ferocious critique of our social system in history. One suspects that the mordant, sardonic tone of this criticism owes a great deal to Brecht, as his style and attitudes gradually began to infiltrate American culture. The highly successful, long-running off-Broadway revival of *Threepenny Opera* in the fifties— the first to expose Brecht to a wide American audience—was performed in the style of *Pal Joey*. But it would not be long before Brecht's true spirit would begin to dominate the schedules of the resident companies, the directorial essays of the experimental the-atres, the satirical sketches of the cabarets, the syllabi of university drama courses, even the techniques of Broadway itself—first in Charles Laughton's Epic version of Shaw's *Major Barbara*, later in such musicals as *Cabaret* and *Evita*. Brecht helped to turn our Pepsodent smile into a Weimar sneer, altering our sense of ourselves and our society in a manner that has yet to be measured or chronicled. America's Brecht—I hope that fertile unexplored country will be the subject of Mr. Lyon's next book.

Yet, much as we owe to Brecht, he surely owes something to us. It is a paradox, considering how unhappy he was here, that Brecht did the most important writing of his last years during his American exile; in East Germany, he wrote no more original plays, limiting his theatre activity largely to adapting and directing. This new emphasis resulted in the development of a great theatre, the Berliner Ensemble, where Weigel, the "kitchen slave," would have the opportunity to show that she was a great world actress. But it was the Hollywood years that produced *Schweyk in the Second World War*, *The Good Woman of Setzuan*, *The Caucasian Chalk Circle*, and *Galileo*. Perhaps opposition was a stimulus to Brecht's dramatic instinct; perhaps a morbid discontent was the spark of his creative genius.

In few of the photographs included in Mr. Lyon's excellent book does Bertolt Brecht look happy. He sits squinting in his Hollywood Tahiti mortuary as if being tortured by the sun. Only in his New York photographs does he permit himself the trace of a smile—particularly in one picture, where we see him sitting on the roof of an apartment house. His head is thrown back, he is smoking a cigar, he looks totally relaxed against a background of concrete, smog-encircled skyscrapers. This is his element, the one aspect of American life that did not betray him, the *Asphaltstadt* that originally inspired his cold, his mean, his merciless art.

THE PRODIGAL CLIFFORD ODETS

Years before he died in 1963 at the age of fifty-seven, Clifford Odets had assumed a symbolic role of considerably more significance than his position as a writer. Calling himself "the foremost playwright manqué of all time," he allowed, perhaps even encouraged, a myth to evolve that identified him as an artist of great promise who had made a corrupt Faustian contract with the film industry. A television interview conducted in the year of his death shows him, his eyes bulging exophthalmically, his hands working nervously building a mountain of cigarette butts, as he tries to persuade the interviewer to regard him as a "technician" who turns out movie and TV work for money, and finds his fitful moral purpose, his rare creative satisfactions, in the theatre. Odets's career would seem to confirm his inglorious place in the moral melodrama of our cultural history; it tells a now-familiar tale of early auguries and failed achievement, of high expectations dashed by personal ambitions. He considered the Group Theatre, out of which he was born and in whose bosom he was nourished, one of the last embers of a fading American idealism; and like many of his Group colleagues, he helped extinguish those embers by abandoning the company for Hollywood.

In 1935, when Odets was barely twenty-nine, *Time* magazine called him, in an unfortunate phrase, the White Hope of the American theatre; five of his plays were running simultaneously in New York—among them *Waiting for Lefty*, *Till the Day I Die*, and *Awake and Sing*. A year later, he had gone west to work on *The General Died at Dawn*, where at a Hollywood party he met a movie star (Luise Rainer) whom he later married. For a few years, he continued to shuttle back to New York between screenplays to supervise (and support) productions of other plays with the Group. But to his increasingly hostile critics, he had become an artistic pariah and political hypocrite whose premature death was merely the corporeal extension of a prematurely dead talent. Before he died, the headlines on his notices already had the quality of obituaries: "White Hope Pales," "Odets Takes a Holiday," "Odets Where Is Thy Sting?"

One of the purposes of Margaret Brenman-Gibson in the first volume of her new biography (a second is expected shortly) is to show that the story of Odets as a Hollywood sellout is not a melodrama but a tragedy. *Clifford Odets: American Playwright* takes us up to the playwright's thirty-fourth year, right after the failure of *Night Music*; it is a meticulously detailed, prodigiously researched account of Odets's frailties and strengths—a heroic project, considering the current lack of interest in his work. One wonders how many people would be interested in wading through 748 closely printed pages of biographical material on a writer generally conceded to be of the second rank—his early notes and memorabilia, the brand of his typewriter, his mother's fondness for giblets, his numerous sexual conquests, his conscious and unconscious methods of attempting suicide. Dr. Brenman-Gibson's almost personal affection for Odets (she writes of his "haunting eyes" and "long, beautiful fingers") is unlikely to be shared by many of her readers, who may react to her continual probes into the hidden corners of his life the way Lenny Bruce recoiled from a middle-aged lady wearing a see-through dress—"only you don't *wanna*."

Conceding that Odets is rather unfashionable today, Dr. Brenman-Gibson nevertheless doesn't make much of an aesthetic case for him, preferring instead to deal "essentially with the underlying psychological conflicts and their resolutions." This decision accounts for the weakest element of her book—it is abubble with psychobabble. A practicing analyst herself, Dr. Brenman-Gibson calls her work a psychohistory—a treacherous genre that only her mentor, Erik Erikson, and his mentor, Freud, managed successfully, and then only with figures long dead. Dr. Brenman-Gibson's method illuminates Odets's neurosis at the risk of obscuring the plays and losing our attention. In a passage typical of many that stud the text and the notes, she describes the "sensual Hennie-Moe relationship" in *Awake and Sing* as

> representing Odets' "profane" fantasy about his father. When in the original *I Got the Blues* Hennie gives Moe up, resigning herself to a life with the frightened, ineffectual, and scorned Sam Feinschreiber, this expresses Odets' fear that if he were wholly to give himself up to his identity as a Writer, he must

renounce not only a wild sensuality but all passionate relationships. Such renunciation of the relationship to his fraudulent,
passionate, seductive, high-stepping father, however, means
that he would exist only half-alive like his weak, depressed,
withdrawn, tubercular mother.

Similarly, Hennie's abandonment of her baby suggests to the
author "Odets' chronic terror of abandonment and betrayal, plus his
lifelong search for a woman who would not betray him as he
consciously felt his mother had," while Moe's remark to Ralphie that
he wouldn't trade him for "two pitchers and an outfielder" she
interprets to be "Odets' fulfillment of his yearning for the love of his
baseball-fan father," for whom he had contracted a "fantasy of a
profane love affair." This psychocritic sometimes has her psychofoot
in her mouth.

The author is perfectly capable of lucid critical analysis (and
eloquent prose, as suggested by her moving opening chapter on
Odets's death); her clinical readings may be a tactical way to avoid it.
For a more literary, nonpsychologizing approach might well have
revealed why history has not been kind to Odets. If he helped to
create a time, he was eclipsed by the passing of that time; serious
audiences today find it hard to share the electrical thrill that flowed
through audiences at the opening of *Waiting for Lefty* or *Awake and
Sing*. Odets's highly charged urban characters and pungent, nervous,
colloquial, gritty dialogue can still evoke an age drenched in blues and
jazz; but the plays have something, too, of the quaintness of that age,
the same crackle we hear in the sound track of 1930s movies, the same
artifically pitched voices. Odets's sloganeering politics, congenial to
those who embraced him as a revolutionary playwright, are embarrassing today (they were embarrassing even to him—he joined the
Party out of a hatred of injustice and inequality, and similar abstrac-
tions, but left it after discovering he had been duped into an ill-fated
trip to Batista's Cuba). But his treatment of American materialism and
alienation—the obsessive theme of his later work and thought—was
also weakened by circumstance. Dr. Brenman-Gibson is short with a
Time magazine interviewer who, responding to Odets's remark that
"the American people don't know who they are or where they're
going," said: "Clifford Odets knows where he is going—to NBC as a

television writer." But Odets's contradictions made his social pronouncements unusually vulnerable.

Odets's critique of America was easy to dismiss because he was
himself so implicated in compromise and corruption. But the curious
thing is how Odets's own capacity for self-loathing—unsparing and
elegiac—sometimes exceeded that of his detractors. Dr. Brenman-
Gibson's clinical method may not vindicate Odets's writing, but it
does persuade us to respect Odets's suffering. She demonstrates the
awful personal effort it cost him to sustain his convictions, since they
were based on perceptions of his own failings. The author has chosen
for her epigraph Odets's remark "I will reveal America to itself by
revealing myself to myself." This she makes the basis not only for her
exhausting investigation of the playwright's emotional problems but
also for an excellent study of the social, cultural, and historical
conditions that produced him. If such an examination does not fully
rehabilitate Odets the man or writer, it nevertheless reveals that he
shared his failure with his society. The book's greatest value lies in
exposing direct links between his problematic career and the problematic qualities of our nation, as immediately reflected in the equally
problematic American theatre. It is the context that continues to
fascinate long after the reader has tired of the subject and his work.

Odets's story is inextricable from that of the Group Theatre, and in
telling it, Dr. Brenman-Gibson has succeeded in writing the best
history of this embattled company to be found outside of Harold
Clurman's *The Fervent Years*. Like Clurman, she provides abundant
evidence that this legendary art theatre, so justly celebrated in
cultural and theatrical histories, had a record of continual commercial
failure and financial emergency, of dismal treatment by the press and
rejection by the public. Aside from the odd aberrant success like *Men
in White*, only Odets's plays attracted any sustained attention to the
Group—and, remarkably, only *Awake and Sing* and *Golden Boy* could
be considered box office successes (*Waiting for Lefty* was produced at
another theatre). After that first glorious year, Odets shared with the
Group the repeated experience of short runs and bad notices, despite
the enormous amount of personal attention he had earlier received
from the media.

It was this attention that may have caused his ruin. Temporarily
lionized, eulogized, and glorified, Odets soon became a praise-addict,
a victim of what Clurman called "the desire for this-and-that." Odets,

Clurman added, "wanted to run with the hares and hunt with the hounds; he wanted to be the great revolutionary playwright of our day and the white-haired boy of Broadway. . . ." Running on this double track made him particularly vulnerable to the critics; he generally regarded them with the same ambivalence as a junkie regards his dealer. After the negative notices for *Paradise Lost*, he wrote to all the reviewers begging them to attend new rehearsals he had called in an "effort to work several of your critical statements into concrete theatre practice" (he tried this tack again later—unsuccessfully once more—after the failure of *Rocket to the Moon*). He cajoled his critics, solicited their advice, pleaded with them to keep him in the theatre, wheedled and whined, all the time feeling a profound contempt for their values. Writing to Bernard Shaw, he told him there is no "first-rate theatre critic in New York . . . one who writes from a constant point of view . . . who looks at writers on a long-term basis . . . who has in his work any continuity of ideas or approach to the theatre."

From Hollywood, he complained that "reviews are driving me out of the theatre." Every time he wrote a play, the critics condemned him for not having produced another masterpiece. "I'm *not* a genius," he moaned. "I can't write like a genius." At the same time, he was declaring that people of great gifts are inevitably stifled and strangled in America: "We live in a strange dry country. A strong heart is needed, iron nerves, to continue to be a serious writer here." He made plans to write a tragedy about "the way America treats its artists."

Odets had scented what he was later (in the title of one of his screenplays) to call the "sweet smell of success," and the odor hung in his nostrils like a sickly cologne. "America keeps you keenly conscious of success . . . ," he wrote. "Before you were free; you are a prisoner now." Odets's "America" was now less a geographical entity than a vast Gentile abstraction—an omnipotent provider that had offered a banquet to this hungry Jewish outsider before, like Prospero, making the table disappear. For one year, he had enjoyed both fame and respect, both money and admiration. Now he was obliged to choose between material needs and spiritual satisfactions, between Mammon and God, between Hollywood and the Group. Still greedy, still famished, he continued to hunger for both.

Bertolt Brecht had fewer illusions about his American reception: "Why should they pay," he asked, "for their own extinction?" But like so many radical-minded American theatre people, Odets was unable to apply his Marxist theories to his career expectations in a capitalist culture. He believed he could continue to attack materialism and captivate audiences, to speak of alienation and surround the Critics Circle. The failure of *Night Music* thus evoked in him the rage of a bewildered, disappointed lover: "So, friend, this is the American theatre, before, now and in the future. . . . How can it happen that this small handful of men can do such murderous mischief in a few hours?"

It is curious that Odets should still have been asking such questions. The power of the New York press had been bestowed on it by market needs he had been among the first to analyze, by a consumer demand he had been among the first to identify. His anguish reflected internal confusions that he shared with his company. The failure of Odets and the Group lay not so much in trying to maintain a collective identity in a competitive society. It was the result rather of trying to establish a permanent theatre within the structure of the commercial Broadway system. It remained for the percipient Harold Clurman to express this frankly: "The basic defect in our activity was that while we tried to maintain a true theatre policy artistically, we proceeded economically on a show business basis."

Odets, therefore, was not alone in his ambivalent attitude toward the commodity culture, just a little more extreme. His plays rejected, his money running short, he left New York for Hollywood in 1936 to join Franchot Tone, the Group's first defector. Odets, in turn, would soon be joined by every major member of the company: Stella Adler (who changed her name—and nose—to adapt to her new surroundings), Luther Adler, John Garfield, Bobby Lewis, Lee J. Cobb, J. Edward Bromberg, Elia Kazan, even Clurman himself for a time. Odets, like all his colleagues, always maintained his loyalty to the Group and continued to contribute money and plays until it dissolved. But these defections—along with internal quarrels, continual financial worries, defective leadership, ideological battles, and, worst of all, the consistent failure of society to recognize and support the importance of the work—puzzled the collective will, and eventually resulted in the dissolution of the theatre and the permanent Diaspora to Broadway and Hollywood.

For Odets, Hollywood provided not just a dependable source of income, but also a dependable source of indignation. He hated the fascist mentality of such magnates as Louis B. Mayer (who was soon cooperating with the Dies committee and trying to placate Hitler), and he loathed the voluntary servitude of the contract system. These feelings he shared with his new wife, Luise Rainer, one of the few stars with a distinguished theatre background (she had acted under Max Reinhardt); Miss Rainer's antagonism toward the film industry, in fact, may even have exceeded her husband's. Having twice earned the Academy Award—for *The Good Earth* and *The Great Ziegfeld*—she demanded the right to choose her own roles, and when this privilege was denied, she announced to Mayer her decision to walk out on Hollywood.

"Luise, we've made you," Mayer responded, "and we're going to kill you." Miss Rainer replied: "I was already a star on the stage before I came here. . . . Besides, God made me, not you." This rejoinder suggests some of the dignity and strength of will that originally attracted Odets. It also displays the element of "queenliness" that was eventually to help ruin their marriage. Luise, Odets complained, continually made him feel uncouth and vulgar; he found her tasteful delicacy a form of aggression, her faultfinding a way of absolving herself: "It's sugar, sugar, sugar . . . that's all you want." But Odets's behavior toward his wife was even more awful. He was insanely jealous of every man she met—including Einstein and Stieglitz—and he responded to her letter announcing that she was going to have a baby with a cable that read: "Dear Luise will wire you Monday because now I don't know what to say love Clifford." Not surprisingly, she immediately decided to have an abortion and file for divorce.

Dr. Brenman-Gibson is interesting on the subject of Odets's marriage and affairs; she is even better describing Odets's involuted relations with his father, "L. J.," a financial ne'er-do-well and moral bankrupt whose letters to "Big Boy" are as colorful as any dialogue his son produced. But her most valuable contribution, to my mind, is the way she manages to establish Odets's place in the pantheon of blighted American careers. Odets was not the first American writer to prove a poor caretaker of his talents. He was, however, among the most poignant regarding his wasted life and his compromised gifts, among the least forgiving regarding his own artistic trespasses, among the most knowledgeable regarding the forces contributing to his ruin. Today, when the values by which Odets measured his personal failure are considered either obsolete or futile—when our invincible system has absorbed most of the opposition and annihilated most of the alternatives—Odets's nostalgia for a pure life seems almost archaic. Even the seventeen-year-old heroine of Woody Allen's *Manhattan* is ruefully aware that "Everybody gets corrupted."

At the end of his life, dying of cancer of the bowel that had metastasized to his stomach, he was visited in the hospital by Marlon Brando, who, as a former member of the Actors Studio, could be considered a direct descendant of the Group and one of the heirs of its legacy. In his interview, Brando—who looked on Odets as the very incarnation of the thirties—reported that the dying man "was leaking from all parts of his body, his life running out in ugly fluids." Odets didn't seem frightened; in fact, he spent most of the time making bitter jokes. At one point, he looked at Brando and said, "Life is about shitting in a towel." He was referring to his own incontinence, but it was an odd thing to say to an actor who, like many of his contemporaries, was already giving a new dimension to the notion of prodigal waste.

THE VITALITY OF HAROLD CLURMAN

The American theatre has suffered many losses recently, but none so impoverishing as the death of Harold Clurman. A sound theatre critic and an inspiring stage director, Clurman will perhaps be best remembered as the prime begetter of the Group Theatre, which, flourishing in the 1930s, created the foundation for a whole new American stage tradition (Clurman chronicled its history in that splendid account of early triumph and eventual disappointment, *The Fervent Years*). Clurman, who began his theatre career as a reader with the Theatre Guild, provided the inspiration, the aesthetic, the purpose, and, above all, the dynamic for this revolutionary theatre enterprise. A voluble talker and energetic intellectual, he had the capacity to identify and attract like-minded theatre artists and, in a culture not particularly notable for its collective strengths, created the

conditions—for at least a decade—in which such intrinsically independent spirits as Stella and Luther Adler, Clifford Odets, Bobby
Lewis, John Garfield, Elia Kazan, and Franchot Tone could work and
develop together as a collaborative unit.

Clurman not only led the Group, he staged many of its productions. But like his artistic leadership, his production process was
largely a matter of exhortation and indoctrination. Some say he talked
plays onto the stage; others say he occasionally talked them off. But
his genius for speechifying was the real adhesive of his ensemble.
How this adhesive came unstuck is the true subject of *The Fervent
Years*, and constitutes its most melancholy commentary. Clurman
knew precisely where his company had succeeded; he also knew
where it had failed. He was aware that the Group had made a crucial
error in trying to work within the commercial system, since this
decision made its survival as dependent on creating hits as any
Broadway producer.

The real cause of the Group's demise, however, was not economic
but cultural: the defection of its now-successful members to Hollywood and Broadway. It was Clurman's ambiguous pleasure to watch
the insurrection he had started in the heart of the American theatre
become the basis for its reigning aesthetic, as Group actors and
writers joined the stage and movie Establishment, and another of its
members, Lee Strasberg, used its Stanislavsky-based techniques to
train stars for movies, TV, and the commercial stage (later starting a
chain of acting studios all over the country on the model of Arthur
Murray). "The Group's situation was an impossible one," he wrote
with melancholy candor. "We were carrying on a task that was almost
against nature! . . . My idealism did not preclude my seeing that in a
very real sense we were fools."

After the Group collapsed, Clurman saw the problem through a
wider social perspective: "For a group to live a healthy life and mature
to a full consummation of its potentiality, it must be sustained by
other groups—not only of moneyed men or civic support, but by
equally conscious groups in the press, in the audience, and generally
in large and comparatively stable elements of society. When this fails
to happen, regardless of its spirit or capacities, it will wither." No one
read eulogies or sang dirges over the corpse of the Group, partly
because it never officially announced its own death, but mostly
because few recognized at the time what had been lost. The dissolu-

tion of what was arguably the finest company of actors ever to be gathered together in America was, in fact, received with a certain glee by the "divisive forces of the New York theatre," as Clurman called them, "which through indifference, casualness, need for excitement, malice, and a miserable competitiveness dog the coherence and stability of all organic effort."

Clurman responded to the extinction of his theatre by becoming a Broadway director himself, staging not only American drama—*A Member of the Wedding* and *Incident at Vichy* were among his more notable achievements—but many European works as well. Despite a long-postponed plan to perform *Three Sisters* in a new version by Odets, the Group had concentrated entirely on new American plays. Now Clurman became the man responsible for bringing the plays of such French Boulevard writers as Anouilh and Giraudoux to the attention of New York theatregoers—a service for which a grateful French government awarded him the *Légion d'honneur*.

Clurman was a bit of a boulevardier himself. Conscientiously, he developed for himself the persona of a dashing, flamboyant regisseur on the order of Diaghilev, usually appearing in public with a black slouch hat, a silver-headed cane, and a stylish overcoat proudly adorned with his French ribbon. Short and somewhat stocky, with flat Russian features heightening shrewd, veiled eyes, Clurman was not a conventionally handsome man, but he gave an impression of such confidence about his own personal magnetism that he struck many women as irresistible. As drama critic for the *Nation*—a position he held for many years after serving briefly as theatre critic for the *New Republic*—he would sashay down the aisle of a theatre, usually with a striking young girl on his arm, greet a number of friends and admirers on the way, then take his seat with a great flourish and hold forth in a loud voice about the virtues of the actors he was about to see and the shortcomings of his colleagues in the aisles—one of whom he always characterized (a slap at this critic's copious output) as "the best typewriter in America."

Clurman never had much use for the American theatre reviewer, who, he wrote, "represents nothing definite [and] has no intellectual identity; his mind is a private affair, and his change of mind may be an accident. . . . Unlike other people, our reviewers are powerful because they believe in nothing." But when he became a critic himself, he displayed the capacity—not shared by many of us second-night bruisers—to speak his opinions without leaving blood on the floor. As a theatre man, he knew how easy it was to wound the people who made their living exposing themselves on the stage. And while he rarely lost his heart to actors, he never cut their hearts out either. His criticism was invariably gentle, mellow, and instructive—offered with a caress rather than carved with a scalpel. A bit of a slasher myself at the time, I sometimes thought that he was a little *too* gentle, that his friendships with people of the theatre were softening his judgments. Only later I learned that these were the qualities of his temperament, that only a genuinely kind man could have navigated so well the treacherous shoals of practice and perception. His kindness and generosity even extended to his own critics, myself included. Once, after making some ungracious remarks about his style in one of my articles, I sent him a copy of the book in which these were included. He responded by commending the work highly—goodnaturedly adding that the only thing he disagreed with was my harsh judgment of him.

By the time I had the good sense to invite Harold Clurman to teach at the Yale School of Drama, he was disqualified because of age from holding an academic post—a rueful example of shortsighted university retirement regulations. He did come up to New Haven—about once every other year—to lecture to our students, and invariably exhausted all of us with his limitless energy. Speaking without notes, without so much as a breath between sentences, he would launch into some tirade about the current state of the theatre, flailing his arms like a windmill, shouting at the top of his lungs, huffing and puffing like a human bellows. And he was no less passionate in the living room than in the lecture hall. Listening to him was tantamount to being trapped in a wind tunnel: You found yourself whipped about by gusts and blasts of ideas, passions, opinions, anecdotes, jokes, exhortations. Despite his prodigious learning and intellectual disposition, he held an idea of the theatre that was of the flesh, fleshly. "The stage is life, music, beautiful girls, legs, breasts," he would roar at us, "not talk or intellectualism or dried-up academics." Because of these opinions, Clurman struck some of our more demanding students as somewhat middlebrow, especially when he submitted as a "shocking avowal" his discovery that "*Waiting for Godot* is a more significant play than *The Diary of Anne Frank*." Nor were they impressed by his unapologetic devotion to the theatre "as a place of entertainment." But Clurman was simply trying to say that the stage was an affirmation of life. "Art alone does not create art," he wrote once; "our living experience is what matters most. I am hospitable to all forms of theatre which spring from a life-inspired and life-giving source."

Clurman himself was one of those life-inspiring and life-giving sources, but it was impossible not to worry about his health whenever he started to talk. Surely, no human arteries could endure such exertions, no human heart could take such strains. To see Clurman survive his own lectures was to have one's faith revived in the indestructibility of natural tissue, the invincibility of mortal flesh. When I heard he had died, I assumed he had pushed his energy too far, that Death had clapped him on the shoulder in the midst of a speech. But at seventy-eight his heart was still strong, his blood pressure still sound. He had died instead of overhospitality to life, from the multiplication of cancer cells within his body. To the end, he was the center of energy and inspiration. He had had a theatre on Forty-second Street named after him; he had recently completed a book on Ibsen and was in the middle of a book about O'Neill; he was still reviewing plays. I don't doubt he was also holding forth, and brilliantly, until the final moment.

Shrewd but kindly, penetrating and humane, Clurman had the same combination of warmheartedness and tough-mindedness as Chekhov—a playwright whose works he loved but never had the chance to stage. It is sad enough that the Group never produced *Uncle Vanya* or *The Cherry Orchid*—and puzzling also, since Stanislavsky and Chekhov were its patron saints. But by the time Clurman was ready to direct such works of art, he was working in a commercial theatre that had lost its nerve. Clurman criticized this theatre from within its walls. Beginning as a theatre revolutionary, he eventually became the mediator—both as critic and practitioner—between intelligent people and Broadway. The bridge was down for quite a few years before he died, but Clurman never ceased in his efforts to repair it. Without his generative presence, the commercial stage has lost an important spur to its intent, criticism has lost a major voice, and all of us who work in the theatre have lost a warm, ebullient friend.

LEE STRASBERG: PORTRAITS
OF THE MASTER

Lee Strasberg has always been the subject of considerable myth-making, but in the last decade, and particularly since his death in 1982, a number of writers have begun carving icons out of his bones—idolatrous or malevolent, depending on the observer's point of view. The latest addition to the Strasberg bibliographical industry is a new history of the Actors Studio—the institution with which he was identified for over thirty years—by Foster Hirsch, a Brooklyn College film professor. It joins a long list including Cindy Adams's celebrity biography *Lee Strasberg: The Imperfect Genius of the Actors Studio*, the Robert Hethmon–edited *Strasberg at the Actors Studio*, and, most recently, David Garfield's *The Actors Studio: A Player's Place*, not to mention innumerable books, articles, interviews, collections, and tape-recorded sessions with the Master. Predictably, Hirsch's book is called *A Method to Their Madness* (Robert Lewis's anti-Strasberg lectures in 1957 were collected under the title *Method—or Madness?*, while a 1979 *Times* article was called "Can the Method Survive the Madness?"—even unfriendly writers tend to cast themselves as Polonius to Strasberg's Hamlet).

Like the titles, the prefatory material of these books is often remarkably similar—first, an account of the Stanislavsky system, then a history of the Stanislavsky-oriented Group Theatre and the quarrels (especially with Stella Adler) over whether Stanislavsky would have approved Strasberg's use of affective memory and private moments, and finally the story of how the Group tradition was reawakened when three of its members (not including Strasberg, who joined later) formed the Actors Studio. Aside from Bobby Lewis's bitchy swipes at Strasberg in his recent memoir, *Slings and Arrows*, most of these works have been reverential portraits of an inspired if flawed teacher responsible for a naturalistic style associated with the most famous American actors of the postwar period.

Hirsch's book is not as well written or researched as Garfield's and covers much the same territory, but it carries the history of the Studio up to the leadership of Ellen Burstyn. Yet another rehearsal of the issues at this late stage would seem superfluous, especially when the institution was arguably moribund, or at the least sapped of its force and vitality, following the collapse of the ill-fated Actors Studio Theatre in 1965. Still, the subject continues to exercise its fascinations, since the conduct of Strasberg and the Studio has been the focus of controversies about the moral and aesthetic direction of the American theatre that are still being argued today.

I participated in these debates. As reviewer for the *New Republic*, I was a persistent critic of Strasberg and his Method, and later of the Actors Studio Theatre when it stumbled badly through some maladroit productions. I did not believe I was prematurely judging a budding theatre company, since Strasberg had been working with these actors in cloistered sessions for more than fifteen years. No, the performance of his long-promised practical theatre cast doubt on the theory behind it, reinforcing an impression that the celebrated Method was inadequate to anything other than naturalistic, neurasthenic, personalized roles. More depressing than the artistic failure, however, was a failure of vision. Unlike the Group Theatre which, despite its economic structure, was trying to create a serious permanent ensemble as an alternative to Broadway, the Actors Studio was merely another arm of the commercial system, supine before stars, dazzled by celebrity, riddled with ambition. In an article called "The Keynes of Times Square," I likened Strasberg's acting reforms to those of a prose stylist who raised the quality of advertising copy or an interior decorator of a crumbling structure whose foundations he did nothing to change. I felt these impressions confirmed when, at the height of his own fame, Strasberg founded a chain of lucrative acting schools offering classes in TV commercials, after which he virtually abandoned the Studio to act in movies.

Where both Hirsch and Garfield are interesting is in their behind-the-scenes investigations of how these apprehensions were shared by many Studio members, as well as by Strasberg's most severe critic, his son John. Virtually all of Strasberg's actors praise his capacity to free and expand their talents, but his behavior in relation to the Actors Studio Theatre almost traumatized them. To start the season, he chose a long-winded O'Neill play *(Strange Interlude)* as a vehicle for Geraldine Page, followed by a sketchy Costigan piece *(Baby Want a Kiss)* as a vehicle for Paul Newman and Joanne Woodward; he cast non-Studio stars such as Franchot Tone and Betty Field for the value of their names and allowed Jane Fonda and Ben Gazzara to sign on for brief periods despite his stricture that everyone else contribute at least five months to the project; he turned a weak script by June Havoc (*Marathon 33*) into an even weaker one by waffling over revisions; and when he directed *Three Sisters* with a star-studded cast, he astonished his own people with his rude dictatorial behavior, violating almost every precept of Studio training. Worst of all, following the disastrous reception of *Three Sisters* and *Blues for Mr. Charlie* in London, he joined in the criticism of Baldwin's play, adding that these productions "are not necessarily representative of the work of the Actors Studio. . . . We are not a repertory company, and have had a company for only a year." The actors, already demoralized by a bad press, were appalled by this betrayal, and George C. Scott almost took a swipe at him.

His choice of plays was also questionable. With the exception of *Three Sisters*, a standard repertory item, and *Dynamite Tonite!*, an experimental actors' opera cravenly shut down after one performance off-Broadway because of a sour review from the *Times*, none of the plays of the Actors Studio Theatre was of much quality. It is shocking to learn that Strasberg decided not to start his season with *Who's Afraid of Virginia Woolf?*, which Albee had offered the theatre to the delight of most of its members. Cheryl Crawford, the theatre's executive administrator, was frightened by the play's bitterness and brutality, the theatre's leading lady, Geraldine Page, objected to playing another "drunken loudmouth," and Roger Stevens, the theatre's general administrator, rejected it as "a dull, whiny play, without a laugh in it . . . one big yawn," adding, "I will never be a party to subsidizing the speaking of those dirty words on the stage."

It was inevitable that play selection would be weak, since whatever its interest in actors, the Studio seemed to have little interest in plays. Strasberg was said to be extremely learned, and amassed a huge library of theatre books. But, fixed on techniques rather than texts, he was totally undiscriminating regarding the choice of scenes to be acted or scripts interpreted. "Struck by the disparity between the Studio's inner technique and the play it is being applied to," Hirsch is nevertheless awed by an actress doing a monologue from Gibran's *Life of Jesus* (!) in which, playing Mary Magdelene, she brought the scene through a series of "drafts," at one point taking off all her clothes and saying, " 'Fuck you, you son of a bitch!' . . . as she began to act out, at a primal level, the pain of sexual rejection. . . . With only marginal attention to the actual words of the text," Hirsch sighs on, "she had captured the essence of the character."

Granting all the differences between the concert hall and the theatre, imagine a violinist or a flutist treating a composer, even the musical equivalent of Kahlil Gibran, in this cavalier manner. In Strasberg's Studio, the medium (the actor) was the message, and the object (the text) was simply a pretext for behavior. Even in the Directors Unit of the Studio, according to one observer, "most people tried to play safe. . . . There was a lot of Williams and Inge, the classic fifties and sixties slice-of-life school. There was practically no Shakespeare, very few classics, and few comedies." It was what these directors thought Strasberg wanted of them, and it was doubtless what was wanted of them in the commercial theatre. Although the Studio attracted many artists eager to develop their craft, it was more often a magnet for those interested in breaking into Broadway and Hollywood rather than interpreting great roles.

Strasberg at first lamented the impact of Hollywood on such gifted actors as James Dean: "Talent has to be maintained with personal progress," he said, "and combined with a contribution to the theatre." But Studio members were usually conscious of the contradictions in his position. "Despite all his idealism," said Jack Garfein, "he wanted money and success too. . . . When the opportunity came to be popular, he took it, which is what he counseled us against." "Lee was in love with stars," noted Estelle Parsons, with Madeline Thornton-Sherwood adding, "Lee knew his reputation was based on movie actors he produced." Not to mention those he didn't produce, but whose acting ambitions he exploited, such as Marilyn Monroe, whom Garfein called "a sign of Lee's lust for success." "The ones who made the sacrifices for art were not the Rabbi's favorite," Garfein added. "Those who *made* it were the Rabbi's favorite." He died dancing in a celebrity chorus line during a "Night of a Hundred Stars."

Like most Studio biographers, Hirsch is dazzled by the luster of these stars and devotes a generous section of his book to such celebrated alumni as Brando, Pacino, and Dean. "Strasberg's rapport with the camera underlined the fact," he says, "that it is through the film work of its most famous members that the Studio has made its most enduring contribution to the history of American acting."

Although hardly unexpected from a biographer who expresses his preference for plays set in the "real world" with "characters who are . . . every bit as neurotic as the people in the audience," this is an accurate statement—behaviorist techniques, private moments, and internalization are much more appropriate to the personality acting of movies than the character work of the stage. But it makes the Actors Studio seem like an accomplice of Hollywood, a feeding ground for the film industry. It is a common weakness of teachers to boast about their most successful students, but it is also a teacher's obligation to encourage such students to put their talents in service to something greater than their careers. For all his immense power and influence— and Studio members liken him to Jesus, Buddha, Moses, and the Great Sphinx—Strasberg possessed neither the moral beauty of his great mentor, Stanislavsky, nor the artistic passion of his warm-hearted colleague, Harold Clurman.

The fault seemed to be in the personality. There is something pinched and disappointed in the face of Lee Strasberg; photographs never show him smiling, even during the most festive occasions. A singularly private individual, he attracted awe and admiration from his members but very little love. If his son, John, is to be believed, he didn't excite much love from his family either. "My father's work dealt almost exclusively with the expression of feeling," he says, in the most insightful remarks to be found in these pages. "That's not the same as creating life on the stage. He was incapable of expressing his own feelings, so he always reverted to that in his work. He simply couldn't express himself on deep levels except in his work. Some actors will tell you he could, that he was a warm man: I know he wasn't."

He is also interesting when talking about Strasberg's inability to collaborate: "My father could never work with anybody else on an equal basis. . . . You have to work out your dream with everyone else. Yet to have an ensemble spirit you need a strong leader. . . . His whole history in the theatre was leaving it when the going got tough, as in the Group. . . . Doing it bigger and better and being famous were more important than the Theatre and the organization. They were all self-serving, with no one big enough to rise above their own needs. It's the problem of America."

John Strasberg formed his own theatre a few years ago, the Mirror Repertory Company, partly in an effort to throw off the Strasberg inheritance and correct that "anti-literary bias" he blames on his father. It is one of a number of new theatre institutions in this country devoted to texts, and to creating opportunities for intelligent actors concerned less with analyzing their own lives and dredging up their private emotions than with interpreting the great literature of the theatre, past and present. Strasberg considered his son's act a betrayal and refused to talk to him or let him near the house. That's sad for many reasons, but especially because his son, John, may yet prove to be an important Strasberg legacy. "The Studio is passé and everyone knows it," comments John. "There's no new force there. New artists don't seek it. . . . In its heyday, up through the Actors Studio Theatre, it was a focal point for the *best* in American theatre. . . . [Now] Ellen Burstyn runs it as a homage to my father: everything she does is in his honor." But there are many ways to pay homage to such a brilliant, defective man, even through the revisionist efforts of a rebellious son.

JOHN HOUSEMAN: MEMOIRS OF A MOONLIGHTER

Toward the conclusion of the third and last volume of his memoirs, *Final Dress*, John Houseman writes: "I could look back with satisfaction on a series of utterly unpredictable achievements, of which directing Henry Fonda in a Broadway smash hit [*Darrow*] marked the climax but which also included the creation and administration of the country's most advanced theatre school [Juilliard], a starring role in a major Hollywood film [*The Paper Chase*] and the formation of an acting company [the Acting Company] that stood alone in the contemporary American theatre." One might argue about the accuracy of some of these claims, and question the importance of others. But the passage still manages to suggest the remarkable range of a wildly eclectic career, through which are reflected some of the victories, and a few of the defeats, of American theatre history.

In his two previous books, *Runthrough* and *Front and Center*, Mr. Houseman gracefully described his youth as a Rumanian émigré, his associations with Orson Welles, the Mercury Theatre, and the Federal Theatre project, and his career as a Hollywood producer. In *Final Dress*, he tells the story of his later years, when he rescued the congenitally troubled Shakespeare theatre in Stratford, Connecticut, started a professional theatre company at UCLA, acted as advisor and director with the APA company, and, at the age of sixty-six initiated a whole new career as founder and chief administrator of the drama division at Juilliard—not to mention its youthful offspring, the Acting Company, which still continues to tour the United States each year with a repertory of classical plays.

In addition to all his other activities, Mr. Houseman has now played a role in the formation of at least seven separate theatre companies. But although fate (and occasionally a hostile board of trustees) often intervened to affect his decisions, Houseman's inability to remain with a single activity or institution was largely a result of his own restless nature. It may also have been influenced by the seductive quality of American culture. At the same time that he was applying himself to serious artistic ventures, he was accepting invitations to return to Hollywood to produce movies, to coproduce a television series, and to direct Broadway plays, when he wasn't staging operas, serving on boards, advising foundations, writing memoirs, making personal appearances, or, finally at age seventy-one, becoming an Academy Award–winning motion picture star (later starring in the spin-off television series) for his portrayal of Professor Kingsley in *The Paper Chase*.

Mr. Houseman is understandably proud of his capacity to achieve success in a variety of media, as he suggests through extensive quotations from his reviews. He is also proud of what he calls "my professional transformation from a respected but neglected veteran in the theatre to one of the most sought-after and highly paid aging male performers in the mass media." But he also recognizes the contradictions inherent in his desire for private glory and financial gain in contrast to his capacity for public sacrifice, and includes some interesting self-reflective passages attributing these vacillations to an early conflict between creative yearnings as an artist and business ambitions as a grain dealer. Whatever the explanation, Houseman seems almost congenitally incapable of turning down an offer or holding a single job. Even at the moment he is developing the Juilliard program, he is expressing interest in becoming director at the Met and artistic director of the Vivian Beaumont.

Yes, this is the work of an ambitious and gifted achiever, self-satisfied but also capable of self-doubt, particularly in regard to his family. Houseman, for example, is genuinely devoted to his wife, Joan, but regrets that his itinerant life has robbed her both of his companionship and of a stable home, while his bemused, distant relationship with his two sons ("perplexed but mildly affectionate") suggests that he never really got the chance to know them very well. He affected a similar distance from his Juilliard students who there-upon described his playing of Professor Kingsley as no performance at all, simply "the way you behave around here." But if he displays Kingsley's aloofness toward people, he also shares the character's intelligence, urbanity, and weight. What was said of Lear might almost be said of Houseman: "We that are young shall never see so much, nor live so long."

Yet, something troubles me—not about the character of this admirable man, not about his long and often valuable career, but about the cultural atmosphere in which he floated. For example, a curious omission in Houseman's account of the innumerable shows he did with Stratford or the Theatre Group of the Acting Company is the element of urgency. No matter how expertly they were done, no matter how successfully received, we never learn why it was essential at a particular moment in history for him to produce *Much Ado about Nothing* or *Don Juan in Hell* or *Ring Round the Moon*, apart from the fact that the play would balance the season or provide good roles for actors. (Neither do we learn much about the purpose of the training program he developed at Juilliard with Michel Saint-Denis.) These are not ignoble ends, but great theatre is rarely created simply out of professional or even aesthetic imperatives, as Houseman surely remembers from his experience with Orson Welles's antifascist *Julius Caesar* and his anti-Hearst *Citizen Kane*. It is almost always engaged, whether directly or obliquely, with the current anxieties and dilemmas of contemporary society.

I'm not saying that theatre production is a form of political activism, simply that it must be informed by suggestive and relevant metaphors if it is effectively to challenge audiences or have any value aside from cultural display. Houseman, who had leftist leanings in his youth, expresses civil libertarian outrage whenever an associate is tarred by prejudice or red-baiting, but his passion for social justice does not seem to extend into his concepts or choices any more than the disturbances of the Vietnam period play much part in his account of the Juilliard training. This discontinuity between one's political and professional life is not unusual in the theatre—it has been with us, except for a brief spell in the sixties, since the McCarthy era—but it may explain why so few of the productions with which Houseman was associated, solid as they were, have become a vivid chapter of theatre history.

What I'm missing, I guess, is a sense of obsession, which translates into commitment to a single passion, idea, or overwhelming purpose. The absence of such obsessiveness accounts, to some extent, for Houseman's rootlessness and restlessness, his fondness for media moonlighting. If a man of so many talents is not consumed by a passionate calling, then he will inevitably fall back onto personal satisfactions. And when society is slow to acknowledge the accomplishments of serious artistic work, then he may grow less discriminating about where such satisfactions are to be found.

In his final chapter, Houseman quotes Garrick Utley of NBC as saying that "when in his seventies, John Houseman finally found Professor Kingsley—he found himself." Houseman does not mention Professor Kingsley's later incarnations as a TV salesman for McDonald's hamburgers, Smith Barney investments, and Chrysler cars. These are probably annuities for a time (far off, I hope) when he is ready to retire, and Houseman doubtless understands their proper value. But there are signals, nevertheless, that Kingsley is taking over John Houseman's life. The climax of *Final Dress* is an account of the night on which he received his Oscar for *The Paper Chase*. He has dutifully lobbied for the award through interviews and talk shows, and now the precious moment has arrived. Numb with apprehension, he hears the overwhelming applause of the audience ("it can be verified in decibels on the tapes of that night's proceedings"), then rises to his feet and reads his acceptance speech, feeling "much as the frog must have felt just after he'd been kissed by the king's daughter and turned into a prince."

His creative energy undiminished in his eighties, Houseman may very well discover many more selves in the remainder of his professional career. But without wishing to deny him his well-deserved rewards and recognition, indeed in order to salute his lifetime of achievement in the theatre, I am obliged to say it would be a shame if the strongest image perceived by the young people for whom he is a role model was as "one of the most sought-after and highly paid aging male performers in the media," measuring the decibel count of his applause, and hugging his gleaming brass statuette.

LILLIAN HELLMAN: EPILOGUE TO ANGER

Even in passing, Lillian Hellman engendered controversy—even over her age at time of death. A well-respected playwright and Hollywood screenwriter whose confrontation with the House Un-American Activities Committee in the fifties was legendary, she survived the penury and neglect of the blacklist to establish herself, late in life, in a new career as author of a series of impressionistic memoirs. This brought renewed fame, wealth, and the respect of a few in the literary community, besides making her a model for independent women everywhere; it also, inevitably, made her the focus of renewed contention. A former friend, Diana Trilling, angered by Hellman's rash and hurtful imputations regarding her husband Lionel's relation to McCarthyism, wrote a convincing rebuttal in a memoir of her own. Its rejection by the publisher they shared inspired new accusations (denied by Hellman) that she had blocked the book. Others accused her of distortion and misrepresentation. And on the Dick Cavett show, Mary McCarthy delivered her scathing judgment that Lillian had never written a truthful word in her life, including *and*s and *the*s. This brought a libel suit in response.

Previously characterized by her enemies as a fellow traveler who continued to support Stalinism long after most other American intellectuals had abandoned it, Lillian was now being called a liar and a bully. Herself a former victim of blacklisting, she now stood accused of helping to muffle the free expression of others, leading some to say that she embraced the First Amendment only in her own defense. It was a miserable epilogue to what should have been a respected old age. Although she remained an inspiration to the radical young and gifted women (Marsha Norman was among those testifying to Lillian's seminal influence on her playwriting), she was embroiled at the end in bitter quarrels and troublesome litigation with dozens of people, many of them former friends.

Much as they saddened those who loved her, these broils, I believe, are what kept her alive. Stricken first by blindness, and then—chain-smoking to the end—by emphysema, heart attacks, paralysis, a stroke, and the loss of her dearest friend and close companion, Hannah Weinstein, Lillian Hellman was dying for over four years, fighting death with mounting rage and determination. Her friends watched her grow frailer and feebler from month to month, fearing that each would be her last; yet, every June she returned to Martha's Vineyard after a winter of illness to hold a joint birthday party with John Hersey and Kingman Brewster, though she usually had to be carried into the house, placed in a chair, and fed her food. Two years before her death, her pacemaker popped out of her chest—by this time her skin had become like papier-mâché—but before it could be replaced, she had to have two carotid arteries operated on in her throat. She was now anorexic and nearly died from malnutrition, a bedridden Job imprisoned inside a broken bag of bones; yet, a day before the operation she insisted on putting on makeup, leaving the hospital, and cooking two geese for a friend's dinner in Boston.

She hated death; she defied it; and she kept it at bay through blind fury. I had an image of her blood congealing, and then set coursing through her veins again by means of her reaction to some new outrage, real or invented. She quarreled with everyone, often over the most trivial issue—she broke with Bill Styron for an entire summer in a dispute over the proper way to cook a ham. She even had a quarrel with her "adopted son," Peter Fiebleman, the mildest of men whom she had known and loved for forty-three years. In a touching grave-side eulogy, Fiebleman reported the opinions of her nurse: "This lady is half paralyzed; she's legally blind; she's having rage attacks that are a result of strokes; she has no way of stopping. She says things to people she doesn't necessarily mean and then she regrets them. She cries at night; she can't help that. She can't eat. She can't sleep. She can't walk. . . . I think, frankly, she's dying" (to which Lillian added, when asked how she was feeling, "Not good, Peter. . . . This is the worst case of writer's block I ever had").

But the rages that the nurse attributed to her physical condition her closest male friend, John Hersey, interpreted as "a rage of the mind against all kinds of injustice—against human injustice and the unfairness of death." Before the onset of pain and illness, her anger was more focused; after, it became a free-floating, cloud-swollen tempest raining on friend and foe alike.

But throughout her life, even near the end, she remained the most hospitable of women, the most gracious of friends. An inspired cook, though she barely tasted her own dishes, she loved to see her friends well fed (another birthday party had been scheduled and rescheduled just days before she died). This preoccupation with nourishment, perhaps reflecting her blocked maternal instinct, was the sort of thing that attracted people regardless of political differences or momentary conflicts; and, anyway, her opinions were really irrelevant to her friendships, except as a pretext to start a fight (among her oldest comrades was the conservative columnist Joseph Alsop). For this reason, I guess, I never took Lillian Hellman's politics very seriously, even when she attacked me, as she often did—once for giving "the most conservative speech I ever heard." I was always amazed when people, particularly American intellectuals waging fifty-year-old wars, treated her as a dangerous left-wing thinker.

Lillian Hellman's opinions were an outlet for her witty, sharp, satiric nature; I think she was always more interested in personalities than issues. She liked nothing better than to fish and, while sitting in the boat with her line on the bottom waiting for a fluke to bite or a rock bass, to gossip about the frailties of acquaintances. She responded to warmth and thoughtfulness with the gratitude of a childless woman who invested all her emotions in friends, but she went straight to someone's weaknesses with the eye of a peregrine falcon pouncing on a sparrow. What her enemies saw were the envenomed talons, not the warm heart. "Forgive me," she would always say, before discharging a poisonous fusillade of contradiction concerning some innocent remark by one of her guests. But somewhere, I believe, she truly wanted forgiveness for whatever wounds her opinionated nature inflicted.

As a playwright, Lillian wrote eight original dramas and four adaptations before abandoning the stage in the early sixties. None of the first rank, at least three, I believe, have a permanent place in American drama: *Toys in the Attic*, *The Autumn Garden*, and, of course, her classic *The Little Foxes*. Skillfully constructed and nailed together with strong scenes, crisp dialogue, and powerful characters, Lillian's theatre was fashioned largely under the influence of Ibsen, an unvarnished tribute to contemporary social realism. Like Ibsen, she believed the drama to have a function beyond mere entertainment, that it could be a vehicle for social commentary, psychological insight, and, above all, sharp incisions into the diseased body of a corrupted society. Later in her playwriting career, Lillian made a conscientious effort to loosen up her style—hitherto as carefully arranged as her impeccable coiffure—by employing the more indirect, apparently plotless techniques of Chekhov. But she never wavered in her conviction that theatre could be a force for change in what she considered an unethical, unjust, essentially venal world.

Aside from power, Lillian's major theatrical subject was money, how it is made, how it changes lives, what people will do to acquire it. Money, in fact, is usually an additional shadow character in her plays, often the most important one. It can function symbolically, but it also has a tangible, concrete, almost organic nature—in *Toys in the Attic*, money is stroked as if it were a domestic animal. Lillian sometimes seemed to divide the world according to how people's loyalties and values were affected by money (though she loved money herself and usually maintained a sneaking admiration for her villains). This led critics to accuse her of being a melodramatist. It is true that her plays, in the tradition of melodrama, often seem to be confrontations between good and evil, paralleling the passionate friendships and bitter enmities of her life. Her capacity for friendship, in fact, was probably the force that originally drew her to the stage, the most collective of all the arts, just as her quarrels and disappointments eventually repelled her from it. Fiercely loyal herself, she could not abide disloyalty in others. And it may be that her life, with its strong alliances, combative courage, and abrupt domestic scenes, will eventually be considered her greatest theatre.

She died on the downside of her reputation, feeling herself under siege in a society where recognition and respect are always being tossed about by the winds of fashion. "Dear Lillian," said John Hersey at her funeral in a hillside cemetery in Chilmark, "you are a finished woman, now." The bitterness was quenched, the physical pain, the mental anguish, over. Her capacity for anger, about which almost everyone spoke, had hurt herself and others at the end, but it had been a more accurate weapon once, at times a fresh and liberating force. "Jonathan Swift has sailed into his rest," wrote W. B. Yeats about another irascible literary figure. "Savage indignation there / Cannot lacerate his breast." One wishes the same peace for Lillian Hellman, but many of us will sorely miss that reckless heart, that rude, cantankerous tongue.

LAURENCE OLIVIER: ONCE MORE INTO THE BREACH

> As far as I know, *Henry V* might as well have been the first Shakespeare film. To me, it *was* the first Shakespeare film. Somehow it worked, and I think it had much to do with the way I adapted the sound of the lines to the modern ear. . . . I appealed to a new public, to those who had thought that Shakespeare was not for the likes of them.

These lines from Laurence Olivier's new book *On Acting* transported me back to the mid-1940s when, an untutored lout of eighteen who shared the general conviction that "Shakespeare was not for the likes of him," I discovered the reality of classic theatre through a sublime film. I saw the movie twenty-seven times and labored for a time under the delusion that *Henry V* was the greatest play ever written. I committed to memory every word of Shakespeare's text and every bar of William Walton's score. I knew the names of every actor and the behavior of every performance, including the four subsidiary characters Olivier anonymously played in addition to Henry. Like many young actors of the time, I was persuaded by this film to make a career on the stage, and my own performances were apish imitations of Olivier's stirring cadences and Robert Newton's extravagant, eye-popping Pistol.

With *Henry V*, Laurence Olivier did for my generation what rote memorization in high school, college Shakespeare courses, and the resonant warbling of Maurice Evans and John Gielgud on Broadway could never accomplish—he made Shakespeare immediate, coherent, engrossing. By God, those lines actually *meant* something, they were related to actual human emotions, and the people who spoke them were inhabitants of the earth, not brocaded humanoids from some far-flung planet. Olivier's *Henry V* authenticated theatrical history. Yes, scholars could quarrel with his reconstruction of the Globe Theatre and liberals would criticize his celebration of English jingoism. But who could fail to respond to the rich profusion of ideas and imagination—the way he managed the subtle transition from Elizabethan stage to metaphorical medieval landscape, the heroic battle at Agincourt with yeoman arrows whistling through the air at the French charge, the sexy languorous wooing of Princess Katherine, or his sensual-robust appeal as Henry, the chiseled features and lazy eyes half hidden by neck armor as he roused his soldiers into the breach while skillfully managing an unruly white stallion?

I had a crush on the man, and his playing of Henry impelled me toward all his available performances, whether on stage or screen. Up till then, I had imagined Olivier to be an engaging British film personality in the style of Ronald Colman or Robert Donat—lots of silken charm, no inner depth. Now I searched his work—*Clouds over Europe*, *That Hamilton Woman*, *Rebecca*—with new eyes, seeking hints of that power and intelligence I found so riveting in *Henry V*. Soon after this film, Olivier arrived on these shores with Ralph Richardson and the rest of the Old Vic company to demonstrate his remarkable powers of transformation as Hotspur and Justice Shallow in both parts of *Henry IV*, as Puff in *The Critic*, and, preeminently, as the title character in *Oedipus Rex* (forty years later, people would swear they could still hear his offstage scream). The man who first made his reputation in the United States as an appealing matinee idol was now saying something significant about the actor's obligation to his craft, to the theatre, to the great classical roles.

I saw his movie of *Hamlet* only five times and his *Richard III* only three, though both were far more challenging roles. *Hamlet* was somewhat marred for me by pseudo-Freudian interpolations (influenced by Ernest Jones), by self-conscious art direction, and by a certain posturing in his playing. Olivier's idea of introspection was to hood his eyes, dentalize his consonants, and let the camera circle his blondined head like a sparrow looking for a place to deposit its droppings. His Richard was a startlingly original re-creation of the role he had already claimed as his property on stage (compare Barrymore's recorded falsetto shriek on "Tut! Were it further off" with the way Olivier nonchalantly throws the line away), but the movie as a whole failed to cohere. Olivier now believes that he miscast Richardson as Buckingham, but the problem may belong to the play, which departs from its fascination with a diabolical hypocrite to become a desultory series of battle scenes. Perhaps I was now approaching this actor with a more demanding eye, but while I continued to admire him this side of idolatry, I began to think his vocal and physical mannerisms were preventing him from truly inhabiting his roles. On tour in this country with his wife, Vivien Leigh, in alternating performances of *Antony and Cleopatra* and *Caesar and Cleopatra*, his hooknosed Caesar seemed somewhat thin after Claude Rains's philosophical depth and cordiality in the movie, and his Antony, though considerably more textured than the rather immature Cleopatra of Miss Leigh, captured the wounded lover more convincingly than the ruined warrior. Many of his greatest triumphs were also technical stunts—one could not help but admire his majestic Othello, for which he lowered his voice an octave, or his James Tyrone, played like an Irish version of Molière's Harpagon, or his "breakthrough," as he properly calls it, in *The Entertainer*, when this theatrical aristocrat, soon to be a peer of the realm, joined forces with the new working-class spirit in English theatre emerging after Osborne's *Look Back in Anger*. (Soon he was to institutionalize this spirit when he founded the National Theatre at the Old Vic with such Royal Court stalwarts as Albert Finney, Alan Bates, Robert Stephens, Peter O'Toole, and his new wife, Joan Plowright).

Perhaps because of the now-legendary aura surrounding his person in later career, one sometimes found him less identified with his roles than running alongside them on some parallel track. Although Olivier's book is called *On Acting*, the information about acting technique and interpretation is scanty. It is valuable rather for informative anecdotes about Olivier's life and performances, recounted role by role. The style is chatty, almost gabby, as if the author were sitting by the fire and dictating nostalgia into an editor's tape recorder over a glass of port. He seems to have perfect recall regarding old friends and past memories. Many stories, like the time Noel Coward cured him of giggling on stage, are repeated from his autobiography, *Confessions of an Actor*. Others, like his hair-raising account of the time he contracted stage fright playing Shylock, and wouldn't permit the other actors to look him in the eyes, have already entered theatrical legend.

Sometimes Olivier sounds like one of those long-winded Garrick Club thesps who like to reminisce about the "Bard" and the noble deportment of the other actor laddies ("Every man Jack of them") who inhabit the boards. Occasionally he gets to maundering, and his diction becomes banal and his metaphors confused ("[Shakespeare] writes roles that any actor worth his salt would find the means to play by hook or by crook"). But good-natured as it is, the real energy of the book is in its anger, particularly in Olivier's resentment over his enforced retirement from theatre: "I should be soaring away with my head tilted slightly towards the gods, feeding on the caviar of Shakespeare. . . . I was made to perform, and it is not easy to be put out to grass, left to feed on memories and friendships. An actor must act." The refrain of this book—it is heard throughout in one form or other—is "Gone. All gone." (It is shocking to be reminded that he hasn't performed on a stage since 1973, the year he was unceremoniously fired from the National Theatre he had founded at the Old Vic.)

But the book is lovely despite its literary and structural faults, for the beauty of this man comes through on every page. Olivier thinks through memories, and his memories of himself and his friends in the theatre are unusually warm and affectionate. At times, he allows himself a momentary snarl, as when he admits he modeled his Richard III on Jed Harris and calls him "the most loathsome man I ever met," or when, remembering his troubles with Marilyn Monroe on the set of *The Prince and the Showgirl*, he castigates her "spikiness and spite," or when he lets go a well-placed uppercut at Lee Strasberg and the Method (" 'He's got so many faults,' Lee said [about a good character actor], and went off into a lot of hot air, sprinkled with clichés. 'The only fault he's got is the confidence you are draining from him,' I said"). And sometimes he takes credit for achievements that may not belong to him—the idea of a nineteenth-century setting for *The Merchant of Venice*, for example, which Jonathan Miller (in his new book, *Subsequent Performances*) says he persuaded a reluctant Olivier to accept, but which Olivier suggests he discovered all by himself: "Fortunately, Jonathan and my other associates agreed with my vision." (He also claims as his the decision to play the part without the traditional hook nose, though Miller remembers that Olivier brought the nose to the first rehearsal, along with a set of artificial teeth that he was reluctantly allowed to wear.)

But usually Olivier is extremely warmhearted toward his friends and collaborators, most of whom return the favor (and repeat the anecdotes) in their own memoirs. He and Gielgud seemed always to share something of a friendly rivalry. Gielgud was scornful of Olivier's Romeo, and Olivier believed Gielgud too much infatuated with his own beautiful voice (". . . if he was lost for a moment, he would dive straight back into its honey"), though he concedes that Gielgud has become a much finer actor since he developed a sense of humor. About Richardson's talents and comradeship, he speaks nothing but praise, though it is alarming to read that the amiable knight, resenting Olivier's success in *Richard III* in Paris, almost threw him off a balcony in a drunken fit of envy. As for Kenneth Tynan, Olivier gives him full credit for many National Theatre successes, most notably *A Long Day's Journey into Night* (contradicting Jonathan Miller's contention that Olivier hired Tynan as his literary director only in order to neutralize his criticism). He is inordinately warm about the charm and talents of his second wife, Vivien Leigh, and courteously neglects to mention the grief she caused him. And he concedes to William Wyler everything he learned about film, whether it be acting, directing, or simple respect for the medium.

What he learned about film was the virtue of minimalism. For Olivier, the theatre always represented the opposite: "My stage successes have provided me with the greatest moments outside myself," he writes, "my film successes the best moments, professionally, within myself." The stage, in short, was for character actors, the movies for star personalities. Partly because he lacked confidence in his own personality, Olivier always preferred the stage. It is where he has the opportunity to lose himself in accretions of externally applied characteristics: a walk, a nose, an accent, an eye patch, a tone of voice. But if Olivier praises Wyler for teaching him screen acting, it is Tyrone Guthrie who provided him with his greatest insight into the art of acting as a whole—the now-celebrated advice (offered when Olivier was playing Sergius in *Arms and the Man*) to love the character he is playing, regardless of how odious or dumb.

It is hard to believe that Olivier loved the succession of dismal film and television roles he was forced to perform following his premature retirement from the stage, though he defends them as vital—and not just for financial reasons. His physical resources depleted by a series of dreadful illnesses, sorely in need of trust funds for his children and his wife, he nevertheless claims to have embraced the opportunity to play in such movies as *The Betsy* and *The Boys from Brazil* and ridicules those critics "who said I lowered myself playing these parts." But it is not the parts or pictures that pain a critic about Olivier's latter-day career—he is more than entitled to a relaxed actor's life in sun-drenched locations. It is his growing affiliation with superficial acting choices and uninvestigated characters. The hobbling, balding, frail old man who resorts so often to unconvincing high-pitched German or Jewish accents while drilling into Dustin Hoffman's cavities or chasing down Nazi doctors sometimes strikes one as an impostor who runs the risk of obliterating precious memories of more ambitious achievements: his dead-eyed, gap-toothed Archie Rice, his serpentine Richard of Gloucester, his athletic Henry Plantagenet.

The invention of film has given our generation the dubious advantage of watching our acting heroes deteriorate before our eyes. Movies have the unusual capacity to catch an animated moment in time; they also have the unpleasant capacity, when seen sequentially, to catch the ravages of time. In Olivier's case, it is not a question of age but of physical transformation, as if he were playing one of his more extended character parts. (In his television *King Lear*, one sympathized less with Lear's feebleness than with the actor's mighty effort to control his own.) Unlike, say, James Mason, who carried his youth in his face until he died, or Cary Grant, who to the end looked like a snowy-haired C. K. Dexter Haven, Olivier has exposed us to the vagaries of the aging process. The passage of years, and ghastly physical disorders, have made him virtually a different human being from the springy swarthy brooder of *Wuthering Heights*, and one grieves for his lost youth and vitality in the same way Colette's Cheri grieved for his beautiful mistress, Leah, when he came upon her many years later buried inside a mountain of wrinkles and fat.

Still, if Olivier today lacks his old stamina or charisma, he more than compensates for them with a valiant heart and a gallant spirit. And however weak his ability to muster up a potent performance, he still retains a passionate devotion to the stage. Of this, *On Acting* provides abundant testimony. The book aches with nostalgia—over dead friends, lost opportunities, the loving relationship with a live audience, all those great Shakespearean roles ("What a shame I can't play them again"). But it is also pulsing with good memories and a deep concern for the living theatre. *On Acting* may not offer much in the way of concrete information for young people: the epilogue (a letter written in 1947 to Joan Plowright when she was playing in *Major Barbara*) contains the book's only specific technical advice aside from admonitions to exercise daily and avoid dissipation. But what is exemplary is the man himself—his past achievement, when he inspired me and my kind as the greatest actor in the English-speaking world, and his continuing inspiration for the young as one who never lost his passion or respect for the profession he helped to mold and transform. Toward the end of a great career, staring into the abyss, he still has the spark that ignited our hearts before the mighty victory at Agincourt.

Part II

Productions

Contemporary American Playwrights
Children of O'Neill

TWO COUPLES

(Talley's Folly; Marie and Bruce)

If you're looking for new trends in the American theatre, I think I've got one for you—the hour-and-a-half play featuring two mis-matched people in the throes of courtship or divorce. Forgive my generalizing on the basis of slight evidence, but I saw two such works on the same day. One of these, Lanford Wilson's *Talley's Folly*, is now sitting comfortably on the stage of the Brooks Atkinson, adored by Broadway audiences and hailed by critics as diverse as Walter Kerr and John Simon. The other, Wallace Shawn's *Marie and Bruce*, has just fallen off the stage of the New York Public Theatre where it tottered precariously for a few weeks, making audiences miserable and enrag-ing critics as diverse as Walter Kerr and John Simon. At the risk of magnifying a growing reputation for perverseness, let me enter my customary dissent. I found Wilson's play a wittily written, carefully manufactured fake, while Shawn's piece struck me as powerful and heartbreaking.

Talley's Folly is best described as a cute meet. Set in 1944, in an abandoned, ramshackle boathouse near Lebanon, Missouri, it is a ninety-seven-minute wooing scene between a bearded, middle-aged Jewish accountant, Matt Friedman, and a thirty-one-year-old nurse's aide from a wealthy family, Sally Talley. The setting, the situation, and the unlikely twosome promise a stage blend of William Inge and Paddy Chayefsky, which Marshall Mason's production dispenses with the consistency of an egg cream mixed with Gilbey's gin. As played by Judd Hirsch, with Yiddish inflections and a voice that snaps through the house like a revolver report, Matt Friedman combines the function of chorus, stage manager, protagonist, comic relief, and focus of interest for Jewish audiences. He describes the time and place, dallies with Sally Talley, imitates Humphrey Bogart, and tells a bunch of Yiddish stories. He is, in short, one of those wise, witty, wonderfully unforgettable stage characters you pray you never have to meet, and despite the clever efforts of the gifted Mr. Hirsch to endow him with depth, is less a living personage than a treasury of Jewish folklore.

Trish Hawkins, playing Sally, has even less to work with, so she is forced to settle for the familiar stage spinster with the cloying ingenue voice as invented by Julie Harris. Her role consists primarily of reactions—listening to Friedman's anecdotes and disapproving of his impersonations—when she is not engaged, for reasons that constitute virtually the entire plot, in resisting his amorous advances. Since Matt loves Sally and Sally is perceived to be coyly interested in Matt, most of the playwright's energy and ingenuity are expended in finding devices to keep them out of each other's arms until the end of the play. Matt makes a confession—characteristically in the form of an anecdote—about the fate suffered by his European family at the hands of the Germans. Because of this "border tragedy," he has resolved "never to bring into this world another child to be killed for a political purpose." (This decision you may recognize from your readings in other literature, fiction being the only place where people resolve to be childless because of the world situation). For her part, Sally reveals that, as a result of a fortuitous hysterectomy, she is now unable to bear any children. This makes these two characters just about perfect for each other, in spite of their contrasted backgrounds. As soon as Matt is able to persuade Sally that he didn't invent his own story because he knew about hers, they both go off to live happily ever after in St. Louis, having discharged their debts both to world politics and to the inscrutable benefits of modern medicine.

Wilson has obviously hit on a happy formula for playwriting, if not for marriage brokering, and one can hardly fault his genius for creating symmetrical solutions to artificial problems. What one might question, however, is why he has expended his talent for fastidious craftsmanship on such a shallow situation. The historical setting seems devised more for nostalgia than for cogent social commentary, and the "sound design" (barking dogs, chirping crickets, lapping water) is of the kind that used to drive Chekhov up the wall when Stanislavsky used it in 1901. Worse, the characters seem to have no life beyond their function in the plot. I mean, we don't expect Dostoyevski in our stage confections, but surely people have more depth than this, even in Lebanon, Missouri. In *Talley's Folly*, Lanford Wilson is functioning less as a dramatist than as a theatrical efficiency expert. Why, the play even ends on time, its last line (spoken by Mr. Hirsch with a glance at his watch) being: "And so, all's well that ends well . . . right on the button." Precisely.

Marie and Bruce does not observe the clock very well at all. It is messy and sprawling, but it left me, nevertheless, quite limp and vaguely depressed at its end. I'm not grateful to the author for this response, but I have to concede that he achieved it honestly. Though not identified as such, Marie and Bruce are genuinely Jewish characters (unlike Matt Friedman, who is too benevolent to pass). And what Shawn has created here—with the aid of two splendid actors, Louise Lasser and Bob Balaban—is the agony of a really intolerable Jewish marriage. I don't mean to say the situation is typical, but it is recognizable as a piece of the truth blown up to monstrous proportions. Performed in a simple, modular white setting that revolves the scenes from a bedroom to a cocktail party to a Chinese restaurant, *Marie and Bruce* begins and ends with a shriek of marital agony by the female protagonist that does not subside in pitch or volume until the final curtain. "Let me tell you something," she says, sitting up suddenly in her marriage bed, her hair decorated with two awful red plastic bows. "I find my husband so goddamn irritating that I'm planning to leave him."

This remark is the signal for a long monologue about her "worthless piece of shit" of a husband who, when he emerges from the bed-clothes, seems much too mild a Milquetoast to warrant such fury.

Yet, the odd thing is how Bruce eventually reveals himself as pretty much the monster Marie says he is, not from any active malevolence so much as from his maddening detachment from his wife's unhappiness. At one of those endless, mindless New York cocktail parties, where leering life-size puppets are indistinguishable from the actual guests, Bruce circumnavigates the room like a horny Ulysses, immobilizing his wife by loading her down with six or seven highballs that she is then forced to juggle on her thighs, her dress, in the crooks of her arms. Getting drunker and drunker, Marie suddenly conceives a new sexual passion for Bruce while he soliloquizes about the other women he has been attracted to, asking her, when she finally passes out: "Why is it that whenever we have a conversation, you get sick?"

The final scene, in the restaurant, shows us this marriage is just about hopeless. As a group of homosexuals discuss their stomach troubles in sickening detail at the adjoining table, Marie launches into her ultimate assault on Bruce. He keeps his attention fixed on the egg rolls and noodles. "This is very sad," she says. "I mean our dinner is spoiled, but my life was spoiled because I met you." "I don't imagine you'll be wanting any dessert," he replies, as the two sit wanly, desperately, amidst the rubble of their dinner and their marriage. Bruce has proven Marie's contention that he is not a "living person," and when she proceeds to strike him violently about the head, all he can do is hold her hands. It is as if Shawn has taken all the Jewish self-irony previously expressed with affection by Woody Allen, Jules Feiffer, Mel Brooks, Marshall Brickman, and numerous others and shown us its underside in ferocious, sardonic self-loathing. The gold in the streets, which Jewish immigrants expected to find when they first came to this country, has turned into ashes in the bed. *Marie and Bruce* is one of the most savage assaults yet on the failure of American promise.

The acting is very hard to assess by conventional standards. When Louise Lasser begins to speak, she seems television-size, barely audible, and she rarely gives the audience the benefit of any vocal range. But I find it difficult to describe how deeply her performance affected me. Critics have commented on her obesity, unjustly I believe; the weight she is now carrying, while inappropriate for Mary Hartman, is a perfect manifestation of Marie's depression. Miss Lasser's characterization has all the failings and all the strengths associated with "private moments." At times, we feel we are invading her soul; at others, we are witnesses, and sharers, of unbearable stress. I can understand why people have had strong reactions to this performance; I can only tell you that I found it overpowering. Bob Balaban, in a more diffident role, is only slightly less effective—coldblooded, frozen, immobile, like an engine that has run out of oil and clutched. As for Wilford Leach's direction and design, for all their jagged edges, they loyally serve this appalling, traumatizing play.

THE PLAY YOU'RE NOT ALLOWED TO HATE

(Children of a Lesser God)

Mark Medoff's *Children of a Lesser God* at the Longacre is a supreme example of a new Broadway genre—the Disability Play. The origin of the species, I suppose, was William Gibson's *The Miracle Worker*, written twenty years ago—but only after the success of such recent extensions of the formula as *The Elephant Man*, *Joe Egg*, and *Whose Life Is It Anyway?* has the Disability Play taken Broadway by storm as its dominant "serious" drama. It's not hard to understand the success of the genre, since it has everything going for it: (1) *Unforgettable Characters*, including spastics, paraplegics, the deaf, and the blind, (2) *Intriguing Conflict* between the handicapped protagonist and the "normal" person who invites contempt by trying to help out, (3) *Love Reversal* the moment the conflict between these two characters ends in an embrace, (4) *Terrific Breakthrough* when the protagonist reveals that he/she can speak/feel/read lips/walk, and (5) *Inspirational Theme* after we learn we all share a common humanity, regardless of our defects. The impact of this on the tear glands is dynamite. I haven't seen audiences leaving a theatre with such wet faces since the last revival of Bette Davis in *Dark Victory*, though I mistakenly believed Peter Sellers had put an end to this sort of stuff forever when he rose from his wheelchair in *Dr. Strangelove* to announce to the American president, "*Mein Fuehrer*, I can walk!!!"

The other built-in success factor is that the species is really a subgenre of a time-tested Broadway artifact—the Play You're Not Allowed to Hate. In the past, this used to be a political drama—people resisting a corrupt political system or fighting for the Loyalist cause during the Spanish Civil War. More recently, it has almost exclusively featured ethnic and sexual minority groups, thus increasing the quota of moral extortion. To fail to respond to plays about blacks or women or homosexuals, for example, is to stand accused of racism, sexism, homophobia, or getting up on the wrong side of the bed. Now that the handicapped have organized themselves into another minority pressure group, they have access to the same kind of blackmail. Meanwhile, the theatre becomes an agency for consciousness raising, with audiences alternately being tutored and entertained for considerably less money than a modest contribution to an effective rehabilitation program.

Medoff's version of this formula is successful because it combines the features of two current types you're forbidden to dislike—the Disability Play and the Feminist Play. Its male hero is James Leeds, a speech therapist who works in a clinic for the "nonhearing" (the word *deaf* having been consigned to the same dusty lexicon of archaic English as *Negro* and *Mrs.*). One of his charges is a feisty woman named Sarah Norman, "nonhearing" since birth, who resolutely refuses to learn to speak or read lips (the two communicate entirely through signing). What is more, she dislikes everybody who does, including the baffled Leeds, who can't understand why the recalcitrant Sarah continues to refuse his help. Nevertheless, he continues to offer it, and, endlessly, to discuss it (*help* is the most frequently uttered word in the play). A former Peace Corps officer, he is attracted to support functions "because it feels good to help people." When he goes to bed with Sarah, it feels even better, and his efforts at helping enter a new phase.

Eventually, they get married. Leeds, who has a weakness for pop psychoanalysis, concludes that Sarah's hatred of "hearing" people is related to her hatred of herself, while she confesses that she has refused his therapy because "I don't do things I don't do well." One gathers sex is not among these (she has had an active history before she married him), but the two soon fall to quarreling. He hasn't turned on his stereo in months, and she seems more interested in fighting for the rights of the "nonhearing" than in saving the marriage.

These personal battles lead to two dramatic revelations. His is an admission that he feels guilty over the suicide of his mother—not surprisingly since it occurred right after he announced to the unfortunate woman that if he lived with her one more day, he would put a gun to one of their heads. Her revelation comes when he forces her to utter sounds, and she confesses she has been reading lips for years. In a scene you may recognize from about fifty other plays (beginning with *A Doll's House*), she then tells her husband that until she becomes an "individual," "we cannot be joined, we cannot share a relationship." The payoff comes when Leeds, after trying to help Sarah for the entire length of the play, is forced to admit his own dependency ("Help me—teach me . . . be brave, but not so brave that you don't need me anymore"). She leaves anyway. Will she return? Tune in tomorrow. In the ambiguous conclusion, Sarah reaches out to James in a half-light, signing, "I'll help you if you help me," following which the spectators helped themselves to their hankies and I helped myself to my coat.

Obviously, only a stony heart could remain unmoved by such a story, especially when it is delivered with such conviction by the two principal actors, John Rubenstein and Phyllis Frelich. Rubenstein, who has the sharp angular features of a young Fred Astaire, carries the burden of virtually the entire play on his talented shoulders since he not only speaks his own lines but translates Miss Frelich's signs as well. This double task he discharges with such wit and passion that he almost succeeds in feeding some suppleness into the cardboard goody two-shoes he is forced to impersonate. As for Miss Frelich, she is an accomplished mime, with a mischievous smile and an instinct for deviltry that reminds one of Harpo Marx, and she demonstrates how spiritual beauty and intelligence can be articulated without the aid of speech. Indeed, the whole play is a good argument for the return of the silent film—perhaps with subtitles by W. C. Fields. Expertly crafted, and directed with considerable skill by Gordon Davidson, it successfully disguises its soap-opera origins by being a chic compendium of every extant cliché about women and minority groups, where speech operates not to inform or reveal but rather to manipulate emotions and reinforce conventional wisdom.

DON'T READ THIS REVIEW!

('night Mother)

Since the theatre with which I am associated originated this production of Marsha Norman's *'night Mother*, I should really disqualify myself from writing a review. Well, I'm going to commit a questionable journalistic act and submit one anyway. I have two excuses for this totally self-serving decision, neither very exculpatory. One is that ever since I first read *'night Mother* it has filled me with the kind of exaltation I experience only in the presence of a major dramatic work, and how many new plays can you say that about in the course of a reviewing career? The other is that since my judgments have little influence on Broadway theatregoers, it is unlikely that anything I say will start a box-office stampede. Still, there's no question I'm involved in a conflict of interest however I proceed. I can't very well pretend to be objective about the production, so I will forego comment on it, but I simply can't resist writing about the play. (You may have an easier time resisting my review).

'night Mother occupies about eighty-five minutes of stage time without intermission, as measured by three or four clocks that tick away remorselessly on the surfaces of the set. Scrupulously realistic, the play is also chastely classical in its observance of the unities, especially the unity of time. It not only measures its own time, however (like the movie *High Noon*), but also the time of the audience. Matinees excepted, the clocks on stage display the same hour as the watches on the wrists of the spectators. This sounds like a gimmick, but it gives the play the density and compression of an explosive device, and accounts in part for its remorseless power (it also validates the enduring truths of the *Poetics*).

The clock collection belongs to Thelma Cates, the aging mother of Jessie Cates; the two have been living together in a tackily decorated country house somewhere in the New South. In the brief course of the play, these two women will share a profound life crisis, a catalytic experience designed to reorder the chemistry of a familiar relationship and expose both character and destiny. The crisis is initiated by

Jessie. Having retrieved her dead father's rusty revolver from a shoebox in the attic, she announces calmly to her mother that she has decided that very night to use it on herself.

At first, Thelma is disbelieving, but Jessie's determination is unmistakable: the play is actually an extended death scene, preceding an inevitable, inexorable act. Jessie says she has informed her mother of her suicide plans in order to prepare her, both emotionally and domestically, for life without her. But even as she is outlining the shopping routine and inventorying the kitchen utensils ('night Mother is a minutely detailed mosaic of the commonplaces of everyday domestic life), Jessie is also trying to justify and explain the root causes of her extreme decision. Her passion for the quiet and darkness of death is fed by real misfortunes—her husband has left her, her son is a petty thief—but more incurably by a free-floating despair; "I'm just not having a very good time and I don't have any reason to think it'll get anything but worse. I'm tired. I'm hurt. I'm sad. I feel used." When her mother presses her further about the source of her misery, Jessie answers: "Oh, everything from you and me to Red China."

The Red China issue we share with Jessie, but the "you and me" is personal. Having made her decision, Jessie wants to use her last moments to explore her relationship with her mother and recall their past. She is full of recrimination, particularly about Thelma's failure to inform her fully about her epileptic condition. But underneath the bitterness and complaint lies a curious form of symbiotic love. Her suicide is perhaps meant partly to punish her mother, but it is also a means of reaching out to her, and in the agony of their parting there develops a deeper understanding between the two women than they could ever have achieved in life. But it is not enough. Jessie feels like someone who just failed to arrive. She waited and waited to fulfill the promise of her childhood, but it never happened; "I'm what was worth waiting for and I didn't make it. Me . . . who might have made a difference to me. . . . I'm not going to show up, so there's no reason to stay, except to keep you company, and that's . . . not reason enough because I'm not . . . very good company. . . . Am I?" To which Thelma must truthfully answer no.

But Thelma is not simply trying to understand her daughter's suicide, she is also trying to stop it, and she uses all the strategies and arguments in her possession to stay the course of necessity. Thelma is a salty, shrewd, good-natured country woman who represents a strong force for survival. Having allowed her damaged daughter to take care of her in order to give her a purpose, she is now being brought to realize that nobody can organize or possess another's life; but she still thinks she can prevent another's death. In an incessant stream of chatter, she tries to distract Jessie's attention with jokes and anecdotes, resorting then to tantrums, exhortations, derision, pitiful pleas, even physical threats. Nothing works for her—not even her poignant effort to prepare hot chocolate "the old way," which is Marsha Norman's version of J. D. Salinger's "consecrated chicken soup." (Both women admit they never liked it, since both hate milk.) For Jessie has no real appetites, another symptom of her anomie. Wondering what might keep her alive, Jessie muses: "If there was something I really liked, like maybe if I really liked rice pudding or cornbread for breakfast or something, that might be enough," to which Thelma replies softly, "Rice pudding is good." "Not to me," answers Jessie.

In the climax of the play, Thelma's positive force finds expression in a resounding affirmation of life as she screams her refusal to die until they drag her screeching and screaming to her grave. But it is not enough to counteract Jessie's pitiless and terrifying "No." Realizing that Jessie is already dead—"I'm looking right through you. I can't stop you because you're already gone"—Thelma crumples into helpless resignation, weakly absorbing her daughter's instructions about how to behave after she hears the shot. And when, following Thelma's final desperate attempt to restrain her daughter, Jessie says good night, closes her door, and fulfills her destiny, Mama is left forlorn on stage, her left had gripping the hot-chocolate pan, as she picks up the phone to inform the rest of the family and confront the wreckage of her life.

It is a moment that must happen; yet we continue to believe that it won't, as in the highest tragedy. *'night Mother* proceeds with the relentless force of a juggernaut, displaying not a single moment of artifice or contrivance or self-consciousness. In the absolute truthfulness of her treatment and dialogue, in the unforced poetry of her modern speech, and in her capacity to create major climaxes out of petty quotidian affairs, Miss Norman has followed the path of Chekhov, who believed that the great stakes of modern drama must emerge from under the trivial course of the daily routine: "Let the things that happen on stage," he wrote, "be just as complex and yet just as simple as they are in life. For instance, people are having a meal at a table, just having a meal, but at the same time their happiness is being created, or their lives are being smashed up." But the playwright to whom she in bound to be compared in future, in power, style, and intention, is Eugene O'Neill. In the way it exhumes buried family secrets, exposes the symbiotic links among parents and children, and alternates between bitter recriminations and expressions of love, 'night Mother is a compressed, more economical version of A Long Day's Journey into Night.

I am invoking some great names in describing this play because I believe Miss Norman, consciously or not, is writing in a great dramatic tradition and, young as she is, has the potential to preserve and revitalize it. Nothing reinforces one's faith in the power and importance of the theatre more than the emergence of an authentic universal playwright—not a woman playwright, mind you, not a regional playwright, not an ethnic playwright, but one who speaks to the concerns and experiences of all humankind. Implicated as I am, I have grown convinced that Marsha Norman is the genuine article—an American writer with the courage to look unflinchingly into the black holes from which we normally turn our faces. I hope you will, therefore, forgive me my ethical trespasses as I try to welcome her with all the awe and humility and gratitude that I think her work deserves.

SHOW AND TELL

(Death of a Salesman; Glengarry Glen Ross)

To see the revival of Arthur Miller's *Death of a Salesman* back to back with David Mamet's new play *Glengarry Glen Ross* is a compelling and enlightening experience—the coupling of these two events is like a cultural broadcast of what is past and passing and to come. Mamet follows Miller in making salesmen the metaphorical victims of a ruthless, venal, and corrupt system, but the two approaches, divided by a gulf of thirty-five years, reflect significant differences in politics and practice, telling us more about the changing nature of American drama (and society) than a dozen theatre histories.

Mamet has unwittingly accentuated a long-criticized flaw in Miller's conception, and I don't mean Willy Loman's failure to achieve tragic stature. It's hard to imagine anybody, including the author, still prepared to anoint his poignant Brooklyn drummer as the lower-middle-class equivalent of Oedipus. No, the years have proved *Death of a Salesman* valid not as a new democratic "tragedy of the common man," but as a social realist melodrama with roots in the Yiddish theatre of Jacob Adler (estranged father and son reconciled in an emotional embrace) and the Group Theatre of Clifford Odets (rebellious young man abandons his oppressive home for a place where life is not printed on dollar bills). Miller's stage technique seems to depart somewhat from linear realism when investigating Willy's memories, but these episodes are more akin to movie flashbacks than interior dream journeys since—like the climactic encounter with Biff in a Boston hotel room—they usually recapitulate actual events in Willy's past life.

No, the flaw I am referring to is Miller's failure to tell us what Willy Loman sells. This no longer sounds like a quibble after *Glengarry Glen Ross*, which fashions powerful epiphanies precisely out of dramatizing what the salesmen sell (real estate), and, more important, how they sell it. Mamet's theme is subtly assimilated within accumulated details of action and character; for Miller, these elements are often secondary to pontifications and pronouncements ("Nobody dast blame this man," "He's only a little boat looking for a harbor," "Attention must finally be paid to such a person," etc.). It is the difference between a writer with the qualities of a dramatic poet and one who tends to use the theatre for oracular rhetoric. It contrasts the writer who *shows*—who understands the effectiveness of understatement, who knows how a totally honest realism can transcend itself, that the truth is concrete—with one who *tells*—who manipulates his material for the sake of emotional effects, sententious flourishes, and social generalizations.

Still, *Salesman* remains Miller's most potent play, for all its well-rehearsed faults, and I am glad it's being revived if only to see the author reinstated in the fickle affections of his countrymen. Under

Michael Rudman's respectful, deliberate direction, the current production is an honorable one, though the evening has its longueurs and the central character is miscast. Dustin Hoffman's rasping gravelly delivery features a strong Brooklyn accent in puzzling contrast to his brother Ben's orotund Players Club diction, and he waddles across the stage like a graying, pleated, unsteady penguin looking for his nest. Hoffman's effort is gallant, but he is playing a role for which he lacks sufficient histrionic weight. Expending his energies in a detailed impersonation of late middle age, he often gives a studied, technical, curiously cold performance. John Malkovich as Biff, in a subtle, shrewd display of naturalistic underplaying, by turns soft-spoken and menacing, immediately identifies himself as the media heir to Brando and Pacino—but in witnessing the actor's instant leap to stardom I sometimes stopped concentrating on the character, as if I were reading a feature follow-up rather than watching a performance. Kate Reid does what she can with the impossible role of Linda Loman— patience darning socks on a monument, awaiting manumission by the woman's movement—and Stephen Lang's Happy, David Huddleston's Charley, Ben Edwards's lyrical tenement set, and Alex North's thirty-five-year-old flute music all contribute to warm feelings of nostalgia, if not of *déjà vu*.

Ah, but Mamet, bless him, has written a play without a single soft spot, that once again allows you to believe that American playwriting, at its best, can hold its place with the finest in the world. Mamet's ear is uncanny. Nobody today has a more flawless gift for reproducing overheard colloquial speech. But Paddy Chayefsky had this too (so, indeed, does a tape recorder). What distinguishes Mamet's dialogue is the purpose to which it is put. Without a single tendentious line, without any polemical intention, without a trace of sentiment, Mamet has launched an assault on the American way of making a living at the same time savage and compassionate, powerful and implicit, radical and stoical.

The first act of *Glengarry Glen Ross* consists of three short scenes in a seedy Chinese restaurant. The first of these—between the salesman, Shelly Levene, and the officer manager, John Williamson—is materially similar to, yet significantly different from, the vaguely agitprop climactic scene in Miller's play where Willy gets fired by his boss, Howard. Levene is aging, flagging, on his way out. What he needs from the bloodless Williamson is access to the prime leads so he can recover his past affluence and self-esteem. Williamson, his face cold with distastes, agrees to give him the leads provided Levene returns 20 percent of his commission and fifty dollars a lead, with a hundred dollars down. Levene accepts the deal but doesn't have the down payment. In a similar condition of helplessness, Willy Loman moaned, "You can't eat an orange and throw the peel away"; Levene responds by pouring a flood of contemptuous invective on the head of his hated tormentor.

The second scene features another orange refusing the rubbish heap. Dave Moss, a bald dynamo, is discussing with another salesman, George Aaronow, the possibility of stealing the leads and selling them to a competitor—"Someone should rob the office . . . trash the joint, it looks like robbery." George half listens until he realizes that Dave expects him to do the job. He is implicated now, an accessory before the fact. When George asks why he is doing this to him, Dave answers: "It's none of your fucking business," and then, "Because you listened." In the third scene, the salesman Richard Roma lines up a potential mark, James Lingk, by engaging him in sexual small talk, then hauls out a brochure for Glen Garry Highlands, a tract of land in Florida. This apparently insignificant action ends the act.

Written like obscene vaudeville riffs, these small Mamet mosaics become the basis for a large, ambitious narrative in which the pursuit of the leads assumes the magnitude of a quest for the Holy Grail. The second-act setting is the real estate office. It has been thoroughly trashed; the leads have been stolen; a police detective is questioning the suspect salesmen. Both Levene and Roma have closed big deals, and they are exultant. But before the day is over, both men will lose their advantage. Levene's customers prove to be incorrigible eccentrics who sign worthless checks. And Roma's mark, Lingk, has come to cancel the sale by order of his wife, who controls the checking account. Through a masquerade so inventive it almost establishes Roma as a Zen master of the art of conmanship, he manages to stall Lingk long enough to make cancellation impossible—only to have his con queered by the malignant Williamson. In the mayhem that follows, the true thief is exposed and apprehended (Mamet's only implausible plot twist), while Williamson regains his dominance over the beleaguered salesmen.

Those salesmen, however, for all their ruthlessness and competitiveness, have meanwhile managed to assume a kind of unexpected camaraderie, largely in opposition to such "fucking white bread" as Williamson. Except for him, Roma tells us, "everyone in this office lives on his wits." But the race is becoming extinct. "It's not a world of men," reflects Shelly, "it's a world of bureaucrats, clock watchers, office holders—we're a dying breed." Dying they may be, but for Mamet this sleazy, smarmy race of losers still has a volatile energy, even an elegiac aura of heroism. The powerful tensions he has uncovered between the ethnic underlcass and the WASP functionaries who administer its employment opportunities pick the scabs off a lot of ancient half-healed wounds.

The production comes from the Goodman Theatre in Chicago and it is excellent. Gregory Mosher, Goodman's artistic director, has capitalized on his association with Mamet to create a forward momentum that is relentless while deepening each of the performances. Robert Prosky as Levene maintains a manly resolve and courage in the midst of squeezed gray defeat; Joe Mantegna's Roma, with his patent leather hair, gold cuff links, and pinkie ring, essentializes the splendid vulgarity of a merchant of manipulation; James Tolkan is wired and taut as Moss; Mike Nussbaum plays Aaronow like a forlorn beagle, his sad eyelids drooping over his perpetually woeful countenance; and J. T. Walsh is steely cold as the meticulous Williamson, whose only physical defect is a spreading bureaucrat's bottom. Michael Merritt's sets are brilliantly rendered disaster areas, especially the cinder block office, and Nan Cibula's costumes provide an authentic polyester look for men who have a weakness for terrible clothes.

Like *American Buffalo, Glengarry Glen Ross* is to my mind a genuine Mamet masterpiece, a play so precise in its realism that it transcends itself and takes on reverberant ethical meanings. It is biting, pungent, harrowing, and funny, showing life stripped of all idealistic pretenses and liberal pieties—a jungle populated with beasts of prey who nevertheless possess the single redeeming quality of friendship. It is a play that returns tragic joy to the theatre—the kind of understanding O'Neill gave us in his last plays, facing painful truths with courage and thereby leavening profound pessimism with profound exhilaration. It is a play that shares the secret implicit in all fine works of dramatic art—that such truths are much more potent shown than told.

PAINLESS DENTISTRY

(Hurlyburly)

I had the unusual opportunity to read David Rabe's new play, *Hurlyburly*, in typescript before I saw the production. It was then called *Spinoff* and so powerfully written that I sent a letter to the playwright, whom I had never met, congratulating him on his achievement. I had not been kind toward some of Mr. Rabe's previous work, characterizing it as formally linear, thematically manipulative, morally self-righteous—smug mechanisms for producing guilt. This new play was either a major departure for Rabe or I had been wrong in my previous assessment. Either way, I felt obliged to write an apology, hoping thereby to encourage the playwright in what was bound to be a difficult progress toward the stage.

Doubtless, he needed more than my encouragement. Mike Nichols's production of *Hurlyburly* at the Promenade reminds me of the original production of Tennessee Williams's *Cat on a Hot Tin Roof* insofar as, like Elia Kazan, he has managed to give his playwright a hit only by altering the tone of his play. I don't mean to suggest that Nichols's treatment of Rabe's material is cheap or meretricious. Actually, few contemporary directors could have directed his actors with more skill. But in trying to make the work viable for the stage, Nichols has inadvertently managed to remove much of its impact and most of its meaning.

The text of *Hurlyburly* covers 152 typewritten pages, which makes Rabe still another child of O'Neill, with a play as long as one of O'Neill's late works, and equally repetitive. Like those of his model, however, Rabe's repetitions have a purpose, if only to expose the audience to the same ordeal as the characters. Structurally, they form a centripetal pattern, bringing us closer and closer in diminishing circles to an explosion at the center. In cutting this lengthy four-hour work to manageable length, Nichols has spared the audience's buns but left us wondering just what in hell the evening is all about.

What the play is about, I believe, is how the disintegration of American values has created a pronounced loss of purpose. Rabe's metaphor for this is cocaine, which functions in *Hurlyburly* much as do the "leads" in *Glengarry Glen Ross*, a play to which it bears a stylistic resemblance. (Previously under the hortatory influence of Arthur Miller, Rabe is now adopting the implicit *verismo* of Mamet—and the late O'Neill.) *Hurlyburly* takes place in the Hollywood Hills home of two casting agents, Eddie (William Hurt) and Mickey (Christopher Walken). Both are divorced, and their house is a center for casual sexual encounters and male friendships. Chief among the visitors is Phil (Harvey Keitel), a second-rate itinerant TV actor with a psychotic streak whom Eddie has virtually adopted. Women—including a postpubescent hippie (Cynthia Nixon), a balloon dancer (Judith Ivey), and a photojournalist (Sigourney Weaver)—wander briefly through their lives, but these are not males with a capacity for abiding relationships; their strongest connections are with other men.

Or, more accurately, with drugs. From the very first moment of the play, which starts in early morning, everybody is "getting ripped" through a wide variety of orifices, using a wide variety of narcotics, among them cocaine, marijuana, mushrooms, and Quaaludes. These "pharmaceutical experiments," as Eddie calls them, impart to the atmosphere an eerie zonked air of disengagement. People converse, but in a stream of meaningless talk, a species of underwater conversation, about broken marriages, sexual betrayals, blighted careers. Artie (Jerry Stiller), a middle-aged Jewish screenwriter, brings in Donna, the underaged hippie, for a gang bang; Eddie tries to break through the jargon of his photographer girlfriend ("I mean, I mean, you know, weird, weird, weird") to get her body arranged on the couch for sex. The language play grows ritualistic—repetitions of "blah-blah-blah" and "rapateeta" become a form of incantation.

The only plot concerns Phil, whose behavior grows increasingly erratic as the drug fog closes in ("Phil has got violent karma," says Eddie, "that's all, it's in the cards"). He has beaten up his estranged wife; he has mauled a stranger just for looking at him. Teaching Donna to play football (an ugly scene cut from the production), he butts her in the head. When he takes the balloon dancer out for a quickie, he throws her out of her own car. Eddie's affection for Phil is inexplicable; perhaps, as Artie says, he likes him because Phil is "safe"—"no matter how far you manage to fall, Phil will be lower." Whatever the case, Eddie excuses every instance of his friend's inexcusable behavior until, in the second-act climax, he turns on him, brutally destroying Phil's already shaky belief in his acting "potential" ("They just use you to make the bullshit look legitimate").

Eddie quickly reconciles himself with Phil. But in the final act, his doomed friend fulfills his inevitable destiny by killing himself in a car crash. Eddie, wiped out by guilt and drugs, feeling somehow responsible, begins analyzing Phil's suicide note for anagrammatic messages. He is trying to establish coherent causal connections between his own state of mind and the state of the world. But whenever he comes up with reasons, Mickey ridicules him ("Eddie, it's a rough century all around. . . . It's not the times that are dark, it's you"). Still, Eddie's bitter reflections on television brainwashing, the neutron bomb, and the Nestle formula milk invasion of Africa are apparently intended as serious social indictments (they are the only remaining traces of Rabe's former accusatory style and uncharacteristically explicit). At the end, Eddie is blowing coke in front of his television set, talking back to Johnny Carson, and blearily confessing himself to the bubble-headed Donna.

Mike Nichols has excavated all the humor available in the text, and added a considerable degree of satire. But in providing so much laughing gas, he has anaesthetized the toothache. Under his direction, the all-star cast sniffs out the jokes like truffles, but I don't think Rabe conceived *Hurlyburly* as such a madcap romp, nor were the three women originally intended to be such Nichols and May caricatures. Misses Nixon, Ivey, and Weaver fulfill their assigned tasks gallantly, but their characters are so lacking in human dimension (Miss Nixon, in particular, has been reduced to a set of physical and vocal flower-child clichés) that one ends up feeling it is the playwright, rather than his male figures, who has no understanding of women. Christopher Walken, brilliant as the cynical Mickey, dances effortlessly through the role with assumed accents, ironic twists, and irresistible charm, and Harvey Keitel's Phil is a delayed-action fuse of surface calm and repressed fury. But William Hurt, very credible when playing Eddie's drugged stupefaction, substitutes (at least on the night I saw him) whines and whimpers for Eddie's lacerating self-disgust, without which his coldness and cruelty are simply inexplicable.

As a result, Eddie seems indistinguishable from the character Hurt played in *The Big Chill*—a deadened survivor thrashing about for meaning—and this makes the playwright seem to be thrashing about as well. But Rabe has conceived Eddie as fully in his bitter elegiac desperation as any character since O'Neill's James Tyrone, Jr. in *A Long Day's Journey into Night*. The young Jason Robards, as a matter of fact, would have been ideal for this role, though Christopher Walken could play it equally well today, since he is clearly one of a few contemporary American actors unafraid to explore the dangerous swamps of his own soul. Hurt's failure is only partial, but, along with Nichols's evisceration of text and adjustment of tone, it works to subvert theme, purpose, and relationships, leaving us with an entertaining but ultimately hollow comedy-drama of male bonding, populated with goofy Hollywood tintypes.

I think Rabe intended something a great deal deeper than that. Besides displaying a dazzling new technique—not just a flawless command of dialogue, but an improved understanding of the nuances of human conflict—he has documented a chronicle of post–Vietnam War American life pieced together from the shards of our shattered beliefs. Probing the social-metaphysical secrets revealed to only the most visionary playwrights, he has correctly seen that the plague of cocaine, which has infected virtually the entire entertainment industry, is less a disease than a symptom of a much larger malaise that is infecting virtually the entire country, thus giving us insights into our fall from grace, if not into our capacity for redemption. Not much of that is now evident on the stage of the Promenade Theatre, where *Hurlyburly* remains a dramatic masterpiece in search of a faithful uncut production and an audience more interested in theatrical issues than gaping at Hollywood stars. But just to see it produced in the same year that featured *Glengarry Glen Ross* suggests that 1984 may well go down in theatre history as a watershed of American playwriting.

THE BEST OF BROADWAY

(Biloxi Blues)

Theatre critics I respect have proclaimed that Neil Simon's *Biloxi Blues* may signify the reawakening of the commercial stage from a year-long (decade-long?) coma. But traveling down to see the best that Broadway has to offer, I couldn't shake off thoughts of David Denby, the movie critic who recently assailed, in the pages of the *Atlantic*, the pretensions and artificialities of American theatre. Would this highly touted show simply be further documentation of his "theaterphobia," more grist for his bilious thesis that the best of Broadway adds up to less than the worst of Hollywood?

It would be easy enough to write Mr. Denby's sequel for him, though I still resist his extreme conclusion. I found *Biloxi Blues* mildly meretricious. But the occasion also reinforced my sense that quality judgments by disenchanted critics such as Mr. Denby (or myself) are beside the point of a problem that has passed the boundary of aesthetics into the realm of sociology. One must first recognize that Broadway theatre has lost its local audience. The passionate New York theatregoer who used to dominate dinner converation with chat about Broadway shows is now leading the table in discussions of *Purple Rose of Cairo* and *Jewel in the Crown*, while those who today buy tickets to the holdover hits are not an audience but a congeries—an aggregate of tourists, expense-account entertainers, refugees via bridge and tunnel. Under such circumstances, every show that opens in New York has an obligation not just to entertain but to reconstitute that scattered native community, and this I think is what critics wishfully forecast when they announce a Broadway resurrection.

Has Lazarus risen as a result of this new production? Well, maybe he's wiggled his toes a little. At least the patrons at *Biloxi Blues* bear some vague resemblance to a collective. I'm not sure this means Neil Simon is now ready for installation in the pantheon of the blessed, but this theatrical memoir of his days as a raw recruit in World War II certainly deserves points for momentarily bringing the spectators together in some kind of unity. The trouble is (can't suppress those opinions) that the very jokes that unify the audience manage to disunify the play. Mr. Simon sometimes reminds me of Witwoud in Congreve's *Way of the World*, a character who is always interrupting polite conversation with Restoration one-liners (then called epigrams). That the conversation Simon interrupts is his own makes the habit no less maddening, for there are times when he seems on the verge of generating real dramatic tension.

Biloxi Blues announces itself early when Simon's surrogate, Eugene, (the stripling from *Brighton Beach Memoirs*) declares his intention to survive the war, to become a writer, to lose his virginity, and to fall in love. If the last two ambitions suggest a romance or farce, the others augur something more penetrating, and it is Simon's ability to engage his characters in issues of consequence that has encouraged critics to speak of a new dimension to his talent. This emerges mainly in the conflict between the sickly but stubborn Jew, Epstein, and the Southern spirit-breaking sadist, Sergeant Merwin J. Toomey. But it is also reflected in Epstein's relations with the other trainees, a familiar roster of dumb ethnics, urban deadbeats, would-be crooners, and sensitive homosexuals, most of whom subject Epstein to a variety of anti-Semitic humiliations. The plot reaches its climax in Epstein's final encounter with Toomey. Brandishing his pistol, the drunken Toomey challenges Epstein to report him for threatening the life of a recruit, in an altruistic last-ditch effort to turn "a subhuman into a soldier" (a Herman Wouk–like character reversal designed to vindicate the villain). Epstein gets his delayed revenge by sentencing the sergeant to two hundred pushups.

Although this hardly original plot is frequently Simonized with gags (falsely accused of homsexuality, Epstein thinks of "an Agatha Christie story—*Murder by Fellatio, Fellatio on the Orient Express*") or with sententious sermonizing (he warns Gene not to censor his memoir because "once you start compromising your thoughts, you're a candidate for mediocrity"), it carries the only authentic moments of tension and electricity. Regrettably, however, Simon has wrapped these moments up in a conventional service comedy, a compound of *M*A*S*H*, *Stalag 17*, and *Sergeant Bilko*, revolving around Eugene and his cohorts in the Biloxi barracks. Many of the jokes stem from their incorrigible habit of breaking wind—there is enough farting in *Biloxi Blues* to reinflate the *Hindenburg*. There is also the obligatory put-down of the mess-hall chow, particularly the chipped beef ("They ought to throw this stuff over Germany—the whole country would come out with their hands up")—funny enough until it culminates in the defiant Epstein's punishment for refusing to eat it. These extraneous flippancies turn into outright comic pandering in the second-act brothel scene where Simon virtually abandons his concern with truth of character in order to reactivate his laugh machine. Morons evolve into wits, sexual innocents into studs, anything to watch the meter rise. One male virgin announces there are "at least fifty-two [sexual] positions. . . . I saw a dirty deck of cards once." Another protests: "My first time? Are you kidding? My second time. The first time they were closed." The same character who has just told Eugene you don't lose interest in sex after five or six orgasms tells him not to give it up for good if he doesn't like it the first time.

If the sexual aspects of the play seem the most forced, it is partly because the two women in the cast are such stick figures—the good-natured whore with whom Eugene loses his virginity, the idealized virgin with whom he falls in love. Seeking "the perfect girl," Gene finds her at a USO dance in the person of a parochial school bobby-soxer whose "all-time favorite book" is *The Great Gatsby*; his puppy-love courtship during a clumsy dance ("Would you get insulted if I told you I thought you were pretty?") is out of high-school prom movies of the forties. This uncertainty of tone, this compound of nostalgia, kitsch, and farce, ultimately undermines one's confidence not just in Simon's seriousness of intention but in the authenticity of his memories, and even Gene's final accounting of the fate of the characters (Daisy marrying a Jewish doctor, Gene beginning to write for *Stars and Stripes*, Epstein missing in action) seems to be lifted from the ending of *American Graffiti*.

The production almost manages to conceal these schizoid splits. It has been meticulously directed by Gene Saks, whose sense of theatrical placement and style is unassailable, and features a handsome minimalist setting by David Mitchell that conjures up images of trains, barracks, brothels while preserving a gracious atmospheric distance. The acting is also wonderful, from Bill Sadler's menacing Toomey, his jaw muscles flexing like biceps, through the spectrum of oafish recruits, to the Epstein of Brian Miller, a performance of exemplary control, particularly in the way the actor manages to maintain the integrity of his character through a hailstorm of comic schtik.

Matthew Broderick's Eugene is wonderful too—at times too wonderful. Shambling through the play like a sloppy schlemiel—Holden Caulfield as played in turn by Jerry Lewis, Stan Laurel, and Eli Wallach—Broderick has become to Neil Simon what Jean-Claude Leaud was to Truffaut, the very personification of his youthful hopes and tribulations. Unfortunately, the actor is also beginning to personify Simon's shrewd capacity to manipulate audiences. Broderick's broad takes, his shuffling walk, his urban accent, even the way he often appears to be breaking up on stage, sometimes seem more calculated than real, especially by contrast with Miller's uncompromising portrayal of Epstein. Like his author, Broderick is not always certain whether he is creating theatre or vaudeville.

Still, one must respect the spirit of those spectators, more lively, more engaged, more *at home* than any Broadway crowd in years. Someone once said that the success of popular art is measured by whether or not it demeans the audience, and on the basis of that criterion, *Biloxi Blues* for all its slickness, comic engineering, and ambivalent tone, is surely worthy of a muted cheer.

COMBATING AMNESIA

(The Marriage of Bette and Boo)

During his brief sojourn in the Sunday pages of the *New York Times*, the English drama critic Benedict Nightingale indicated a central strain of current American drama as "diaper plays," by which he meant works that ignored the urgencies of the political and social world, focusing instead on a surrogate hero's problems with his parents. It was a fundamental criticism of recent American playwriting from which only Mamet, Rabe, and Sam Shepard (and not always they) were spared, and it suggested that most of our younger writers were stuck at some premature, essentially narcissistic stage of development.

At the time, the name of Christopher Durang, whose last childhood trauma play was culpably called *Baby with the Bathwater*, stood high among those accused of an infantile obsession with dirty nappies. But while I agreed with Nightingale's general observations on the regression of much American playwriting (and even Durang's celebrated *Sister Mary Ignatius Explains It All For You* could be construed as a fantasy revenge exacted for humiliations experienced during childhood), something troubled me about Nightingale's inclusion of this domestic satirist, and not just because of my personal affection for a former student. After seeing Durang's masterly *Marriage of Bette and Boo* at the Public Theatre, I think I know what it is. *Bette and Boo* is another anguished comedy about growing up in a demented household, but if this is a "diaper play," then so is *A Long Day's Journey into Night*.

It is not entirely frivolous to cite O'Neill when discussing Durang for both are Catholic writers who know that the past is the present, and that until you understand your personal history you will be doomed to repeat the errors of your parents. Nor is this subject without political implications. It suggests how we can elect a Reagan after suffering a Nixon, how we can contemplate intervention in Nicaragua after failure in Vietnam, how we can again neglect our poor, how Bitburg is possible after Buchenwald. The American amnesia regarding the past spreads over every aspect of our lives, our political blunders being bred first not in the political womb of a society that ignores its own history but in the unexamined transactions of parents and children.

Milan Kundera has said that the primary struggle of the artist against tyranny is the struggle of memory against forgetting; he was not just referring to totalitarianism. Durang has learned from bitter experience how closely domestic and political amnesias are linked. Facing an effort generated by religious groups (including the Anti-Defamation League!) to suppress *Sister Mary*, he has recently become an advocate of another traditional memory in danger of being forgotten, the rights of the First Amendment. Perhaps this explains why a new poignance has entered his work in *The Marriage of Bette and Boo*, with no loss of cutting edge. An expanded version of a short play produced when he was a drama student at Yale, *Bette and Boo* is a remorselessly sad, achingly funny assault on the vanities, inanities, and insanities of family life, as seen from the cool, vaguely lobotomized perspective of a college student steeped in Thomas Hardy.

It's safe to say that Durang (who plays the part in this production) bears some resemblance to that student and that the family depicted in the play share some qualities with his own. But whereas O'Neill entered his past in order to lay his ghosts to rest, Durang, though engaged in similar acts of absolution, has not yet enacted that rite of exorcism. The play vibrates with absurdist satire, all the more funny for being true, and bitter recriminations, all the more savage for being unresolved. At the center is Bette, the mother, like her own mother passionate for children, and the father, Boo (short for Bore), a drunk like his father before him. At the opening curtain, they are married to the strains of composer Richard Peaslee's strained-glass chorale as Boo's father throws rice in his face. Boo's father is a cheerfully cruel man (his wife, Soot, he calls "the dumbest white woman alive"), while Bette's father is a zombie whose speech defect is an outrage to his family ("I've asked you not to speak—we can't understand you").

Their first child is Matt, the narrator, nicknamed Skippy because Bette loved the movie. When the doctor brings him in, he is dropped on the floor: "It's dead, the baby's dead." Matt survives ("Oh, you're right, it's not dead. You have a son"), but a series of five more infants, born dead, are successively pitched to the floor. Bette is RH negative and Boo is RH positive; the incompatibility of their blood groups effectively symbolizes their relationship. At a disastrous Thanksgiving dinner, Book drunkenly spills gravy all over the rug and enrages Bette by trying to vacuum it up. Nevertheless, Bette, congenitally a *Kindernarr* (she loves babies more than people and names all the dead infants after characters in *Winnie the Pooh*), simply can't repress her desire to increase and multiply, and neither physician nor priest nor psychological counselor can stay these stillborn couriers from their appointed rounds.

Impassive, detached, Matt manages the chronological narrative, acting as a Brechtian legend board, analyzing Hardy's *The Return of the Native*, listing his favorite nun movies (*The Nun Also Rises, Nun but the Lonely Heart, The Nun Who Shot Liberty Valence,*) and otherwise trying to keep his distance from the encircling lunacy. His father, Boo, falling on and off the wagon throughout the play, makes desultory efforts to communicate with his son which inevitably end in failure. Finally, some years after Bette has filed for divorce, she contracts cancer, followed by chemotherapy, prayer, even Christian stoicism, which she rejects ("I don't think God punishes people for specific things; I think he punishes people in general for no reason"). When Boo comes to visit, Bette remembers the past ("All the dead babies," to which Boo absentmindedly responds, "Yes, we had some good times"). Bette endures a spasm of pain, cheerful as ever, then quietly expires. Matt's requiem imagines her united with the unborn babies in a place where she waits for Boo, for all the dead Pooh children—"and for me."

It is an oddly touching coda after such satiric chaos and anarchic disorder. Durang has earned it by subtly weaving threads of genuine emotion through the pattern of his comic non sequiturs and absurdist turns. All of his characters are quite mad, yet somehow not without appeal. Even Matt's brutal paternal grandfather enjoys his moment of twisted redemption ("Don't try to change anybody—if you don't like them, be mean to them"). *The Marriage of Bette and Boo*, for all its anger and reproaches, is suffused with an aura of understated forgiveness, and it is this element that seems to me new in Durang's work.

The cast assembled at the Public Theatre, and the production, are perfect—American theatre at its best. Jerry Zaks, an ideal Durang interpreter, has directed the play with exactly the right wash of zaniness without neglecting the darker colors of its grim reality, and Loren Sherman's design scheme—a series of rolling panels revealing successive locations—provides the evening with pace and fluidity. As Bette and Boo, Joan Allen and Graham Beckel enact the quintessential union of hysteria and dopiness, their marriage doomed not by any of the usual foibles but by invincible shallowness and armor-plated stupidity. Bill Moor, as Boo's callously indifferent father ("I never wanted much from life. I wanted to get my way in everything, and that's about all"), and the brilliant Olympia Dukakis, her blond hair piled atop her head like a mud pie, playing his bubbleheaded mother, Soot ("I think I'm going deaf—God, I hope so"), enact another kind of American marriage, that of brutal master and dumb slave. Patricia Falkenhain plays Bette's mother, looking like Diana Trilling stoned on methadrine, and Bill McCutcheon, as her father, manages to amuse without pronouncing a single coherent word (he is equally amusing after he has died from an indigestible slice of birthday pie and sits on stage with a sheet thrown over his head). Splendid also are Kathryn Grody and Mercedes Ruehl as Bette's sisters, the one forever on the edge of breakdown, the other always on the verge of parturition. And finally, there is Durang as Matt, the cherubic innocent with curare on his fingernails, desperately trying to find some strategy for coping with an incomprehensible world, as he remorselessly proceeds to chronicle its deliriums.

The Marriage of Bette and Boo is a significant advance for its author. All of Durang's works (excepting *Beyond Therapy*, his only screwball comedy) have been satires built on a mound of pain, but *Bette and Boo* represents a greater effort to leaven this pain with understanding. As such, it is just as American as the poisoned apple pie that kills the maternal grandfather of the play and, for all its domestic venom, just as universal in its appeal.

THE SHEPARD ENIGMA

(A Lie of the Mind)

A Lie of the Mind is Sam Shepard's most ambitious play to date, the closest he has come to entering the mainstream of American drama. Directed by the playwright in association with professional producers, it has been mounted at the Promenade Theatre with a strong cast. Like David Rabe's *Hurlyburly*, whch also played that off-Broadway theatre with box-office actors, it stands a good chance of moving later to a Broadway house. Thus, Shepard seems to be following the pattern of all serious American dramatists since O'Neill—beginning with a small but passionate coterie of devoted admirers, and then achieving popular support and media recognition. In Shepard's case, this recognition has been enhanced, and complicated, by his celebrity as a movie actor, which has exacerbated the tension between his public and private careers. A similar tension was partly responsible for that neglect suffered by most reputable American playwrights after their greatest success (followed perhaps by a revival of interest when the playwright died or reached some venerable birthday). Clifford Odets got smothered by Hollywood; Arthur Miller ran out of usable material; Tennessee Williams lost control of his form; William

Inge turned to increasingly hysterical plots; Edward Albee sacrificed his absurdist power for mystical drawing-room comedies modeled on T. S. Eliot. On the other hand, O'Neill, with whom Shepard is most frequently compared, wrote his greatest plays years after Broadway had abandoned him.

For that reason, any cautionary remarks about Shepard's future are premature, though I must admit I found *A Lie of the Mind* disappointing—a big canvas on which the colors run in smeared, sometimes slipshod fashion. True, Shepard's playwriting has never been neat, but then it has never been very accessible either. What is strange for Shepard enthusiasts is how closely this one resembles a play by Lanford Wilson or Tennessee Williams. Ever since *Curse of the Starving Class*, Shepard has been moving away from extravagant characters, dream actions, and hallucinatory riffs into a more domestic style; with *Buried Child*, arguably his finest work, he managed to make the family play a structure for subterranean probes into the American nightmare. Now, however, those relationships between violent and sensitive brothers, loony mothers and children, fathers and alienated sons, husbands and estranged wives, have increasingly moved to the center of his plays, while whatever was fantastic and demonic has gone to the fringes. *A Lie of the Mind* goes delightfully haywire in the last of its three long acts, but for most of its four-hour length the action and the characters are relatively recognizable, even endearing eccentrics.

In short, Shepard is beginning to domesticate himself as a writer—ironically, at the very moment when, as a movie actor, he is being catapulted into legend as the iconic lonely Westerner. Composing more and more out of his actual as opposed to his dream experience, Shepard is moving inexorably toward the heart of American realism,where audiences have the opportunity to identify him as a family member like themselves—son, brother, lover, husband. This has advantages in greater clarity, concentration, and recognition. It also has disadvantages in that Shepard is now displaying what he has in common with the spectator rather that what the spectator unwittingly shares with him. Another disadvantage is that as Shepard's life gets increasingly familiar from interviews, his work seems to get increasingly biographical—and confined. The brothers from *A Lie of the Mind* remind us of the ones in *True West;* the husband and wife recall the brother and sister in *Fool for Love;* the California family comes from *Curse of the Starving Class,* the Montana family from *Buried*

Child. Worse, one finds oneself speculating about more personal links: whether the enmity between the dead father and his son is based on Shepard's own published filial feelings, whether the hero's jealousy over his actress wife has any bearing on his relationship with Jessica Lange, whether the character's brain-damaged dialogue has been influenced by that of his close friend, Joseph Chaikin, a recent stroke victim. One is tempted, in short, to confuse fiction with reality, imaginative creation with biographical gossip.

A Lie of the Mind begins with a frenzied telephone call from Jake to his brother, Frankie, saying that he has killed his actress wife, Beth. Objecting to the way she identified with her roles, Jake imagined that, Method-like, she was sleeping with her leading man, and beat her about the head. Beth, however, is alive, though the assault has damaged her brain; hospitalized and visited by her own brother, Mike, she can speak only nonsense syllables ("I'm above my feet. . . . How high me? How high up?"). Jake is having his problems too; he refuses to believe Beth has survived and suffers catatonic fits. His Mom, a menopausal vamp, tries to cure him by feeding him cream of broccoli soup, but he is in a fever of jealousy over a past affair he imagines between his brother and his wife.

Meanwhile, Beth has moved from a California hospital to her Montana home, where her father spends his days hunting venison. When Frankie arrives to try to reconcile Beth to Jake, her father, Baylor, mistaking him for a deer, shoots him in the leg ("In my prime, you'd have been dead meat, son"). Beth's family, particularly Mike, are primed for vengeance. Beth, alternating between moments of clarity in which she confesses her love for Jake and periods when she thinks they cut out her brain, dresses up like a hooker and tries to seduce the wounded Frankie, while Mike gleefully hauls in the hind end of a deer and drops the carcass on the living room floor.

Back in California, Jake is preoccupied with the ashes of his own father, an alcoholic air force officer who had abandoned the family. In a long revelation scene, Jake confesses his responsibility for his father's death, whom he led from bar to bar, then encouraged to run down the middle of the highway. When Jake finally goes to Montana to find Beth, Mike trusses him like a horse, putting an American flag in his mouth for a bit (Baylor is mighty upset by this desecration of the "flag of our nation"). While Baylor and his dotty wife carefully fold the flag, Jake announces his love to Beth—"I love you more than this earth. . . . Everything lied—you—you're true. I love you more than life"—then, to prove it, delivers her to his brother Frankie and leaves in the snow.

This is essentially the plot of the play, though there are dozens of other scenes, many irrelevant, including one in which Jake's Mom leaves home with her daughter and, in order to avoid packing, sets fire to the house (in Montana, Beth's mother thinks she sees a fire in the snow). It may seem odd to describe such idiosyncratic characters and bizarre behavior as "normal," but the eccentricities, while often amusing, sometimes seem willed, like the studied Gothic in Beth Henley or Tennessee Williams, and at the heart of this work is a rather conventional, even somewhat banal, love story. "I love you more than this earth" is not a line one would ever expect to find in a Shepard play.

Nor would one expect to find such crude symbolism as the flag business at the end. Even his title lacks the customary, instinctual Shepard resonance. What *A Lie of the Mind* could use is a really exacting editor, one who might have persuaded the playwright to pare away irrelevancies and obesities from his rather bloated text, while encouraging him to examine more closely its themes and situations. This is a director's function, and, much as I admire some of Shepard's work with the actors, I think it was a mistake for him to stage his own play. The setting, for example, apart from being crude and unsuggestive, leaves the central area of the stage virtually unused, with most of the scenes being staged in the two rooms on the sides.

I did not see Harvey Keitel play the part of Jake; perhaps to counteract his image (following a similar role in *Hurlyburly*) as a woman-beater, he was away assisting his own wife give birth to a child. Instead, his understudy, Bill Raymond, performed Jake, script in hand, in a display of guts and talent that drew cheers, though it made one attend more to the achievement than the play. People have a tendency to miscast Amanda Plummer, and she seemed to me again miscast as Beth, too spiritual and stentorian to capture the ripe steamy voluptuousness of the character. As Frankie, Aidan Quinn adds to his growing stature as an intelligent performer; Will Patton is a strong, vaguely simian Mike, roaring out the fury of an unsatisfied revenger; and James Gammon brings a hoarse crude authority to the deer-stalker, Baylor, whether having his bare feet rubbed with an ointment made to soften leather boots or giving his wife her first kiss in twenty years.

But the acting honors of the evening belong to the two Moms: Geraldine Page as Jake's mother and Ann Wedgeworth as Beth's. Her talent and control increasing with her age, Miss Page is a fearless and accomplished actress. She brings a bleary dissociation to the role—her belly swollen into a pot, bobby socks on her feet, a flower in her ear, whining like a fire siren—that tells us more about Jake's genetic disorders than Shepard's writing. As for Miss Wedgeworth, equally amnesiac about the facts of her past—demure, wan, trembling on the edge of hysteria—she emerges somehow as the most delicate member of the family, and the sanest, too, for all her flakiness ("Please don't scream in this house; this house is very *old*").

But, ultimately, despite the felicities of the acting and the writing, this play wears you down rather than works you up; the dialogue is a little too declarative, the plotting a little too undisciplined, the characters a little too artificial, to persuade you that the motor energies come out of inspiration rather than will. Critics are saying that Shepard's double role as playwright and movie actor is providing that missing link in American culture between high and popular art. I wonder. It must be very hard to write plays when people are staring at your hands to see if your nails are dirty. How does one perform the private act of creation under the blinding glare of publicity? How do you base your work on experience without making it a subject of gossip or speculation? How can Shepard find the freedom to separate himself as a writer from the role determined for him as a movie star? Perhaps those Pirandellian questions might form the subject of his next play.

ADDRESSING A HOSTILE AUDIENCE

(Aunt Dan and Lemon)

In the days when colleges required public speaking courses, students had to practice a debating technique known as "Addressing a

Hostile Audience." It consisted of arguing the virtues of some position—legalized infanticide, superannuated homicide—guaranteed to enrage the listener. Wallace Shawn's new play at the New York Shakespeare Festival Public Theatre, *Aunt Dan and Lemon*, seems to me less a dramatic work than a two-hour version of that public speaking procedure. Constructed almost entirely of provocative monologues, it concludes with a long speech by the sickly young heroine, Lemon, extolling German death camps. She finds the extermination policies of the Nazis "refreshing" because killing is something that has to be done, and "why not be truthful about it?" Killing is always unpleasant, but you have to admit people squash cockroaches without much remorse. After a while you get used to watching people die. You secretly even enjoy it. There's something inside all of us that likes to kill.

I suspect the author anticipated a reaction to this speech not unlike those thunderstruck gapes with which the audience in Mel Brooks's *The Producers* greeted the storm-trooper chorus singing "Springtime for Hitler"—maybe even a piece or two of ripe fruit shied at the scenery. How else does a debater "addressing a hostile audience" measure his effectiveness? But nobody raised a peep the night I was present. We all just sat there, as listless as late-summer flies, receiving these arguments, then applauding them at the end—like the audience applauding Peter Shaffer's arguments for mutilating horses in *Equus*—tolerating sentiments in the theatre we would never accept in life.

Because Lemon's speech is a monologue, nobody is allowed to suggest that, sickly and weak (if not because she talks too much), she herself would have been among the earliest victims of the Nazis. But then I suspect this play has very little to do with credible realities or logical thought. It is really about Wallace Shawn's relationship with his audience. So much of *Aunt Dan and Lemon* is directed out toward the house rather than in toward the other characters that it appears Mr. Shawn is trying to position himself in relation to the sorely besieged pieties of prevailing liberal thought.

For the intellectual heart of this play is a defense of the Vietnam policies of Henry Kissinger. Aunt Dan, an American friend of Lemon's mother and an Oxford don, is infatuated with our former secretary of state not just on account of his mournful countenance but because, Christ-like, he took upon himself the sins of an entire nation. "The whole purpose of government," she argues, "is to use force so we don't have to." How dare the "filthy, slimy worms, the little journalists" attack him for killing peasants? They just "sit in their offices and write their little columns" instead of expressing gratitude to Kissinger for making shattering decisions on America's behalf. Lemon's mother raises a small protest against this reasoning ("Are you saying government or Kissinger can do anything?"), but for the most part she, like everyone else in the play, is a mute recipient of totally unchallenged, totally arguable opinions.

It may be exceeding my critical privileges to mention that, as editor of The *New Yorker*, Wallace Shawn's father, William Shawn, published not a few "little columns" by those "little journalists" protesting Kissinger's policies; I bring it up to suggest some reason why these arguments seem aimed at an audience presumably composed of some of William Shawn's readers, and why these arguments seem so irritable and confused. Seeing the play doesn't lead one to reargue the virtues of the Vietnam War or even to dispute Aunt Dan's defense of Kissinger. It simply stimulates questions about authorial attitude toward the issues raised in light of what later prove to be their consequences. For Lemon's defense of the Nazis following Aunt Dan's death seems a direct result of Dan's teachings that governments survive and prosper through the use of violence: "I was on my own," Lemon says. "My education had been completed."

If you think this shows Shawn himself refuting Aunt Dan by proving that a policy that justifies force leads to a policy that justifies extermination, the play also includes a subplot, otherwise irrelevant, that could be construed as confirming Lemon and Dan's position. This involves some underworld friends of Dan, particularly an attractive blond demimondaine named Mindy who, largely for thrills, poisons and then strangles a foreign drug dealer in the midst of having oral sex with him (echoing raunchier writings by the son of an editor of a chaste periodical popularly known as Aunt Edna). Dan and Lemon are both fascinated with Mindy, and Aunt Dan even has an affair with her—an unconvincing mismatch between an elegant middle-aged Oxford scholar and an amoral party girl who have in common only their mutual recognition of the necessity for violence.

I have been discussing *Aunt Dan and Lemon* more as an argument than as a play since it is impossible to evaluate it in dramatic terms. Its failure to create any real engagement between characters, lack of organic development, directionless twists and turns of plot, tortured structure, unending exposition, confusing flashbacks (within flash-backs), and extreme talkiness all suggest an aesthetic disaster of considerable proportions if judged by any existing standards of theatrical form. Wallace Shawn, potentially one of our finest drama-tists, is perfectly capable of creating a strong dramatic action: *Marie and Bruce*, though occasionally disjointed, is a penetrating radiograph of a collapsing marriage. He is also capable of writing a work of genuine intellectual power, as demonstrated in the dialectical *My Dinner with Andre*, where Shawn, playing Sancho Panza to Andre Gregory's Don Quixote, countered his partner's grandiose mysticism with wry mordant realism. But the talk in *Aunt Dan and Lemon* is far from dialectical. It is more like a bleary soliloquy in a college dormitory, interrupted by the merest gesture toward theatrical con-text ("As we were talking," says Lemon in a typical aside, "night would fall"), causing one to leave the theatre as you might stumble into Harvard Yard after having been verbally assaulted by an espe-cially garrulous undergraduate proposing particularly provocative premises.

There is, no doubt, a vein of truth in Shawn's presentation. Human beings *are* destructive and violent; governments *do* reflect the aggres-sive qualities of their constituents. So what else is new? But it is also true that humankind has been struggling since the beginning of civilization to overcome its discontents and control this violence with compassion and understanding, lest we all end up in clumps of corpses or piles of ashes. Liberalism, however discredited, and for all its admitted hypocrisy and frequent silliness, remains committed to the life principle and the quest for peace in an aggressive world. And so does conservatism, for all its confrontational "realism" and para-noid style. But this is not true of the ideological extremism expressed in *Aunt Dan and Lemon* with its effort to elevate a strain in human nature into a general all-embracing dark principle. Which tempts one to say to Wally Shawn, "Don't hang back with the brutes."

I'm not really suggesting that Wallace Shawn endorses the reaction-ary ideas of any of his characters, or seriously entertains their positions. He's more engaged in fashioning acts of provocation. But open season on liberals has been licensed for many years now and the trophy room is getting crowded. I suspect that it might be more daring in the present climate to defend liberalism than to ridicule it, since the hostile audience Shawn is eager to address can be safely assumed now to be at least partly conservative.

Just a word about the production. It reveals the desperation of trying to make something theatrical out of essentially nondramatic material. Max Stafford-Clark, the director, has tried to adapt this disquisitional play to an English drawing-room tradition by putting it on a creaky turntable surrounded by wing-and-border scenery decorated with green fields and fall flowers, and isolating scenes through generalized lighting. The music (the "Barcarolle" from *The Tales of Hoffmann*, *The Songs of the Auvergne*) seems arbitrary and so does much of the invented business, such as Aunt Dan putting Lemon to bed while she is bending her ear off with opinions. As for the actors, they have very little to play except the dialogue. Kathryn Pogson as the retiring anorexic Lemon makes the most of limited opportunities by expressing her fascist sympathies with delicacy and shyness; and Wallace Shawn engagingly lisps a variety of roles, particularly Lemon's embittered father ("His teeth were rotten, his shit was rotten, and of course he stank"). But most of the other characters are reduced to sponges absorbing Dan's venomous opinions, and Linda Hunt, burdened with discharging these, is too mannered and monotonous to sugar the poison with the necessary charismatic charm.

It's puzzling why this play is set in England, even though Dan (despite Miss Hunt's elegant cadences) is supposed to be American, Lemon is half-American, and the political issues are native. But then *Aunt Dan and Lemon* strikes me as an entirely puzzling performance by a valuable writer, trying to create a play of ideas but too confused by internal contradictions to compose a coherent work.

HIGHBALLS AND BALLUPS

(Rum and Coke)

The subject of Keith Reddin's new play at the Public Theatre, *Rum and Coke*, is coded in the title. Rum and Coke proportionately blended is a concoction known in senior-prom circles as a "cuba libre." *Free Cuba*—a descriptive adjective misconstrued by the Kennedy administration as an imperative verb. *Rum and Coke* concerns the U.S. effort to liberate this island ninety miles to our south from Castro communism through an aborted invasion by Miami-based Cuban exiles backed by the CIA—surely one of the most idiotic enterprises in a long catalogue of absurd government adventures. It was Philip Roth who first remarked that the behavior of contemporary Americans, whether official or civilian, had become so extreme that it was outstripping the writer's capacity for satire. The challenge to any playwright addressing an event so incredibly botched, so ludicrous in planning and execution, as the Bay of Pigs fiasco is to discover an appropriate tone. Reddin's solution mixes baffled innocence, ironic indignation, and documentary facts in proportions as sweet and potent as his titular mixed drink.

I suspect his unconscious model was Stanley Kubrick's *Doctor Strangelove*, another comedy of disaster about government agencies gone temporarily mad. While Reddin's wrath is considerably milder than the lunatic fury of that surreal farce, his scalpel has its sharp edges. In place of Group Captain Mandrake—Kubrick's personification of impotent exasperation—he substitutes a young Yale graduate named Jake Seward to witness, and to participate in, the events leading up to the Cuban invasion. Jake spent some time in Havana as a child, and later ran a radio program in Caracas, playing records and making jokes, where he met Vice President Nixon during his ill-fated visit to Venezuela. This makes him a ripe candidate for the CIA, which recruits him to train exiled Cubans in broadcasting.

Under other circumstances, Jake would probably grow up to be George Bush. He has (aside from the habit of wearing white socks with his pinstripe suits) a perfect Ivy League finish combined with the capacity to rationalize the more barbarous behavior of his own government. He also has an older sister, Linda, a reporter for *Time* magazine, who functions initially as his political conscience ("What's your country? Connecticut?") until she too is co-opted by the promise of a government job. In the course of their meetings around Miami pools and restaurant tables, Linda, the liberal investigative reporter, gradually transforms physically and spiritually into an administration apologist and press secretary for Jackie Kennedy. What attracts her is the First Lady's chic—"She's class; we could use a little class around here"—in contrast with the style of the previous administration, symbolized by Ike walking around on polished White House floors in golf cleats swinging a nine-iron.

Jake is first recruited for his new position by a smooth functionary named Rodger Potter, and by Tod Cartmell, a Texas redneck with a ferocious hatred of Sinatra; the latter tells stories about a four-foot worm that once dropped out of someone's backside into a pan of milk ("You guys hungry? You want something to eat?"). At a CIA board meeting, Jake is apprised of the plans for overthrowing Castro—planting LSD in his double corona, spraying his beard with a strong depilatory to make it fall out overnight, hiring a member of the Mob (syndicate money being tied up in Cuban casinos) for purposes of assassination. Bizarre as this sounds, it is the stuff of history, if not of *Godfather II*. But Jake nevertheless proceeds with his obligation to train "freedom fighters"—exiled Cubans stationed in Guatemala whose hatred for Castro is surpassed only by their unrequited lust (until the whores arrive, they have to be satisfied with Kim Novak movies).

Jake's patriotism has been fueled by his personal contact with Nixon in Venezuela. Reddin intercuts scenes from this besieged meeting—where Nixon, dodging stones, admits, "People don't take to me; I'm not the life of the party"—with brief shots of Castro, complete with beret, cigar, and fatigues, teaching baseball to kids playing anti-Yankee war games. Later, when Jake begins developing doubts about the invasion and telephones Nixon, now a defeated presidential candidate, for reassurance, he is answered with character-building bromides and invective against Eastern Ivy League professors who watered down his original invasion plan.

Jake has qualms not over the act of overthrowing Castro but rather over the means. He knows the CIA has overestimated the extent of native Cuban discontent with their government, and without a local uprising, his Cuban exile friends will be left behind on the beaches, expendable sacrifices to a callous and careless bureaucracy. He attempts, unsuccessfully, to expose the situation to Linda for publication in *Time*. But the administration has already asked Time-Life to kill the story on security grounds ("Hey, we're all patriotic Americans") and, anyway, she's more occupied with persuading Jake to dress like a Kennedy. Eventually, he tries a Deep Throat maneuver, handing stolen memos to a newspaper reporter who turns out to be a CIA contact. He is apprehended by Rodger for breach of security.

"We're fucked," he moans, and when the smoke clears, it is obvious the Cuban invaders have been fucked too. American support has faded away. Fidel stands over the survivors gloatingly, meting out sentences ranging from imprisonment to death. The opposition has vanished but, as Fidel says, "I am still here." Nixon calls it "a bigger fuckup than PT 109." Linda has lost her job; Jake faces trial. Brother and sister, both now dressed Kennedy style, reminisce over the good times they once had in pre-Castro Cuba, over its pleasures and corruptions: "It made me feel special." When the investigative report of the invasion was issued in 1961, Jake cried and threw up. "How could we have been so dumb?"

Rum and Coke ends as an elegy for lost innocence and lost honor. For the young Reddin, Cuba represents a historic event as catastrophic to patriotic ideals as Suez continues to be for young Englishmen (*Rum and Coke*'s English counterpart is David Hare's *Plenty*, another elegiac study of the subversion of personal values by official duplicity). But although the play has a political subject, it is not strictly speaking a political work. Reddin takes no stand regarding the ethics of overthrowing Castro. What fires him is the betrayal of committed Cuban patriots in a stupidly contrived adventure. In common with previous work by this developing dramatist, *Rum and Coke* deals with historic subjects largely in an effort to humanize them, conforming to Chekhov's dictum that "writers and artists must concern themselves with politics only insofar as it is necessary to put up a defense against politics." In short, the play is a document more eloquent than most of the speeches at the recent PEN conference about the adversary relationship between the "writer's imagination" and "the imagination of the state."

Rum and Coke has its flaws, most of them confirming Roth's remarks about the inadequacy of modern satire in the face of contemporary reality. Often, Reddin can invent nothing more ludicrous than the established facts, which gives his work the feel of newsprint scraped off the front page. Some of his characters—the redneck Texan, for example—are stereotypes. His portrayal of Nixon ("Maybe you don't know it, but I sweat") is conventional and facile, little better than a stand-up impersonation, and his cruel paternalistic Castro is not fully imagined. His intercutting and flashback techniques are more cine-matic than theatrical. And his tangential comic monologues—Tad's story of the four-foot worm, the exile leader Miguel's account of a Guatemalan woman smoking a cigarette "with her thing"—while providing the wildest, most virtuosic moments in the play, occasion-ally seem extraneous to the action.

Still, *Rum and Coke* is never less than intriguing, and sometimes very moving. It is also enjoying a dynamic, fluid production at the Public under the direction of Les Waters. John Arnone's design makes economical use of a small stage, with set pieces gliding in against a corrugated background. Peter MacNicol's glandular Jake, partly based on the playwright himself (also a gifted comic actor), is two parts nerd to one part hero; the actor somehow manages to evoke sympathy for his character without ignoring his shortsightedness. Polly Draper has a hoarse-voiced Debra Winger appeal as the mature Linda, and, playing her as an adolescent in Havana—a debutante stick with a corsage, shoving a hankie in her bra in preparation for a date with a Cuban Lothario—she displays considerable comic talent as well. Tony Plana as a betrayed exile spokesman, Larry Bryggman as the insensate CIA chief, Michael Ayr as Rodger, John Bedford-Lloyd as a variety of characters—indeed, virtually the entire cast—deliver a performance that extracts the last ounce of outraged humor from this engaged and engaging play.

A SHAGGY DOG STORY

(The House of Blue Leaves)

After years of feeling marginal—he once called himself the oldest promising playwright in America—John Guare is about to experience a vogue. *The House of Blue Leaves* has been revived in New York, in a production so highly acclaimed that it was elevated from the minia-ture Mitzi Newhouse in Lincoln Center, where it opened, to the more glamorous and underoccupied Vivian Beaumont, accompanied by full-page fanfares in the *Times*. Guare is now destined to become the subject of newspaper features, magazine tintypes, TV talk shows, radio interviews, and all those other celebrity rituals that constitute the American version of ancient puberty rites and walkabouts. Or perhaps they're the Gentile adult version of Jewish bar mitzvah parties where relatives and guests circulate around the confirmation boy to praise his speech, admire his blue suit, and pinch his cheeks before leaving him, bewildered, isolated, forlorn, amidst the stacked plates and soiled tablecloths.

John Guare is young enough to enjoy these rituals and seasoned enough to be prepared for the inevitable end of the party. He knows success is always accompanied by backlash, if not whiplash, and he will keep his good nature when the ballroom empties out. He will also keep his admirable devotion to the stage and unwavering commitment to playwriting, which he's courageously maintained in the face of unkind evaluations and sour reviews of the type I am about to offer.

I think I once compared John Guare to a big shaggy dog whose paws get all tangled up in its efforts to befriend you. In *House of Blue Leaves*, this kindly creature seems to be standing on your shoulders and licking you all over the face. I can't recall, when I first saw this play in the early seventies, that it worked so hard to ingratiate itself with the audience, so part of the problem may be Jerry Zaks's curiously coy production (surprising in the light of Zaks's much more hard-nosed approach to the sharper style of Christopher Durang). Whatever the reason, the intervening years have turned *House of Blue Leaves* from a provocative off-Broadway comedy into an eager-to-please middlebrow commodity.

I realize that "middlebrow" is no longer a term in the critical lexicon, but what else do you call the divided tone of this calamity-packed laugh riot? *House of Blue Leaves* is black comedy seen through rose-colored glasses. It ends with a shock, when the trapped husband, Artie Shaughnessy, throttles his dippy wife, Bananas, in the midst of her puppy impersonation (why didn't Torvald think of this when Nora started her squirrel bits?). But it's tough to accept a tragic climax after having been encouraged all night to regard murder, madness, physical affliction, adultery, and assassination as occasions for gags. Yes, I know about Joe Orton, but Orton never deviates from his remorseless japery. More like Peter Nichols in *Joe Egg*, Guare wants it both ways here—to exploit the absurdities of his maimed characters, and then to draw down the mouths of their comic masks. But you don't establish dramatic empathy after two hours of farcical alienation.

"Alienation" is probably too lofty a phrase to describe a style that mixes arch one-liners ("Orion—the Irish constellation") with droll characters and whimsical situations, and turns the audience into a laugh track. Zookeeper Artie is a would-be songwriter who sometimes speaks in couplets; his consuming ambition is to compose movie music for his boyhood chum, the Hollywood director Billy Einhorn. Artie's guilty concern for the mildly insane Bananas (she occasionally tries to commit suicide by slashing her wrists with spoons) is the obstacle to this ambition ("You wish I was fatter," she says, "so there'd be more of me to hate"). And his peroxide tootsie, Bunny, doesn't offer much in the way of consolation by refusing to cook for him ("We've gotta save some magic for the honeymoon. . . . I want it to be so good, I'm aiming for two thousand calories"). On this particular day, the pontiff is coming to visit New York, and the couple's psychotic son, Ronnie, is planning a papal assassination. Like his nonfictional Turkish successor, Ronnie botches the job. He blows up a couple of hip nuns instead, along with Billy Einhorn's girlfriend, the deaf starlet Corinna (Bananas has mistaken her hearing aid transistors for lithium and swallowed them). Billy decamps with Bunny, leaving Artie frustrated enough to strangle Bananas. And the play ends, as it began, with Artie in a blue spotlight, crooning songs.

It's too bad that Bananas gets killed at the end, because the *dramatis personae* of *The House of Blue Leaves* is cute enough, and the plot sufficiently contrived, to be recycled for a TV sitcom (the ultimate fate of Lanford Wilson's *Hot l Baltimore*). Billy consoles Artie for his blighted career by telling him he has "the greatest talent in the world—to be an audience—anybody can create." This flattering nod to the noncreative consumer, unequaled on the stage until Salieri's tribute to mediocrity in *Amadeus*, is the assumption underlying mass culture, and it spells the difference between art created out of need and kitsch created out of need for endorsement. The very good actors in this production—and Swoosie Kurtz, Stockard Channing, and Julie Hagerty are especially fine American performers—have also all been directed to sniff out that endorsement. Virtually nobody—the exception is Christopher Walken's silken suffering Billy—behaves normally, because virtually everybody is behaving for the sake of audience approval. Just once, a character—the assassin Ronnie—gives the spectators the raspberry. But even that mild breach of conviviality is followed by a quick "Sorry."

The play is better constructed than the later work of Guare, who has a lot more feel for New York local color than for Nantucket or Civil War history, the subject of his more ambitious *Lydie Breeze* cycle. One also has to respect the playwright's effort to locate humor and vitality in the desperate careers of the dispossessed and uncelebrated, though it's not always clear how detached he is from their one articulated value, which is to get on a plane to Hollywood. Dammit, I like John Guare, I really do, and I'm glad he's having his moment in the sun. I'd like him a lot more if he'd just get his paws off my chest and romp freely around the yard.

SOULS ON ICE

(The Iceman Cometh)

When *The Iceman Cometh* was first produced by the Theatre Guild in the mid-forties, hostile intellectual critics unflatteringly compared it with Ibsen's *The Wild Duck* and Gorki's *The Lower Depths*. After it was successfully revived ten years later by Circle in the Square, commentators began to recognize that, for all its clumsy dialogue, repetitiveness, and schematic plotting, the play was a great work that surpassed even those distinguished influences in depth and power. Today, almost forty years after its initial appearance with James Barton and Dudley Digges, *The Iceman Cometh* has been restaged at the Lunt-Fontanne Theatre by the original director of the Circle in the Square revival (José Quintero) with the same Hickey (Jason Robards) and, despite arthritic moments in the production, emerges not only richer than ever, but as the inspiration for much that has been written for the stage since.

The play resonates. It is at the same time familiar and strange. One is caught in its potent grip as by a gnarled and crippled hand.

Robards, with his past history of alcoholism and air of personal suffering, has always been the American actor showing the greatest affinity with O'Neill's spiritual pain, and this blood kinship, coupled with a valiant heart, carries him through the handicaps of playing Hickey in his late sixties. Hair darkened, face rouged, mouth dentured, energy flagging, Robards would now appear to be too old for the part, and there are times when he seems less to be living his role than remembering it. Still, if the performance is a bit of an overpainting, Hickey has belonged to Robards for many years, and when this remarkable actor makes his first entrance in a straw boater and off-the-rack pinstripe suit, throwing his bankroll at Rocky the bartender and exhorting the inmates of Harry Hope's saloon in his slurred whiskey bass, there is a thrill of simultaneous immediacy and recognition.

Age has given Robards an extraordinary luminescence—pallid skin, transparent eyes. His Hickey continually promises his drunken friends the reward of spiritual peace (each act but the last ends on the word "happy"), but for all his drummer's energy, finger-snapping, vaudeville physicality, and carny-shill delivery, he is a ghost from the moment he walks on stage. Robards is continually undermining his character's professed optimism, as when he gets "sleepy all of a sudden," trips over a chair, and falls into a faint; Robards's face goes slack as though he's had a minor stroke. For while Hickey has the remorseless cheeriness of an American evangelist (he was no doubt inspired by Billy Sunday or by Bruce Barton's characterization of Jesus as the world's greatest salesman), only Larry Slade looks as deeply into the abyss of life without hope or redemption.

Robards is surrounded by a fine cast, the one weakness being Paul McCrane's rather flaccid Parritt. Barnard Hughes is a roistering Harry Hope, John Christopher Jones an intellectually degenerate Willie Oban, James Greene a gaunt Jimmy Tomorrow, and Donald Moffatt a dignified Larry Slade, and most of the smaller roles are also played with strength. Still, Robards's realism, even when unfulfilled, is of such intensity that it sometimes makes the others seem a little "classical." Take Barnard Hughes, so ingratiating and roguish when holding court in his saloon but not quite anguished enough when his "pipe dream" is exposed. Or consider Donald Moffatt, quietly eloquent and detached throughout the play, yet resorting to languorous legato cadences in his time of agonizing self-recognition.

And I wish that Quintero had been a little bolder in his approach. Ben Edwards's bar setting is selectively seedy, and Jane Greenwood's costumes really look like secondhand clothes that have been rotting on the bodies of the characters. But apart from the opening scene, with the stubble-bearded living-dead derelicts sleeping openmouthed under Thomas R. Skelton's pasty light, there has been little effort to suggest that this is a world at the bottom of the sea or that *The Iceman Cometh* has a reverberant symbolic interior as well as a naturalist facade. Quintero acknowledges O'Neill's hints (in his archaic title and elsewhere) that Hickey and his twelve companions bear a strong resemblance to Christ and his disciples—Parritt being Judas and Larry suggesting Peter, the rock on which he builds his church—and that Harry Hope's birthday party is based on the Last Supper (his actors fall into poses inspired by da Vinci's painting, Hickey hovering over them with his palms outstretched). But otherwise the production is a retread of the one staged in 1956, as if nothing had happened to the theatre in thirty years. Even the exits and entrances seem designed for Broadway applause. I don't mean this version is old-fashioned—it has too much life for that—and I admit that a more imaginative interpretation might very well have obscured the play's intentions. Still, O'Neill was a very reluctant convert to Ibsenite realism ("holding the family kodak up to ill-nature," as O'Neill called it) and never truly abandoned his devotion to symbolic substructures. A play as thickly faceted (and familiar) as this one deserves more audacious treatment.

Even conventionally staged, however, *The Iceman Cometh* has lost none of its consuming power. The play is long—it lasts almost five hours—and sometimes painfully repetitious, since each character is identified by a single obsession that he continually restates. Thus, each act offers a single variation on the theme of illusion; the action never bursts into spontaneous life; and the characters rarely escape O'Neill's rigid control, as, say, Falstaff escapes Shakespeare or Mother Courage escapes Brecht. Still, one must recognize that the work consists not of one but of thirteen plays, each with it own story; O'Neill has multiplied his antagonists in order to illuminate every possible aspect of his theme and every rationalization, whether religious, racial, political, sexual, psychological, or philosophical, with which humankind labors to escape the truths of raw existence. And in some crazy inexplicable way, the very length of the play contributes to its impact, as if we had to be exposed to virtually every aspect of universal suffering in order to feel its full force.

This exhaustiveness of design probably accounts for its influence on so much subsequent work; seeing the play today is like reading the family tree of modern drama. Surely, *Death of a Salesman*, also recently revived (superbly) as a film for television, owes a strong debt to *The Iceman Cometh*, with its O'Neillian theme of an illusory tomorrow embodied in another hapless drummer cheating on another saintly wife in out-of-town hotels (the name Willy Loman even echoes that of O'Neill's character Willie Oban). Hickey's long-delayed entrance ("Would that Hickey or Death would come") may have inspired a similar long-awaited figure, Beckett's Godot, who, like Hickey, stands in an almost supernatural punitive relationship to helpless derelicts. And there is no question that Jack Gelber's dazed junkies in *The Connection* owe a great deal to O'Neill's drunks in Harry Hope's End of the Line Café, just as it is likely that if the play were written today, the characters would be drug addicts.

I cite this partial list of influences not to swell the secondary reading list of the dramatic lit. syllabus but to suggest how a great play over time becomes a seedbed of seminal riches. And *The Iceman Cometh* is as great a play as the modern theatre has produced. The current production brings no new insights; it is occasionally badly paced and laborious, especially in the overly schematic third act; and the actors, gifted as they are, sometimes draw back from the precipice. But by the conclusion of this long evening, this masterwork has managed to cut to the bone, and that makes the production a signal event in any Broadway season.

AN ENGLISHMAN IN NEW YORK

(Fifth Row Center)

During the 1983–84 theatre season, an English drama critic, Benedict Nightingale, was invited to become Walter Kerr's temporary replacement in the Sunday culture pages of the *New York Times*. He has now recorded his impressions of that year in *Fifth Row Center: A Critic's Year on and off Broadway*, and it makes for instructive reading. Nightingale is a humane, intelligent man who believes that theatre is a central art; perhaps that is why his book is such a lamentation over the quality and marginality of the New York stage. After nine months in the job, he fled to London, and no amount of arm-twisting by the *Times* has yet been able to lure him back.

Alternately bemused, puzzled, and indignant over our sorry theatrical climate, Nightingale keeps searching throughout his "querulous journal" for the sources of the drought, generally using the relatively healthy London theatre as his divining rod. What can account for the drop in attendance, the burgeoning production expenses, the closing of the theatres, the loss of "traditional" theatregoing audiences, the paucity of new plays, the reliance on pretested products, the pinched horizons of American playwrights, the absence of great actors, and all the other well-publicized woes of the New York stage? Curiously, the 1983–84 season was a comparatively rich year for American theatre. It included Mamet's *Glengarry Glen Ross*, Shepard's *Fool for Love*, Durang's *Baby with the Bathwater*, Rabe's *Hurlyburly*, Sondheim's *Sunday in the Park with George*, and (with Nightingale as one of its lonely admirers) Kopit's *End of the World* among new American plays, not to mention such successful revivals and imports as *The Real Thing*, Peter Brook's *Tragédie de Carmen*, *A Moon for the Misbegotten*, and *Death of a Salesman*. Nightingale writes appreciatively, though discriminatingly, about many of these works. Yet, his tone is invariably that of someone performing extreme unction for a theatre in its death throes.

Although he often tends to confuse American theatre with New York, and New York with Broadway, Nightingale is undoubtedly correct in his diagnosis of our stage, and, being a foreigner, he brings an unclouded eye to his subject. One may quarrel with his opinions of individual plays and productions—in fact, he invites disagreement—but his real value is as a sociologist of an ailing species. "What my masters at the *Times* seem to want," he writes, "is generalization," and Nightingale is not reluctant to fashion sweeping statements. True, he occasionally displays the limitations of the social scientist, particularly in his environmental emphasis. Insisting properly on a "public dimension" for drama, he may be a touch insensitive to its metaphysical dream nature, preferring plays that engage social-political subjects to those embarked on subterranean interior journeys. Correctly chastising the "relentless domesticity" of American "relationship" drama, he is not sufficiently critical of the externality, editorializing, and stylistic showmanship of his own countrymen, Michael Frayn and Tom Stoppard. A really fine modern play for Nightingale is something like *Jumpers*, while the *locus classicus* of modern drama is still Osborne's *Look Back in Anger*. He is capable of praising Shepard and Mamet, but one suspects he would be happier if our playwrights could write more like Clifford Odets or Arthur Miller ("If *Awake and Sing!* has dated," he asserts, "then so has *Death of a Salesman* and *All My Sons*, and much else that seems quite as eloquent to me as it did to my seniors").

I would also quarrel with his protectionist view of the classics—a myopic conservatism he shares with many American critics. Claiming to recognize there is no such word as *definitive* in a good critic's vocabulary ("Anything with richness, resonance, or even ambiguity can be performed in different ways, with different emphases, different lights and shadows, peaks and deeps"), Nightingale nonetheless is consistently hostile to the reinterpretive deconstruction being performed these days on classical plays by experimental directors (his first extended review was a trashing of Andrei Serban's *Uncle Vanya* for its "chutzpah" and "perversity"). He makes an exception of Peter Brook's *Carmen*, defending it against hostile music critics by drawing lines between "work that can on occasions be subjected to surgery and work so momentous that it can never be tampered with"—a distinction that restricts theatrical investigation to second-rate plays.

The real distinction, as Nightingale admits later, is a subjective one. The reason he will defend Brook's *Carmen*, and not Serban's *Vanya* (apart from knowing Chekhov better than Bizet), is because he *likes* it—though when he returns for a fourth time and hears it in English, he finds it cruder, coarser. His new opinion makes him speculate about the whole nature of a critic's judgment when confronted with the "exhilarating" changeability of the theatre. Is it possible for an observer outside the process to distinguish errors in production from faults in a play? He is aware that reviewers will often attack actors for the decisions of directors, just as they will blame playwrights for distortions introduced by their collaborators. Gradually developing a healthy skepticism about the value of absolute critical judgments, he determines to devote more thought to analysis and less to unformulated opinion. Nightingale's Socratic modesty is his most winning quality; would that it might infect the rest of us opinionated wretches!

Fifth Row Center is generously larded with judgments, but these are usually pretexts for analyses; every new production inspires a digression on some new theatrical problem. Reviewing Dustin Hoffman in *Death of a Salesman*, he observes that while the cream of the profession will occasionally return to theatre, most American actors are imprisoned by television and movie careers. Noticing that five months into his job only two new plays have opened on Broadway, he suggests that conditions in America do not favor the encouragement or development of playwrights. Seeing yet another work on Broadway that originated in London, he wonders about the health of a theatre so dependent on English imports. During dark days, he interviews Hal Prince, the Nederlanders, and the Shuberts (who defend New York as the most creative theatre city in the world, but can cite only technical advances), continually looking for explanations of the disarray he sees around him. He concludes sadly: "I never quite managed to find the New York theatre. It always seemed to be out when I called."

Nightingale acknowledges the abundant talent, wealth, and enthusiasm around. What he misses is "the algebra that will bring all these elements together in a nice, satisfying equation." The algebra he favors is the source of Britain's theatrical health: generous government subsidy and the development of a national theatre. And the person who gives him greatest hope is Joseph Papp, "probably the most important figure in the New York and, indeed, in the American theatre," whose scheme for a "National Theatre on Broadway" Nightingale warmly endorses. This was 1983. What Papp proposed then was a string of new American plays produced for limited runs of eight weeks each in a chain of perhaps ten Broadway theatres, drawing actors from Hollywood and TV during short breaks in their careers, along with playwrights lured by a promise of twenty-five thousand dollars, whether or not their plays succeeded. Low ticket prices, union concessions, private and public subsidy, air rights, these were the elements required to make the idea work in an arena that had recently proved inimical to untried new plays.

Papp's plan, while grandiose, was not impractical, and he undoubtedly possessed the entrepreneurial skills to realize it. That it still lies dormant years later suggests that, like not a few of Papp's announced policies, it was displaced by some other project ranking higher on his agenda at the moment. I hope it is implemented soon because the commercial theatre needs new plays. But Nightingale should realize it's a formula for Broadway producing in subsidized form, thus no more qualified to be called a "National Theatre" than such old-line Broadway cooperatives as the Playwrights Company or the Theatre Guild. As I've frequently written, a "National Theatre" is not likely to materialize in a country as large and diverse as ours; it's even less likely to materialize out of a press conference announcing a company of vacationing Hollywood stars.

The chances are it won't materialize in New York either, for reasons that drove Nightingale back to London. (Divining these reasons, his countryman, Tyrone Guthrie, established a repertory theatre in Minneapolis). Nightingale expresses regret that he was unable to travel much to review theatres throughout the country, and, apart from seeing some soporific exercises by the virtually defunct Living Theatre, he didn't see much avant-garde work either. I doubt if he would have appreciated it much—he displays, for example, typical British insularity toward such visionary innovators as Robert Wilson, whom he finds without "moral or social purpose." Yet, it is in a handful of decentralized resident companies and itinerant perfor- mace artists that Nightingale might have found the theatre he sought without success in New York. It is there, too, that he would have encountered a passionate, engaged audience—a true community fol- lowing the progress of an artistic institution, rather than the hit- happy tourists he sees at Broadway shows. And it is there he might have met some dedicated theatre artists—playwrights, directors, actors, designers—who have continued to care more about the ongo- ing process of their work than about the ongoing progress of their careers.

Such artists exist in New York, but lacking continuous employ- ment and critical appreciation, they don't form a coherent community there, except in isolated pockets like Mabou Mines and the Wooster Group. Many have therefore chosen to refuse New York—and that means refusing the promise of celebrity—believing that the answers to our plaguey theatre questions are not to be found in this traditional center. What results will not resemble the British model where the National Theatre and the Royal Shakespeare Company coexist com- fortably in London with a thriving commercial theatre. Rather, it will be formulated in response to the fact that for almost two decades now no major resident theatre company has been able to survive in New York City, where even our most celebrated actors and playwrights have no assurance of regular work. American theatre must sow the seeds of its growth in soil that is welcoming, and this means finding communities where theatrical art is not treated like disposable merchandise. As Benedict Nightingale acknowledges in this wry, warmhearted, and ultimately depressing account of his visit here, we have the talent, the wealth, the enthusiasm, and the vision to build a great theatre in America. The gifted artists whose work he saw in New York showed him everything but continuity. I suspect the missing algebra he could not identify in his equation was a fertile site.

HERE ARE THE PLAYWRIGHTS

Perhaps the question most frequently asked in the American theatre is, "Where are the playwrights?" Each generation believes that the past was a golden age of dramatic writing and the present is barren by comparison. I remember hearing the question in the fifties, when Williams, Miller, Hansberry, Gibson, and Inge were dominating the stage. It was asked again in the sixties, when Albee, Gelber, Kopit, Bullins, Feiffer and Ribman were generating plays. And it has been insistently posed in recent years—a period, paradoxically, when American playwriting may very well have been entering a renaissance. Even American playwrights are sometimes prone to accept the legend of their invisibility. In a recent article in the *New York Times*, Albert Inaurato bemoaned the cultural conditions that were making it impossible for dramatists like himself to work: insufficient royalties, indifferent audiences, unavailable actors, unadventurous producers. The situation sounds dismal—until you notice there are more talented playwrights around the theatre today than at any other time in our history.

Playwrights are a stubborn breed. Potentially the most ballyhooed writers in our society, they rarely enjoy consistent public or critical approval. One day they are lions, the next day goats. They can work for years on a script, rehearse it for months, and see it die in a week. They may experience every form of discouragement known to a writer; yet, unlike our actors and directors, they rarely abandon the stage permanently for movies or television (many have the option to moonlight in these lucrative fields). Playwriting is not so much a craft as an obsession. Playwrights often seem to have no other choice than to write plays.

I know good dramatists who haven't had a work produced in New York in over ten years. Yet, every season, like clockwork, they submit a new script. In the past, one could argue, they were playing the odds. With one Broadway hit, followed by tours, out-of-town productions, and publication in the Samuel French catalogue, their financial future was assured. Nobody expects this anymore. Today, a serious American play stands as much chance on Broadway as a classical revival, which is to say a brief run at best, even in the unlikely event it gets produced. American playwrights are exiles in their own land, their traditional territory having been usurped by British imports, formula musicals, and lightweight comedies.

Yes, it's true that Marsha Norman's 'night Mother, David Mamet's Glengarry Glen Ross, August Wilson's Ma Rainey's Black Bottom, and David Rabe's Hurlyburly, perhaps a few others, have enjoyed productions on Broadway in the past five years. All of them originated at resident theatres and none, I believe, made profits on their commercial runs. John Guare's The House of Blue Leaves will transfer to Broadway after successful showings first at the Mitzi Newhouse, then at the Vivian Beaumont in Lincoln Center. My guess is this play won't make a profit either, though it's closer than most to having a successful formula. With this kind of record, even the most adventurous Broadway producers are being forced to recognize that they can't return investments with serious plays, and this in turn inhibits any desire to risk capital in the hope of advancing American theatre. The situation will not improve, it will deteriorate further.

So where are the playwrights? They're here, all right, though not in commercial venues. They are still being welcomed by resident companies, off Broadway and beyond, and by the various playwriting festivals in Louisville, Waterford, and the Berkshires. Their fees range from pin money to modest royalties, but the possibility of the Big Bonanza is becoming more and more remote. A Broadway playwright once remarked that you can't make a living in the theatre, only a killing. Now you can't even make a killing. Your best hope for a living is an NEA or Rockefeller or Guggenheim grant, or a play that makes the rounds of the nonprofit theatres, possibly followed by a modest movie sale.

I am going to propose a strange hypothesis; I hope it will not be construed as showing insensitivity to the American playwright's material needs. But it is my growing conviction that the very conditions blocking commercial success are proving responsible for artistic developments of a very high order. In the past, the pattern of American playwriting has usually been one or two major successes, accompanied by phenomenal media acclaim, followed by a succession of disappointing failures and a critical write-off. This was the pattern of O'Neill, who was forced to abandon the stage for almost a decade and afterwards watch his masterpiece *The Iceman Cometh* rejected by press and public alike. It was the experience of Clifford Odets, who couldn't ring a cash register on Broadway after *Awake and Sing* and *Golden Boy*. It was the fate of Arthur Miller after *All My Sons* and *Death of a Salesman*, a dramatist of world acclaim who hasn't managed to make a significant theatrical impact in almost twenty years. It was the biannual response to Tennessee Williams, whose later offerings were met with continual discouragement and impatience. And it was the pattern of Edward Albee, who hasn't even had a minor success since *A Delicate Balance* in 1966, or launched a commerical production since five or six years ago, with the short-lived *Man with Three Arms*.

The criticism most frequently heard about the playwrights of past generations, particularly Williams, was that they were repeating themselves. If this was true, it was less an artistic choice than a consequence of immeasurable cultural pressure to match their past triumphs. The successful American playwright was forced to pay dearly for his momentary fame, largely because it was so incredibly inflated. More than the novelist, certainly more than the poet, the Great American Playwright became a source of hopes and expectations so magnified it was virtually impossible to fulfill them. Perhaps because plays reached the public more directly than novels or poems, the hit playwright was instantly catapulted into the kind of celebrity usually enjoyed only by movie stars and sports heroes. But just as fatigue invariably follows familiarity, so the reputable playwright soon discovered that nothing he could produce, not even clones of past hits, would satisfy the sensation-hungry palates of a fickle public, a jaded press.

Now, of course, whether by choice or circumstance, even a Miller or an Albee has little access to the commerical stage. No wonder, when Sam Shepard, one of our most celebrated writers (and movie actors), has yet to see his first Broadway production. But this has not limited Shepard's powers. Indeed, unlike those predecessors who wilted under such conditions, Shepard has flourished in a state of marginality. With the exception of his most recent play. *A Lie of the Mind* (the first to show overt signs of self-consciousness), Shepard's work has been a model of growth and variety. The same may be said of his gifted contemporaries—I suspect for much the same reasons. David Mamet's initial Broadway production of *American Buffalo*, a masterpiece of writing and acting, was greeted with critical jeers and audience incomprehension, which may be why he followed that work not with more naturalistic proletarian dramas but with new departures: the theatrical *Life in the Theatre*, the socially explosive *Glengarry Glen Ross*, the mysteriously metaphysical *The Shawl*. David Rabe, following his somewhat self-righteous off-Broadway Vietnam plays, *Pavlo Hummel* and *Sticks and Bones*, went on to develop a passionate drama of social documentary, culminating in the scorchingly written (though superficially produced) *Hurlyburly*. Ronald Ribman, whose only Broadway entry was the realistic *Cold Storage* in the mid-seventies, has been developing quietly, methodically, and meticulously into one of the most haunting dramatic poets our stage has ever seen, with three new plays announced for next season that have the capacity to make theatrical history.

With *Marie and Bruce*, savaged by the New York press, Wallace Shawn emerged as a playwright of courage and intellect. And although I was not among the admirers of *Aunt Dan and Lemon*, it could not have been predicted by anything Shawn had yet written. Christopher Durang has been distilling his special brew of denatured venom for about a decade now, each new work a deeper incision into the source of the pain that produced it. Arthur Kopit has moved gracefully from absurdist comedies to the interior journeys of *Wings* to the satiric indignation of *End of the World*. These, I believe, are all major playwrights. But even less ambitious, less versatile, or less prolific writers—Lanford Wilson, Marsha Norman, Terrence McNally, Keith Reddin, Albert Inaurato, Robert Auletta, A. R.

Gurney, Beth Henley, August Wilson, Richard Nelson, Charles Mee, Jr., Harry Kondoleon, William Hauptman, and many others—are composing plays with serious intentions, powerful themes, rigorous craftsmanship, and subtleties of character and action.

The numbers alone suggest that something unusual is happening in our theatre, but the general quality and intelligence of the work is the real measure. Because they so rarely have Broadway hits, few of these playwrights have found their way into the feature sections of newspapers and magazines. Their existence is not a significant fact in the minds of the literate public at large. But this may be the very reason why they continue to write with such obdurate intensity, with such astonishing unpredictability. Obscurity has advantages as well as disappointments, just as sudden fame can prove to be the greatest enemy of promise. In the past, a few notable writers—J. D. Salinger, Edmund Wilson—made a conscious decision to refuse celebrity on the premise that it was death to talent. In Salinger's case, so far as we know, the talent died anyway. At the present time, celebrity is electing to refuse quite a few notable writers—with somewhat more encouraging results. The effect on the income of such writers is damaging, the drain on their egos debilitating. But the impact on the development of their gifts has been unquestionably salutary. Today's playwrights may not have as much chance as yesterday's to get momentarily rich and famous. But they have a better shot at something more elusive and more satisfying—the capability to last the course with dignity, without compromising their talents. So the next time you hear someone ask, "Where are the American playwrights?" tell him, "They're here!"

The Auteur Director
The Avant-Garde and the Classics

SHAKESPEARE IN EXTREMIS

(The Tempest)

The Lee Breuer version of *The Tempest* (directed with his wife, Ruth Maleczech) was performed in Central Park during the month of July as part of the New York Shakespeare Festival. With the notable exception of Jack Kroll of *Newsweek*, few had a kind word to say for the production, not even Michael Feingold of The *Village Voice*, who wrote an open letter to his personal friend and sometime colleague expressing concern over his creative misbehavior. The night I saw the show, the house was half-empty (for *free* Shakespeare!), and not a few walked out after the first act. When I spoke with the actors afterwards, they seemed dispirited, demoralized. The rehearsal process had been difficult, with the two directors sometimes giving conflicting instructions, and the performances were fighting a losing battle with the technical apparatus (including a real helicopter that had been substituted for the ship in the storm scene).

111

Quite a mess, in short, and one has to concede the mess was discernible on stage. Yet, I came away from the production feeling pretty happy. For one thing, this *Tempest* was evidence that Joe Papp was back in the ring, as feisty and unpredictable as ever, after a year (if my speculations are correct) when he was less preoccupied with supporting talent than with trying to line up another *Chorus Line*. Perhaps the commercial success of *Pirates of Penzance* had liberated Papp from the ledger sheets, again permitting him the kind of risk-taking for which he once was justly celebrated. Whatever the case, to commission an avant-garde tiger to gnash his teeth on Shakespeare in this age of conservative backlash was bound to be considered a provocation, if not the artistic equivalent of a terrorist act. Breuer's reinterpretive techniques are more extreme than most. But the very idea of the "concept" classic is under heavy attack today, as scholars and critics place themselves before the sacred texts like an army of Switzers guarding the doors of the Vatican. It's almost as if the eighteenth-century battle between the Ancients and Moderns were being reenacted; I wonder how such landmark reinterpretations as Brook's *Midsummer Night's Dream* or Serban's *Cherry Orchard* would fare in this sour present-day climate.

Obviously, the Guardians differ over what is considered permissible, but in an episode typifying the current atmosphere, Lord Noel Annan was recently invited by the English departments of various Ivy League universities to excommunicate such heresiarchs as Peter Brook and Peter Hall (also Lord Olivier and Sir John Gielgud) for desecrating the holy relics of the Bard with their sacrilegious concepts and readings. Lord Annan took the opportunity to deliver himself of his own version of how Shakespeare passages should be rendered, declaimed in sonorous Cantabrigian accents that nailed every comma and semicolon into place. And in a stirring conclusion that left his auditors positively shimmering with gratitude, he then thundered out a paraphrase of General de Gaulle's patriotic admonition to his laggard countrymen: "Honor the Word! Respect the Text!"

Few of the distinguished English professors who listened to Lord Annan with such rapt agreement were prepared to ask how the theatre—a medium not only of language and intonation but of gesture, characterization, visual design, action—could ever respond to a demand so exclusively textual it could be satisfied only on radio. But then few people know what they mean when they speak of "traditional" Shakespeare. Is it to produce the plays in an authentic Elizabethan manner? We have no knowledge of Shakespeare's original intentions and very little is known about the production style of his company at the Globe (well, yes, we do know that the first Cleopatra wore a hoopskirt). Is it to revert to the declamatory, brocaded, Hamlet-brooding-in-a-chair conventions of Maurice Evans and Margaret Webster? It may be that our notions of "tradition" are influenced by thirty-year-old playgoing experiences, but I can't imagine anyone who would be happy today with all that posturing and elocution. This is not to say that the acting style of our own time is necessarily superior, but at least it belongs to us. Classical production will invariably bear a contemporary stamp because actors, those "abstracts and brief chronicles of the time," are our contemporaries. It is in the study and the classroom only that the text can be "respected" in the way Lord Annan desires, because only there are we free from actors and directors with their insistent fleshly intrusions, their regard for the "form and pressure" inherent in the body of the time.

To return to the matter at hand, Lee Breuer takes Hamlet's description of the purpose of playing literally—and therein lies the root of his current problems. His approach to *The Tempest* is virtually an act of translation. Without changing the language (though he is not loath to reinterpret it), he has transformed Shakespeare's characters, action, and images into an idiomatic modern glossary. Breuer's contemporary references are almost entirely influenced by the media, particularly movies of the thirties and forties. His primary device is to discover recognizable parallels for the characters among the heroes and legends of popular culture (ironically, Breuer, like Sam Shepard, is often charged with being difficult and inaccessible when both are merely trying to find a vernacular language for the stage). Thus, Trinculo (played by a woman) speaks in the hip-swaying accents of Mae West; Stefano drawls and swills like W. C. Fields; Caliban has the cockney nerviness of Sid Vicious; and the shipwrecked (more accurately, helicopter-wrecked) villains of Naples and of Milan wear the slouch hats and three-piece suits of Italian godfathers. Meanwhile, the background music consists largely of songs from old Disney movies, and Ferdinand and Miranda perform their tasks to the tune of "Whistle While You Work."

You're probably recoiling just from this description, and it is true that the production often looks like a media blitz by a Wizard of

Sleaze. For me, however, the technique was less offensive than wearing. Once Breuer establishes a cultural parallel, he does not provide sufficient wit or variety to sustain our interest in it; the comic shock is soon vitiated by repetition. In his effort to cut through the vapors of conventional Shakespeare, Breuer risks substituting a miasma of relentless unconventionality; even the constant effort to astonish becomes predictable. Still, it would be a shame if the flashy surface of this production obscured some of its real qualities, because there are aspects of the interpretation that go beyond novelty to touch something deep. One is the set, a revolving globe against the beautiful background of Central Park, which keeps the action continually mysterious, off-center, disorienting. Another is the startling entrance of a samba band during the Masque scene, which starts everybody on stage (and off) swaying and rocking. Still another is the presence of children in the play, as symbols of freshness and renewal: Prospero's relationship with Miranda includes a flashback that shows her on the island as a young girl. And among the eleven Ariels (one a hefty sumo wrestler), four or five are delightful, spunky sprites who charm the audience as much as they do their master.

The ending also discourages us from regarding Breuer's production merely as an engaging bag of tricks. Prospero (coolly played by Raul Julia) has been reinstated in his dukedom. Costumed throughout in a stocking cap and sarong, he is now dressed in the clothes of a diplomat: shirt, vest, pinstripe suit, buttonhole carnation. The other noblemen, similarly dressed and wearing name tags on their coats, come to join him for champagne and cigars, and to have their pictures taken by an official photographer, before flying back to Naples in their helicopter. Prospero is left alone on stage to let his Ariels free. A Prospero double, wearing identical clothes and a Raul Julia mask, is the last Ariel to be liberated. Having burned (rather than drowned) his book, Prospero then comes forward for the epilogue—removing the body mike that he and the others have used throughout the evening, speaking for the first time without the aid of amplification: "Now my charms are all o'erthrown, / And what strength I have's mine own / Which is most faint." It is a moment that returns the human element to the play, a self-mocking commentary on the very "charms" of the production, its excessive reliance on technical aids, slight of hand, and media transformations.

Breuer's self-consciousness here is curiously moving, and the way it moves one suggests that something subliminal has been going on throughout the evening beneath the high jinks and the magical tricks. Even without these deeper resonances, however, the production would have deserved a less universally brutal reception. Shakespeare is sturdy and impregnable. He has survived a hundred thousand conflicting interpretations; he will survive Lee Breuer as well. The history of theatre is not a compilation of definitive productions, but rather a dialogue, even a debate, among people of different perspectives, among people, let us remember, of different times. Breuer's work on *The Tempest* is an honest effort to create a Shakespeare for our time. It is by no means a successful effort, but it was made by a gifted theatrical artist laying himself on the line. Instead of savaging it and other productions like it, we might reflect on why the most violent critical reactions are usually directed against not what is conventional, mind-deadening, and banal, but rather against those very rare occasions when an artist dares to risk, and fails through a surplus of imagination and invention.

SERBAN UNDER SIEGE

(Uncle Vanya)

The Rumanian director Andrei Serban recently completed the fourth in his cycle of Chekhov productions, *Uncle Vanya*, this one at La Mama, and was rewarded with a storm of criticism, including a double whammy in the *New York Times* (daily and Sunday), and a Dresden firebombing from John Simon in *New York*, who concluded his attack by insinuating that Jean-Claude van Itallie's translations might be plagiarisms. Serban is a friend and associate of mine—his previous Chekhov production was performed last season at the American Repertory Theatre—so I can hardly pretend objectivity in the matter. Still, I am willing to take my lumps from those who want to charge me with prejudice or self-interest if it will help correct what is arguably an artistic injustice.

Not that I expect to change any minds. Opinions about Serban are too emotional to respond to reason and there is a notion abroad that one shouldn't dispute prevailing opinion. Debates of this kind were once considered a lively form of discourse; now critical disagreements are often regarded as breaking ranks. The current passion for consensus may explain why Serban's controversial productions evoke such heated reactions: such passion presumes an authorized interpretation of the play. The received opinion about Serban is that he delights in vandalizing cherished classical works and desecrating the memory of helpless playwrights: "Would Chekhov Have Embraced This Vanya?" is the rhetorical headline question in Benedict Nightingale's inaugural review as Walter Kerr's replacement for the *Times*. The question suggests that the critic, not the artist, is the best reader of the playwright's intentions, the most faithful defender of his text.

The tumult over *Vanya* reflects the traditional uneasiness between the analytical intelligence and the interpretive imagination. One does not have to believe that a play can support any harebrained or lunatic interpretation in order to recognize that theatre is not absolute, not immutable, not frozen, but rather in a continual state of process and change, and therefore not subject to fixed concepts of authorial intention or "definitive" production.

Precisely because plays are written to be staged rather than read, there is always more to be learned from the explorations of a fine creative instinct than from the analytical studies of even the keenest critical intelligence, though in the best of worlds these would not be incompatible. Since the territory explored is uncharted, this sometimes requires a leap of faith—not so difficult to make when the director enjoys a record of genuine achievement. Such a record even his most severe detractors would hesitate to deny Serban. Not all of his productions have been completely fulfilled, but in the last decade he has altered our vision of innumerable classical and modern works, subjecting them to a fertile imagination that is at the same time traditional and contemporary. It is true that his imagination is sometimes excessively fertile, but the road of excess, Blake tells us, leads to the palace of wisdom.

Serban's *Uncle Vanya* is occasionally excessive, but it is also often wise, perceptive, penetrating, funny, and, in my opinion, very tender. Whether Chekhov would have approved I cannot say, though this is a question Serban continually asks himself. But considered strictly as an exploratory "essay" rather than the final word on the play, Serban's version emphatically adds to our knowledge of the text. For one thing, it is a strong corrective to Stanislavsky's morbid behaviorism, the basis for most "definitive" Chekhov productions of recent vintage, though Chekhov himself detested it. Whereas Stanislavsky is basically psychological, Serban is metaphorical. The Stanislavsky actor pursues "existence," the intentions and objectives of his character; Serban's actor looks for "essence," a characteristic gesture or style. Stanislavsky leaves Chekhov squatting amidst the painted flats and Victorian upholstery of the nineteenth century. Without doing violence to the playwright's spirit, Serban brings Chekhov into the twentieth, in company with artists he influenced, such as Samuel Beckett, and even those he didn't, such as Bertolt Brecht.

Serban's metaphorical strategy begins with the setting. As he said in an interview, his inspiration for the design of *Vanya* came from a passing remark of Serebryakov's that the house was like a maze. Serban turns the simile into a metaphor—Santo Loquasto's design *is* a maze, a large wooden labyrinth of ramps and gullies and platforms, with a single depressed area in the center like a sunken cellar. The apparent intention is to envelop the spectator in the action, as if he were another inhabitant of the house. But even though the characters often address the audience directly, the effect is curiously distancing: Sonya begins the play reading her final speech from a book as though it were already part of literature, the stage manager calls out the offstage cues from a visible booth, and much of the action is viewed from above.

It is obviously Serban's plan to withdraw *Uncle Vanya* from realism and return it to the theatre. Thus, he never lets the spectator forget that the actors are acting or the director directing. For this purpose, he has devised self-conscious extensions for his company, primarily derived from broad farce and high melodrama. Farce and melodrama are the prime ingredients of Chekhov's style, for all his efforts to conceal this through buried actions and complicated characters. And in *Vanya*, an extreme example of the mixture with its onstage shooting and interrupted love scenes, Serban pushes this style to its extreme limit, excising everything, in this hundred-minute version, that does not accommodate broad strokes. Yelena, in a remarkably volatile performance by Diane Venora, is played as a woman continually on the verge of a swoon, by turns neurasthenic, vacant, and flamboyant, striking poses out of nineteenth-century fashion magazines and declaiming her lines (sometimes accompanied by tenor arias from Bellini's *I Puritani*) as if she were being played by Arkadina in *The Seagull*. It is a performance that makes the operatic Yelena seem at the same time extremely shallow and yet somehow oddly touching, particularly when she grabs Sonya's feet before departing and begs her forgiveness. F. Murray Abraham's Dr. Astrov is intelligence in decay, a drunken sot who really does loathe his moustache, doing a precarious tightrope walk on one of the ramps before falling in a heap and saying, "Excuse me, I'm not wearing a tie." Frances Conroy, as Sonya, is severe and strained, on the verge of breakdown, yet never lacking the compassion that brings Vanya his only solace.

Vanya himself, as played by Joseph Chaikin, is a sad clown, an aging child, out of silent-film comedy. Chaikin's Vanya has been severely criticized by virtually every reviewer for a single piece of stage business—he sits on Serebryakov's lap after being told of his intention to sell the estate. Yet, this is clearly Serban's effort to essentialize how it feels to be a helpless child in a disintegrating household. Chaikin, who has a heart condition, did not achieve the required peaks of hysteria in his climactic scene the night I saw it. But the actor enjoyed at least one really stunning moment, when he came upon Yelena and Astrov embracing. In his slept-in suit, his pants flopping over his shoes, holding a bunch of flowers in his hand, he stood watching his betrayal for minutes, soundless, expressionless, motionless, until, a Chaplinesque stoic, he turned helplessly on his heel and walked away. The same mute despair concludes the play. Sonya, in a passionately angry outburst, exhorts Vanya to work as the only antidote against despair, after which the two of them set about their tasks like robots—the mechanization of meaningless labor—as Telyegin, playing the balalaika and singing, whirls in ever-widening circles.

If you open yourself to these images, some of them will etch themselves indelibly on your mind, even when at first they seem gratuitous. Van Itallie's (wholly original) adaptation is the crispest and most powerful extant (I love the "He says no" that ends the second act). Jennifer Tipton's lighting is luminous, and the company, despite a few weaknesses in the cast, is stylistically uniform. This *Vanya*, in short, is another genuine achievement by Serban, who remains one of a handful of authentically innovative directors in a field normally characterized by flat, prosaic, unadventurous dullness. Remarkably, it is not the drones but the directors with the courage of their imaginations who are now being driven from the theatre by a discouraging press.

THE PREMATURE DEATH OF MODERNISM

(Through the Leaves; Laurie Anderson in Concert)

The demise of modernism is frequently proclaimed these days—most eloquently by my futurist friend Daniel Bell—but the news of its death has been vastly exaggerated. An upstart movement that likes to thumb its nose at conservative established trends, modernism often behaves like a spiteful teenager daring you to smack him. And, like many such rebellious postures, it may be that these sassy attitudes disguise a secret desire for attention and approval. The obligatory provocativeness of the avant-garde can no doubt be impudent, annoying, even self-serving. But the modernist movement won't evaporate by pretending it doesn't exist. In the theatre, at least, modernism is still responsible for a great deal that is vital and original in contemporary dramatic expression, even though most of its discoveries and inventions are within minutes conveniently co-opted by commerce and the media, often with the connivance of its creators.

A surprising development of one recent form of modernism has been the revival of a meticulous painstaking realism. This, after all, was how the modern dramatic movement began—out of the naturalistic novels of Zola and the domestic plays of Ibsen—but for over a half century now realism has been primarily identified with mainstream theatre. In the United States, however, largely thanks to David Mamet, a faithful verisimilitude is gaining new respect among serious critics, while in Germany, largely thanks to Franz Xavier Kroetz, such realism has recently been identified with the most advanced form of playwriting.

Kroetz's *Through the Leaves*, a joint presentation of Interart Theatre and Mabou Mines, represents a good introduction to modernist realism, since it is being offered in a superb production by JoAnne Akalaitis. As in most of his work, Kroetz is here concerned with moments of crisis in the lives of desperate depressed people living barely at the level of consciousness, and, again as in most of his work, his treatment of this victim class is pitiless, harsh, remorseless, cruel, redeemed only by fitful flashes of compassion. Annette is a middle-aged spinster who makes her living by cutting up "utility meats" for dog food; Victor is a coarse unemployed roustabout who occasionally services her crudely in a room behind the shop. Annette keeps a diary of their relationship, recording her longings for romance with all the punctuation marks intact ("Is there still a chance for love when you're forty—question mark?"). But not only is Victor frequently unfaithful, he also deserts her frequently for long periods of time ("Come back!" pleads the diary, "exclamation point and period"). Each time Victor returns, however, he is more abusive, insensitive, and violent. Witnessing the lovemaking of this unappealing, overweight couple is sometimes like watching two sides of beef having their loins rubbed in her butcher shop; at one point he tries to take her while she is chopping up a mess of calves' liver.

Annette's generous if bovine love for Victor, however, is not entirely free of resentment, and there are occasional hints that she would like to carve him up with her cleaver. Still, in exchange for his intermittent company and occasional spurts of pleasure, she passively accepts her role in what amounts to her complete abasement and humiliation, never totally at a loss for cheer even when he deserts her for good at the end ("All alone—longing—period").

Kroetz, a Marxist, makes little effort to dramatize the dignity of working-class people, whom he shows to be leading lives of noisy desperation. Relatively tender toward women, he displays no feeling whatever for his males, who are almost invariably depicted as human brutes living at the lowest scale of existence. As a result, his plays are usually laborious documentaries of man's inhumanity to man (more often, to women), making no concessions either to theatricality or to the pleasure principle—grimly squalid vignettes of humanity in extreme circumstances, a poetry of aesthetic abstinence.

But Kroetz provides rich occasions for production, and this one is exceptional. In Douglas Stein's extraordinary double setting—the butcher shop complete with cow's head and animal organs in the display case, and the back room decorated with plastic furniture, crocheted calendar, and a forlorn green rubber plant—Miss Akalaitis creates an atmosphere that is convincing and uncompromising in its realism, yet always rhythmic and stylized. As Annette, Ruth Maleczech simpers and cajoles, her face frozen in the blank look of a grinning marionette as she saws away at a thigh bone, while Fred Neumann as Victor sketches a harrowing portrait of a brutal sexist male who uses female flesh purely as a source of friction. Roger Downey's translation sensibly transfers the action to an American working-class suburb, where clamorous rock music ("This is not a love song") crashes through the tainted air like splintering glass.

Laurie Anderson represents an entirely different species of modernism, one much more indebted to the current techniques of rock concerts and therefore capable of drawing large mass audiences. A lot has already been written about this *sui generis* performance artist; I managed to see her for the first time at the Boston Opera House during a recent tour. The first thing one encounters upon entering the theatre is a massive media board monopolizing two or three rows of seats, while the open stage, monitored by an army of technicians, is festooned with bizarre musical instruments, pipes, wires, screens, lights, courtesy telephones, and synthesizers. Miss Anderson is entirely a creature of technology, which constitutes both her medium and her subject. When the performers enter, greeted by a screaming audience, they are wearing strangely decorated ski masks recalling those seen on the terrorists at the Munich Olympics. Their leader is dressed in a white silken suit and begins to speak in an unctuous baritone voice about the differences between the numbers 0 and 1 ("Being a zero is no worse than being number one").

This is Laurie Anderson, her voice treated by a synthesizer, and the monologue is a prologue for her first musical number, "Shorty's Day." As in most rock concerts, the overamplification makes it impossible to gauge the quality of the music—everything is electrified in this evening, including Miss Anderson's auburn hair. But whereas such traditional groups as The Grateful Dead, for example, eschew costumes, props, and light shows, concentrating almost exclusively on an aural impact, this is a highly complicated mixed-media event, similar to video rock productions, combining film, animations, dramatizations, projections, lights, and thumping acoustical rhythms to create a synaesthetic influence on the eyes and eardrums.

Miss Anderson is clearly an original, with a sly sense of humor, which makes it difficult to tell whether she is satirizing the Computer Age or acting as its agent and volunteer. Playing such instruments as a synclavier, a vocoder, and a violin that uses magnetic tape instead of strings, she alternates between songs, dances, and monologues, as images of multicolored trees, snowy television screens, people moving down subway escalators, Japanese ideograms, revolving radar screens, airplanes skywriting "Aloha," dancing dolls, and her own haloed talking features swarm behind her. In one monologue, documented with a series of "While You Were Out" phone messages, she speaks to herself on a courtesy phone while playing a huge electric sitar; in another, she sings to the accompaniment of illustrated doodles concerning her upcoming tour ("Banana hats for the musicians are a waste of money—they'll probably refuse to wear them"). The voice of William Burroughs comes over the loudspeaker telling us that "language is a virus from outer space." And the screen fills with the various ways we use the alphabet to create shorthand words (G-string, K rations, ZZZZZZs, etc.).

Miss Anderson connects best with the audience when she takes it into her confidence ("I don't know about your dreams, but mine—are really hackneyed—the themes are infantile"). But what she is continually communicating, in her cool, winsome, appealing style, are messages of anomie and tedium. I came away impressed by effects but feeling as affectless as the performer, and totally puzzled about her purpose. For Laurie Anderson, at present, the medium really *is* the message, though, somehow, her personality manages to be the message too.

There is no predicting the future development of such a gifted innovator, but watching her I began to understand a little better why people so often proclaim the death of modernism. Like a few other avant-garde artists of her generation I could name, Laurie Anderson is an offspring of the recent marriage between modernism and the media, where the feverish need for new products, new personalities, new cover stories is creating a condition in which embryonic genius is prematurely canonized and embryonic art gets stuck at the level of technological effects and synthetic dazzle. When modernism becomes just another agency for selling tickets, or for increasing the circulation of newspapers and magazines, then the alternatives for the avant-garde artist are either to be eclipsed by the next newly discovered genius-personality or to invent even wilder attention-getting mechanisms. What gets lost in this process are the tranquil conditions required for any penetrating exploration of experience, so necessary to artistic growth. Still, modernism will continue to survive, if only because it contains within it great diversity not only of forms and approaches but of artists dedicated to pressing against the boundaries of the possible. And all those with a stake in a healthy culture know that it *must* survive; it is our most effective antidote against stagnation.

EXPANDING EINSTEIN'S UNIVERSE

(Einstein on the Beach)

Eight years after its two performances at the Met in 1976, *Einstein on the Beach* was revived for one week in December as the climactic event of the Next Wave Festival at the Brooklyn Academy of Music. It confirmed a now legendary reputation as one of the masterpieces of modern opera and theatre. This extraordinary collaboration between the composer/lyricist, Philip Glass, and the conceiver/director/designer, Robert Wilson, has a spoken text devised by Christopher Knowles, Samuel M. Johnson, and Lucinda Childs (who also did the choreography). In these synthesizing collective hands, it represents one of those rare moments in cultural history when the most gifted people at work in the performing arts combine their resources to wallop us into an oceanic perception of our relation to the cosmos. Few contemporary works have penetrated so deeply into the uncreated dream life of the race. Pulling ecstasy from boredom, finding insight through repetition, alternating mechanical rhythms with pulsing climaxes, *Einstein on the Beach* manages to burrow into your mind and work on you like a wound.

Wilson and Glass have correctly identified Albert Einstein as the seminal maker of the modern consciousness who, over a relatively brief historical span, not only witnessed a major change in our understanding of physics and philosophy, but was himself largely responsible for it. Choosing random incidents from Einstein's life, the work creates a world where everyone is Einstein—not only the company, identically attired in baggy trousers, watches, suspenders, and tennis shoes, but also the white-maned, bushy-moustached solo violinist, who sits playing impassively on a chair—perhaps even the audience itself. Einstein's interest in time and light permeates the triadic structure of the evening. Following the initial Knee Play, one of the five connective episodes featuring Lucinda Childs and Sheryl Sutton as two automatons tonelessly repeating disconnected phrases, the first three acts alternate between "Train," "Trial," and "Field" sequences, inchoate evocations of Einstein's physics or biography. The earliest "Train" sequence opens on a boy on a tower, examining a plastic cube and floating paper airplanes onto the ground. He is soon joined by a woman (Lucinda Childs) dancing in spastic patterns across the stage, a boy listening to the sounds of the sea in a conch, and finally a cutout locomotive engine, driven by a pipe-smoking engineer, that moves at an infinitesimal pace onto the stage. This slow progress of a train, a vehicle normally identified with high rates of speed, suggests how the discoveries of Einstein, who may be the two boys in the scene, have altered our perceptions of time. Throughout the length of this evening, we are locked in the interstices of the temporal world, folded into the space between one millisecond and the next—forced to reflect how very slowly even the fastest earthbound objects move by contrast with objects in space or with the speed of light.

One must be willing to tolerate a different order of time in order to enter this work. In contrast with Samuel Beckett, whose recent writing is an effort to compress experience into a single essential image or phrase, Robert Wilson is dedicated to expanding our sense of what is permissible in the theatre. Brief by contrast with some of his other works (one of which takes three days to perform), *Einstein on the Beach* is nevertheless something of an endurance test for the bladder. It not only lasts four and a half hours by the clock (the audience is encouraged to wander in and out of the theatre at will), but repeatedly emphasizes its own length. Numbers are the sole subject, for example, of the first and final sequences, where choruses count backwards and forwards between one and six, and each gesture, each movement, is precisely calibrated to the second. Timepieces, furthermore, are everywhere on stage, and not just on the wrists of the characters. The centerpiece of the first "Trial" scene is a faceless clock, which is gradually eclipsed by a dark object, like the moon eclipsing the sun. Another stage clock runs backwards. And that old-fashioned instrument of dimensional space, a compass, descends at one point to remind us how our traditional devices of earthly measurement have been radically altered by the new science.

The "Trial" scenes invoke the forms of the courtroom without the substance. In the first one, a woman defendant sits stonefaced on a high stool at a proceeding presided over by two bewigged judges— one an old black man, the other a child—the spectators read newspapers and jiggle nervously, the robotic jury slumps, and two court stenographers mechanically run their fingers over recording machines—normal enough, except for the presence of a huge bed and a bolster in front of the judge's bench. In the next "Trial" scene, as the word *Bang* elides into *Bank*, the defendant transforms into Patty Hearst, complete with beret, peacoat, and rifle (*Einstein* was first performed in the year of Hearst's conviction for robbery and terrorism). As she is being tried, sentenced, and imprisoned, she repeatedly intones snatches of that hypnotic incantatory dialogue that constitutes the text: "I was in this prematurely air-conditioned supermarket. There were these bathing caps that had these kind of Fourth of July plumes on them. . . . I was reminded of a time when I had been avoiding the beach." It is one of the few references to the mystical title, which was reportedly inspired by an early photograph of the physicist on some distant seashore. In the associative manner of the work, we are reminded of the Nevil Shute novel, *On the Beach*, set in the future after a nuclear catastrophe.

The "Field" scenes (a reference to Einstein's unified field theory?) are essentially choreographed dances featuring the Lucinda Childs company, twirling to wild jazz saxophone riffs or frenetic Hebraic melodies played on a violin; both climax with the appearance of a saucer-shaped spaceship floating overhead. The opera is gradually working its way toward outer space. A crowd gathers in front of an industrial warehouse, all of them—with the notable exception of a woman engrossed in a book—staring up at the top window of the building where a young person scribbles equations (you may safely assume that one of them is $E = MC_2$). In one of the most striking episodes of the entire evening, the huge bed from the "Trial" scene becomes a horizontal shaft of white polarized light that, to the accompaniment of powerful organ arpeggios, ever so slowly assumes a vertical position, levitates, and then gradually disappears into the flies.

The image reminds one of the mysterious monoliths in Kubrick's *2001*; in fact, the entire opera resonates with echoes of that seminal film. Kubrick contrasted the technological advances of the future with a profound anomie, where human feeling had atrophied and only HAL, the computer, was capable of strong emotions. Wilson and Glass see the future as a series of spasms and dislocations dominated by a language based on the speech of autistic children, dreams, solfeggio, and popular songs (notably Carole King's "I Feel the Earth Move"). What the two works share in common is a genius for imagining images for meditation, images that are unique and startling, yet somehow permanently enter our waking and dreaming lives: Kubrick's star child, for example, a placid embryo with huge eyes and folded stunted fingers, soaring endlessly through space.

In the splendid final scene before the final Knee Play, as the music turns demonic with Einstein sawing away on his violin, we are in an enormous spacecraft. Hibernating astronauts in transparent Plexiglas boxes designed like modernistic grandfather clocks sail through space horizontally and vertically. In dozens of square cubicles, space workers manipulate patterns of circular and diagonal light. The Glass music transforms into a contemporary "Ode to Joy." The two women from the Knee Plays, still costumed like Einstein, emerge from plastic bubblelike cocoons in a semisupine position, bound to the floor. And suddenly a drop falls, decorated with an etching of an airplane, a large explosion, and an undecipherable text that gradually comes into focus. It is the Enola Gay, and the text is an account of the Hiroshima disaster. We have been shuttled through history from locomotives to rocket propulsion, from paper airplanes to space travel, from firecrackers to nuclear explosions—all in the lifetime of a single man of genius.

And yet, as the final Knee Play suggests, not everything has changed. The music and lyrics reprise the numerical countdown with which the opera began; it is now ineffably melancholy. A streamlined cutout bus moves slowly into view. Speaking into his microphone, the driver describes not the passing scenery, but rather a "soothing story to banish the perplexing days." It is an "old, yet new story, the old old story of love." He tells of two lovers sitting on a park bench in silence, their bodies touching, holding hands in the moonlight, saying, "You are my sun, my moon and stars, you are my everything." To estimate the scope of this feeling, you must count the stars, measure the heavens, for it is beyond language, beyond physics, a passion that maintains its elegiac force throughout all technological change, despite all scientific discovery.

Not all the elements of this monumental work are equally dazzling. A feminist parody by the judge in the second "Trial" scene seems rather out of place; I don't understand the relevance of the Patty Hearst sequence; and I'm unsure of the cogency of a long episode in a train caboose involving a man and woman in 1920s dress clothes (the Einsteins on honeymoon?) that culminates with the woman wielding a pistol. Still, even these lacunae compel attention because the control is so confident and the material so evocative. Robert Wilson is an artist who paints magnificent images in motion, and Philip Glass is a composer who drives musical nails into your soul. Together with a dedicated cast and the magical lighting of Beverly Emmons, they have fashioned a piece that launches the theatre into new dimensions of the unknown, propelling our imaginations into the expanding universe of art.

THEATERPHOBIA

(The Garden of Earthly Delights)

David Denby, film critic for *New York* magazine, has written an extended attack on the stage that compels a response, since it is so agreeably argued it may well become a *locus classicus of theaterphobia*

It appears quite appropriately in the *Atlantic*, a Boston-based monthly whose Brahmin disdain for the stage is long-standing—with roots perhaps in the antitheatrical prejudice of the Puritans. Denby's bias is hardly Puritan. He speaks for a whole class of smart people, largely sophisticated New Yorkers, who love books, music, and movies but have long turned off to the theatre, more for aesthetic than for moral reasons.

Denby's arguments are not unfamiliar and many are true. Movies are a superior medium for realistic representation; even the worst films are exciting at some level whereas bad theatre makes you feel miserably trapped; stage actors fail to convince audiences they exist in real time and space; realistic settings are inauthentic, contrived, and mechanical. Denby is not only exasperated by bourgeois domestic realism; he also pummels the alternative theatre for its self-conscious use of shock tactics, metaphors, and alienation effects. "The avant-gardist's concentration on the *means* of making theatre," he writes, "is intellectually exhausting at best, a pretentious bore at worst. The avant-gardist is locked into a stance of pure aggression."

To research his article, Denby went on a New York theatregoing binge. He suffered mostly through the more celebrated middlebrow products of the commercial stage—*The Real Thing*, *Death of a Salesman*, *The Glass Menagerie*, *Baby*, *Sunday in the Park with George*—though he also ventured into *'night Mother*, which he disliked, and into such current avant-garde offerings as Brook's *Carmen* and Pina Bausch's *1980*, both unsatisfactory. The only production that aroused any enthusiasm from him, aside from *Noises Off* and *My One and Only*, was Mamet's *Glengarry Glen Ross*, primarily because its dialogue (like that of *Hurlyburly*) reminded him of good movie actors improvising. I cannot honestly quarrel with most of his play judgments. I not only share many of his opinions, I find his expression of them witty and trenchant. It is refreshing to see a member of the film generation, with no scales on his eyes, taking a good look at what passes for hit plays these days (his review of *The Real Thing*, for example, is right on the mark regarding that fashionable exercise in deep frivolity). It is saddening to think how many good potential theatre critics have been lost to celluloid who, thirty years ago, might have been naturally drawn to the stage.

Still, while some of Denby's premises may be winning, his conclusions are all wet. For one thing, he's been sitting in the wrong seats.

It's not just that so much of his attention is directed toward Broadway where, by common consent, virtually nothing of real interest has happened in years; his description of alternative theatre is also inaccurate, indeed woefully out of date. Denby's main gripe about the avant-garde is that its only subject is itself—which is to say, the drama of action gives way to metaphors of process, experiment, the making of theatre: "The closer [the theatre] comes to realistic representation, the more it betrays how inadequate it is next to the cinema; the further away from representation it moves, the more it loses contact with what interests us in the world and becomes preoccupied with the means of its own existence. . . . Devising an acceptable mode of being on the stage becomes a philosophical, rather than a dramatic, problem." Most theatre artists would agree that the movies have preempted realistic representation; but it is tautological then to condemn the alternative by the standards of movie literalism. And if philosophy and metaphysics are unfit subjects for the stage, where do we put *Hamlet, Life Is a Dream, Six Characters in Search of an Author, Waiting for Godot?* Denby's notion of a self-reflecting, lacerating avant-garde, furthermore, fails to recognize the extraordinary new developments in performance art, which have moved as far from the aggressive and narcissistic Artaud-inspired Living Theatre, Performance Group, and Grotowski Laboratory Theatre as those companies did from Beckett and Brecht.

I doubt if these would give much pleasure to an observer who concedes the theatre's superiority over movies only in the preeminence of the "word" (scratch a movie critic and you find a literary humanist). But it is silly to ignore the achievements of a growing cadre of experimental performing artists and groups. These, together with recent developments in playwriting—not just Mamet, whom Denby admires, and Rabe, whom he grudgingly praises for his "mastery of language," but Shepard, Norman, Durang, Ribman, others—begin to suggest not that the theatre is languishing but that it is experiencing a genuine renaissance. The "operas" of Robert Wilson, for example, formed in collaboration with people as diverse as Philip Glass and Heiner Mueller, have opened up entirely new dimensions of theatrical time and space; Mabou Mines—under JoAnne Akalaitis, Lee Breuer, and Ruth Maleczech—has been experimenting with forms ranging from political satire (*The Dead End Kids*) to classical updates (*The Gospel at Colonus*) to a new brand of neorealism (*Through the Leaves*) by contrast with which films appear cheesy and grainy; the Wooster Group, in such works as *Routes 1 & 9* and *L. S. D.*, has been investigating the polity by rearranging such familiar American texts as *Our Town* and *The Crucible*; and an army of imaginative young directors have been deconstructing classics in ways that uncover fresh sources of vital strength.

David Denby fails to mention these, as he passes over Laurie Anderson, Ping Chong, and resident repertory theatres, not to mention *The Garden of Earthly Delights*, an exquisite work of art that originated at the Lenox Arts Center before moving to St. Clement's Church in New York. I suppose he could challenge the theatre credentials of this last named, largely a dance piece with no obeisance whatever to the "word," but there is little question that it belongs to that burgeoning group of collective artworks that are beginning to transform our whole notion of what constitutes "theatre." Conceived and directed by Martha Clarke, and featuring music by Richard Peaslee that is virtually a dramatic character in itself, *The Garden of Earthly Delights* is a collective creation of everyone associated with it, including the dancers, the musicians, the designers, and an aerial magician named Foy who has devised feats of flying for the performers—generally over the heads of the audience—that remind us why the theatre remains potentially the most magical of all the arts.

The work, based on the paintings of Hieronymus Bosch, is in four parts: "Eden," "The Garden," "The Seven Sins," and "Hell"; and I have witnessed few greater theatrical contrasts than that between the lyrical innocence of the opening and the carnal brutality of the episodes after the fall from grace. To the accompaniment of wind sounds and a brass choir, delicate creatures in white leotards wander through the garden on their fingers and toes, their behinds raised like ethereal fawns. A musician places his marimba under one of the dancer's legs and plays her; another turns a dancer into his cello. An unearthly half-light suffuses the scene as Adam and Eve enact their agony in the garden. An angel flies above their heads. Banished from Eden, they turn into boats and sail away; two nymphs begin whipping themselves with branches; a woman becomes a tree; a man (Jesus?) is led onto the stage lashed to a huge stick.

As the music turns percussive and dissonant, the scene changes to a location much like Puritan New England, where loutish characters haul a load of raw potatoes out of a burlap bag. One puts an empty bucket on his head; another urinates on the floor. Characters begin shitting and vomiting potatoes. A man coldly copulates as others fight over the potatoes. The music shrieks and pounds. One man is hitting a bass drum; the drum is then used as a weight to crush another. The dancers begin to rotate in air like planets. One brute practices shoving a stick into a victim's eye; another hits a nail into his partner's head. The familiar strains of *Dies Irae* accompany a battle over the chimes playing it. Two men kill each other with single blows of a mallet. The original theme of Eden emerges played on a lonely cello. A woman pulls the cellist's arm and makes him miss his note. The music becomes foul and ugly. She breaks the strings, grabs his bow. He stabs her with the sharp end of the cello and plucks at it grimly as she writhes on the ground. A man is hanged. The piece ends with a chorus of flying figures. The audience departs, stunned both by beauty and brutality.

This sublime metaphor for the human condition could, I suppose, be considered philosophical or metaphysical; it is also powerfully dramatic. Admittedly, it is not realistic; yet, this imaginative adventure has plucked, as no veristic anecdote could, at the very strings of our existence. With her gifted performers and with Peaslee's musicians, Miss Clarke has concocted a one-hour creation that essentializes everything that is unique and inimitable about the theatre—its compactness, its concreteness, its immediacy, its grace, its capacity for inspiring awe. A few blocks to the east, in Broadway theatres, playwrights, composers, actors, and designers are still laboring with old outmoded forms in a style that, as Denby correctly notes, has been long expropriated by films. But *The Garden of Earthly Delights*, like so many recent works of inspired theatrical imagination, shows us theatre in the act of regenerating itself, exploring realms that have thus far been uncharted, beyond realism, beyond representation, entering the very source of creation itself.

CARMEN WITHOUT CHORUS, CHEKHOV WITHOUT WALLS

(Le Tragédie de Carmen; The Seagull)

War is raging again as a result of two unusual new theatre productions, Peter Brook's version of *Carmen* at the Vivian Beaumont in
New York and Lucian Pintilie's reinterpretation of Chekhov's *The
Seagull* at the Minneapolis Tyrone Guthrie Theatre. The trouble with
these theatre controversies, as with Marxist quarrels in the thirties
and neoconservative polemics today, is their unfortunate tendency to
make judgments of quality conform to ideological prejudices. (It is as
likely for *Commentary* or the *New Criterion*, for example, to praise the
work of a writer who favors détente and nuclear freezes as it once was
for the *New Masses* to approve the verse of a conservative poet).

Having thus cleared my throat, I must nevertheless admit an
ambivalent attitude toward these two adventurous productions, beginning with Brook's *La Tragédie de Carmen*. One thing at least has
been accomplished by this show. It has knocked all the talk about the
structural inadequacies of the Beaumont into a cocked hat. With the
most economical means, Brook has created a space that can be used
there for virtually any kind of production simply by removing a few
seats and extending the stage into the auditorium. This creates an
atmosphere of intimacy at the same time that it instantly improves
acoustics and sight lines. The space is a circular dirt floor, intersected
by crude unstained wooden panels that half conceal the musicians
while functioning for exits and entrances. The roughness of the
setting provides a striking contrast to the plush upholstery of the
auditorium, not to mention the plushly upholstered audience (another
contrast is the price of the tickets at the Beaumont—forty dollars—as
compared with the eight-dollar top Brook charges at his own theatre
in Paris). But no matter how impressive the environment, it is not
sufficient, finally, to conceal the limitations of the event.

The beginning is promising. A bunch of burlap rags on the dirt
floor begins to move, a hand emerges turning tarot cards on a rope
circle and sprinkling the area with black powder: the rags take human

form as Carmen, the gypsy sorceress. A sultry unwashed beauty, she vamps a taciturn Don José by rolling a fat cigarette on her bare stocking, sucking it, and throwing him suggestive looks. When Micaëla protests, she taunts her, squeezes her cheeks, then fights her to the ground and cuts her face with a razor. Enter Lieutenant Zuniga. Carmen holds him at bay with a knife, knees him in the balls, and pitches dirt in his eyes. This Carmen is no sloe-eyed soubrette bedizened with lace and mantillas, but a tough broad from the streets, part-time hooker in Lillas Pastia's stable of whores, with a particularly strong appetite for food and sex.

Brook has reduced the opera to eighty minutes without intermission, cut the choruses, supporting roles, and all but fourteen members of the orchestra, and stripped the story down to its bare essentials. He has also turned the characters (including some from Prosper Mérimée's novel) into hard-boiled eggs out of a naturalistic saucepan. This, in theory, is a brilliant conception, and Brook executes it brilliantly. The trouble is with the recalcitrant material itself. Whatever *Carmen* is, as an opera or a literary work, it is not a "*tragédie*," but rather a melodrama garnished with local color. Brook's reduction succeeds in complicating character, but it simplifies the already rather absurd plot, the bony structure of which is hardly sturdy enough for such penetrating radiology. In outline, Carmen is about a jealous soldier, infatuated with a promiscuous gypsy, who slices up anyone who ogles his girl and inevitably kills the girl herself. Take away Bizet's lush orchestration, his spirited choruses, the sunlit splendor of Seville, and the excitement of the bullring, and all you are left with is the outline, a silly anecdote of considerable implausibility.

Brook has directed *Carmen* with five separate casts. In the company I saw, the part of Carmen is sung and performed well by a fine black actress-singer (Cynthia Clarey). But Don José is such a wimpy creature, baby faced, expressionless, that his uncharacteristic temper makes him look like Henry Aldrich on a rampage. Finding Zuniga embracing Carmen, he forces him to the floor and strangles him. After Escamillo moves into Carmen's orbit, Don José tries to stab him with his knife (passes that Escamillo successfully dodges with his cape). When Carmen's husband, Garcia, appears, demanding his conjugal rights, José rewards his request with a shiv in his ribs. And for a finale, he shoves a knife in Carmen's back as they both kneel on a dusty road after Escamillo (in Brook's interpolation) has been killed in the bullring. Although Brook has directed this massacre with his customary brilliance (the staging of Garcia's death is as fine an example of casual violence as anything I have seen on stage since Mike Nichols's treatment of Carlyle's murders in *Streamers*), the accumulated slaughter ultimately becomes both ludicrous and wearing: Charlie Chaplin, in his version, at least had the sense to make fun of it. It is clearly Brook's intention to rescue *Carmen* from the tedious artificiality of grand opera. But when I looked over my shoulder at the audience I saw so many snoozing husbands I thought I was back at the Met.

Pintilie's *Seagull* at the Guthrie does not allow one to nod—the ideas come at you like a shower of meteors. In Pintilie's cinematic approach, the play begins with the final act, and then goes into flashback, as perceived through the mind of a hallucinating Treplev. In the tradition of his Rumanian countryman, Andrei Serban (and *his* teacher, Peter Brook), Pintilie gives us Chekhov without walls—a glittering dreamscape of memory and desire. Radu Boruzescu's setting is a gorgeous environment—a burnished metallic mirror that becomes transparent to reveal a ghostly Nina surrounded by a forest of birches (and later Treplev's improvised stage covered with twigs and branches)—and Miruna Boruzescu's gauzy lace, linen, crinoline, and velvet costumes, festooned with boas and ostrich-feathered hats, are equally shimmering.

Whatever is implicit in the play, Pintilie makes explicit. When Irina admits she has never read a word of her son's work, Treplev is behind her to absorb the insult. When Nina returns to the house, Treplev mounts her in a clumsy effort to consummate his love ("Give me a glass of water," says the unresponsive girl after he rolls off her, as if asking for a postcoital cigarette). Treplev's first suicide attempt is performed before the audience. And when Treplev catalogues his mother's faults ("She's a psychological case"), he speaks the indictment within earshot as Irina floats lazily on a swing.

"How lovely it used to be—do you remember?" asks the distraught Nina, and the stage transforms in preparation for the beginning of the play—for the ending, too, because the fourth act is repeated in its entirety, creating a rather tedious sense of *déjà vu*. At the climax, Nina is surrounded by Irina and Masha, who stain her face with black makeup, dress her in a feathered seagull costume, and crucify her on Treplev's stage—a stage that trolleys behind the panels immersed in fog and smoke, with Nina screaming, to the accompaniment of high-pitched electronics, "Now I am a real actress." Having witnessed this, there's nothing left for Treplev to do but burn his manuscript and end his life.

Some of these interpolations are perverse, some ridiculous, but this *Seagull* nevertheless describes an important symbolic arc for a theatre that, under pressure from subscribers, has recently shown signs of reverting to its conservative past. The only thing Liviu Ciulei really needs from the Guthrie past is its abandoned permanent company, because the weakest aspect of the event was the performance. No matter how brilliantly produced, *The Seagull* belongs to actors and cannot succeed without an ensemble. This production collected a disparate group of strangers together for the first time, and asked them to become a family in five short weeks. Irina brought vocally limited and neurasthenic luggage from the Actors Studio; Polina was a giggling yenta; Masha reminded me of the battle-ax Domina in *A Funny Thing Happened on the Way to the Forum;* Trigorin was performing for TV; Nina was mannered. Only David Pierce as Treplev successfully combined the phantasmagoric dream with the passionate reality. "I didn't understand a word of it," says Dorn about Treplev's play. "But I enjoyed watching it. You were very sincere and the scenery was lovely." That's as good a judgment as we'll get on this bizarre and irritating, yet always absorbing and provocative, experiment.

A BOTTOMLESS DREAM

(A Midsummer Night's Dream)

It could be argued that productions of *A Midsummer Night's Dream* (like those of *Hamlet*) help to define a decade—or at least to reflect its styles and issues. The all-white environment of Peter Brook's *Dream*, where Athens became a freestyle gymnasium, lovers wooed on swings, and rustics behaved like working-class pub stiffs, characterized the playful side of England in the late sixties. Alvin Epstein's *Dream*, with its Purcell score, Uccello battle paintings, and a dangerous wooden scoop peopled with reptilian spirits, reflected the radical contentions of the early American seventies. And now Liviu Ciulei's *Dream* at the Minneapolis Guthrie Theatre suggests the feminist revisionism of the middle eighties.

Perhaps because our current decade has not yet fully declared itself, Ciulei's production lacks the conceptual overview of its predecessors, but in freshness of approach and layered detail, not to mention a freedom from traditional ethereal delicacy, it is certainly their equal in every other respect. Enclosed within Beni Montresor's shiny red vinyl setting furbished with two central doors that open, at one point, to reveal a large cutout moon, this *Dream* begins with a black Hippolyta, as spiky as her insolent brush hair, being forcibly divested of black cotton battle fatigues, which are then incinerated on a brazier of coals. Her conqueror, Theseus, wearing a long Victorian motoring coat, has not so much gained a bride as captured a sullen war prisoner, one who resists being assimilated in the white robes of the Athenian court. Power and subjugation are the major issues, and black, red, and white the primary colors—shades that suggest the bold strong choices of the production.

The interpretation makes jumps in style and time. But however contemporary in feeling, the environment is too generalized to live in any particular period. The rustics rehearse their play wearing derby hats, caps, and academic gowns, as if the Supreme Court were preparing to enact *Pyramus and Thisbe*. Puck is a punk street kid, her arrogant fingers pulling at the armholes of her leather vest as she argues with the First Fairy, a lisping poof mincing about with a flower in his ear. Enveloped in a black cape, Oberon, the black husband of another racially mixed couple, engages in a power struggle with Titania, also dressed in black, though her fairy retinue wears white. Lysander and Demetrius fight with switchblades. Helena and Hermia, those two combative Shakespearean heroines, are even tougher, more contentious than in most recent productions, with no trace whatever of Elizabethan modesty (Helena tells us women "were not made to woo," then makes a serious attempt to seduce Demetrius).

The mechanicals—I've seen them played more deftly and amusingly, but rarely more good-naturedly—share an oafish fraternity similar to that of De Niro's chums in *The Deer Hunter*, enjoying the same rough male bonding: Flute is a half-pint wiseacre, Quince an Arnold Stang intellectual, Bottom a vain self-satisfied stand-up comic with a passion for one-liners. It is Bottom's humor, in fact, that appeals most to Titania after—almost suffocated by Cupid's flower (it gives Puck hay fever)—she falls for his asinine appeal. His every word reduces her to helpless laughter, and when he trades quips with her fairies, she rolls on the bower shrieking hysterically and pounding her fists on the floor.

But Ciulei's emphasis is mostly on "the fierce vexation" of this dream, its aches, its sorrows, its furies. The first encounter of Oberon and Titania is a ferocious marital spat (over a long dinner table) that gets so heated that Titania knocks over a decanter of wine. The same table is finally the scene of reconciliation, but not before Theseus and Hippolyta sit there to watch the play-within-the-play, and Puck, stealing wine, spills the same decanter. The domestication of the strife between the two matched couples not only makes their arguments parallel and immediate but also suggests that nothing is won when sexual mastery is at stake. Oberon achieves his original goal—the possession of the changeling boy—but it is a victory without satisfaction, just as Theseus's conquest of Hippolyta is unlikely to prove the basis for a very serene marriage.

As a result, the pervasive tone of Ciulei's *Dream* is not one of joy or enchantment, but rather of disappointment, a mood enhanced by the use throughout of Philip Glass's *Music in Twelve Parts*, with its hypnotic repetitions and mournful Hebraic saxophone figures. High spirits are almost always followed by melancholy reflections; Oberon is not pleased when Puck tells him "my mistress with a monster is in love"—the "sweet sight" of Bottom and Titania entwined in each other's arms grips him with wretchedness and self-hatred. When Titania, released from enchantment, sees the ass she's been embracing, she is possessed by a morbid state of grief, as if broken by the experience (the same fine actress, playing Elmire in Pintilie's *Tartuffe* at the same theatre, experienced the same psychic deterioration after her husband Orgon forced her into the embraces of another man). Oberon comforts Titania, as he in turn is comforted by Puck, but the wounds don't heal. Nor do Helena and Hermia easily forgive Lysander and Demetrius for the ordeals they have been made to suffer; and Hippolyta, though she finally offers Theseus her hand at the end of the play, is hardly going to prove a pliant wife. As for Puck, that "merry wanderer of the night," she is sometimes in such a deep state of depression she seems in need of lithium treatments. Even Bottom has a depressed moment when he reflects on his transformation—before waving off the whole experience with a dismissive "Nahhh."

The *Pyramus and Thisbe* sequence—played by the rustics in cutaway coats and bow ties—evokes the customary laughs, with Flute's Thisbe (as usual) running off with the show. But even this raucous episode ends on a dying fall: the clowns return to dance the bergomasque before an empty house, the entire audience having disappeared. It is, in fact, the moods that change in this production rather than the settings. Possibly cued by Oberon's reference to "the eastern gate, all fiery red," the whole show is played against that same striking Chinese red surround, occasionally decorated with broken designer's mannequins representing the court or rolling transparent silks representing the forest, while Titania's bower (and Bottom's stage) is a square of glass and steel that raises and lowers on cables.

This is Ciulei's final production at the Guthrie, which is a shame for many reasons, not the least being that he has now assembled a strong young permanent company. Harriet Harris is a passionate and tempestuous Titania with a rich emotional voice that seems to come from deep inside her roots. Lynn Chausow plays Puck like a sardonic tomboy with a duck waddle, bored by her job, laid-back, and rebellious, her head a punching bag for Oberon to bang against the bower whenever he gets angry. The lovers—Katherine Leask, David Pierce, Brian Hargrove, and Kathryn Dowling—are strongly individualized and energetic. Peter-Francis James's debonair Oberon is thickly textured. And while I was not entirely charmed by Jay Peterson's somewhat oily Bottom, he was the spirited leader of an appealing group of rude mechanicals, distinguished by John Madden Towey's wily Flute.

People may dispute this production, but not its air of confidence: Ciulei and his actors have freshly rethought every line of dialogue, every line of action. Don't expect a definitive version of *A Midsummer Night's Dream*. There is no such thing. Ciulei's layered work reminds us that the play, like Bottom's dream, is bottomless, that there are many ways to interpret great art. Still, however enjoyable, something was missing from the evening, perhaps what I mentioned earlier, a unifying metaphor. One remembers details of interpretation rather than general concepts, specific meanings instead of universal themes

Brook's *Dream* was about acrobatic vitality and high spirits, Epstein's about music and conflict. Ciulei's *Dream*—for all its scenes of sexual strife, for all its racial and feminist overtones—is largely about . . . red.

I guess I'm saying that this beautiful contemporary production doesn't always transcend its concrete referential function to create a fuller meaning. Updated classical productions are usually built on the prose principle of simile: *Julius Caesar* may remind us of Mussolini's Rome, so is set in Fascist Italy; *All's Well That Ends Well* could suggest Freud's Vienna, so is placed in nineteenth-century Austria. The more poetic classical productions function like metaphors, reverberating in a manner similar to nondiscursive poems. I prefer the latter, and Ciulei's *Dream*—both in and out of time, specific in style and general in setting—falls somewhere in between.

RUMANIA, RUMANIA

(Hamlet; The Wild Duck)

The supremacy of English-style classical theatre, virtually unquestioned in this country for the past forty years, is now being seriously challenged in the United States by a group of expatriated Rumanians concerned with deconstructing sacred dramatic texts. A number of English-speaking directors, notably the internationalist Peter Brook, has also worked this vein effectively. But it is essentially an Eastern European phenomenon that started in Soviet Russia during the twenties with Vsevolod Meyerhold's celebrated production of Gogol's *The Inspector General*, and then spread west to the satellite countries. Following the appearance of the Rumanians Andrei Serban, Andrei Belgrader, Liviu Ciulei, and Lucian Pintilie on our shores, classical deconstruction became a native movement dominating the American avant-garde and some of our resident theatres.

The establishment of this movement, as well as its nervous reception by critics and public alike, grew clear during Joe Papp's brief control of the Vivian Beaumont—when Serban was invited to stage radical productions of *The Cherry Orchard* and *Agamemnon*—and during Ciulei's auspicious, if controversial and short-lived, reign as artistic director of the Guthrie. If it was Ellen Stewart of La Mama who first invited Serban to the United States to evolve his masterpiece on Greek classical themes *Fragments of a Trilogy*, it was Ciulei who imported Pintilie to direct *The Seagull* and *Tartuffe* (which Pintilie later restaged at the Arena). Now Ciulei, set adrift by the Guthrie, has resurfaced at Papp's Public Theatre with a production of *Hamlet*, while Pintilie has just opened a new version of Ibsen's *The Wild Duck* at Arena Stage. (As for traditional classical production, the American Conservatory Theatre, its chief native exponent, has faltered following a series of dull seasons and the resignation of William Ball. No other major company has taken up the baton.)

The Rumanian conquest, however, is far from complete—at least to judge by Ciulei's *Hamlet*. It is a production at once carefully modulated and curiously safe—not exactly a surrender to traditional directorial styles, but obviously informed by traditional caution. Papp has an obsession with *Hamlet*, which he seems to produce about every three years (last with Diane Venora in the lead). This version was apparently commissioned for the promising classical actor Kevin Kline. Kline is not yet ready for the role; like the young prince, he lacks advancement. The only time he seemed able to join his own experience with that of his character was during an athletic duel scene with Laertes, beautifully staged by B. H. Barry in a swashbuckling manner suitable to *The Pirates of Penzance*.

Kline first appears holding his head in his hand, his hair wild, his body wrapped up inside a black Victorian greatcoat. His physical model is the Russian Raskolnikov, but what he gives us is Rotarian blandness. Kline's Hamlet has no overdrive in his internal motor, neither mercurial passion nor suppressed hysteria. He is pleasant, good-natured, intelligent, but too self-assured to suffer, and less anguished than annoyed by the problems that plague him. He is flat and perfunctory with the ghost, mildly upset by his mother's adultery. He can glare at Claudius and twit courtiers but shows little hatred for the bloat king or pangs of conscience over Polonius's murder. More at home with players than aristocrats, he joins them as a jester, applying clown-white pancake. With Ophelia, he's a stand-up comic, but the humor's unleavened with irony or wit. This Hamlet is a bit of a yuppie, destined to be a stockbroker or a lawyer. You can't help liking him, but you share his impatience over the obstacles impeding his career.

This is a failing of emotional commitment, not of intellect; Kline's reading of the text is remarkably clear, and on two occasions even original. I never realized, until the actor stressed the word *set* in the passage "The time is out of joint" ("O cursed spite / That ever I was born to *set* it right!"), that Shakespeare's metaphor referred to resetting dislocated limbs, while Kline's expression of astonishment on "The rest is silence" made this line the resolution of Hamlet's internal debate on the nature of death in "To be or not to be."

For the most part, however, the actor managed to avoid facing any of the knotty problems of the play, and so did the production. The directorial interpolations were usually decorative rather than interpretive—Gertrude removing her wig to reveal gray hair beneath, Ophelia going mad during a dinner party while buttering bread and pulling flowers from the centerpiece, the First Player reading his Hecuba speech to the accompaniment of a cello, Claudius coming on like a portly U. S. Grant, Laertes goose-stepping like a Nazi youth. Ciulei has set the play in the late nineteenth century in a mythical country resembling Graustark or Zenda, and the minimalist scenery (mobile burnished columns and a diagonal screen upstage lit with abstract forms by Jennifer Tipton) provides fluidity and crispness. But the generalized environment puts the burden of specificity on the Victorian costumes (richly designed by William Ivy Long), and adds a peculiar fleshliness to all the characters, not excluding the usually incorporeal ghost.

Like Kline's Hamlet, the acting is competent without being particularly charged. Two young people stand out, both from Ciulei's period at the Guthrie, one of them miscast. Harriet Harris, a passionate Titania in Minneapolis, is too mature for Ophelia, whom she endows with an incipient neurasthenia more appropriate to a Tennessee Williams character. Still she manages to provide the truest, most powerful emotion of the evening. And David Pierce's Laertes—a prissy, cold-blooded cadet from a fascist military academy—has a repressed ferocity that is menacing and dangerous. These excepted, the actors usually slide along the surface of their roles. Ciulei shows more interest in moving the action along than investigating the text, keeping us more occupied with stage business than with thematic interpretation or character plumbing. Shakespeare's story is clear enough; what is less clear is the animating impulse driving the performance.

At the Arena Stage in Washington, Lucian Pintilie's version of Ibsen's *The Wild Duck* is a genuinely new look at that play that pulls it out of canvas realism into a world of poetic metaphor and savage farce. The opening act in old Werle's house is not altogether promising. But then it's a fearfully difficult piece of exposition (the second act of this five-act play is largely expository too). Pintilie tries to distract our attention from two servants shoveling background material at us by using strained devices, including a sumptuous banquet seen through transparent mylar mirrors, and an anachronistic slide show of vacation photographs conducted by Mrs. Sorby while the Chamberlains sing "Harvest Moon." (Though the play has been updated to the twenties, I don't believe Kodak color carousels had yet been invented.) Here the director appears to be forcing visual interest on a talky drama.

When the scene changes to Hjalmar Ekdal's lodgings, however, the play begins to develop a cumulative power. Pintilie's setting is much too spacious to suit the humble means of the Ekdal family—it has the dimensions of a fashionable loft in Soho—and the metal stairway leading to the "attic" containing the denizens of old Ekdal's simulated forest, wild duck included, is high enough to suggest they own the whole piece of real estate, substantial holdings for such impoverished people (Pintilie made architectural modifications in the Kreeger in order to accommodate this ambitious design). Still, the furnishings of this enormous room are gritty enough, including a metal desk and filing cabinet, a clothesline, and a huge arc lamp used for Hjalmar's photography. And the squalor is enhanced, despite Gina's heroic efforts to keep the place clean, by eggs periodically splattering on the floor from the attic above.

For all his concern with grandiose environments and visual punctuation, Pintilie keeps us focused on the theme of *The Wild Duck*, which is the malignant effect of utopian idealism on those who need illusions in order to survive. In his effort to lead the Ekdals toward "a true conjugal union," Gregers Werle exposes Gina's adultery with his father, old Werle, and the dubious paternity of their daughter, Hedwig. It is a story that concludes morbidly with Hedwig's suicide. But Ibsen nevertheless realizes it is an occasion for ferocious satire, even farce, especially since Gregers (played by Christopher McCann with flattop haircut, Trotsky whiskers, and mealymouthed self-righteousness) is such a priggish wimp and Hjalmar (played by Richard Bauer with the flamboyance of a road-company Cyrano) such a histrionic poseur. The confusion of styles is precisely what gives the play modernity, and the way the director treats the climax adds postmodern touches as well.

Despite prophetic warnings from Dr. Relling (played with sardonic brilliance by Stanley Anderson, looking like a squashy, whiskey-soaked Anthony Hopkins), Gregers's meddling has destroyed the entire family. While Hjalmar vacillates between abandoning the household and completing his breakfast, Hedwig commits suicide in the attic to the accompaniment of frightened barnyard sounds. Her body falls to the floor like another splattered egg; the arc light begins to turn in circles around the room; old Ekdal stands babbling on the stairs. Hjalmar, in an orgy of self-pity, shouts hysterically at the ceiling ("How could you do this to me?") and turns to Gina for comfort; she shrinks at his touch. The spoiled priest Molvik starts praying; Dr. Relling hurls a drink in his face. Relling then drags Gregers the length of the stage to the couch and, shaking him like a puppy, forces his face into the dead body of his victim. Rising, Gregers pulls violently at Relling's nose, Relling pulls Gregers's hair, and with the two locked in a clumsy grappling match, Hedwig's body falls slowly off the couch. Gregers runs from the room, hitting his head on the doorframe, as Relling shouts after him, "Go to hell," (adding, with a grin, "See you tomorrow").

This inspired scene, where the audience is alternately juggling pathos, laughter, and surprise, is, in retrospect, the moment toward which the whole production moves, and it redeems whatever casting flaws, longueurs, or directorial excesses occasionally plague it. Using his own free stage version based on a translation by David Westerfer, Pintilie has made the work entirely contemporary and immediate without altering its essential structure. And that, of course, has been the major contribution of our expatriate Rumanian friends to our perception of the classics: to make us see them as fresh works of art rather than as anthology pieces or curatorial artifacts. Ciulei, perhaps daunted by the sour critical atmosphere of New York, has momentarily flagged in his approach; but his protégé, Pintilie, has picked up the fallen pennant and waved it proudly aloft.

ADVANCED MACHINES

(Hamletmachine)

Heiner Mueller's *Hamletmachine* is a six-page response to Shakespeare's *Hamlet;* Robert Wilson's production with NYU students is a two-and-a-half-hour response to Mueller's six pages. Although this suggests that the original object is receding further and further into the distance, the results are dazzling, a significant advance in a historic collaboration.

Mueller is a celebrated East German dramatist/director whose works are just becoming known in this country, largely through the translations of Carl Weber and the ministrations of Wilson himself. Occasionally performed in off-off-Broadway venues, he has lately achieved wider recognition in the United States for his contributions to Wilson's epic *The CIVIL warS* and for his prologue (a twelve-page continuous sentence) to Wilson's recent *Alcestis*. For Wilson, who usually regards texts as fanged animals preparing to leap at his throat, Mueller represents a writer who stimulates rather than threatens his imagistic imagination. Paradoxically, the apolitical Robert Wilson has developed into the ideal director for the politically engaged Heiner Mueller.

This happy relationship is based on deep mutual respect, combined with total artistic autonomy. What they share in common is a storehouse of dream imagery. Increasingly, Mueller's "plays" have become less conventional dialogues than hallucinatory poems designed to disorder the senses; increasingly, the hallucinations are being inspired by the myths and characters of classical dramatic literature. Reordering Greek drama has typically been one of the central concerns of modern playwrights—Cocteau, Sartre, Anouilh, Giraudoux, O'Neill, T. S. Eliot among them. But it was not until Brecht's *Coriolan* that contemporary playwrights began trespassing imaginatively on Shakespeare's plays. Since then, Edward Bond produced a meditation on *King Lear* (called *Lear*) and Eugene Ionesco turned *Macbeth* into the absurdist farce *Macbett*. Now Heiner Mueller has begun using the materials of Greek and Shakespearean tragedy—

Medea, Macbeth, Titus Andronicus, Hamlet, etc.—more freely than ever classical dramatists used myth or story.

Mueller's approach is to drag the shadows and silhouettes of classical characters into the twentieth century, dumping them into a maelstrom of contemporary issues—female subjugation, terrorism, revolution, madness, and nuclear panic included. Like Eliot's, his pieces are assemblages of shards and fragments shored against his ruin, the shattered memory of history running through them like a nagging, demented refrain. His text can feature five-page soliloquies or uninterrupted silence, as his figures split, multiply, advance, and recede in waves of heroic anonymity. *Hamletmachine* features only five characters from Shakespeare's play (Hamlet, Ophelia, Gertrude, Claudius, and Horatio/Polonius) and only one line of dialogue ("Denmark's a prison"). But it includes a barrage of quotations by other writers, from Karl Marx's introduction to his *Critique of Hegel's Philosophy of Law* ("The main point is to overthrow all existing conditions . . .") to the mutterings of Susan Atkins at the Manson trial ("When she walks through your bedrooms carrying butcher knives you'll know the truth"). Assailed by monstrous events, bombarded by the "daily nausea Nausea" of the media and "prefabricated babble," characters like Hamlet are no longer able to function or play out their parts: "My drama didn't happen. The script has been lost."

As for Ophelia ("the one the river didn't keep"), she refuses her part entirely: "I eject all the sperm I have received. I turn the milk of my breasts into lethal poison. I take back the world I gave birth to. I choke between my thighs the world I gave birth to. I bury it in my womb. Down with the happiness of submission." She will neither accept her fate nor take refuge in suicide. She will tear up the photos of all the men who made love to her (even the author's photograph gets torn in the course of the play). Entombed in history, she and all the characters are beating their wings against the cage of their captivity.

Mueller's motor impulses are deeply political, though nondidactic. He is given to asking questions without providing answers, confronting the audience with the butt end of its own traditions. His charnel-house imagery, which establishes his links with his countrymen Buechner and Brecht, is the language of German neo-Romanticism. It comes from the butcher shop, but it is also inspired by the deliquescence and putrefaction he sees in the modern world. Mueller's borrowed characters, therefore, are not dramatic figures so much as figures in a muddied historical landscape—where they resonate with the experience of gas ovens, revolutionary violence, nuclear terror, and radioactive contamination.

Robert Wilson has been doing similar things in his own work, not just with such classical characters as Medea, Alcestis, or Lear, but also with actual historical personages: Stalin, Freud, Einstein, Patty Hearst, Queen Victoria, Frederick the Great. In *Hamletmachine*, he treats Mueller's *dramatis personae* with the same combination of care and indifference as he treats the real lives of his own people. Every line of Mueller's text is there, and every stage direction, but the stage directions are announced rather than enacted, while the spoken lines are never accompanied by the anticipated illustrative action. Neither Wilson nor his actors attempt to "interpret" Mueller's text (much to the delight of an author who prefers his words unfreighted with the impressions of others). What they offer instead is a parallel reinforcing event.

The results are remarkable. Performed in a tiny seventy-four seat theatre after only three and a half weeks of rehearsal with undergraduates in John Wulp's experimental theatre program, *Hamletmachine* is a model of theatrical discipline. Wilson has choreographed the piece within an inch of its life, each beat signaled by the stage manager with the click of a Chinese baton. The setting is simple: a long table where sit three women, overly made up like forties movie stars (I thought of Linda Darnell, Esther Williams, and Hedy Lamarr), a bare tree stroked and attended by another woman, and screens on each of the three visible walls of the stage. On a nearby rolling office chair sits another woman, a wraith with powdered blown hair and powdered skin. Accompanied by the sound of barking dogs and a melancholy piano obbligato for one finger, this setting, like the hands of a moving clock (Mueller's "machine"?), changes position four times in the course of the evening, each time uncovering a new screen.

The stage is full of Ophelias, the most prominent being a lovely young girl with a long black pigtail. There are also a number of Hamlets, including a swaggering young man in leather jacket and boots, a boy in a yellow jogging suit, another in torn tee shirt and jeans who knocks down a book on each of his appearances, and the young lad who speaks most of Mueller's text. Gertrude is represented by a woman in a Victorian ballroom gown, Claudius by a top-hatted man in a frock coat, his face coal black.

What happens is not easy to describe because it is more a sensory trip than an ordered series of events. You fasten on a detail—a raised finger, the book falling on the table, the three women scratching their heads or, fists in mouth, emitting piercing screams—and enter a new form of time and space. Your eye wanders along the set, across the joins and holes of the curious furniture, with the leisure enjoyed at a museum. Suddenly, a screen is lowered and the whole space changes. As a Schubert piano piece is played, the action is transferred to film, with Mueller's lines functioning as subtitles. The screen images catch fire, then turn purple; the women transform into apes. The image goes cubist, as if seen through the mottled glass door of a shower; then the projection minifies, turns white, and disappears. The evening ends abruptly, as all three wall screens are simultaneously revealed, and a fourth is drawn in front of the audience.

Not all of this is of equal interest. The production has its longueurs and the undergraduate actors, though physically adept, do not always show sufficient vocal authority. Still, they appear remarkably mature on stage, and, strictly from a training perspective, their Wilson experience is bound to affect them deeply, even those whose eyes are looking West Coastwards. Some members of the audience will no doubt be confirmed in their conviction that Wilson turns actors into puppets; but the precision work of these young people after four weeks with their director is more expressive, and more valuable, than three years of high emoting.

Major changes in theatre usually happen imperceptibly—the progress from the epic style of Shakespeare to the proscenium realism of Ibsen took almost three hundred years to accomplish. We are presently witnessing a theatrical revolution that is dramatically rapid, in which our conventional notions of character, action, plot, and theme are being fundamentally altered and our perception of causal reality radically shattered. Mueller's *Hamletmachine*, like all of his works, is another step in that process, and Wilson's production of *Hamletmachine*, like all of his productions, is another landmark in the modern theatre's exploration of the hidden corners of life.

VIENNESE DREAMS

(Vienna: Lusthaus)

Martha Clarke demonstrated her unearthly theatre instinct two years ago with *The Garden of Earthly Delights*, a work of almost bestial beauty created in collaboration with the composer Richard Peaslee and based on the famous triptych of Hieronymus Bosch. Following human "progress" from Edenic grace before the Fall to a condition of Hobbesian brutality, the piece was a compound of movement, acting, music, and aerial gymnastics, a wordless (though not soundless) collage that led some to question whether it was properly called theatre—or dance. Yet, it undeniably belonged to the stage, just as clearly as Wilson's operas and Foreman's phantasmagorias. *The Garden of Earthly Delights*, in fact, was arguably one of the most significant works of postwar American theatrical art.

Miss Clarke has now followed this with a piece composed of similar elements (excluding flying). It is called *Vienna: Lusthaus* and, while not yet as fully imagined as its predecessor (being still a work in progress), confirms her stature as a major American theatre artist.

Vienna is a dream play inspired by a piece of architecture—the *Lusthaus*, or Pleasure Pavilion, originally built in the Austrian capital before 1556—"an octagonal structure," as the program tells us, "located at the far end of the Prater." Clearly, Miss Clarke's imagination is aroused by visual stimuli (the work was also influenced, she says, by the nude drawings and paintings of Egon Schiele and Gustav Klimt). And if my admiration for *Vienna* is not total, it is partly because this brilliantly imagistic work has not yet fully assimilated Charles Mee, Jr.'s gnomic and flattened text. Mee's tangential narrative, intoned by the actors Robert Langdon-Lloyd and Brenda Currin as if they were sleepwalking, speaks of fountains, rivers, trips to the opera, rat killings, and human habitations ("Man is born in a hospital and dies in a hospital; he ought to live in a place that looks like a hospital"). But it intersects with Miss Clarke's imagery only at one crucial point—the erotic. Love—whether heterosexual, homosexual, lesbian, narcissistic, incestuous, or bestial—is the articulated and unarticulated theme of the evening; it also forms a junction with the other subject of *Vienna*, death.

Miss Clarke appreciates the dangerous beauty of naked human bodies, especially with their limbs entwined in what Blake called "the lineaments of gratified desire." For her, *fin-de-siècle* Vienna represents sexuality (and perhaps Jew-baiting) on the rampage: After lulling us with the elegant civility of military officers, demure ladies, and Strauss waltzes, she evokes dream images of increasing coarseness and violence. A soldier sits with a lifelike puppet on his lap, caressing and undressing her. A man and woman locked in embrace roll on the floor in slow ecstasy. Another man, wearing woman's shoes on his hands, literally becomes his own lover. As musicians wander blithely through the action, a soldier lying on the ground peeks under the skirt of a noncommittal girl; another slaps a rival in the face. That soldier is later killed, perhaps by him who got slapped, and is visited by mourners. At the conclusion, snow falls on the living and the dead, and the performers first skate, then waltz, through the drifts. The evening ends on a decomposing query: "What colors does a body pass through after death?"

These episodes have been arranged in a nonlinear, nonsequential manner that sacrifices cumulative narrative power to unity of mood. This is not a dream with a story, however fractured or fragmented, like Strindberg's *A Dream Play* or Cocteau's *Blood of a Poet*, but rather variations on a reverie designed to make a subliminal appeal. It is, as a result, abstract and allusive—and somewhat unanchored. Because the shards of text are so divorced from the movement, the mind sometimes divorces itself as well, and the spectator finds himself not so much engaged in the proceedings as a detached admiring witness.

Still, the imagery is extraordinarily lovely even at its grossest, and the control of the performers is breathtaking: the lissome slender nymph Paola Styron, the expressionless puppet Lila York, the virile blond lover Robert Besserer, the deliciously corrupt Marie Fourcaut, the dead soldier Timothy Doyle, nay all the dancers, and all the actors, represent models of discipline. Richard Peaslee's music, more diffident here than usual, has a haunting grace, even in dissonance, and the visual environment is stunning. Robert Israel, responsible also for the striking Viennese military tunics, shifts, and ballroom gowns, has designed a tilted white room, glimpsed always behind a scrim functioning as a transparent shroud. It helps dislocate your sense of reality, as Paul Gallo's eerie, luminous shadowy lighting helps disorient your psyche. Whatever my reserve about *Vienna* in its present phase of development, it is a performance piece of consequence that poises Martha Clarke for greater leaps in future.

THE CENTURY OF DIRECTORS

(Great Directors at Work; Grotowski and His Laboratory)

Lately, the most rabid controversy in the theatre has been over the role of the modern stage director—often characterized by outraged actors, critics, and even spectators as an upstart careerist determined to usurp the traditional function of the playwright. "Director-auteurs" have been raising temperatures for over a hundred years now; yet, discussion of their work has rarely risen above the levels of snarls and grumbles. Now two new books approach directors not as egoistic intruders but rather as prime movers of the theatrical occasion, indeed as among the most original artists working in the modern theatre.

David Richard Jones believes our time will be celebrated as the "century of the director." He argues that no theatre history can be complete without careful analysis of directorial achievement. *Great Directors at Work* is a study of four groundbreaking productions as created by four seminal theatre figures—Stanislavsky, Brecht, Brook, and Kazan—based on a careful reading of their casebooks, model-books, notebooks, interviews, and other pedagogical material. Zbigniew Osinski's *Grotowski and His Laboratory*, on the other hand, concentrates on a single figure, the Polish visionary Jerzy Grotowski, whose work was a vital influence on world theatre in the sixties and seventies, and whose life was a significant model of self-abnegation and dedication. Both the American and the Polish critics share a conviction that directors are no longer simply playwrights' adjutants, obliged to render faithful interpretations of written texts, but rather creative figures in their own right, with the license to approach plays as freely as playwrights approach their source material.

Jones would like to establish a directorial "canon" that can then be studied as scrupulously as the great modern plays. A director himself, he is openly dismissive of any limits on the director's power, and regards all challenges to directorial authority as essentially reactionary: "I am inclined to accept the historical fact that directors have become central to modern theatre and then to consider a corollary, that modern theatre is no doubt more sophisticated and more artistic for that change." Instead of viewing the creative-interpretive tension as an obstacle to the theatrical process, Jones chooses to see it as fundamental. He rejects the familiar analogy between the way the director serves the playwright and the orchestra conductor serves the composer on the premise that musical notation is precise and stage directions are not. For Jones, a stage director is not a subordinate but a genuine artist in the Coleridgean sense, one who creates original matter out of his own imagination. To those literary humanists (and these include most theatre critics) who uphold the primacy of language, bemoaning the way the written text is staled upon the stage, he answers with the famous remark of Meyerhold, "Words in the theatre are only a design on the canvas of motion." Theatre, in short, is a nexus of symbols, many of them visual, and dramatic literature cannot find its true form until embodied in the stage imagery of inspired directors, not to mention the flesh of actors. Because this was recognized most vividly in the period from 1880 to 1980, he calls this era "the third great age of Western drama."

Jones's introductory essay contains ideas that deserve wide circulation, but the rest of the book does not always fulfill the promise of the opening argument. For one thing, having drawn the lines of battle, he enlists a squad of soldiers who are not all fighting for the same cause. Of his four "great directors," for example, only two—Bertolt Brecht and Peter Brook—can be considered auteurs, and Brecht is an auteur primarily by virtue of being an author. As for Stanislavsky and Kazan, they belong, by declaration and intention, more properly to the interpretive tradition, however playwrights might have protested their "creative" interpolations. Jones claims unity for these four disparate directors because they are all "stylists" and "intellectual figures, artists full of ideas about art and work and culture." But I find this a strange way to describe the anti-intellectual Kazan—a man who, asked to define his style, answered, "Poetic realism I call it when I'm in an egghead mood."

Given the visionary artistry of so many present-day directors in America—Robert Wilson, Joseph Chaikin, Richard Foreman, the Mabou Mines collective, the (naturalized) Rumanian Andrei Serban, among others—I find puzzling the choice of Kazan as the representative American of the book. This is not a comment on his talent, but on the level of his aspirations. With the exception of a disastrous production of *The Changeling*, he never aspired beyond contemporary Broadway plays; and while I share Jones's admiration for *A Streetcar Named Desire*, the production was hardly in a class with Stanislavsky's *The Seagull*, Brecht's *Mother Courage*, or Brook's *Marat/Sade*, being the product of an entirely different system of which Kazan was a leading, if not always uncritical, proponent.

Jones recognizes this when he describes Kazan's *Streetcar* as an example of "high-wire directing in the high-pressure commercial zone." He acknowledges that in staging this show Kazan was required to do more than please himself; he "had to produce a hit." But his account of *Streetcar*'s production history, unlike the language he employs in the rest of the book, is full of chitchat, backstage gossip, and star talk. Much of this is interesting—Kazan's initial choice of John Garfield for the part of Stanley (he rejected it because the role was too small and the contract too long), the rehearsal tensions between Jessica Tandy and Marlon Brando, who felt miscast, the celebrity-studded opening, the critical response, the ensuing awards (excluding the Tony, which went that year to *Mister Roberts*). But Jones is too enchanted with Kazan's magnetic wizardry, too infatuated with his success as opposed to his achievement, to question the limitations of his macho realism or the manipulative nature of his effects.

If the vocabulary of this chapter seems lifted from *People* magazine, this is because, by contrast, Jones's discussion of the other directors in the book is centered on critical issues rather than personalities. His chapter on Stainslavsky, and the way this remarkable artist grew from an autocrat—"forceful composition dominating weak acting"—to a "midwife," bringing a production to birth through patient Socratic methods, is a more cogent critical exercise. Jones reminds us that Nemirovich-Danchenko (Stanislavsky's literary partner) directed fifteen of the twenty-six rehearsals of *The Seagull*, a play Stanislavsky initially believed to be unperformable (he called the characters "half-human"). It is well known that Chekhov objected to Stanislavsky's treatment of his work, particularly the director's relentless naturalism and excessive sound effects. Jones makes a half-convincing effort to defend Stanislavsky by saying Chekhov was not present at rehearsals and, anyway, the controversy has been blown out of proportion by those with antitheatrical prejudices. (He also argues that Stanislavsky, like Chekhov, was a naturalist only on the surface, that the success of *The Seagull* was due to its transcendant spirituality as expressed through the "unvoiced inner life of characters"). But in his eagerness to redeem Stanislavsky, he fails to resolve a gnawing question, which might limit his defense of directorial prerogative: How free should an imaginative director be with an early production of a living playwright's work?

The question does not apply to his discussion of Brecht's *Mother Courage*, where the playwright is staging his own play; but the chapter is mainly a recap of Brecht's own modelbook (based on three separate productions), which adds little to the source material. His treatment of Peter Brook's evolution of *Marat/Sade*, on the other hand, is the one instance in the book that begins to fulfill the promise of the introduction. Brook, in a sense, is the father of the modern auteur director. Beginning as a clever boy wonder, shuttling between opera, classical production, and commercial plays (he directed such infinitely forgettable trifles as *The Little Hut* and *Irma la Douce* on Broadway), Brook made a radical career shift in 1970 when he founded the International Center of Theatre Research (CIRT) in Paris. Even before this conversion, Brook was doing radical versions of the classics with the Royal Shakespeare Company, including fundamental reinterpretations of *King Lear* and *A Midsummer Night's Dream*. It was in the workshops preceding the production of the RSC *Marat/Sade*, in fact, that he evolved the experimental process that characterized most of his later work.

Brook wrestled with all the pressing theatrical issues of the day: the death of the word, the self-consciousness of modernism, the transaction between actors and audiences, the need to disarrange consciousness—all in an effort to make the theatre *central* once again to the modern sensibility. Drawing on Brecht, Artaud, Chaikin's Open Theatre, and the Beck-Malina Living Theatre, he was on a continual quest for prophetic new forms; and when he began work with the RSC on Genet's *The Screens* (after doing a preliminary workshop of Artaud's *Spurt of Blood*), he had evolved the theatre-of-cruelty techniques that were to culminate in the hallucinatory *Marat/Sade*.

Jones's description of this production—and the way the actors prepared for it by visiting asylums, exploring vocal sounds and physical transformations, using primal screams—evokes all the sensory memories of that extraordinary theatre event. Its major effect was to disturb the audience, politically, emotionally, morally. "Starting with its title," Brook wrote, "everything about this play is designed to crack the spectator on the jaw, then douse him with ice-cold water, then force him to assess intelligently what has happened to him, then give him a kick in the balls, then bring him to his senses again." It was a complete realization of the play in a style the playwright, Peter Weiss, never imagined, and as such, a powerful demonstration of the way the director's art can transform a literary text into an experience both immediate and transcendent.

In his later experiments with the CIRT, Brook frequently stumbled, especially when he abandoned texts for collective creations. The directorial artist with whom he developed the closest affinity, Jerzy Grotowski, also lost his way when he gave up texts, though even in his most celebrated productions he showed scant respect for the written word: "I believe," he wrote, "that a dramatic script should provide only a theme for the director who will use it as the basis for a new, independent work, or theatre production." *Grotowski and His Laboratory* follows Grotowski's painful quest for new forms through initial critical hostility ("to much faith in the theatre and too little faith in the playwright") to the triumph of the Polish Theatre Lab as the major (at first the only) experimental company in Poland, evolving brilliant productions of Wyspianski's *Akropolis*, his own *Apocalypsis cum figuris*, and Calderón's *The Constant Prince*. Osinksi's account of Grotowski's personal sacrifice in achieving his vision is moving in the extreme. Attacked for "elitism," for apotheosizing pain and suffering, for idealizing ugliness, for "creating a utopia for masochists," and for provincialism ("If it's so great," said one critic of the work done in Wroclaw, "show us in Warsaw"), Grotowski eventually attracted hordes of admirers and imitators and, after highly acclaimed world tours, passionate critical support.

Grotowski's continuing theme was human loneliness and the inevitability of death; even as a world celebrity, he spoke of being an "eternal wanderer without a homeland." It was perhaps out of this sense of perpetual alienation that in the mid-1970s, at the pinnacle of success, he stopped being a director—a decision he said he made "in order not to be my own follower." He began spending more and more time in the forest, searching for that "other pole of theatre . . . where human beings stop acting." He conducted a series of "paratheatrical experiments" (people chanting, performing yoga, walking in wide ellipses, lying on each other as a "Tree of People," improvising melodies) with a number of adoring disciples, including a representative of the Rockefeller Foundation.

This is the holy ecstasy Andre Gregory described to Wallace Shawn in *My Dinner With Andre*—Woodstock for theatre gurus, EST for intellectuals (no wonder Grotowski ended up in California). Shawn expressed a kindly skepticism; one Polish critic said Grotowski should be supervised not by the Ministry of Culture but by the Ministry of Health. You do not need to adopt so harsh a view to recognize something aberrant in Grotowski's messianic behavior. It represents the dark side of the visionary directorial quest—confusing the search for a new aesthetic with the founding of a new religion. Grotowski's sincerity is not in question—he remains, like Peter Brook, a true saint of the theatre. But even saints seem to lose their way in the weightless modern confusion. Grotowski's progress reveals the terrible price inspired directors must sometimes pay for their newly gained authority.

Neither of these books resolves the continuing debate over who should have supremacy in the theatre, the director or the playwright. But the truth is there is no resolution to this question, nor can there be, unless composite theatre artists, such as Bertolt Brecht and Robert Wilson, command the entire occasion. Nor should there be. Living playwrights—with certain exceptions—will be better served by interpretive directors such as Stanislavsky or Kazan. Classic dramatists—with certain exceptions—will find a fresher life in the hands of creative directors such as Meyerhold, Brook, or Grotowski (even oft-produced plays by living playwrights can sometimes benefit from reinterpretation). It is chastening to remember that the theatre began with neither of these upstarts, but with the actor—and some would argue that it was healthier when dominated by great actor-managers. Still, the compelling thing about the theatre is its pluralism. It is a collective art where collaboration is the password, and every dog can have his day.

The Broadway Musical

NOSTALGIA GLANDS

(42nd Street)

Recent revivals got me thinking a lot lately about the Pavlovian effect of remakes on the nostalgia glands of contemporary Americans, so it was interesting to find a powerful example of this chemical reaction—*42nd Street*—on view at the Winter Garden. To judge from the audience clamor and the tumult at the box office, listening to the melodies and wisecracks of an earlier age is tantamount to soaking for three hours in a steaming tub filled with lemon verbena bath oil. Still, this particular equation represents something more than the commercial exploitation of an earlier popular success (the formula of most remakes). It has been put together (and discussed) as if it were the reworking of an ancient myth. *42nd Street* offers itself in relationship to its thirties source original in much the same manner as, say, T. S. Eliot's *Family Reunion* does to Aeschylus's *Libation Bearers*. If you chew on this for a while, you'll get something of the flavor of a culture that—lacking a heroic past or a shared body of literature—has no better place to go for traditional materials than the myth and magic of fifty years of Hollywood movies.

It's the show's assumption that every spectator knows the deathless line at the climax of the old Dick Powell–Ruby Keeler movie, after the leading lady has twisted her ankle, when Julian Marsh, the producer, says to the gallant little hoofer from the chorus whom he wants to replace her: "Sawyer, you're going out there a youngster, but you've got to come back a star." Irresistible stuff like that—and the marvelous old tunes of Harry Warren and Al Dubin—get the audience so drunk on memories that they even start applauding the strobe lights. Not too long ago, in a somewhat tougher age, kitsch of this kind was considered more appropriate for satire. My own nostalgia extends back to a sketch on *Your Show of Shows* called *92nd Street* ("where for every broken window there's a broken heart"), when Sid Caesar sent Imogene Coca out on stage to replace the backer's girlfriend (a female giant with a deep bass voice), and watched as Coca's quavering soprano knocked out everybody in the theatre, including the janitor, the ushers, and the company dog (who inclined an ear toward the stage like the old trademark for His Master's Voice).

Though it permits a little camp, the current version rarely satirizes its source material, which is fair enough considering how much money it is making off it. *42nd Street* comes on, rather, like an affectionate historical re-creation, right down to wry references to the astronomical price of theatre tickets ("They're paying $4.40 a seat out there!"). The names on the marquees that light up at the end of the show feature such contemporary hits as *Alien Corn* (starring Katherine Cornell), *Mary Queen of Scots* (starring Helen Hayes), *As Thousands Cheer*, and *The Threepenny Opera*. Apart from the Brecht-Weill piece— an inglorious flop when it first appeared—this Broadway honor list is hardly decorated with deathless plays. But at least in aspiration, available acting talent, and sheer number of productions, the list suggests that the Street was considerably more lively fifty years ago than today. It may be, as Julian Marsh gushes elegiacally to his new young star (right before warbling "The Lullaby of Broadway" into her ear) that the phrase *musical comedy* constitutes "the most glorious words in the English language." But a large number of other glorious words have disappeared from the Broadway vocabulary in the period between the time of the action and the date of the revival.

It is as a tribute to the old musicals, however, that *42nd Street* finds its energy. There are Busby Berkeley reproductions, choral tap dances on a bunch of silver dollars, a torch song delivered by the soubrette (Tammy Grimes) to her own shadow, soft-edge Art Deco sets where even the mirrors have voluptuous curves, and an acting style (anachronistically amplified) that delivers everything directly to the audience, even that obligatory final moment when the producer, having achieved his hit, is left solitary on stage, wistfully contemplating the darkened lights of Broadway. On opening night, we are told, the real producer, David Merrick, came on stage to announce that the show's director, Gower Champion, had died that very afternoon— thus laying the mythical groundwork for the remake of the remake. *42nd Street* is the kind of simple lively entertainment that *Oklahoma* was supposed to have forever laid to rest. It reminds me, in fact, of that glitzy top-hatted musical we glimpse during the curtain call of *A Chorus Line*. It is not of our time—which may be the ultimate explanation of its enormous appeal.

MUSICAL INTO OPERA

(Candide)

The Broadway musical has long been touted as America's one original contribution to world culture, on the theory (*pace* Walt Whitman) that we are obliged to invent indigenous art forms in order to validate our identity as a nation. It is true that the American theatre has attracted a wealth of talented lyricists and composers—Cole Porter, Rodgers and Hart, E. Y. Harburg, Kurt Weill, Jerome Kern, Marvin Hamlisch, Stephen Sondheim, et al. But if we have not yet been catapulted into the pantheon of the culturally blessed on the back of the American musical, the blame lies with the written word. With a few notable exceptions, the literature of musical comedy is an embarrassment—subliterate in a way that even the most extravagant

Italian opera is not (just compare the Giacosa-Illica adaptation of Henri Murger's autobiographical sketches for *La Bohème* with the way Kopit/Tune mutilated Fellini in *Nine*). I recently had occasion to reexamine about thirty of these celebrated contributions to universal art. And while the music almost always retained its original freshness, the books were usually as crumpled and soggy as overroasted marshmallows.

There are exceptions. Such musicals as *Guys and Dolls* and *A Funny Thing Happened on the Way to the Forum*, because they draw nourishment from the healthy roots of American comedy and burlesque, manage to remain vital and unpretentious. The more ambitious undertakings, however—those with underground reputations like John LaTouche's *The Golden Apple* or Moss Hart's *Lady in the Dark*— look exceedingly feeble today: the one an unbearably folksy adaptation of *The Iliad*, the other a journey into pop psychoanalysis so superficial it makes a movie like Hitchcock's *Spellbound* seem authorized by Freud.

Leonard Bernstein is among the most gifted of the serious composers for the musical theatre, but he too has been hamstrung by pretentious collaborators. Arthur Laurents's book for *West Side Story* is *Romeo and Juliet* seen through the eyes of an urban sociologist who never left Sutton Place, and *Candide*, which may very well have one of the best scores ever composed for a musical, was weighed down in its 1956 production by an army of Broadway celebrities (Lillian Hellman, Richard Wilbur, Dorothy Parker, John LaTouche, Tyrone Guthrie). They turned Voltaire's satire on the best of all possible worlds into a raging battlefield strewn with the worst of all possible egos. Later, in 1973, with a new book simplified by Hugh Wheeler, additional lyrics by Stephen Sondheim, and a sharp production concept by Harold Prince, *Candide* was restaged by the Chelsea Theatre Center in an intimate one-act version that ran on Broadway for two years. Now, restored to its original two acts and with an expanded orchestra, the work is being revived by the New York City Opera at the State Theatre, Lincoln Center, where it has been changed from a musical comedy into a witty Viennese light opera.

Candide has always had something of this quality—"Glitter and Be Gay" is a brilliant coloratura aria, and "The Old Lady's Tale" has the form of a barcarolle. But the ambience of an opera house helps to highlight the scope and ambitiousness of the score in a way denied to a

Broadway theatre. It also, unhappily, introduces a note of formality that tends to dampen its charming nature and lighthearted spirit. The New York State Theatre, let's face it, is a monster—designed, like the Met, more to flatter the audience's self-image than to house a musical performance. The sumptuous chandeliers are enormous simulations of the diamond pendants swinging from the necks of its dowager patrons, and the chased gold walls and balconies look like the materials Tiffany uses for its more expensive bracelets. In this atmosphere of luxury and privilege, Harold Prince tries manfully to relax the occasion. His performers amble through the audience, sometimes accompanied by pink sheep; the conductor helps an actor change his costume; the production has the sweep and swagger of a three-ring circus. But Prince's efforts are continually vexed by the stiffness of the operatic event, and he makes an unwise decision to keep his huge chorus on stage at all times, with precious little to do except stand, watch, and react.

I don't think, either, that the New York State Theatre has entirely solved its acoustical problems, since I had difficulty hearing most of the spoken dialogue, and even some of the lyrics. The house is not kind to baritones or contraltos; only the more piercing soprano and tenor tones seem able to penetrate its aural fog, which may explain why I was more beguiled by Erie Mills's wide-eyed Cunegonde, Deborah St. Darr's delicious Paquette, and David Eisler's disingenuous Candide than by John Lankston's Voltaire/Pangloss or Muriel Costa-Greenspon's Old Lady. This is a shame, since the book is often quite clever, and the lyrics have a winning insouciance. But it is the price one pays for staging anything vaguely subtle in that massive, daunting barn.

On the other hand, what opera offers best is music and spectacle, and in these respects, *Candide* cannot be faulted. Although Clarke Dunham's design is a little garish, it is a functional setting for an action that whisks us halfway round the world, from battlefield to ballroom, from cathouse to cathedral, from volcanic eruptions and *autos-de-fé* to voyages on the bounding main. Prince's direction is broad and often very funny, particularly in the Slavic-Spanish tango number, "I Am Easily Assimilated." This features a chorus of super-annuated, superherniated caballeros buckling at the knees as they try to hoist the corpulent Old Lady aloft while she warbles her song. And the finale, "Make Our Garden Grow," a utopian pastoral fantasy complete with horses, sheep, and country wagons, is a genuinely rousing, even thrilling climax to this epic undertaking.

Candide has long had a legendary reputation as an undervalued musical, especially for those who knew the work exclusively on record. It reveals Bernstein at the top of his powers, eclectic without sacrificing singularity, melodic without turning saccharine, capable of borrowing complex musical formulae without vulgarizing them. It succeeds in a way that eluded *On the Town*, for all its jazzy razzmatazz, or *West Side Story*, for all its streetwise sentimentality, or *Mass*, for all its rock-and-roll religiosity. It succeeds because it is written by a composer no longer condescending to a "native American art form," but rather expanding into a classical style more appropriate to his substantial talents and training.

ARGUING WITH A TANK

(Dreamgirls)

Trying to criticize *Dreamgirls*, the new Michael Bennett musical, is like arguing with a tank. The damn thing just rolls over your body, leaving you flat as a pancake with Caterpillar tread marks on your brain. I saw it in Boston, where it received much the same reaction from the audience it is getting in New York—people rising to their feet, their brows feverish, their hands raw from applause, to stomp, stampede, and scream with the moist fervor of true believers. Europeans act like this at mass political rallies; we usually reserve such behavior for sports events. It reminded me of a time, many years ago in Ebbets Field, when the old Brooklyn Dodgers won their first National League pennant in decades. There was primal energy rushing up from under the seats, and God help you if you happened to be a fan of the New York Giants.

I'm not a fan of *Dreamgirls*, but having been run over by it, I consider my opinion a lot less interesting than the audience reaction. One reason I can offer for the mass hysteria is the relentless Motown music, a mixture of rock, disco, and soul, consciously engineered to turn respectable theatregoers into frenzied Jacobins. Every time the overamplified brass and percussion start thumping away, and the singers screech out those hyena sounds from their upper registers, you can hear responsive growls forming in the throats of the audience. The people who put this musical together could change the social system if they wanted to, because they really know how to use rhythm, sound, light, and sensory effects in order to get us rattling our cages.

I am told that some musicians consider Henry Krieger's rhythm-and-blues score one of the best ever composed for the musical theatre. To my bruised ears, it sounded extremely monotonous, each new number indistinguishable—in pitch, tone, and rhythm—from the last, though I suspect the uniformity and tunelessness are responsible for the Pavlovian effect. As for Tom Eyen's lyrics, here is a sample quatrain: "You are horribly satanic / The way you lead me around. / I feel just like the *Titanic*, / I always run aground." Socko, huh? (I feel just a touch satanic mentioning that the *Titanic* ran into an iceberg).

Mr. Eyen's book is as witless as his lyrics when examined away from the evening's pulsations. The musical concerns a trio of backup singers, reputedly based on the Supremes, who, after an inauspicious tryout at a talent show in the Apollo Theatre, acquire a ruthless manager and rise to the top of the charts. This is done at the sacrifice of some honor, since these black singers have to accept white compromises in order to get ahead. They also sacrifice their original leader, Effie, a corpulent creature considered too hefty for the media, who is therefore replaced—not without a lot of showstopping musical agony—by a more slender singer. The Dreamettes (not to be confused with the Harlettes) are now called the Dreams, a sign of their growing maturity. They perform in Miami, though they are not allowed to stay in the hotel where they work, then on the *ABC Star Cavalcade*, then in Vegas, gaining in fame what they lose in "Negritude." At the end of the show, in their final performance before their breakup, they score a triumph at the legendary Met, apparently turning into legends themselves, since they have been costumed like Egyptian princesses preparing for entombment.

The plot has a few more complications—not to mention occasional philosophical ruminations on the comparative merits of "pop versus soul"—but the directorial emphasis is on sights and sounds, on fluorescent signs, white hand-held mikes, and magnificently gussied-up gowns. You find yourself following the story less than the quick changes, and leave the theatre humming the wigs and costumes rather than the songs. Tharon Musser's lighting is literally dazzling, since the multicolored Lekos bounce off the singers' metallic dresses right into your eyes, and Robin Wagner's set—a flexible construction that doubles as a lighting grid—though the most imaginative thing in the show, is designed to keep the environment changing lest you pause for a moment to peek under the flash.

It would be silly to examine the values of such an event, except they are so equivocal they are almost intriguing. We learn that fame demands a high moral price but is also very rewarding. We learn about the symbolic significance of the Cadillac car in the cultural life of America ("Got me a Cadillac, Cadillac, Cadillac car" is the memorable number that hits the pop charts). It is bought by the "Negro brother to prove he too belongs to the human dream." And we learn from Effie's eventual success as a soloist (also from her torch song, "I'm Changing") that you can conquer even a hard-drug habit if you have sufficient determination and volume.

What I learned, in addition, is that despite the occasional nod toward social matters, Broadway is still primarily interested in black people who can display a nice sense of rhythm, along with a little singing and dancing. These capacities the young cast has in abundance, especially Jennifer Holliday, as Effie, who is already on her way to becoming one of the great loudmouth belters of the musical theatre, in the wake of Merman, Channing, and Streisand. Like the rest of the cast, she's not much of an actress. But the art of acting is not of great importance to a musical that makes its impact not on your mind or emotions but almost exclusively on your nervous system.

THIS "MONEY-GOT, MECHANIC AGE"

(Cats)

Cats, the new Andrew Lloyd Webber musical, surely represents some kind of end product; British theatre skills have hitherto been essentially verbal and technical, but they have never been so totally mechanical. This spectacle could have been manufactured by Disney World, using audio-animatronics instead of actors; I perceived no sign of flesh-and-blood behavior beneath the glitter and flash.

I confess to being a dog man myself, and I've never been too captivated by the whimsy of T. S. Eliot's *Old Possum's Book of Practical Cats*, on which the musical is loudly based. But the problem lies not in the original material so much as in the failure of the adaptors to honor its modest values. With the help of talent, imagination, and a little taste, *Cats* could have been effective as a small cabaret piece. Instead, it has been inflated into a four-million-dollar extravaganza with a relentlessly brassy score and a superfluous visual strategy that virtually prohibits any life from trespassing on the scenery.

The chief miscreants, aside from the composer, are the director, Trevor Nunn, and John Napier, his designer, whose collaboration on *Nicholas Nickleby* hardly prepared us for this vulgar manufacture. Mr. Nunn has established an enviable record over the years as leader of the Royal Shakespeare Company, though I am reminded of his shaky start at Stratford in the early seventies when (by contrast with the Brechtian simplicity of Peter Hall's RSC) he also traded heavily on expensive mechanical effects. Possibly influenced by cuts in his British Arts Council grants, his later work became considerably more Spartan. But with the generous assistance of his American producers, he seems to have suffered a relapse. *Cats* shows his artistic soul grown fat and scant of breath.

Whatever the case, Mr. Napier's design is a multimillion-dollar exercise in junk culture. He has broken through the proscenium for the purpose of turning the entire theatre into a huge garbage dump decorated with a wide variety of found objects—boxes of cat chow, high-heel shoes, tennis rackets, paper plates, TV sets, Coke signs, you name it. Seen from the perspective of small felines, everything is naturally outsize. But apart from being unpleasantly garish, the design has the effect of dwarfing any other activity. Clearly, the set is intended to be the star of this show (Napier admits as much by including his signature onstage in the form of a license plate bearing the inscription NAP 2). It is always being encouraged to perform, particularly during the overture when thousands of cats' eyes strobe in the darkness and a mammoth lighting fixture rises to the ceiling, and at the climax when Old Deuteronomy ascends to heaven on an enormous tire that flashes spotlights through fog effects like an extraterrestrial chandelier. One could feel the audience fighting back the impulse to wave and say goodbye through flooding tears, like the child in Spielberg's *Close Encounters*.

In *Nickleby*, Dickens shows us adults incapable of identifying with children; *Cats*, like most of our popular culture, is engineered for adults unable to do much else. But if popular culture tends to sentimentalize childhood, this musical is not even very faithful to cats. For all the tails and whiskers and fur, few of the performers have actually bothered to study feline behavior. The acting reinforces the impression that, despite all the money and effort expended on exterior artifacts, little attention was being paid to the cat beneath the skin. Kenneth Ard gives a strong frenetic energy to Macavity, the Mystery Cat, but Rum Tum Tugger, the Curious Cat, played by Terrence V. Mann, becomes a simpering Mick Jagger, and Ken Page plays Old Deuteronomy, the Prophet Cat, like a parody of Peter Ustinov (already a parody) twinkling and squinting in *Logan's Run*. There is one extended vaudeville pirate number called "Growltiger's Last Stand," which has some charm as a Christmas pantomime. And "Memory," a romanticized, overplugged, but lyrical adaptation of Eliot's "Rhapsody on a Windy Night" is well and throatily sung by Betty Buckley as Grizabella. But the Radio City Rockette choreography, the manic direction, and the derivative music bury whatever subtleties or delicacies there are in Eliot's light verse under visual and aural rubble.

There are those who say he would have enjoyed this travesty of his work. I think he would have been appalled. Ben Jonson, a Jacobean dramatist Eliot admired immensely, once found himself in a similar situation when his poetic contributions to a masque were in danger of being obliterated by spectacular scenic intrusions (those of Inigo Jones). Fearful that the literary "soul" of the work on which they had collaborated was being eclipsed by its "bodily parts," Jonson launched a savage attack on Jones's "omnipotent design" that could very well have been the response of his dead and helpless successor, T. S. Eliot. It could also stand very well as the definitive review of *Cats*:

> *Oh shows, shows, mighty shows!*
> *The eloquence of masques! what need of prose,*
> *Or verse, or sense, t'express immortal you? . . .*
> *Painting and carpentry are the soul of masque.*
> *Pack with your peddling poetry to the stage,*
> *This is the money-got, mechanic age.*

No less money-got and mechanic, our own age likewise continues to bury poetry and sense beneath the carpentry and the show.

MUSICALIZED PROPAGANDA

(La Cage aux Folles)

In my profession, nothing is more alienating than going to a smash hit and not being able to share the good time everyone seems to be having. Contrary to opinion, it's no fun for a reviewer to be in disagreement with an audience. It's about as satisfying, in fact, as entering a foreign country without a passport. There you are, morose and crestfallen, surrounded by hordes of natives who not only understand the language but greet it with roars of laughter, screams of approval, and standing ovations. Deafened by all these noises recently at the Palace Theatre, I felt very lonely indeed in the presence of *La Cage aux Folles*.

I don't resent the pleasure this new musical is giving to large audiences, but I continue to be a little disturbed by how easily these audiences are manipulated by transparent tricks. Harvey Fierstein's book, based on a long-running French farce, is designed to gain acceptance from middle-class heterosexuals for flamboyant homosexual lovers. This suggests it is also meant to function as musicalized propaganda for the gay liberation movement. There is virtually nothing in Mr. Fierstein's representation of homosexual marriage to distinguish it from conventional family life, except for the fact that the spouse who applies mascara, wears women's clothes, and puts on high heels is a male. On stage, Albin (Zaza) and Georges, the aging lovers of *La Cage aux Folles* (they also work as the M.C. and star of a gay nightclub in Saint-Tropez), merely hold hands and look romantically into each other's eyes in front of a Magritte drop, while the motor of the plot is activated by nothing more daring than Albin's desire to be treated as the true mother of Jean-Michel, the young man Georges (hoping to learn "what the fuss was all about") once sired on a real woman.

Albin's temporary exclusion from a meeting between Jean-Michel and the parents of the girl he wants to marry inspires an Act I curtain number called "I Am What I Am" ("Life's not worth a damn till you can say, World, I am what I am"). It is already being hailed as the homosexual national anthem. But although few would wish to deny to gentle monogamous Albin his right to be accepted as his own "special creation," he hardly represents the large variety of homosexual life or typifies its more revolutionary sexuality. As in *Equus*, audiences are maneuvered into condemning those who reject the unorthodox behavior of the central character, without being fully informed of what that behavior implies or involves—which is pretty much the way George Meredith defined sentimentality.

I'm not suggesting that a Broadway musical should include songs about fellatio or anal intercourse or sex with boys or leather or "recreational" bathhouse activity. But surely there is something more radical about the drag subculture than its love of transvestism or its capacity for bitchy humor. It also has a conscious political component involving flagrant rejection of straight sexual and social conventions. *La Cage aux Folles* might have been a real breakthrough had it been more honest about the range of homosexual life-styles instead of suggesting that these are merely differences of costume or manners. But what audiences are applauding in this musical is a relationship indistinguishable from those in TV sitcoms—notably *The Odd Couple*, of which *La Cage aux Folles* is an inverted version (there are also occasional thefts from *Charley's Aunt*). Virtually every Fierstein joke is a homosexual twist on conventional domestic one-liners (example: "First you start missing meals . . . and then separate bedrooms"), and there is even a black homosexual who doubles as a wisecracking maid. I'm taking bets that shortly after this musical closes, Albin and Georges will end up on a network series.

Of course, every revolution in our society eventually ends up as an income-producing commodity, providing it can be packaged smartly, and this one has some canny merchandisers. A long introductory nightclub number by a chorus of drag queens ("Les Cagelles") gets the audience used to applauding everything that moves (they have already cheered a series of opening set changes). Theoni V. Aldredge's clothes have that atrocious bad taste that distinguishes camp, and so does David Mitchell's garish nightclub decor with its chaser lights, illuminated staircases, rain curtains, treadmills, and pink spots (though Mitchell is certainly capable of creating quiet tasteful environments, as he does with a lovely riverside setting against an Impressionist backdrop). These along with the transvestite choreography provide the glitter and flash of the evening, and the visible signs of its five-million-dollar investment. But the stage is so continuously crammed with moving objects that I half expected to see Harpo Marx riding down one of the flats and going to work on the equipment with an axe. As for Jerry Herman's score, his music is tuneful, if bland, but his lyrics embody the same neutered quality as Fierstein's book—even "I Am What I Am" is designed to hit the charts as a heterosexual ballad on the order of "I Did It My Way."

The director and prime manipulator of this spectacle is Arthur Laurents, apparently still as optimistic about the warmth of the human heart and the redemptive qualities of love as he was as a playwright. In a recent interview, Laurents disputed "the mistaken notion that to be positive is to be inartistic, and that cynicism and a bleak view of life equal art," adding, "I don't know why Beckett doesn't jump out of a window, given the way he sees the world." Although Laurents is hardly prepared to appreciate the complicated nature of Beckett's ambivalent worldview, his remarks about the power of positive thinking are particularly maladroit in view of the fact that *La Cage aux Folles* bears so little relation to anything recognizably human or real, much less artistic. Its only convincing quality, in fact, is the overwhelming need of its characters (and creators) for approval. The villains of the piece are the parents of the bride—the father is a French deputy from the party of Family, Tradition, and Morality—who are little more than homophobic stick figures, while most of the remaining characters are caricatures from the world of low camp.

By contrast, the two leads, Gene Barry (Georges) and George Hearn (Albin), are permitted to perform in a relatively subdued manner as a way of establishing their tender normality against a background of screeching queens and disapproving moralists. Barry carries himself as stiffly as a clothing store mannequin, and his voice was raspy on the night I saw him, but Hearn performs with an air of cool relaxed reality that accounts for the only authentic moments of the show. Dragged out like a huge dowager or an operatic soprano, wobbling in his shoes when forced to wear male clothes, he introduces elements of genuine pathos and comedy. And when, after having been excluded from the meeting of the prospective in-laws, he bites his lip, pulls himself together, gestures the chorus off the stage, belts out his defiant credo, and marches through the audience in rage and disappointment, he provides a stirring, if spurious, first-act curtain. It was a shrewd move to cast heterosexual actors in these central roles, because it was a way to help the audience accept the homosexuality of their characters. But this is precisely the kind of evasion that makes *La Cage aux Folles* often seem so crudely manipulative, so dishonest, so crass.

I began this review by saying I felt alienated in the presence of this musical. I realize that this is nothing compared to the alienation experienced by most homosexuals in our society. Anything that reduces feelings of marginality and loneliness is by definition a positive accomplishment, and by that measure, I suppose, *La Cage aux Folles* is an effective piece of propaganda. Like most propaganda, however, it seriously misrepresents the cause it is advancing. It is the homosexual community that will ultimately have to determine whether it is better served by "positive" and pretty evasions or by the unadorned, if sometimes "bleak," truth.

SINGING THE SET

(Sunday in the Park with George)

In the halcyon days of Gershwin, Porter, and Rodgers and Hart, Broadway musicals used to be about music. Beginning with *Oklahoma*, and culminating with *My Fair Lady*, Broadway musicals usually featured the book. *Sunday in the Park with George*, a new work by James Lapine (book and direction) and Stephen Sondheim (music and lyrics), is the first Broadway musical that is mainly about the set.

This show has a very good set—indeed, a brilliant one—by Tony Straiges, and since the design is primarily intended as a stage canvas for the reproduction of the large pointillist painting *A Sunday Afternoon on the Island of the Grande Jatte* by George Seurat (costumed actors substitute for the original figures), one could sit and look at it for hours. This, in fact, is precisely what the audience finds itself doing at the Booth Theatre. A popular joke about heavyweight musicals was that you came out of the theatre humming the costumes. Stephen Sondheim's score is designed to send you out of the theatre singing the set.

And you would were the music just a little more tuneful. Once again frowning on lyricism, Sondheim is here composing in a minimalist, vaguely serial style that functions primarily as a setting for his surprising, often witty lyrics. This disdain for melody, coupled with a certain emotional coldness and remoteness, explains, I think, why so many Sondheim musicals have a large following but not a large audience. I suspect that *Sunday in the Park with George* will share that fate. The idea is original—to bring the advanced techniques of such works as the Wilson-Glass *Einstein on the Beach* into the commercial mainstream—but although the evening is packed with succulent ocular feasts and crammed with vibrant theatrical images, the show is ultimately wearisome, even a little silly.

The problem, as usual, is the book—what book there is. *Sunday in the Park with George* begins in the park, where the artist (Mandy Patinkin) is sketching his model (Bernadette Peters) as the future characters of his painting wander among the trees. The model is named Dot—a reference, no doubt, to Seurat's pointillist method. George is her lover, and all she wants him to do is look at her. This he steadfastly declines to do unless he is painting her figure. Since he is always painting someone's figure, she can't command his attention long enough to engage her in argument or even to take her to the Follies. Soon he impregnates her, doubtless without looking; his eyes remain glued to his canvas. He refuses, in fact, even to look at his own daughter after the baby is born, complaining that mother and child are blocking his light. Unsurprisingly, Dot soon takes up with another man, a baker, more responsive to her personal charms ("In bed, George—I mean he kneads me—like bread, George"), while George proceeds to use her, the baker, and the baby as additional figures in his grand design.

We are familiar with stories of artists—Gauguin is the most famous—who sacrificed family, love, and personal relationships for the sake of their art. But whereas Bernard Shaw was able to provide this nineteenth-century theme with some philosophical relevance as a deadly struggle between the artist-man and the mother-woman, *Sunday in the Park with George* reduces the whole issue to a trivial domestic squabble, like a wife complaining that her husband would rather watch TV than tell her what happened that day at the office. Still, George's passion for "color, design, tension, balance, composition, life, light, and harmony" does have a certain relentless urgency. And the first-act climax, when human figures, trees, sailboats, cutout dogs, and a humpbacked monkey come together to simulate the completed canvas, is a stunning *coup de théâtre*.

There is a second act—unfortunately, since it seems to be an afterthought. Set in modern times, it begins in an American art museum where another artist named George, the great-grandson of Seurat and Dot, is paying homage to his distinguished ancestor through the medium of a technological display called a Chromolume. A combination of laser light, moving images, and slide projections emanating from a huge domed machine, this is a dazzling sound and light show designed by the ingenious Bran Ferren. George is criticized by various people for wasting his talents on such marginal artistic pursuits ("Light shows," says one critic, "are getting to be more and more about less and less"), but it remains for Dot's daughter—George's grandmother—a benevolent, forgetful old lady in a wheelchair, to identify "children and art" as the only worthwhile memorials. While the museum crowd inanely chatters away ("What's a little cocktail conversation / If it's going to get you your foundation"), George withdraws from these human encounters by sending up photographic cutouts as surrogates of himself to pretend interest in these banal conversations—another aloof artist, cold and alienated, shrugging off fashionable armies of superficial bores.

In the last scene, George has gone to the island park where Seurat created his masterpiece. Another Straiges stroke, it is surrounded now by high rise modern buildings; only one tree and a portion of grass remain from the original vernal scene. Filled with yearning and nostalgia, utterly melancholy, utterly alone, George encounters the figure of Dot, his great-grandmother, holding her umbrella, while the painting slowly reconstitutes itself on stage for the finale.

Sondheim and Lapine have returned to their original image because that image is the essence of the work; the rest is landfill. Having developed an exquisite idea, and possessing the theatrical resources to realize it, they somehow lacked the ultimate resolve to let it find a natural shape, molding it instead to routine forms—a case of the imagination trying to do the work of the will. Without the second act, and without the modest but foolish plot, *Sunday in the Park with George* might have been a genuine breakthrough in American musical theatre. At the moment, it seems more like an effort to adapt the insights of serious art to the entertainment needs of popular audiences.

The production is subject to the same compromises. Offering magnificent visual opportunities, fascinating when it ruminates on color and line, the book suffers nevertheless from sketchily written scenes and slick dramatic caricatures, particularly a fat American couple from the Deep South who wander through the park gorging on pastries and insulting the French. Bernadette Peters, with her lovely pout and soft chin, always maintains a robust energy and charm, and Dana Ivey, as the unappreciated wife of a competing artist, contributes another of her edged portraits of elegant snobs. But the men tend to speak in those stentorian sonorities left over from old-fashioned musical comedy, where the execution of the dialogue is often indistinguishable from the rendering of the songs. Even the gifted Mandy Patinkin (bearded as Seurat, clean-shaven as his great-grandson), though always intense and concentrated, suffers from excessive emotional reserve, occasional inaudibility, and those bleating chest and throat tones identified with professional stage tenors.

Forced to a judgment, I would like to find some way to express my admiration for this effort, so unique in a musical theatre dominated by the noisy displays of *Dreamgirls*, *Cats*, and *La Cage aux Folles*, but also my disappointment over how the achievement of these talented people is sometimes vitiated by facileness and slickness. I suspect that if *Sunday in the Park with George* had been a short musical piece exclusively concerned with the execution of a painting on stage, it would have been a masterpiece. In its present inflated form, it is merely a handsome, pleasing, occasionally meretricious entertainment.

BLURRING THE EDGES

(Pacific Overtures; La Bohème)

There has recently been a concerted effort to break down the boundary lines separating opera and theatre, a development that sometimes advances both forms, at other times threatens to blur the already smudged edges between commercial and serious art. In the past, the Met might temporarily loan out Ezio Pinza to *South Pacific* to wash "Some Enchanted Evening" with operatic phrasing, while Broadway would reciprocate by sending Jack Gilford to brighten up the Met's *Fledermaus*—but these were aberrations. Now professionals of all types are passing freely between the stage and the opera house, with occasional visits from Tin Pan Alley as well. The most telling example of this interchange is the way stage directors—Andrei Serban, Jonathan Miller, Peter Hall, Peter Sellars—have been startling opera audiences with new interpretations of familiar masterpieces. A reverse example is Peter Brook's recent expropriation of *Carmen* for the theatre, not to mention the New York Shakespeare Festival's Broadway production of *Pirates of Penzance* with Linda Ronstadt. Further evidence is the increasing incidence of musicals such as *Candide* and *Sweeney Todd* in the repertory of the New York City Opera Company and elsewhere (Beverly Sills recently announced a spring season devoted *entirely* to American musical comedies). It is highly symbolic that the institution formerly known as the National Institute of Opera has now changed its name to the National Institute of Musical Theatre.

Two converging problems underlie this growing union: the recent fossilization of opera, which needs an infusion of new energy to relieve its arthritic traditionalism, and Broadway's growing incapacity to mount new musicals or even musical revivals without some prior guarantee of success. The liaison between opera and musicals, therefore, represents a pooling of resources, similar to that between Broadway and the resident theatre in regard to serious plays. It is bound to create institutional anxieties of a similar aesthetic and economic kind.

The Broadway musical has always suffered from being crowned an "American art form" before fully establishing its claim to art. This posed no identity crisis for such early titans as Cole Porter or Irving Berlin or Rodgers and Hart because no one had yet invested musical comedy writers with ambitions beyond creating good healthy tuneful entertainment (though George Gershwin had the native ability to write equally well for the opera and the musical stage). Beginning with the largely hayseed book and play adaptations of Rodgers and Hammerstein and continuing through the sophisticated urban forms of Leonard Bernstein and, particularly, Stephen Sondheim, there has been a noticeable effort to prove the musical worthy of the new seriousness for which it was prematurely hailed.

In Mr. Sondheim's case, this has created the sense that he is writing avant-garde musicals, an illusion sustained by his reductive compounds of serious art forms and Broadway conventions: operatic *singspiel* in *Sweeney Todd*, the painting process in *Sunday in the Park with George*, and Japanese theatre (which is to say, Japanese opera)— Kabuki, Bunraku, and Noh drama—in *Pacific Overtures*. This last effort, which failed on Broadway in 1976, can now be seen again in revival at the off-Broadway Promenade Theatre in a stripped-down version that manages to heighten both its defects and its virtues. Mr. Sondheim and his writers, John Weidman and Hugh Wheeler, lit on a potentially fine subject—the visit of Commodore Matthew Perry to Japan in 1853 and the consequent effects of foreign influences on Japanese culture. They also conceived the notion of having us witness these events through the eyes of innocent Japanese hitherto ignorant of Westerners or Western customs. The original director, Hal Prince, added the splendid concept of making those innocents perceive Perry's ship as a dragon with burning eyes and Perry himself as a pasty-faced bare-chested demon with a blond lion mane extending virtually to his feet.

The whole project, in short, was surrounded by intelligence. But, as often happens in these cases, it was ultimately unable to escape its Broadway roots. What resulted was a curious mélange of Oriental ceremony and American show biz, which is rather ironic considering that the theme of the show is the corruption of Eastern innocence by Western sophistication. (By mixing traditional Japanese conventions with a hint of Broadway kitsch, Sondheim and company are unwittingly demonstrating the truth of this observation.) In the current production, modestly directed by Fran Soeder with respectful nods to Hal Prince, the Reciter—a shaven-headed narrator in a kimono—seems to have wandered in from *The King and I*. There are Oriental actors on stage, but also an inordinate number of chorus gypsies. Men play the women's parts, as in all traditional Japanese drama. But these performers, instead of inhabiting the female characters, seem to be doing drag numbers from *La Cage aux Folles*. Haikus are announced; what we get instead are mundane proverbialisms. Five geisha girls arrive to do a turn that would not be out of place in *Teahouse of the August Moon*. As for the music, it is so full of repeated figures and the composer's insistent tunelessness that the songs grow off rather than on you, while the various numbers sung by the stereotyped French, Dutch, Russian, and American visitors make the score almost seem an act of Western self-hatred. By the time of the finale—it takes place in modern industrialized Tokyo, where the theme is "Do it nicer, do it faster" and contemporary Japanese are threatening to "do to the rest of Asia what America has done to us"—one begins to suspect that among the things "done" by Americans to Japanese culture is not only the spread of digital watches and neon, of computers and Vegas strips, but also of such musicals as *Pacific Overtures*.

Puccini's *La Bohème* at the New York Public Theatre is another effort to expropriate opera for the theatre, and I went to it with all my prejudices poised. There had been much preopening publicity about the casting of Linda Ronstadt, a rock singer, as Mimi, and Gary Morris, a country singer, as Rodolfo, along with stories reporting that

Miss Ronstadt's unsupported voice was inadequate to the taxing demands of the role. The management had invited me to see the alternate cast, which was said to have a better Mimi. I accepted their invitation but could work up no excitement about an enterprise where all the signs suggested that a beautiful work was being mindlessly popularized. Within five minutes, I found myself surrendering to one of the most potent experiences of my theatregoing life.

I'm still trying to understand why this production gripped me so. Judged by technical standards, David Carroll's Rodolfo was hardly a match for Björling or Pavarotti, and Patti Cohenour's Mimi could not be compared in power with that of De Los Angeles or Freni; the voices, though pleasant and melodious, were light, and one could occasionally detect miking. Bob Shaw's rather tacky revolving settings were inhibited by the limited space of the Anspacher; and the orchestra, playing Michael Starobin's orchestrations, was not only seriously reduced, but substituted electric keyboards for the string sections. At first sight, the show reminded me of those pocket productions of Shakespeare one used to see in the Village thirty years ago, where *Hamlet* was performed with a cast of eight, and the producer passed around a hat at the conclusion of the play. Yet, I must confess to having abdicated all critical scruples and reservations by the time of Mimi's first entrance, entering the story in a way I find rare in opera, and giving myself up to what can only be described as powerful emotions of grief.

Wilford Leach, the director, and his cast have managed to find an accessible avenue into the heart of this work by providing it with more credibility, by enhancing its narrative values without diminishing its depth. A problem with such familiar operas as *Bohème* is that one begins to feel awe at voices instead of interest in characters, bravoing the virtuosity of the performers rather than experiencing the drama. This cast renders the music with enough competence to satisfy all but the most discriminating ears, but almost all of them are also superb actors who use the intimacy of the Anspacher and its close audience relationships to penetrate deeply into the recesses of the text. For all its magnificent music, *Bohème* has come to seem a soggy verismo chestnut, featuring arch bohemian local color and unconvincing lovers' quarrels, while Mimi's death becomes that scene obligatory to so many Italian operas where the consumptive heroine mixes her coughs with high C's. In the Leach production, on the other hand, the characters are utterly convincing as genuine people with real occupations and insoluble dilemmas.

Much of the credit for this must go to David Spencer's splendid, though critically abused, new adaptation and lyrics. Its modern colloquialisms may offend some purists (Marcello: "My nuts are freezing." Rodolfo: "Be grateful you still have them. . . . Mine fell off—I'm too numb to feel them"), but it creates a contemporary relaxation and informality that I found totally winning. Spencer does more than adapt or modernize; he actually invents more credible motivations for the characters. For example, I've never been convinced by the reasons Rodolfo gives for leaving Mimi in the third act. First, he tells Marcello she's a faithless coquette, which is obviously untrue; then, he confesses that he feels responsible for her mortal illness since he can't afford to heat his room. This provides him with a rather stiff nobility that Spencer humanizes: in this version, Rodolfo leaves Mimi because he cannot bear to see her die. One more example: At the end of Puccini's story, everyone realizes that Mimi is dead except the person closest to her, Rodolfo, thus permitting his curtain-closing cry over her corpse. In Spencer's version, he *knows* she is dead, but cannot bring himself to admit it ("What are you looking at? She's just sleeping").

The young handsome cast is charming. Patti Cohenour is a delicate waiflike Mimi, and David Carroll's Rodolfo a self-flagellating poet ("Jesus, who wrote this?"). Howard McGillin as Marcello, perhaps the strongest performer in the show, provides a direct American friendliness that makes his relationship with Rodolfo a true comradeship. Cass Morgan's toothsome Musette, somewhat less than thrilling in her waltz, has moments of genuine compassion in her scenes with Mimi; and Keith David as the philosopher Colline and Neal Klein as the musician Schaunard round out the full complement of bohemian friends.

I realize I am in a distinct minority in my evaluation of this production. I can only report a deep personal response. For me, this is one case where the confusion of forms has made something potentially popular without crudely popularizing it, where the blurring of edges has allowed a great piece of music to emerge as a profoundly moving work of theatrical art.

DROODLING

(The Mystery of Edwin Drood)

In life, an unsolved murder is a matter for the police; in literature, it is a matter for critics, cryptographers, academicians, and theatre people digging for Broadway gold. Since Charles Dickens expired before completing the work or revealing the murderer, the real mystery in his last novel, *The Mystery of Edwin Drood*, is who killed the eponymous hero—or perhaps whether he actually died. Edmund Wilson undertook to solve the riddle in an essay in *The Wound and the Bow*. Now the New York Shakespeare Festival has produced a musical that submits the issue to audience referendum.

Because *Edwin Drood* is not a particularly distinguished piece of writing, it's hard to pump up too much critical indignation over the way the novel has been altered for the stage. Still, there have been drastic stylistic changes. The Dickens book, though melodramatic in plotting and sentimental in characterization, is serious in tone; the musical is a camp on the story, the characters, indeed the novel's very conventions. Set in a provincial turn-of-the-century music hall on the amusement pier at Greater Dorping-on-Sea, the show has been equipped with an elaborate induction that includes a preshow escape artist, wandering chorines in girdles, and an ad-libbing "Chairman" of ceremonies who introduces the actors while offering spectators the companionship of his "unsalaried" female employees (contributions gratefully accepted for their "theatrical studies"). He also guides the audience, once the musical finally gets down to business, through the broken structure of the plot, down the skeleton corridors of what's left of the story.

That story, for those unfamiliar with the novel, concerns three men—John Jasper, Neville Landless, and Edwin Drood—all involved with the heroine, Rosa Bud. Rosa is nicknamed Rosebud, though in the novel Drood prefers to call her "Pussy" (those sensing affinities with *Citizen Kane* might be aware that Rosebud was Hearst's pet name for Marion Davies's *mulier pudendum*). Rosa and young Drood are engaged through parental contract, but regard each other more as brother and sister. Jasper, a choirmaster who teaches Rosa music, loves her madly, but apparently loves opium more (during off hours he can be found in the evil den of the Princess Puffer, conjuring sexual fantasies and schizoid mutations out of his long pipe). Landless also has amorous feelings for Rosa—evoking Drood's disdain. Drood's scornful treatment of Landless would appear to be sufficient motive for the lad's murder. But other people have reason to wish him dead, and a mysterious figure named Dick Datchery is later introduced whose curiosity about the murder suggests he has come to track down the killer and bring him to justice.

This background is sketched in the first act. The second act is largely devoted to voting. Declaring "it was at this point that our author laid down his pen," the Chairman then abandons all pretense of dramatic action for exercises in universal suffrage and, in what he calls "a daring and possibly dangerous democratic move," lays the whole problem before the audience. First, the company casts its ballot on whether Drood is dead (the vote is affirmative, sending the actress playing the part home muttering about "envious little shits"). Then the audience is polled on the identity of the mysterious Dick Datchery. And then, after Jasper gets the opportunity to exorcise his doppleganger in a song, after the Princess Puffer tunefully reveals she is Rosa's long-lost nanny, and after several actors eager for election finish their canvassing, the action stops for the big vote of the evening—the identity of the killer of Drood.

As usual, I cast a losing ballot (I voted again for Mondale), but the outcome, I'm told, changes anyway from night to night, the audience tending to elect its favorite actor for the purpose of hearing another song. This preference for entertainment at the expense of plot coherence is pretty much typical of the entire evening, and so is the impulse to elevate the audience at the expense of the author. I know that Dickens was himself essentially an entertainer, but I don't think he ever went so far as to let his readers write his books for him. This approach augurs a whole new epoch in the composition of best-sellers.

Anyhow, Election Night at the show I saw installed in office not Cleo Laine's Princess Puffer (the usual favorite and incumbent) but John Herrera's Neville Landless, who went into paroxysms of ecstasy over the results of the balloting. And after the audience was encouraged to cast a final vote on which of the characters should pair off in duets, the evening was concluded with a rousing production number borrowed from the finale of *A Chorus Line*.

Clearly, the New York Shakespeare Festival is looking for another winner. But while *The Mystery of Edwin Drood* is good-natured, inoffensive, energetic, and ingratiating, I don't think it's likely to become the next commercial annuity for this nonprofit institution. Everything possible has been lavished on this extravaganza, from handsome sets to sumptuous costumes to excellent acting to imaginative direction. What is missing are the minimal requirements of a good book, active lyrics, a decent score. Rupert Holmes, responsible in all three areas, knows how to create the appearance of a hit song, largely through spirited rhythms and Gilbert and Sullivan patter techniques (not to mention the vibrant orchestrations of Michael Starobin). But his melodies are infinitely forgettable and his lyrics are flat, his rhymes forced. This is serious, since the source material is mostly used as a clothesline for the musical numbers (even the Chairman concedes that the show is a "musicale—with dramatic interludes"). And if the songs don't satisfy, then one is likely to grow even more conscious that a work of literature has been debased rather than enhanced on the stage.

The problem, I fear, is that no strong impulse is animating this musical beyond a desire to succeed, and that is why so much of the work seems derivative. The Victorian setting of the novel has been turned into theatrical Victoriana, with the manufactured quaintness of mass-produced antiques, and the characters and atmosphere often seem borrowed from hit musicals of the past, notably *My Fair Lady*. Thus, the show depends on a recognition factor rather than the elements of surprise and originality, which is not inconsistent with organizing the material according to the audience's needs instead of from the artist's perspective.

On the positive side is the production itself—exuberant, attractive, and constantly in motion. Bob Shaw's settings (along with Lindsay W. Davis's costumes) are the most authentic elements of the evening. Sitting inside a false proscenium, the scene designs manage to maintain a music-hall atmosphere while functioning as handsome painted backgrounds on their own, vaguely reminiscent of Magritte. In British sailor dress, the orchestra (under Starobin's baton), maintains a sharp attack, a bright tempo. Graciela Daniele's choreography is consistently lively, particularly during an erotic phantasmagoria in the opium den that has nubile girls in body stockings crawling out of Jasper's bed. And Wilford Leach's direction is always controlled, always witty and imaginative.

There are no infirmities in the acting either. Howard McGillin's John Jasper, gaunt, emaciated, hollow eyed, looking like something out of *An American Werewolf in Paris*, is handled with an assurance that confirms this singer-actor (following his fine work in Papp's *La Bohème*) as one of the strongest musical performers in the business. Betty Buckley plays Drood as an epicene stripling with slicked-down hair, her vibrating voice reminding us of just how much we miss even the one decent song she had in *Cats*. Larry Shue is a commanding Reverend Crisparkle, Cleo Laine a forceful Princess Puffer, Joe Grifasi a twinkly Bazzard, and Jerome Dempsey an inventive Durdles, even though the character as written has been virtually lifted from Stanley Holloway's Doolittle. As for George Rose, doubling as "Your Chairman" and Mayor Sapsea—equipped with top hat, muttonchops, and irrepressible energy—he brings such period charm, such improvisational wit to his part that he almost takes on the status of coauthor. Would that he had written the whole book!

"You stand in place of our author," says the Chairman to the audience, which is precisely what is wrong with the show. Since we are not asked to vote on the scenery, the direction, or the acting, those elements remain compelling in their artistry. The evening falters on the notion that *vox populi* is the voice of creative achievement, that hit musicals evolve under democratic rule.

ADVERTISING A DYING INDUSTRY

(The Tony Awards)

The 1983 Tony Award ceremonies at the Uris Theatre began with a George and Ira Gershwin number from *My One and Only* called "Kicking the Clouds Away." It was an appropriate theme for an evening dedicated to the song's composers, whose past triumphs were endlessly celebrated in song and, at the conclusion of the proceedings, in architecture when the vaguely micturatory name of the Uris was changed to the more euphonious Gershwin. It was appropriate also because the whole enterprise was such an obvious effort to kick away the clouds hanging over the commercial theatre. That very week, *Variety* told us that Broadway was in a major slump, paid attendance being down by approximately 2,500,000 patrons from the previous season, and box office off $18,000,000 despite a rise in ticket prices.

Given these morbid statistics, it was inevitable that the Tony ceremonies this year would partly be an exercise in heyday nostalgia, and partly a two-and-a-half-hour commercial for a depressed industry. Sharing sympathetic vibrations with the industry, the master and mistress of ceremonies also looked depressed—the normally effervescent Lena Horne managing to display her splendid teeth only when she first appeared, and Richard Burton bleating through his nasal passages as if he were delivering a funeral oration for his passed-out career.

Gloomily, they introduced the presenters who, in turn, were entrusted to cite the nominees and winners of the various awards. Each a star of one of the few remaining shows on Broadway, these celebrated survivors materialized before the cameras in full costume, sharing the screen with huge poster blowups of their productions. Bombarded by such hard sell, I found it difficult to distinguish the Tony ceremonies from the commercial breaks, especially when the sponsors were also using Broadway stars to merchandise their products. One moment Frank Langella was bounding on stage in a sweatshirt to advertise *Passion*. The next, Darth Vader Jones was eulogizing the new Polaroid camera, Bernadette Peters was squealing over her American Express card, and Patricia Neal was prescribing Anacin for a stewardess with a headache ("You can fight anything and win," remarked this gallant stroke victim). Even Charlie Chaplin was pressed posthumously into commercial service through the offices of an impersonator peddling IBM personal computers. If it hadn't been for a Planter's Peanut spot, featuring a couple of taxi drivers, you might have thought that everybody in America was in show business.

In such an atmosphere, one could predict the winners by the ticket sales. What the Tony Awards invariably celebrate is not theatre but box-office returns, with the blockbuster musical ("our greatest art form in America," according to one awardee) monopolizing the honors by virtue of being the biggest potential gold mine. Because of its limited popular appeal, serious drama excites very little interest, especially since two of the shows nominated this year for Best Play award had long since expired and the two survivors were commercially marginal. The winner was perfunctorily announced at the start of the ceremonies before most viewers had a chance to turn on their sets. In a competition that included Lanford Wilson's *Angels Fall*, David Hare's *Plenty*, and Marsha Norman's *'night Mother*, the award went to Harvey Fierstein's *Torch Song Trilogy*. The irrepressible author bounded on stage to share his surprise with the rest of us, while his producer, coming out of the closet on national TV to proclaim his eternal devotion to "my partner and my lover," saluted the "stupendous and miraculous moment."

This out of the way, we were in a position to concentrate on the real mission of the Tony ceremonies, which is to increase attendance and income at "our greatest art form in America." In the interstices between a medley of Gershwin songs and production numbers from a period when nobody claimed more for musicals than their capacity to entertain, the awards were presented to a field so thin and uninspired that it made the past seem positively golden. George Abbott ("ninety-six years young" and advertising a revival of *On Your Toes*) appeared on stage to present the award for Best Musical Director to Trevor Nunn, artistic leader of the Royal Shakespeare Company, for *Cats*, which collected seven awards that night. "All I can do is purr," Nunn remarked, adding: "In England, we dream of New York . . . the place where we learn how to do musicals"—a sweet way of thanking Broadway on behalf of all his moonlighting compatriots from the British subsidized theatre for helping to increase their credit ratings, portfolios, and investments.

The poet T. S. Eliot was not present to offer similar expressions of gratitude, having died some years before he could enjoy the unutterable honor, shared with Tommy Tune and Harvey Fierstein, of winning two Tonys in the same evening—one for Best Lyrics for a Musical, the other for Best Musical Book. In collecting his awards, Eliot's wife paused to assure us that he would have been unspeakably proud to see his *Book of Practical Cats* transformed into an overweight, overproduced musical, before carting off the Tony medallions to place them beside his Nobel medal on the family dressing table. Winning a Tony for Best Set for *Cats*, John Napier had the good taste to limit his remarks to a simple "Thanks," probably the most dignified possible response in the circumstances, while Andrew Lloyd Webber, *Cats* winner for Best Score, noted that the band continually replayed snatches of "Memory" every time *Cats* was mentioned: "I'm a bit worried—we seem to be a one-tune show. Thank goodness George Gershwin wasn't nominated in this category." Thank goodness, indeed.

There were a few other isolated moments of dignity in the evening—one, when Matthew Broderick, honored as Best Featured Actor for *Brighton Beach Memoirs*, dedicated the award to his dead father, James Broderick, though this death had been overlooked in the theatre obituaries compiled by the Tony producers. And there was a trace of humor, too, when, winning for *On Your Toes*, Natalia Makarova, in an accent penetrable only in the Russian Tea Room, acknowledged "my husband, who didn't help much, but wasn't in my way." More often, however, the stage groaned under the weight of overripe, overdecorated actresses, impeded in turn by heavy jewelry, sequined gowns, piled dyed hair, and enameled faces that had been lifted so often they seemed three feet off their necks, trying to wrap their vocal chords around the Gershwin tunes. Mercifully, Jessica Tandy, accepting an award for Outstanding Actress in a Play (*Foxfire*), was present to show that what really conquers the aging process is not cosmetic varnish but interior grace, as displayed in the natural, regal elegance of a true beauty.

Finally, one came away from this lavish undertaking, for all its paeans and tributes, even more disconsolate than ever about the future of the Broadway theatre—and especially about the commercial future of the Broadway musical, its last hope. Alone among its competition—*My One and Only*, *Merlin*, and *Blues in the Night*—only *Cats* is a palpable hit. *Blues in the Night* has long since failed, *Merlin* is limping, and none of the four has received any real acclaim. There are those who have considerably more respect for *Cats* than I do, but even they might likely concede that the musical pickings in recent years have been extremely slim—which explains why Hal Prince has announced his intention to abandon Broadway, why Stephen Sondheim is now writing a musical for Playwrights Horizons, and why the New York Critics Circle gave its musical award to the off-Broadway *Little Shop of Horrors*.

By continually plugging Gershwin tunes, the Tony Committee

exposed its unspoken awareness that the glories of this "greatest American art form" were all in the past, in the same dustbin with the serious Broadway drama. And that is why the awards have turned into a gigantic commercial for a dying enterprise. Alone among the various prize committees, the Tony Committee still refuses to recognize that the American theatre exists in other geographical areas than the fifteen tawdry streets between Forty-first and Fifty-sixth. To acknowledge this is to admit that the nature and structure of the theatre have radically changed in the past twenty years. But to ignore it is to transform a once-proud art form into a public travesty, more appropriate for selling used cars.

The British Conquest

THE TRIUMPH OF MEDIOCRITY

(Amadeus)

Peter Shaffer's *Amadeus* (Broadhurst) is about the ravaging of genius by mediocrity. This seems to be not only the subject of the play, but also its prime motivation. At the same time that the central character—a second-rate Kapellmeister named Antonio Salieri—is plotting against the life and reputation of a superior composer named Wolfgang Amadeus Mozart, a secondary playwright named Peter Shaffer is reducing this musical genius, one of the greatest artists of all time, to the level of a simpering, braying ninny. Is the malcontented court composer, Salieri, secretly intended as a portrait of the author as an envious man, caught in a moment of self-hatred? If so, *Amadeus* embodies not only Salieri's revenge on Mozart but also Shaffer's revenge on genuine art and primary artists. In the way it slanders Mozart, *Amadeus* might also be interpreted as achieving for Salieri, one hundred and fifty years after his death, what he could not do in his lifetime. The Pirandellian implications of the situation are positively dazzling; I left the theatre uncertain as to who had actually written the play.

I do not mean to suggest that Mr. Shaffer is another "patron saint of mediocrity"—the self-definition he gives to Salieri. He is far too clever to be dismissed like that—and much too shrewd a writer. He is not, however, a true artist, and like Salieri, he seems to have the sense to know it. Like Salieri, too, he has often been praised for slick, superficial work—for achieving greatness when all he does is impersonate it. In a sensitive man, undeserved praise can generate contempt—contempt for one's deluded admirers, contempt for one's inadequate talent. This contempt gives the play its only real heat and energy. It is the fuel for Salieri's venomous hatred.

It is fairly well known that Salieri plotted against Mozart and successfully blocked his advancement with the Emperor Joseph. Mozart died believing that Salieri had poisoned him; the rumor was current enough to inspire an opera by Rimsky-Korsakov called *Mozart and Salieri*. Most commentators reject the imputation, citing the affection of Beethoven and Schubert for the old Salieri, and the fact that he denied the poisoning on his deathbed. Shaffer also rejects the idea of a literal murder, suggesting instead that Salieri poisoned Mozart with hatred. In *Amadeus*, he constructs a Byzantine maze of intrigue, making Salieri responsible for the near-cancellation of *The Marriage of Figaro* (though it was the emperor who threatened the opera because he felt dubious about the democratic sentiments of the Beaumarchais work on which it was based). He also has Salieri persuading Mozart to include Masonic secrets in *The Magic Flute* so that the Society would repudiate him. Shaffer's Salieri appears to Mozart on his deathbed, in a black cloak and mask, disguised as the mysterious stranger who had commissioned the *Requiem* (Mozart believed this apparition to be the messenger of death, though it later turned out to be the emissary of a Count Walsegg). Shaffer is always prepared to sacrifice historical fact for a good melodramatic climax. Salieri scares Mozart to death by pretending to be the Stone Statue from *Don Giovanni* inviting the composer to supper. Later he admits to having poisoned Mozart because he hoped to achieve immortality with a false confession. And finally, having unsuccessfully attempted suicide, he implicates us all in his hatred of genius and his inescapable mediocrity.

Whether or not Mr. Shaffer has violated history is a question of no great moment; none of his factual liberties would be very serious had he produced a work of genuine imagination. But, and I suspect he knows this, *Amadeus* is no more the important play it has been proclaimed than that spurious Beckett imitation, *Rosencrantz and Guildenstern*. Like Tom Stoppard, Peter Shaffer manufactures smart impersonations—in this case a costume drama masquerading as a tragedy. Both dramatists find their literary antecedents in Beaumont and Fletcher because both disguise their lack of real artistic depth with technical dazzle and smooth surfaces. Like Francis Beaumont (who copied Shakespeare), indeed like Antonio Salieri himself, Peter Shaffer is very good at recognizing genius in others. He has learned his modern drama lessons well. The bargain Salieri strikes with God in which he agrees to remain chaste and virtuous if God will make him a composer ("Go forward . . . serve me and mankind and you will be blessed") is stolen straight from Ibsen's *The Master Builder*, just as Mozart's fantastical deathbed peroration is borrowed from Peer Gynt's speech to his dying mother. Similarly, the cutrate nihilism of the play—issuing from Salieri's quarrels with an indifferent God—are blue-blook renderings of readings in Beckett and Strindberg. Worst of all, perhaps, is his watering down of Freud—the work is riddled with armchair psychoanalysis (Shaffer identifies both the Commendatore in *Don Giovanni* and the High Priest in *The Magic Flute* with Mozart's father, Leopold, and underlines the guilt the composer felt over their complicated relationship). As for the language, it is crammed with bombastic rhetoric and glib metaphors (example: "I wanted my fame to blow like a comet across the firmament of Europe"), that are continually being betrayed by anachronistic colloquialisms (Mozart identifies a rival's music as "the sound of someone who can't get it up"). Shaffer's play is not only about opera; it *is* opera, precisely the kind that Mozart always scorned, warbled in that decorative *bel canto* that tone-deaf people invariably confuse with genuine music.

But none of this would be very important either were Shaffer not joined in Salieri's conspiracy. Salieri is endowed with intelligence, complexity, emotional range, metaphysical *Angst*, and the author's affection. But his genius rival is portrayed as a carrot-topped nitwit with an electrified crew cut which looks the same even when he is wearing a white wig. He is also endowed with a braying laugh, an itchy crotch, and a vocabulary almost entirely limited to baby talk. He stalks Constanze Weber, his future wife, like a cat chasing a mouse, calling her "pussy-wussy" and "squeaky-weaky," meanwhile muttering, "I'm going to bite you in half with my fangs-wangs." At one point, he begs her to beat him on his "botty," as if he had spent his youth in English public schools. (Constanze, for her part, speaks in the language of the English working class—her "Ta very much" is the idiom of a modern Liverpool waitress.) Occasionally, Mozart is permitted a sensible remark or an intelligent insight. More often, he is a raunchy jackass in heat, announcing to all and sundry how he would like "to lick my wife's ass instead of her face." Salieri falls into a dead faint whenever he reads one of Mozart's scores, but the sensibility that produced this music has been buried in an avalanche of contempt.

The best thing about the evening is John Bury's set, a gorgeous shiny blue raked stage with a handsome teak floor, an antique inlaid piano, a huge wing chair, and an inner proscenium that serves as court, interior, and opera house. Peter Hall's production, for the most part, I found externally accomplished, internally empty—like the play. Ian McKellen is an actor whose work I have admired in the past; here, he is doing one of his scornful parts, letting his tenor voice reverberate throughout as if he were applying for Maurice Evans's old job as The Great Resonator. He transforms before our eyes from age to youth, from simulated kindness to snarling rage, never letting us forget for a moment how exquisitely he is carrying the whole thing off. As for Tim Curry's Mozart, it is all exposed teeth and hooded eyes and gangling oafishness—a performance more appropriate for Bottom the Weaver in his incarnation as a donkey. I liked the more simple work of Jane Seymour as Constanze and of Nicholas Kepros as the Emperor Joseph, and Mr. Hall has arranged the rest of the cast attractively on the stage. But the only time I felt in the presence of real accomplishment was when the amplification system offered Mozart's music to supplement the theatrical climaxes. In *Amadeus*, Mr. Shaffer has permitted the audience to feel superior to genius. This allows him to feel superior to the audience, which has given him such unearned success. In one of the endings of the play (it has five or six), Salieri turns to the "Ghosts of the Future"—the middle-class spectators he has been flattering all evening—and says: "Mediocrities everywhere, I absolve you all." Whether history will absolve the author as well, only future ghosts will tell.

GOOD AND PLENTY

(Plenty)

David Hare's *Plenty* is an ambitious effort to create a thoroughgoing X ray of England's soul following World War II. Taking social fluoroscopes is an important, even crucial, dramatic function—it was Chekhov's motive in *Cherry Orchard*, for example, and Bernard Shaw's in *Heartbreak House*—though such tasks have grown more difficult as the diagnostics have grown more complicated. I don't think Hare entirely accomplishes his intention, but I honor him for it, and pray it has a salutary influence on American playwrights, most of whom are still engaged in counting kitchen angels on the heads of domestic pins.

Plenty traces the career of a spirited Englishwoman from her youth as a courier, aiding the French resistance against the Nazis, to her collapse, some fifteen years later, into peacetime disillusionment—paralyzed by anomie, riddled with depression, rotting with despair and psychic rust. Hare's heroine, Susan Traherne, represents a particular example of a general condition, the personification of a hopeful, idealistic generation disaffected by a nation in moral collapse. It is Hare's conviction that World War II represented England's last heroic moment (the play was written before the Falkland victory restored some of the country's lost pride), after which it experienced a series of demoralizing deceptions and compromises, tied to the loss of empire. Ironically, this was a time of affluence, an era of peace and plenty; it was also a period when the relationship between the individual and the family, between the individual and society, began to break down. Susan Traherne is not Everywoman, but her condition is representative of the entire English middle class in showing an intelligent, spirited, delicately poised human being pulverized by the failures of her time.

This demonstration, however, along with a somewhat shaky structure, exposes the most uncertain aspect of the play. It assigns purely social causes to problems that may at least be partially existential. Hare doesn't provide enough information about Susan Traherne to define her conscious or unconscious motivations with any exactitude.

But he intentionally idealizes her wartime experience, and even returns to it in a final flashback when she appears, young and innocent in a flowered dress, to say: "We have grown up. We will improve our world." The postwar world, however, doesn't improve, and neither does Susan. She visits the embassy in Brussels, trying to persuade a diplomat to inform a widow of the recent death of her husband, Susan's casual lover. Next, she propositions a young spiv, during the Festival of Britain, to give her a child ("Deep down I'd do the whole damn thing myself, but there we are"). Then, after this sad attempt has failed for eighteen months to produce progeny, she takes a potshot at the abandoned stud when he rebukes her class for its callousness and condescension.

During this time, Susan has been working at a number of unsatisfying jobs, first in a shipping office, then in advertising, trying to find some commitment commensurate with her memories of the war. She contracts an essentially loveless marriage with Raymond Brock, the diplomat, and effectively ruins his career when she refuses to return with him to Iran. The climactic event in their lives, and the greatest source of disillusion for their generation, is Suez, when Britain under Eden made a halfhearted final effort to preserve the empire: "Nobody will say blunder, international farce," Susan stridently announces at a formal dinner. "Nobody will say death rattle of the ruling class." In the grip of mental illness, embittered, out of control, Susan enacts her "psychiatric cabaret," haunted by memories of wartime France, of the time when British soldiers last landed in a country where they were wanted.

It is the most resonant scene in the play, for it tells the tragic story of many wars after World War II—America's Vietnam, Israel's Lebanon—wars that instead of uniting the people, divided them. It is an event that leads to the death of one of Hare's most interesting characters, Leonard Darwin, the ambassador who served as Brock's mentor, after Darwin has lost all belief in his calling as a result of his country's bad faith. But fiascoes like Suez are not enough to explain Susan's addiction to drink and drugs, her suicide attempts, or her indifference about sleeping, as she says, with men that she knows. Nor does the plea of affluence, though it is one that Susan herself suggests: "Too much money, I think that's what went wrong. Corrupts the will to live." There is truth in the remark, but also the motive hunting of a free-floating, perhaps motiveless, disenchantment, which, like Iago's malignity, is responsible for extreme acts that defy explanation. In one scene (worthy of Strindberg), she decides to give away her house in Knightsbridge, strips it, throwing priceless antiques out of the window, and finally takes a shot at her infuriated husband after he threatens to have her committed.

Still, if Hare is not enough of a poet to penetrate Susan's despair, he is enough of a playwright to dramatize it; and he is a gifted artificer of blistering, lacerating dialogue. Judging from his work here, he is also a strong director, confidently guiding his talented cast through modulated performances. The passionate Kate Nelligan was ill the evening I saw the play, but her standby, Randy Danson, looking like a ripe Iranian queen, demonstrated not only heroism in assuming the role on short notice (one expects an understudy to be gallant), but considerable power and control. Her playing was entirely persuasive, if somewhat generalized due to underrehearsal. Edward Herrmann, as Raymond Brock, proved once again that he is among our most intelligent actors, and also that he has reserves of genuine power under that ingratiating boyishness. George Martin contributed a modest, crisp, wry, and ultimately very touching performance as Leonard Darwin. And I was impressed by Bill Moor as a steely-cold British diplomat, and by Ellen Parker as Susan's confidante, sucking on a hashish pipe and toying with a variety of fashionable political commitments. John Gunter's simple design—a gray pine floor with set pieces, backed by dark historical lithographs of people and ships—was an elegant visual metaphor for an action that moves back and forth through time like brief scenic shudders. And Nick Bicat's music and Arden Fingerhut's lighting were potent enhancements of the brittle mood.

I was reminded of John Osborne before his reincarnation as a theatrical Colonel Blimp—the same nostalgia for lost innocence, the same mournful elegies for an England dead and gone. The alienation of left-wing English playwrights is more that of a disillusioned lover than of a malcontented outsider, which accounts, I think, for an eloquent anger sometimes in excess of the event. *Plenty* is compromised by incompleteness and structural asymmetry (the scenes in France, for example, should have sandwiched the play instead of being internal flashbacks). But it is undeniably alive. For once, the problems come from being too close to the object, not from manipulating it by remote control.

THE PLEASURE OF A COMPANY

(Nicholas Nickleby)

I approached the marathon Royal Shakespeare Company production of *Nicholas Nickleby* prepared less to review a play than to enlist in one: four hours in the afternoon, four and one half hours in the evening, with less than an hour permitted for dinner in between. I got through my basic training less exhausted than exhilarated. You may need steel buttocks to sit through this show, but a stiff behind is the only discomfort you will experience.

Nicholas Nickleby is popular theatre at its best—a great big delicious pudding designed for shameless gorging. It is probably what Brecht meant by "culinary" theatre—consumed without difficulty, easily digested, leaving no unpleasant aftertaste. At last the theatre is offering the kind of pleasures that movies do routinely. What it is also offering—and this is rare in movies—is the spectacle of a great ensemble of actors working in perfect harmony. The company displays not only dash and polish, qualities one has come to expect of the English, but unflagging energy, powers of transformation, intelligence, zest, and ebullient spirits. The production is clearly a group creation. David Edgar is credited with the adaptation, and there is unquestionably a strong crafting hand guiding the plotting and characterization (also some brilliantly original touches, such as a sidesplitting *Beyond the Fringe*–type parody of the tomb scene in *Romeo and Juliet* where all the dead characters except for Tybalt come back to life). But the accretion of detail has been contributed by the directors (Trevor Nunn and John Caird) and a company of thirty-nine splendid actors. As a theatrical adaptation of a Dickens novel, *Nicholas Nickleby* approaches David Lean's movie of *Great Expectations*, still the finest example, to my mind, of a work transferred to drama from literature.

Lean's two-hour movie was a condensation; this production tries to put an entire novel on the stage. Many of the episodes go by too fast to make an impression, and the production sometimes seems impatient with its own ambitions. What keeps one's interest from flagging is the story, which continues to thread through the interstices of the various subplots. This story is not the most subtle Dickens ever told—the coincidences alone are enough to shake one's faith in accident. But it is spread over a vast social canvas, crammed with lovely characters, including the usual Dickensian gallery of the virtuous, the villainous, and the eccentric. The central narrative concerns Nicholas's struggles to combat poverty and injustice in the face of a harsh, unforgiving world as embodied in a huge circus of evil characters, chiefly his uncle Ralph Nickleby. The conflict is passionately acted by Roger Rees, lean and fervent as Nicholas, and John Woodvine as a steely, hooded Ralph Nickleby. Woodvine, especially, brings a Dostoyevskian nihilism to a part that in the writing seems to be an early sketch for Scrooge—cold and indifferent toward suffering, regarding any act of compassion or unselfishness with the curiosity of a scientist examining the reproductive patterns of amoebae. (I should like to see this actor play Bosola in *The Duchess of Malfi*, another vicious character intrigued by idiosyncratic displays of goodness).

Aside from Ralph Nickleby's ultimate disintegration in the face of his own vileness, there is very little process or change in any of the characters. Only Nicholas can be said to develop, and only in the growth and maturity of his social conscience. Employed as a tutor in a school of cruelty and bestiality run by the disgusting one-eyed Squeers and his loathsome family, Nicholas impotently watches the poor wretched boarders being starved, maltreated, and whipped, and takes action only when Squeers brutally beats the twisted helpless runaway Smike. From this point on, he is ready to use his fists whenever he sees an act of cruelty or injustice, whether it is a nobleman insulting his sister, Kate, or his uncle Ralph preparing to sell Madeline Bray to the miserly Gride. The activism of Nicholas represents the awakening of nineteenth-century liberalism. His twentieth-century interpreters have advanced the liberal theme even further, in the final moments of the play, by showing Nicholas—having ended up with love, happiness, money, and all his enemies confounded—holding another wretched foundling in his arms, staring determinedly at an audience that has been brought cheering to its feet.

It is no doubt churlish at this point to note that this is precisely the kind of isolated charitable gesture that makes liberalism look so smug and impotent to its enemies. It also suggests why Brecht was so contemptuous of the "culinary." Is the newly affluent Nicholas prepared for any personal sacrifices beyond taking one more social victim into his home? Similarly, Nicholas's relationship with his faithful, devoted Smike looks to us less like that of a close friend than a kind master petting a crippled puppy who continually licks his hand. And his impetuous nature, curiously violent for a Dickens character, is always justified on the basis of his hatred for injustice. *Nicholas Nickleby* is designed to leave the audience feeling good about human nature, good about the results of social action, good about itself, without exacting any other payment than the price of its tickets. One character makes humorous reference to those Americans who "are much devoted to the grand gesture—I have it on the best authority, they'll pay anything." But the very Americans who are shelling out one hundred dollars a ticket for an evening of entertainment will probably do their best to circumvent the mass of suffering humanity just a few steps away on Eighth Avenue (yes, I do my best to avoid them too). Dickens had a profound understanding of human evil. What he didn't know how to measure was the price of virtuous feelings. The aura of self-righteousness and self-satisfaction that drenches the novel also permeates the production—particularly in the episodes involving Nicholas's sister, Kate, and the dastardly Lovelaces that try to seduce her—scenes that look backwards to Clarissa Harlowe and forward to Little Nell. Still, if there is something almost quaint about the pre-Marxian politics of this work, there is something almost Reaganesque about it too: Ralph Nickleby responds to the outstretched hand of a starving beggar by saying, "I'm sixty and neither worthless nor destitute—work, sir, work." And Squeers feeds his student charges brimstone and molasses and waters their morning milk (well, at least he doesn't pass off the ketchup as a vegetable).

One is, moreover, so grateful for a theatre piece that tries to offer us a fully dimensioned social world that one feels ungracious caviling about the simplified nature of that world. And the actors bring so much belief to their parts, and so much gusto, that they almost have us believing the sentiment too. Part of the joy the audience experiences surely comes from those who perform the play, and perform it with such pleasure. This kind of material is guaranteed to stimulate an English actor's imagination because, along with being pre-Marxian, it is also pre-Freudian. The characters bear no burden of neurosis or internalization. Except for some mild passes by the aristocratic villains, they don't even seem to have any sexuality. What we get instead are 119 confidently sketched individuals whose surface manifestations are instantly conveyed. It is for this reason, perhaps, that the sequences involving the Vincent Crummles troupe of traveling players are among the most satisfying in the production; the Infant Phenomenon, the drunken character actor, the sleek heavy, the aging ingenue—these are known tintypes that experienced repertory actors can depict with affection, amusement, detachment, and authenticity.

Thus, the pleasures one finally takes home from the evening are not just those of seeing a story told well, or watching a lively novel transferred vividly to the stage, or feeling our nodding social consciences awakened, but rather of witnessing a large and brilliant company working skillfully and tirelessly on a highly complicated project. We have seen these techniques of transformation employed before (in Paul Sills's *Story Theatre*) but never so ambitiously. And while the Royal Shakespeare Company has provided us in the past with more profound experiences and more innovative productions—Peter Brook's *Marat/Sade*, for example, and his *Midsummer Night's Dream*—it has offered nothing with wider sweep or more intricate stagecraft. Compared to such endurance contests as Wagner's *Ring* cycle, *Nicholas Nickleby* passes quickly. But it is still a major achievement to keep us so fascinated for eight and one-half hours. This is a triumph of the stage rather than of dramatic art, but it is a triumph nevertheless, and anything that brings so much pleasure to audiences has to be respected. With this production, the Royal Shakespeare Company demonstrates that it is a popular theatre, rejecting our modernistic pessimism for a positive view of life. But it also convinces us that it is a great theatre, capable of doing any play in the repertory. *Nicholas Nickleby* will fill American theatre people with envy; it should also fill us with hope.

THE PARADOX OF ACTORS

(Edmund Kean)

The actor has always been one of the most marginal yet one of the most central members of society. Out of the ranks of those identified with vagrants and gypsies, pariahs once refused burial in sacred ground, can arise a figure who for a time becomes the icon of the age, the glass of fashion, the mirror of conduct and style. That such a reviled profession can also yield such instant fame and influence (and presently even political power) partly explains its continuing attraction for so many aspirants, and the hypnotic fascination it holds for the media. The lives, careers, affairs, marriages, divorces, alcohol and drug problems, and personal quirks of stage and movie personalities virtually dominate the entertainment and feature sections of our newspapers and magazines, while reviewers and reporters seem under some weekly editorial compulsion to identify new idols for a fickle, star-dazzled public.

The intimate nature of these stories, and their celebratory tone, suggest that the relationship between the actor and the public is a pact between the exhibitionist and the voyeur. Acting at its most ideal is a joint activity in which the performer merges his personality with the group and his personal qualities with the role. In each case he reinforces the collective experience through the force of the individual imagination. The media and the public, on the other hand, ever eager to pluck the plum from the pudding, glorify the actor who stands apart from the group, encouraging him to emphasize his own personal idiosyncrasies. The value of a star performer, like that of all commercial products in the market, is measured by a recognition factor. Thus, although self-subordination is an essential element of the histrionic art, our celebrity culture is always beckoning the actor toward a form of self-exposure.

This is one of the paradoxes suggested by *Edmund Kean*, a play by Raymund Fitzsimons currently on view at the Brooks Atkinson Theatre. A one-man show about a notoriously flamboyant nine-teenth-century English star, it is being performed entirely by a singularly modest and unassuming twentieth-century English actor, Ben Kingsley, who in the process absorbs some of the vanity and egocentricity of the character he is impersonating. The ironies implicit in this are boundless, but they are ironies that sometimes seem a lot more interesting than the play.

Edmund Kean, after an obscure career in the provinces, was much admired in London, particularly by Coleridge, who described his acting with that lovely, tantalizing phrase: "To see Kean was to read Shakespeare by flashes of lightning." No less awed by Kean, William Hazlitt was a little more circumspect, writing of his "fiery soul and pygmy body," and adding that he was "possessed with a fury, a demon that leaves him no repose, no time for thought or room for imagination." A dwarfish actor without access to mind or imagination would not seem ideally equipped for greatness. And in addition to his diminutive frame, Kean had a harsh, croaking vocal instrument ("I know of no more irksome noises," noted a contemporary critic, "than those which issue from his breast") that limited him to roles marked by frenzy or malignity—one is reminded of George C. Scott.

Kean dazzled his contemporaries with acting said to be totally free from artificiality. Coming on the heels of the sedate Kemble, whose every gesture looked as if he were modeling for a classical piece of statuary, Kean seemed to be ushering in a new age of histrionic naturalness. A generation earlier, David Garrick was also praised for naturalness; so, in fact, was virtually every celebrated actor in history, including our own Marlon Brando, Al Pacino, and Robert De Niro.

Part of Kean's appeal, though it shocked some upper-class contemporaries, was his scandalous personal life. The issue of "a part-time whore and a drunken Irishman," he was always sensitive about his lowly birth, and falsely claimed a noble lineage. Successful mainly in villain roles, Kean was privately ruthless and unethical. He broke contract after contract to advance his career, and when he finally became the leading tragedian of Drury Lane, he displayed the selfish ego of the small-minded star, refusing to allow any other actor to move in front of him on stage, and monopolizing all the leading roles. He was relentlessly unfaithful to his long-suffering wife, both with grand ladies and with whores; he was riddled with clap; and he was a confirmed alcoholic, frequently staggering onto the stage and performing in a state bordering on narcosis.

How does one make a play out of this *National Enquirer* material? Not very easily. Jean-Paul Sartre tried his hand at one, based on a romantic drama by Dumas, but it was full of bombast and rodomontade, erotic intrigue, and bloated existential musings on the fate of the actor. Fitzsimons's effort is more modest, if more tiresome, a historically correct tintype, which functions primarily as a showcase for Ben Kingsley. Holding the stage with a two-hour semidramatized biography, interspersed with Shakespearean soliloquies, and broken only by a short intermission, Kingsley elicits the same admiration as a marathon runner, for endurance rather than for style. I hasten to add that few actors could hold my attention with a 120-minute monologue; but then how many actors would want to?

The open stage on which this monologue takes place contains a few theatrical artifacts—a trunk, a mannequin, a dressing table, and draped curtains. The passage of time is marked by tinny Elizabethan music. Wearing a leonine wig and a black moustache, Kingsley swings from storytelling to soliloquy, leaping into position to play Harlequin or Shylock, as the lights change to underline the transitions. The author makes some small effort, not much, to create parallels between Kean's life and the Shakespeare roles he is playing. More often, the play is only a clothesline on which are hung the wet garments of a self-infatuated life. Unlike Kean's, Kingsley's vocal instrument is light and flexible; it can also be fervent when the occasion warrants. But although Kingsley could conceivably play well some of the roles from which he reads extracts (particularly Othello), he provides nothing to indicate why Kean was considered such an electrifying performer in his day. What then is the purpose of this evening?

There is one moment, and one moment only, when the shards of this event begin to coalesce into a potentially significant theme. Kean has just discovered that his aristocratic mistress has been unfaithful to him with her husband's clerk. Kean's wife has discovered the affair, and so has the cuckolded husband. A new audience favorite, Macready, is stepping on his heels, threatening to displace him. An outraged mob has come to bait him in the theatre. For the first time in his life, Kean is forced to defend himself on stage. His performance brings no applause, only jeers. Sodden with drink, Kean is reviled as an alcoholic, which for a moment makes him reflective: "They made me drunk with applause and now they want me to be sober."

This thematic germ—the intoxication of the actor by the praise of the audience, the corruption of art by celebrity—could well have been the foundation for an interesting play. To my mind it is among the most poignant facts in the contemporary theatre, one that is daily enacted in a drama of failed and unfulfilled careers. But the moment passes all too quickly before we are back in the tabloid saga of Kean's later years and death, and his collapse on stage while playing Othello. He tells his son: "I am dying—speak to them for me." Too much has been spoken, however, about the actor's squalid life, and too little understood about his battered profession, to make this evening much more than a form of theatrical voyeurism, a peek into the seamier side of an artist's world.

HIPPOLYTUS CAN FEEL!

(The Real Thing)

It has sometimes been said of Tom Stoppard, and not just by me, that there is nothing going on beneath the glossy, slippery surface of his bright ideas and arch dialogue. With *The Real Thing*, he has decided to confound his more jaundiced critics by chipping a hole in the ice for us to peek through—also suitable for fishing. You've probably heard by now what's swimming around this chilly pond. The "real thing" is Stoppard's amorous equivalent of the "right stuff"—grace and style in the performance of a difficult task, in this case the conduct of erotic relationships.

In short, Britain's leading intellectual entertainer is now exhibiting a highly publicized, well-congratulated capacity not just for verbal and literary pyrotechnics but also for *feeling*. His characters actually experience jealousy, envy, sorrow, and passion. Watching and hearing these exotic emotions being expressed, I was reminded of Racine's *Phèdre*, where the lovesick heroine, assuming that Hippolytus is frigid, discovers that all this while he has actually been in love with the young Aricie. "Hippolytus can feel!" says the astonished Phèdre, "but not for me." Mr. Stoppard's display of sentience has seemed convincing for many—but not for me.

The Real Thing begins with a scene from *House of Cards*, a love triangle written by a successful playwright named Henry, enacted by his actress wife, Charlotte, and his actor friend, Max. Brittle enough to be a piece of Stoppard inventory, this is nevertheless not the "real thing" but rather a play-within-a-play (selections from Ford's *'Tis Pity She's a Whore* later form another of these Chinese boxes) about a man exposing his wife's adultery. After Henry's apartment comes in on a revolving turntable, we learn that the "real thing" is actually about the adultery of a husband. Henry has been having it off with Max's wife, Annie, another actress, though one with a bit of a social conscience— she has befriended a young soldier arrested for arson at an antimissile demonstration. By the second act, Henry has left Charlotte and moved in with Annie.

When Max learns of Annie's infidelity, he cries. Henry, who finds Max's misery "in not very good taste," also cries after he discovers that Annie has betrayed him too, with a young actor. Obviously, Hippolytus can feel—but Stoppard is less interested in these lachrymose calisthenics than in demonstrating how it is possible to reveal sentiment without losing one's reputation as a wit. For despite the intermittent weeping, the strongest emotion in the play is a passion for the construction of sentences. Stoppard, ignoring Max's rebuke that "having all the words is not what life's about," is never more fervid than when Henry is celebrating his own verbal felicity. Defending himself against Annie's charge that "you only write for people who would like to write like you if only they could write" (note that even Henry's critics speak in carefully polished tropes), Henry replies that language is sacred, even if writers are not: "If you get the right words in the right order, you can nudge the world a little."

At this point, he has been nudging the world in the direction of quietism by ridiculing soldier Brodie's loutish effort to compose a protest play. Stoppard, whose name was recently used in an ad by British conservatives praising our invasion of Grenada, is as tone deaf before the dissonant inflections of political protest as Henry is in the presence of serious music. After Annie has rewarded Brodie's bad manners by pasting his face with cocktail dip like a slapstick pie, the play ends with a reconciliatory kiss between husband and wife,

Henry writhing to his favorite rock record and Annie entering the bedroom to undress. Thus, love conquers all—even casual adulteries and messy social dissent.

Considering how few people can resist a sophisticated love story, *The Real Thing* is destined to be one of the big hits of the Broadway season and, when the rights are released, a reigning favorite of middlebrow theatre companies. I found it rather coldhearted in its good-natured way, a frozen trifle with little aftertaste. Stoppard has doubtless made some effort to examine his own personal and literary problems, and his writing is rarely defensive or self-serving. But despite the autobiographical yeast leavening the familiar digestible cake mix, *The Real Thing* is just another clever exercise in the Mayfair mode, where all of the characters (the proletarian Brodie excepted) share the same wit, artifice, and ornamental diction. Even Henry's teenage daughter, teasing her father for always writing about "infidelity among the architect class," is fashioning sentences designed for inclusion in a *Glossary of Post-Restoration Epigrams*.

I think I might be less immune to the charms of this admittedly harmless piece of trivia were it not being touted everywhere as the real thing. It comes no closer to being real than any of those other adultery plays recently exported from England—and it doesn't even possess the mordancy of Harold Pinter's *Betrayal* or the ingenuity of Peter Nichols's *Passion*. Born in Czechoslovakia, Stoppard has managed to perfect an expatriate's gift for mimicry. Allied to his ear for language is his unique capacity to imitate playwriting styles. But if he began his career impersonating Beckett and Pirandello *(Rosencrantz and Guildenstern Are Dead)* or Bernard Shaw *(Jumpers)* or Joyce and Wilde *(Travesties)*, he has recently, along with a large number of contemporaries in the English theatre, come entirely under the influence of Noel Coward. The question is whether witty sangfroid is more appropriate to simulating reality or creating escapism, whether, at this critical point in world history, we are more in need of rhetorical artifice—or poetic truth.

Mike Nichols's production is as beautifully manicured as the play and, at times, equally contrived. Nichols has always gotten the best out of good actors, and his casting instinct has not failed him here. Still, there is a natural spontaneity missing from the current production, which suggests the cast is corseted in Stoppard's language. Jeremy Irons, looking like a dissipated D'Artagnan, bearded and baggy eyed, has a plummy time with Henry's dialogue, and commands the stage with authentic theatrical grace. But Glen Close, as Annie, tries too hard to charm us out of recognizing that this is one unpleasant lady. An attractive actress with auburn hair and sunken eyes, Miss Close seems at times too easily persuaded of her own radiance. She smiles too much, and she has a habit of hugging herself. This injects a strain of sentimental self-love into these rather hardhearted proceedings (it is also highly unlikely, though this may be a fault of the writing, that she would be playing the young Annabella opposite a considerably younger Giovanni in *'Tis Pity She's a Whore*). As for Christian Baranski as Charlotte and Kenneth Welsh as Max, they, like the rest of the cast—and like Tony Walton's scenery, Tharon Musser's lighting, and Anthea Sylbert's clothes—function as well as possible to fulfill the assigned task, which is to reflect back the showy brilliance of the two leading characters, not to mention the breathtaking contrivances of their author, in his flamboyant discovery of what it means to be "real."

ROYAL TOURIST ATTRACTION

(Cyrano de Bergerac; Much Ado about Nothing)

What has become of the Royal Shakespeare Company? The productions of Shakespeare's *Much Ado about Nothing* and Rostand's *Cyrano de Bergerac* suggest a great theatre in decline. I'm not protesting a lack of skill or grace, or even visual artistry—indeed, the problem may be related to a surplus of these values. It's just that the offerings are so bloody tame and insipid, from play choices to production concepts, that you leave the theatre with tired blood. What we have here is the New York equivalent of a London show tour—the only element missing is an ad for British Airways. Yes, I know the RSC has always been a rest stop for tourists wandering through Anne Hathaway's cottage and Shakespeare's gardens, but at least in the old days there were some crazy salads at the Aldwych accompanying those Stratford plum puddings. To judge by this visit and even by the superior *Nicholas Nickleby* (and let's not forget Trevor Nunn's mechanical contribution to *Cats*), the RSC directorate has settled into manufacturing pyrotechnical displays for an audience eager to be soothed rather than challenged—an ideal theatre for the Thatcher/Reagan/Bush age.

Both audiences and actors are in a state of extreme euphoria at the conclusion of both these long evenings, largely because the director, Terry Hands, has wrapped the plays in banners and flags, thereby smothering their deeper, darker energies. *Cyrano* is all rodomontade and smoke effects, *Much Ado* simply grandiloquence and elocution. The vocal and visual pageantry is attractive, but like Christian de Neuvillette's good looks it hides a vacant soul. Where is the effort to penetrate character or investigate text? And what has happened to the company's ensemble ideals? *Nicholas Nickleby* was consumer theatre, but at least we saw good actors in a variety of roles. Here two "stars"—Derek Jacobi and Sinead Cusack—dominate the major parts, while the supporting players are often cast to type: the villain De Guiche playing the villain Don John; the clown Montfleury playing the clown Dogberry, etc. We are back in the barnstorming tradition of nineteenth-century Romantic theatre, not a theatre devoted to stretching its actors or pushing forward the boundaries of the stage.

Jacobi is possessed of apparently unquenchable energy; he is also intelligent, good-natured, and likable, particularly in that swaybacked war-horse *Cyrano*, where a lack of genuine histrionic depth is not likely to be perceived. He can't be entirely faulted for playing so much to the house, so little to his fellow performers, considering how he has been cast and directed—and how the audience is being encouraged to applaud his entrances, exits, even his set speeches. Jacobi first came to attention in this country in a TV series as the reticent stammering Emperor Claudius. Reticence is no longer among his stage virtues. True, the posturing role of Cyrano, a character barely off stage a moment after a delay designed to raise our blood pressure for the entrance of a star, is not designed for a modest actor. Supreme in all he attempts, whether poetry, drama, swordsmanship, warfare, astronomy, or braggadocio, "the three Musketeers, Jesus Christ, and Don Quixote all in one," he has but one imperfection (if you discount his impossible nobility)—his nose. An ugly exterior concealing a mighty soul is a popular motif of sentimental drama—in the next century we'll get *The Elephant Man*. But the notion of a Superman possessed of a single flaw is one that belongs in the comic books or the operettas of Friml and Lehar. Jacobi warbles the required arias effectively in a vigorous barking tenor voice, and bites into the plot with full conviction. But he does little to disguise the creakiness of the story or the fake heroics of the central character.

What surprises me is that the audience doesn't care. I am not invulnerable to the charms of this nineteenth-century salute to the age of Louis Quatorze, but I would think that even in our jingoist time a new version would look hard at a hero who has no trouble defeating a hundred ruffians single-handed, or surviving mortal wounds ("It's nothing, it's a scratch"), or daily risking his life to send off a love letter he has written for the vacuous Christian. And what about Roxane, the narcissistic postdebutante who falls for Christian's looks, and then threatens to blow him off because his language is not hyperbolic enough to poeticize love or flatter her beauty? Is she blind not to notice Cyrano dying of a head wound, dropping tears and blood all over his letter, and staggering around the stage like a gored bull? Is she deaf or just simpleminded not to recognize the voice that heated her blood so many years before?

Sinead Cusack plays this role and plays it poorly. It's not just that she's too old for Roxane and a little too frumpy, but that her hoarse simpering delivery substitutes winsomeness for character—an attention to diction rather than depth that makes her sound like Liza Doolittle wheezing over phonetics. But the entire production is a technical display, as if Cyrano had persuaded the director nothing mattered but *panache*. When Hands is not tarting up the battle scenes with smoke pots, fanfares, and colored gels, or underlining tearful climaxes with a humming male chorus, he is sailing dead leaves down from the flies and moving nuns around in pretty formations. In his death scene, Cyrano waves his white plume and calls for "defunctive music." You may recognize the homage to T. S. Eliot; there are more frequent nods to Shakespeare ("Oh that this too too solid nose would melt"). Along with Anthony Burgess's new version, the acting also anglicizes Rostand's text; aside from the usual Oxbridge aristocrats and Cotswold rustics, the Gascons speak in broad Scottish accents. There are well-staged sword fights, movable chandeliers, and lots of bustling crowd scenes. In the unlikely event you've never seen this play, you'll find the production lavish, animated, theatrical. Otherwise, you may wonder just what compelled the RSC to refurbish this antique cannon for yet another assault on the barricades.

Much Ado about Nothing is distinguished by Ralph Koltai's beautiful setting—a high-tech exterior of transparent and reflective mirrors decorated with burnished etchings of Japanese trees. At the very beginning, a striking female cellist sits on a bench beside the tree and plays some mournful music. It is a lovely moment. Nothing in the production ever matches it. One major difficulty is that the purpose of the setting is never established. One anticipates a new avenue into the play; what one gets is just another pretty decoration, later embellished with revolving balloons and twinkling stars. But where are we? And who are all these people? The costumes seem like seventeenth-century Italian and Spanish adaptations, and the period dances are performed with masks and swordplay (a new RSC principle—when in doubt, fence). But nobody has troubled to investigate why Shakespeare set his play in Messina or what may lurk under the surface of the wit contests, horseplay, and melodramatic confrontations.

Again, the performers don't help, for all their elegant speech. Jacobi and Cusack as Benedick and Beatrice bitch at each other sharply but strike no erotic sparks, and Claudio and Hero never display any special reason for wanting to get married. It is a case of actors who clearly prefer to tell than kiss. The vowels are properly placed and the profiles effectively displayed—but I waited in vain for a single moment of surprise or revelation beneath the polished display of ornament and appearance. Terry Hands lights the set beautifully, however, especially in the autumnal conclusion, which turns the stage burnt umber. And it must be said the little concluding dance between the lovers left the audience roaring.

I don't enjoy being severe about productions so admired by critics and spectators, but I can't remove from mind images of Brook's *King Lear* and *Marat/Sade*, Peter Hall's *War of the Roses* cycle, and that great company of forceful, searching RSC actors that included Ian Holm and Paul Rogers and Anthony Howard and Janet Suzman. Why, Trevor Nunn himself was responsible in 1965 for the most penetrating *Henry V* in memory. Under his current leadership, however, a serious falling off must be acknowledged, not just in depth but in the very definition and purpose of the theatre. What accounts for this? Perhaps just the pressure of an age that prefers positive thinking to

critical investigation, technical expertise to emotional depth, complacent fabrications to truthful revelations, soothing appearances to bleak
realities. It is an age in which we are all forced to be tourists
vacationing in the past for nostalgic escape, and the theatre is fashioning pleasant fantasies to match it.

OLIVIER'S LEAR

(King Lear)

   When Laurence Olivier last played King Lear, at the age of thirty-
nine, he was reportedly too young for the role. Now he is essaying the
part again at the age of seventy-five, and, alas, he is too old.
Backbreaking for actors, Lear has the potential to break the hearts of
audiences, and Olivier has wrenching moments when his eyes turn
inward toward some interior landscape of old age and death. But there
is also unintended heartbreak in watching the mighty will of this
afflicted man battering vainly against his feeble frame. Full of courage
and majesty, Olivier's performance is ultimately too weak to capture
the high ground of the part, and Shakespeare's play is overshadowed
by the drama of a very great actor making a valiant but generally
ineffectual assault on his own physical limitations.

   Olivier elected to play this role in a television production directed
by Michael Elliott. Reputedly the most expensive production ever
made for British TV, this *King Lear* looks tacky. On the Museum of
Broadcasting's large screen, at least, it displays the muted orange-and-
browns of faded Ektachrome stock. And although the play is about
nature gone mad, it has been wholly shot in the unnatural confines of
a Granada studio. Clumsy sets by Roy Stonehouse attempt to repro-
duce a ninth-century Stonehenge of mists and fogs (the plaster
dolmens are not even arranged in a Druid circle), while Tania
Moiseiwitsch's surprisingly mundane leather and woolen costumes
could have been designed for Cecil B. DeMille.

The star is supported in this venture by a brilliant cast, some of them, like Robert Lang, Colin Blakeley, and Diana Rigg, alumni of Olivier's National Theatre at the Old Vic, others, like John Hurt and David Threlfall, among the more interesting actors of the younger generation, the rest, like Leo McKern and Dorothy Tutin, solid journeymen of the classical English stage. None of them is ever less than accomplished, but they often seem to be weighed down by their costumes, floundering in a production that lacks an overall conception or integrated style.

Elliott, a gifted director of Ibsen, appears stiff and routine when interpreting Shakespeare, his reverence for Olivier apparently having sapped energies that might have helped to shape the other performances. As a result, the supporting actors often function as Lear's admiring audience rather than his subjects or enemies. The faces of the men, when not buried under crepe hair and spirit gum (the close-ups are particularly unkind to wig joins), are unaccountably well scrubbed, while the women tend to drip tears over their cheeks, lips, and cobra brooches. Leo McKern's jolly Gloucester, with his Father Christmas rotundity and cabbage nose, would be more appropriately cast as Falstaff. David Threlfall's Edgar recalls the dystrophic Smike he played in *Nicholas Nickleby*. John Hurt acts the Fool as if he were still cooking meals for Ryan O'Neal in *Partners*. Colin Blakeley's Kent, though blunt enough, is too youthful to earn Cornwall's scorn as an "ancient knave," or even (since he disguises himself by shaving his whiskers), Oswald's sneering reference to his gray beard. Dorothy Tutin plays Goneril like a pigeon-breasted headmistress rebuking her naughty charges. And the sugar content of Anna Calder-Marshall's finishing-school Cordelia is enough to inflate the stock of diet Coke. The excellent Diana Rigg turns Regan into a sleek glamorous catwoman who rakes her nails over Gloucester's cheek as if she were sharpening them on a piece of wood. But concentrated though she is, her calculated cruelty is still too civilized for this primitive world.

Sir Laurence, however, remains the epicenter of the production, and it is this epicenter that sometimes fails to hold. When he first appears on the screen, bent with age, his eyes beady as an eagle's, in fuzzy yellow whiskers and a flaxen white wig, your expectations rise, fired by memories, until he opens his mouth to speak, smugly demanding flattery in return for territory. That famous instrument proves to be as grizzled as his beard. Olivier's tenor, always a bit thin, has now become wheezy, high, and squeaky, and he doesn't have the breath to express his anger against Cordelia or, later on the heath, against ungrateful humanity. *Hysterica passio*, that climbing sorrow, never manages to rise. A number of his lines he mangles or misremembers, and often he seems merely to be reciting. Frequently, he resorts to familiar mannerisms, such as glazing his eyes and tightening the lines of his mouth in refelctive moments. And there is something a bit antiseptic about his appearance, especially when he awakes in Cordelia's tent, shaved and barbered, looking a bit like a Hindu guru or that "clean old man" of Beatles fame. Walter Huston would have played this role without his dentures; Olivier takes no great risks either with his appearance or his interpretation.

But the great risk is to play the part at all. After the afflictions of gout, cancer, thrombosis of the leg, and a deteriorating muscular disease—not to mention a decade of cheap demeaning parts in movies and television—to take on Lear is an act of gallantry that compels our admiration, despite the several failures. One feels Olivier pushing himself physically through the production, riding bareback on a horse, letting himself be drenched by buckets of water in the storm scene, slicing up a rabbit on the heath and eating its intestines. The character may not excite our pity and terror, but the actor surely does. And if he doesn't always scale the emotional heights of the role, Olivier is nevertheless extremely affecting in its quieter moments. His mad scenes following the storm are both funny and tender. His reconciliation with Cordelia has a broken delicacy. And his last entrance, howling like an animal over Cordelia's corpse, recoiling from the rope burns on her neck, proves that even without its thunderous lamentations, *King Lear* remains the greatest play ever written.

The same might be said of this whole *Masterpiece Theatre* evening. The music is out of Mantovani; the blood looks like Chateau Marmont; the raging wind doesn't ruffle the costumes; and the performers rarely act as if they had anything at stake. But to watch this major artist wrestling so bravely with what might be his last major role is to be reminded once again of the nobility of acting.

"THE FASCINATION OF WHAT'S DIFFICULT"

(Peter Hall's Diaries)

At the same time that he is dictating entries into his own diaries each morning at dawn, Peter Hall—newly appointed successor to Laurence Olivier as director of the National Theatre of Great Britain—is reading the diaries of Lord Reith. "A record of egomania and paranoia," Hall observes. "He hated everybody. He used his diary as a means of letting off steam. I wonder if I'm doing the same. . . ." You bet he is. That's how he survived to tell his story. But the astonishing thing about *Peter Hall's Diaries: The Story of a Dramatic Battle* is how the author manages to preserve his humanity under conditions of unbearable stress. Openly retaliating against enemies and detractors, he simultaneously provides a fairly candid assessment of his own failings.

I liked this man a lot more than I expected to from the uproar accompanying the English publication of his book. Hall's diaries are full of blunt characterizations and uncensored opinions, but the vituperation he attracted from friends and foes alike was aroused less by a lack of veracity than of tact. Once having decided to publish his book while still a relatively young man of fifty-three instead of from a venerable or posthumous sanctuary, he was born to trouble as the sparks fly upward. Yet, Hall's decision is understandable, for all its unfortunate consequences. Fleet Street had created such a malodorous image of him and his theatre (a guide on a Thames pleasure boat regularly described the National on the South Bank to passengers as "a monstrosity run by a pig called Peter Hall") that it was imperative, for reasons both personal and professional, he tell his story while his heartbeat was still regular.

Judging from these diaries, virtually everybody in England wanted the National Theatre on the South Bank to fail, and many in the press, in labor, and in the theatre worked hard to make that happen. Entrusted with overseeing the construction of an arrogant new building, after succeeding a man regarded as an inestimable national treasure, Hall encountered delays, overruns, union shutdowns, protests from the disabled, dissension within his own company, and hostility from the directors of smaller theatres who feared an insatiably hungry National would gobble up their subsidies. As a result, the eight years covered in these diaries often read like a protracted nervous breakdown. "How can I ever run the National Theatre and at the same time direct plays without going mad?" asks Hall in a typical passage. "The organisation is at present small, contained, and the problems are nothing like as vast as they will be on the South Bank. And yet I am at the breaking point; very near the abyss . . . an abyss which everybody faces who manages a theatre and tries as well to be an artist." From the very beginning, Hall is aware he is in a storm center and, fearful of burnout, tries to remain philosophical and understanding: "I was no longer the young revolutionary being discovered, I was the Establishment that needed attacking." But his skin remains paper thin, and no amount of self-examination can stop him from wailing reprises of the artistic director's favorite chorus, "What's-It-All-For?"

Hall receives some encouragement and support, particularly from the National Theatre Board and from such loyal colleagues as Ralph Richardson and Albert Finney. But what he more usually encounters is blank enmity. Leading these hostile battalions is the press, which takes every opportunity not only to batter his productions but to assail his character. Hall is not at all reticent about admitting how badly hurt he and his associates are by the criticism. "John [Andrews] asked me how much longer I could continue to take the punishment I was getting at the National, both physically and mentally. I said not much longer; it wasn't worth it. . . . I am in an extraordinarily emotional state. I keep losing control." At the opening of *The Cherry Orchard* (also panned), the warmth of his company almost makes him burst into tears. When a book is published attacking the conduct of the theatre, the *Evening News* runs the headline "A NATIONAL DISASTER" and challenges Hall's qualifications: "God I am low," he writes. "In a way it's my own confidence, my own awareness that people now regard me as some sort of freak, a failure that has been corrupted, that does all the damage."

Not all his days are like this. Hall takes satisfaction from occasional theatrical triumphs, from his knighthood and awards, and from the fact that nothing in the theatre is ever as bad as it seems. Mainly he takes comfort from the growth of his theatrical friends and associates. Continually accused of egomania, power madness, ruthlessness, and coldness, Hall (while hardly a model of humility) is passionately and genuinely devoted to the flowering of artistic talent. Where he can be faulted—he faults himself—is for stretching himself too thin. Obliged to support a number of failed marriages, Hall is always in financial trouble, and at the very moment he should be fully engaged in getting the National on its feet, he is abroad directing films and Broadway plays, when he is not at Glyndbourne staging operas or serving as host of a TV arts program. "Maybe my hubris," he admits, "is to want to try everything." But this isn't hubris so much as an incapacity to submerge his own career drives beneath the overpowering needs of his theatre, and that in turn suggests, for all his labor and suffering on behalf of the National, some component of ultimate commitment is missing.

Usually personal and envenomed, the press criticism of Hall is just, I think, when it is directed toward the programs he designed for the Olivier, the largest theatre in his three-stage complex and the one for which he bore sole responsibility. Its repertory shows a marked falling off from Hall's more adventurous work a decade earlier as leader of the Royal Shakespeare Company. Hall is conscious that he has grown more traditionalist, that "the radical questioner I was in the sixties is not what I am now." But he is not always aware that his choices may be influenced more by his new status than by any new aesthetic. Those who charge him with failing to take enough risks are right (Hall dismisses too quickly Michael Billington's interesting statement that the most daring plays often turn out to be the most commercial). Yet, Hall himself is full of contempt for safe theatre, particularly the current musicals. His evaluations of *Evita* ("inert, calculating, camp, and morally questionable"), and of *A Chorus Line* ("kitsch at heart. The girl who desperately wants the job, and shouldn't get it, does of course get it. Otherwise the show would not be commercial. Bullshit really, reeking of Broadway double standards") and of *Sweeney Todd* ("Gilbert and Sullivan out of Leonard Bernstein—no balls, New York chic") show a marked distaste for middlebrow commercialism. Regarding his own season choices, however, he is considerably less demanding. Capable of scourging Broadway, he expresses an unexamined admiration for such English Broadway totems as Alan Ayckbourne and Peter Shaffer. Preparing to direct *Amadeus* at the National (and later in New York), he declares it "potentially one of the most remarkable plays I have ever read"—an assessment to be compared with Michael Rudman's judgment of it as "the longest record sleeve" in history. Early in the diary, Hall says his proudest achievements lay in having established a standard of speaking and understanding Shakespeare, and creating an ensemble. These, and much more, were his accomplishments at the RSC, not at the Olivier, where despite some brilliant individual productions he never managed to establish a distinctive style or unified company.

For Hall inherited an essentially Establishment institution from Laurence Olivier and did little to transform it into a theatre of world notice. There is vitality at the National. It has attracted actors and directors of considerable stature, including John Gielgud, Ralph Richardson, Paul Scofield, Albert Finney, John Schlesinger, Christopher Morahan, Bill Bryden, and (before they broke with Hall) Jonathan Miller and Michael Blakemore, along with playwrights from every spectrum of English life—right (Tom Stoppard), left (David Hare), and center (Harold Pinter). But a great theatre needs more than a succession of hits—it requires an identity and a mission, and this the National has signally failed to achieve. Perhaps one has no right to ask such things of a bastion of British pride and tourism. Perhaps Hall followed the only realistic path, given the financial needs, nationalistic expectations, and artistic exigencies imposed on the theatre from the outside. But Jonathan Miller's caustic description of the new building as a "concrete Colditz" is its most fitting epitaph, and Hall often seems less a free artist than another POW imprisoned within its dungeon walls.

Hall himself seems to admit this tacitly when, in the midst of the turmoil and frustration he is invited to the United States and asked to take over the Juilliard school. Comparing the "luxurious and handsome, well-appointed and clean" stages of the school with his own "already run-down, ill-maintained South Bank building," Hall finds himself tempted to take the job—along with the potential artistic directorship of the Vivian Beaumont at Lincoln Center (he spells this "Vivienne" Beaumont—a portent of how he might have anglicized the entire operation). That Hall would consider giving up what is arguably the chief theatre post in the English-speaking world in order to run an American training program, not to mention the job of wrestling with the whitest elephant outside the confines of the Ngorongoro crater, suggests a profound disaffection from his present work, which his rivals always consider a seat of enviable satisfaction. But the entire book documents the punishment Hall suffered in building his theatre. This makes it an invaluable record of the costs exacted of people who try to make culture.

By far the juiciest passages in these diaries, the passages that will doubtless command the most attention, are Hall's reflections on his contemporaries. For those like me with a passion for theatrical gossip, Peter Hall will stand as a clear-eyed source of insight and information about a horde of British celebrities, their motives and their characters. "I'm often astonished," he writes, "how some people whose whole life is devoted to an art form which . . . is meant to encourage human beings to behave better to each other and be more humane, can personally on occasion be such shits: public moralists and private shits." Yet, despite this harsh conclusion and despite considerable provocation, Hall's judgments are rarely cruel or fundamental. Toward old associates like Peter Brook ("one of my few real friends") he is unflaggingly loyal. And his tintypes of those amiably eccentric knights, John Gielgud and Ralph Richardson, are warm and loving. About Olivier he is guarded, largely because his predecessor, who did not participate in his appointment or apparently approve of it, behaved a little like the banished Coriolanus or the sulking Achilles, though it is understandable why a dethroned king would not be eager to cooperate with a regime that had usurped his place. Such siblings as Jonathan Miller and Michael Blakemore, reinforcing my sense that English directors are the most competitive in the world, actively worked to dislodge Hall. And Kenneth Tynan, whom Hall immediately fired upon assuming the directorship, suggested to a variety of American and English newspapers that the National would be better run by a scholar or a critic.

Hall's analysis of theatre, and of the plays he is directing, often assumes the status of criticism, if not of scholarship. He is incisive on the subject of Tyrone Guthrie ("a director whose technique I idolized, but whose work—because of its aridity—I finally hated"). And he is less awed than Tynan and other critics by Noel Coward ("His talent did in some sense become disconnected from reality. Too much showbusiness camp, I suppose. You can't live off the theatre"). His discussions of *Hamlet*, of the *Oresteia*, of *The Cherry Orchard*, and of *Tamburlaine*, among the countless works he directed, are sharp and original. And he remains the final expert on the plays of his closest collaborator, Harold Pinter.

The break with Pinter, a direct result of these diaries, is therefore all the more saddening. Nothing Hall writes about his friend is ever less than affectionate and admiring, but Pinter, whose affair with Antonia Fraser was hardly a hidden subject of British journalism, apparently felt betrayed when it was mentioned by Hall. Such reticence should not be hard for Hall to understand. Open as he is about the private lives of others and his current psychological state, he always remains extremely oblique about his own domestic status—by contrast with Olivier's memoirs, which are often explicit on the subject of his marital crises and sexual inadequacies. It is only in the final pages of the book that Hall admits he has been living with another woman and his marriage has been going on the rocks. Although he prides himself on keeping his diary "professional and unpersonal," Hall is not so chary about invading the privacy of others.

Still, that's an issue for his colleagues to quarrel about and his readers to enjoy. The diaries unquestionably benefit from their author's free-swinging, uncorseted exposures. It will be some time, I suspect, before anyone describes so movingly the dark shades of *Schadenfreude*, the pleasure in the failure of others, that color all theatrical endeavor, or so dramatically relives the constant anguish of running a large theatrical institution in an arena populated with matadors from the press and picadors from the profession. Somewhere in his chronicle, Hall quotes the last lines of Yeats's "The Fascination of What's Difficult" (verses that I—another veteran of theatre wars—once cited in another prematurely published memoir). They are worth repeating here:

> My curse on plays
> That have to be set up in fifty ways,
> On the day's war with every knave and dolt,
> Theatre business, management of men.
> I swear before the dawn comes round again
> I'll find the stable and pull out the bolt.

Those in this country calling for a national theatre modeled on the one the embattled Hall is still trying to run in England might do well to look upon the human ruins described in his book—and despair.

THE INFIDELITY PLAY

(Benefactors)

When the curtain rose at the Brooks Atkinson Theatre on Michael Frayn's new and highly acclaimed *Benefactors*, my blood froze. Addressing the audience were Sam Waterston and Glen Close, two accomplished American actors, speaking in those simulated British cadences that are swiftly becoming the national language of the Broadway stage. Miss Close, through recent practice in a long run of *The Real Thing*, was considerably better drilled in her consonants and vowels than Mr. Waterston. But even to compare them this way suggests the issue that distracted me. Broadway theatre is now so dominated by West End hits and English revivals that our actors must be evaluated less on the basis of emotional power or interpretive depth than their facility with dialects and capacity to project sangfroid.

There's not a hell of a lot more to act in *Benefactors* than sangfroid and dialect. Michael Frayn is already being compared with Chekhov, whom he has translated and adapted. But this is to confuse a journalist with a poet. While *Benefactors* is admittedly a more human product than that intricately manufactured, clackety-clacking apparatus of his called *Noises Off*, it is still the work of an artificer rather than an artist. An editorialist by nature, Mr. Frayn appears to have written a lead article about the evils of social engineering—and it is nice to welcome a play with some kind of public dimension. But the piece is really another story of marital treachery on the order of Pinter's *Betrayal*, Stoppard's *The Real Thing*, and Nichols's *Passion*. The English are apparently becoming obsessed with infidelity dramas about the woes of exchanging wives and husbands, a subject that originated in the plays of Noel Coward, the father of modern English drama. But its lukewarm blood is more appropriate in the veins of a wit comedy, such as in *Design for Living*, than in these well-made domestic dramas about the guilty conscience accompanying successful careers.

Chekhov, too, occasionally wrote about sexual infidelity *(The Seagull)* not to mention adultery, both actual *(Three Sisters)* and failed

(Uncle Vanya). But his purpose was to reveal character, not to wallow publicly in remorse of conscience. And when he dealt with social issues such as the breakdown of classes or the future of progress, he took no sides. "I am not a liberal and not a conservative," he wrote, "not an evolutionist, nor a monk, nor indifferent to the world. I would like to be a free artist—and that is all." Significantly, he added that "the artist should not be a judge of his characters . . . let the jury pass judgment on them." Frayn, on the other hand, is continually manipulating his people into one artificial contrivance or another, since they exist to illustrate a predetermined theme rather than to display a free and independent life of their own.

The theme is announced in the opening remarks to the audience (half the play is audience-directed narrative). David, an architect, tells us he has landed "one of those great slum-clearance jobs" and is going to build a new world for low-income people in Basuto Road. The rest of the play chronicles the degeneration of this urban rehabilitation ideal as a result of rules, ordinances, cables, gas leaks, bad concrete, politics, and ego drives. David's wife, Sheila—an anthropologist in "Basutoland," interviewing the very people David is building for—is bemused about his goals. His friend, a baleful down-and-out journalist named Colin, is actively hostile to them. Colin's wife, Jane, looks on David as some kind of domestic and social savior. As each couple gets increasingly intrigued with the other's spouses, David becomes more obsessed with building skyscrapers than with helping the poor. Colin joins the squatters protesting these master-builder grandiosities, using his journalistic skills to invent anti-high-rise slogans ("Don't scrape the skies, just sweep the streets"). Following the obligatory domestic confrontations, where Jane twice throws a bowl of brown stew in her husband's face, the entire scheme is rejected by the ministry, leaving the four characters to reflect on the human issues: "It was people. That's what wrecks all our plans—people."

Well, as T. S. Eliot would say, that was one way of putting it—not very satisfactory. A sociological study in a worn-out convention. Michael Blakemore has been commissioned to give some active life to this set of architectural disquisitions and marital squabbles, and he does so with a Tupperware production as smooth and enameled as the play. Michael Annals's all-wooden design consists largely of two rooms against a South London skyline—the decaying parlor of Colin and Jane and the little Switzerland kitchen of David and Sheila—

everything but the dishware in shades of brown. The characters mime eating and walk through invisible walls, usually to punctuate a witty speech. The presence of children is suggested by occasional references and crayon drawings on the wall. The three Americans in the cast often seem more British than the single Englishman (Simon Jones), though only Sam Waterston, hangdog and stumbling as David, seems more uncomfortable. Glen Close brings her patented womanly warmth to the part of Sheila, and Mary Beth Hurt has a nice intense doggedness as Jane. Simon Jones, who looks like a crumpled seedy Gene Kelly, uses a tenor voice at the tonal level of Spike Milligan's (one half step higher and he'd be on *The Goon Show*). In short, another British victory in a theatre on the verge of surrender, interesting only for the way it shows the Reagan-Thatcher disdain for social action entering the consciousness of writers for the stage.

THE BRITISH HAVE COME! THE BRITISH HAVE COME!

Not every play that opens in New York these days is written by an English dramatist or performed by English actors—it just appears that way. The British invasion of our shores, a beachhead in the seventies, now seems to have turned into a full-scale occupation, what with *The Real Thing* and *Noises Off* playing to capacity houses, and Ian McKellen's Shakespeare show packing them in downtown. What the English promise our sorely tried commercial theatre owners is a comforting dependability. Critics and audiences alike can be confident they will be watching technically accomplished acting, eloquent playwriting, directing that is elegant and assured. Whatever social or economic convulsions have rocked England lately, English society has managed to remain essentially stable, and that social stability continues to be reflected in English theatre.

It is particularly reflected in the *prose* of English theatre, which ever since Congreve has been Britain's most formidable theatrical instrument. Americans have always admired the way educated English people speak, probably because our own speech is often a compound of stammers, clichés, regionalisms, and syntactical blunders—"the native eloquence," O'Neill called it, "of us fog people"—when it is not a confession of inarticulacy ("you know what I mean?") or of imprecision ("like, man, ya know?"). But English diction provides more than aesthetic pleasures—BBC and Oxford accents are the identifying marks of the English cultured classes. As Shaw demonstrated in *Pygmalion*, speech is even more instrumental than money for marking the boundaries of a rigid system. No wonder language figures so importantly in contemporary English drama, and is now the envy of so many wayfarers through Shubert Alley.

I persist in the heretical opinion that the mounting English influence on the American stage, especially its linguistic emphasis, is not an altogether salutary one, except in momentarily filling a Broadway vacuum. It is a fact that the genuine breakthroughs in contemporary theatre have not been made on the West End or even in the English repertory companies, but rather in the work coming from America and the Continent—from Eastern Europe (particularly Poland and Rumania), from Germany, and from France in the hospitality extended by that country to such American experimental artists as Robert Wilson and (in a paradoxical reversal) to one of the few great English stage innovators, Peter Brook. Some of this Continental theatre has been seen here, and mildly appreciated, in the lofts of La Mama or at Brooklyn Academy of Music festivals. But aside from Brook's *Carmen*, it has yet to arouse our mainstream audiences and arbiters, who instead pay homage to virtuoso acting techniques and proclaim the verbal acrobat Tom Stoppard one of the leading dramatic artists of our time.

A few seasons back it was Peter Shaffer, and before that it was Terence Rattigan and Christopher Fry. Broadway has always needed overseas constellations for its pantheon of shooting stars. The current anglicizing of New York theatre, however, has not only worked to exclude the best work emanating from Europe, but has also managed to eclipse our native traditions. Even such established American playwrights as Miller, Williams, and Albee are usually unable to keep a new play running on Broadway, while the younger dramatists, including Shepard and Mamet, are produced mostly off-Broadway or in the resident theatres. Meanwhile, a whole generation of American actors find continuous employment only by cultivating their English accents. I don't object to this for xenophobic reasons, but rather because the English tilt puts us in danger of celebrating skill instead of inspiration. England can boast of many powerful playwrights—Edward Bond, Caryl Churchill, David Hare, and (for all my cavils) Harold Pinter—and any healthy theatre owes them a hearing. But the most popular models of English theatre on our stage today are usually celebrated for showy rhetoric rather than for any interior strength or beauty.

If I may invoke the *Poetics* for a moment (still the touchstone of dramatic theory), Aristotle did not rate language very high when listing the elements of comedy or tragedy. First he cited *mythos* (usually translated as plot, but more accurately the action of the myth); then *ethos*, or character; then *dianoia*, or thought—and only then did he discuss the importance of *lexis*, or diction. In a truly great play, *Oedipus* for example, these elements are inseparable. But when one of them begins to dominate, it creates an imbalance that robs the drama of its wholeness. Linguistic brilliance alone is hardly the sign of a great writer, yet (perhaps out of embarrassment over our own general inarticulacy) we Americans praise most highly those English playwrights who display the most style. Even Shakespeare is usually honored less for his emotional power or thematic cogency than for his "poetry," though Shakespearean verse functions as a medium for action and character and theme, not a decorative end in itself. Those who listen only to his "poetry" may be missing his true music.

A young Fulbright scholar in the fifties, I once applied to Oxford and Cambridge to do research on a thesis investigating what historical changes accounted for the changes in theatre between Shakespeare's age and the ages that followed. What transformed the English *dramatis personae* from redskins into palefaces? Why did such appetitive characters as Sir John Falstaff and Sir Epicure Mammon give way to such effete epigrammatists as Sir Fopling Flutter and Sir Wilfull Witwoud? What happened in English cultural history to suppress Elizabethan comic lustiness and tragic rage? Understandably, both universities angrily rejected this insolent proposal from an impertinent and presumptuous young American, and the thesis never got written—but these were the same questions being asked by such radical English writers as William Blake and D. H. Lawrence.

I suspect we might find the answers in the Puritan revolution and the Cavalier reaction. But more important than discovering the root of the problem is persuading people it exists, since the symptoms are now occurring here. The reception of *The Real Thing*, for all its lip service to emotional relationships, consolidates the triumph of wit over substance, and will undoubtedly inspire hosts of imitations both here and abroad. Erika Munk, writing in the *Village Voice*, has ascribed its success to a profound political conservatism, and I believe she is right. When the theatrical revolution created in the fifties by the angry young men was overthrown with the Labour government (even John Osborne turned into a Tory crank), the mainstream theatre once again became the plaything of Mayfair gentility, reflecting the political leanings of a Thatcher generation weaned on the Falklands war, nuclear buildups, racialism, and the dismantling of the welfare state. Needless to say, the Reagan generation has been working toward the same goals and applauding the same theatre. The cocktail dip smeared over the features of the badly mannered prole in *The Real Thing* is a custard pie heaved in the face of all that unpleasant political dissent we were forced to endure in the sixties and seventies, while the elegant language of the play functions as a rebuke to the harsh obscenities and crude epithets of recent radical drama.

But Stoppard's conservatism has aesthetic as well as political implications. It represents a return to pastime theatre, where each line of dialogue is a carefully manufactured display of wit, where the only pressing issue is how to get in bed with your lover without alerting your spouse. Adultery among the leisure classes has been a staple of the English theatre since Charles II was restored to the throne in 1660. But whereas Congreve, Gay, and Wilde were able to handle this subject while smuggling in deeply subversive social themes, it is now—as it was before with Noel Coward—an occasion for facile amusement, for celebrating the status quo. Many playwrights from England, the United States, and Europe will no doubt soon be responding, either directly or indirectly, to these artificial theatre conventions. But at the moment, Stoppard has gained the field and enjoys the admiration of a society complacent and secure, unwilling to confront the issues that are eating away at its roots, if not threatening its very existence.

Prospects from Abroad

COMPARING THEATRICAL RESOURCES

(Peer Gynt)

It is unsettling for American theatre people to visit Europe. It makes us too conscious of our limited resources. It's not that European theatre is more original than ours, rather that the European state is so lavish in the way it helps to stimulate and realize artistic adventures. What a pang one feels upon seeing a plaque above a box office reading, "This theatre entirely subsidized by the City of Amsterdam," or "This production largely funded by the Arts Council of Great Britain." Even after cuts, European arts budgets are still fat by contrast with that of the anorexic National Endowment, for the arts abroad are still considered a priority of the national life.

Besides subsidizing its own theatres, Europe is very supportive of ours. Provided they can find their way over, American experimental groups invariably receive more acclaim in foreign cities than at home; there they also receive more funding. The Nancy Festival in 1981 is almost entirely devoted to American experimentation; the Festival d'Automne and Avignon are both underwriting the Mabou Mines.

The latest opera of Philip Glass is commissioned not by the doyens of the Met but by Willy Hoffman of the Rotterdam Theatre Foundation, while Holland is also responsible for the world premiere of the Glass-Wilson *Einstein on the Beach*.

The respect Europeans show toward our artists, however, is not extended to our government, whose notorious indifference to the arts is considered infamous and barbaric. The Netherlands has been trying to create an arts festival in 1982 celebrating two hundred years of Holland-American relations; if it doesn't happen, it's because we're not contributing our share. The State Department has little interest in cultural exchange except for exporting folksy images of happy Americans that will make satellite peoples envious (typically, *Our Town* in the Soviet Union). For us, artists are useful largely as salesmen for the system. France, by contrast, with a Socialist government in office, is increasing its support not for its conservative national monument, the Comédie Française, but rather for such experimental avant-garde groups as the Théâtre Gerard Phillipe in the Marxist suburb of St. Denis, on the implicit assumption that cultural achievements are measured not by embalming the past but by exploring the future.

These advances are presently on view at the Théâtre de la Ville, where Patrice Chereau's extraordinary production of Ibsen's *Peer Gynt* is now electrifying Paris. If you were dazzled by the resources of the British theatre as displayed in the Royal Shakespeare Company production of *Nicholas Nickleby*, you will find this French achievement absolutely blinding. Here it is not the acting that inspires envy; it is the direction and the decor. The company—Roger Planchon's Théâtre National Populaire—is solid and workmanlike, if a little declamatory in the usual French classical style. But Chereau, previously celebrated mostly for opera production (particularly his innovative approach to the *Ring* cycle at Bayreuth), has used these actors to create an entirely engrossing, absolutely novel interpretation of a play that has hitherto eluded even the most imaginative directors.

Peer Gynt lasts six and a half hours and is performed on two successive days. Unlike that other theatrical endurance test, *Nicholas Nickleby*, the tickets are reasonably priced at about fifteen dollars, thanks to state subsidy. Also thanks to state funds, Chereau has created—with his brilliant design collaborator, Richard Peduzzi—a mammoth architectural construction on the immense stage of the Théâtre de la Ville that looks like a universe in transition. Chereau does not believe in subtle set changes. In the dim half-light, where the figures of the actors are further obscured by continuously belching smoke pots, drops are noisily lifted at the same time that others come crashing down to signify a change in scene. Flats move laterally on stage to the accompaniment of an incessant sound track of music, birds, cries, beast shrieks. If Ibsen suggests the presence of an animal—the Sultan's horse or the Troll King Daughter's pig—Chereau finds the largest stallion, the fattest porker, in Paris. The Great Boyg is suggested by a painted drop in the middle of the stage, portions of which are eerily raised and lowered as if by the flexing of giant knees. Ase's death scene is staged in an oaken coffin, sunk into a stage trap, which Peer rides like a reindeer. When Peer chops wood, he hacks away violently at one of the wooden pillars of the set, sending splinters into the house and filling the audience with fears that the whole scaffolding might collapse.

Chereau reserves his most spectacular effects for the second part of the program, for Peer's exile and homecoming. When the foreign traders steal Peer's yacht, a miniature ship sails across the back of the stage and blows up in front of our eyes. Ibsen calls for the statue of Memnon, then the Great Sphinx; Chereau provides large-scale versions of both objects, complete with pyramids. The madhouse scene—where Peer is proclaimed Emperor of Self—is a *Marat/Sade* phantasmagoria featuring a mob of whey-faced madmen (one has a decaying infant strapped to his back) who imprison their keepers and ransack the institution. When Peer returns to Norway, Chereau provides the top deck of a ship, complete with rigging, lifeboats, winches, and the illusion of a great storm. When the ship begins to sink, a huge black billowing drop appears (with a bobbing miniaturized craft on top of it), engulfing Peer while the set is changed *beneath* the simulated waves.

The stage effects, in short, are monumental, breathtaking. What is somewhat less impressive are the stage characterizations. For his Peer, Chereau has cast a gaunt, intense actor named Gerard Desarthe, who accomplishes the age changes so convincingly one believes he is four different people. But whatever his genius for transformation, Desarthe lacks the charm, the whimsicality, the mischief, that make Peer such a bright contrast to his vindictive peasant neighbors. Desarthe's Peer Gynt is more Existentialist than Ibsenite—Beckett's Lucky, lankhaired and scarecrowlike, in a Norwegian setting. The Troll

King, similarly, is more orator than sensualist, and the Button Molder looks and acts like one of Ibsen's comfortable pillars of society. Other characterizations are more successful—Solveig, for example, played by Catherine Retore with slightly spastic, hollow-eyed intensity that takes the blight off her saintliness. And the Lean Person (the Devil) is equipped with enormously long fingernails that he clips nervously while informing Peer he is destined for the casting ladle.

Yes, the production is a little operatic, and more than a little declamatory. But it accomplishes something that nobody—least of all Ibsen—ever believed possible: a complete, convincing, totally faithful stage rendering of an epic dramatic poem.

FESTIVAL FEVER

(Avignon: Ankoku Butoh)

Summer is the season for the international theatre festival, when winter-locked companies get the chance to stretch their limbs in foreign territories, and tourists have the opportunity to combine daytime sight-seeing with nightly theatregoing. The international festival is not an indigenous American theatre event. Here the word *Festival* can be found in the names of individual summer theatres (the New York Shakespeare Festival, the American Shakespeare Festival, the Williamstown Festival Theatre) eager to give their shows a "festive" holiday atmosphere. To be more than a magnet for picnickers and shoppers, the festival requires two things not normally found in our culturally primitive, art-pinched land: respect for the ongoing work of permanent companies and generous government sponsorship. Both of these key elements are abundant abroad, however, where ambitious theatre festivals are happening throughout the Orient, South America, and the Mideast, as well as in virtually every nation of Europe.

I've just returned from Avignon, one of the festivals to which my own company was invited in this summer of 1982; it was an exhilarating trip. This ancient town in the South of France, situated on the banks of the Rhône, is the site of numerous Roman and medieval artifacts, including the famous *"pont"* of the children's song (more a piece of sculpture than a bridge—only half of it is standing), also a marvelously preserved encircling wall, and the palaces and cathedrals of the popes who resided in this *cité des papes* after temporarily abandoning Rome in the thirteenth century. Although there is a municipal theatre in the center of town, most festival activity occurs inside the courtyards of such buildings, on wooden scaffoldings that provide temporary seating and a stage. This testifies to an extraordinary faith in the benignity of the climate, which is mostly justified. It rarely rains in Avignon. The only enemy of the performance is the mistral.

The mistral is a wind that comes from the north, blowing with mighty force down the Rhône, customarily lasting for three, six, or nine days (nobody can explain why it comes in progression of threes). When the mistral is blowing, the audience huddles in chilled misery trying to hear the voices of actors above the wailing of the implacable wind, watching the scenery being shredded and whipped by forty-mile-an-hour gusts. An epic eight-hour production of *The Possessed* by a Paris company consisted of a series of doors and windows that the mistral turned into a wrecked construction site, and our own production of *Sganarelle* had to be performed on a bare stage after the wind not only knocked over the set in the courtyard of the Faculté des Sciences but also pulled down an antique piece of stone masonry to which it had been lashed.

There are usually seven or eight companies performing each night in Avignon, along with an even larger number of off-festival events. The central square, the Place de L'Horloge, is alive with activity twenty-four hours a day, being the site of innumerable mimes, musicians, magicians, mountebanks, actors, acrobats, and political demonstrators. All perform free for mobs of people sitting in the outdoor cafés or loitering in the streets. Most of these acts are awful— someone offered a cash prize and a shotgun to the person who could bag the most mimes. But they testify to the magnetic power of the festival in attracting those with theatrical ambitions. The city also attracts many young people, drawn there in part by the availability of drugs. Their dress and behavior recall Berkeley and Harvard Square in the sixties. In fact, the Avignon summer seems like a hippie paradise until you come upon someone lying facedown in the streets, or sitting forlornly on a corner, wearing a sign that says, *J'ai faim.*"

But the hunger for theatre is the prime motivating appetite of the Avignon Festival, and it is satisfied in a variety of ways. I arrived too late to see Mnouchkine's productions of *Richard II* and *Twelfth Night*, which were generally well received. But *The Possessed* and our own productions aside, the performances that made the most impact on the festival came from Japan. One was a marionette company playing at the Théâtre Municipal, the other a dance company across the river at the Cloître du Cimetière Chartreuse in Villeneuve.

This was the Dairakuda Kan, an ensemble that describes itself as a "movement of revolt" in opposition to such classical Japanese dance and theatre styles as Kabuki and Noh. The revolt seems to be an outgrowth of the "student fever" of the late sixties in Japan. It is not just aesthetic, it is also political, organized around a principle of rejection that includes all American cultural influences, not to mention the Japanese-American security pact. In repudiating both its own heritage and the culture of the West, the Dairakuda Kan is compelled to invent an entirely new imagery of grimace and gesture—presocial, futuristic, subterranean. Its major work, *Ankoku Butoh*, or *The Dance of the Shades*, is a nonverbal piece performed to the accompaniment of a variety of musical forms. Despite the manifesto, most of this music is Western, and features rock-and-roll, electronic sounds, and medieval ballads. Choreographed by its leader and chief dancer, Maro Akaji, *Ankoku Butoh* is a relentless, almost unbearable charade of agony and bondage, a choreographic fantasy inspired by the Hiroshima trauma, a dance essay on the character of survival after the blast.

Ankoku Butoh was played in Purchase and New York City last season. But I doubt if it ever had a more paradoxical historical setting than the Villeneuve Chartreuse, where, in a vast monastic courtyard looking out on a perspective of a medieval fortress, bulwarks of Occidental religious faith are assaulted by images of Oriental nihilism and despair. The abstract scenery consists of redwood panels and a single circular altar filled with a white pasty substance. This might be the pancake makeup that the company wears on its first appearance, as the cadaverous dancers enter naked, holding a rope between their teeth, the men hairless and pierced with arrows, their fingers working like spastic plants. An electronic wail shatters your ears as they move together with painful slowness in a group display of torture and imprisonment. In subsequent scenes, the tiny female dancers, their pupils covered with red lenses, their mouths agape in a toothless parody of merriment, perform a charade of schoolchildren as abandoned, mutilated ghosts; a hefty servant in an incredibly dusty kimono swirls about the stage in circles raising clouds of powder; four male dancers, black from head to foot except for gold painted designs on their faces, navigate around mobile gunnysacks that soon transform into little white-faced girls wearing pink dresses and red hair bows. This grim parody of happy times is followed by a demonstration of the death of the gods (I was reminded of a similar sequence in the Auden-Bernstein ballet, *The Age of Anxiety*): Akaji himself, wearing a huge black wig and walking laboriously on mammoth stilts, is gradually reduced in size and stature until he collapses in ruins on the floor.

The company is wonderfully disciplined and original, but the evening is so remorseless, so monochromatic in its grotesque vision of the nuclear future, that it eventually relinquishes its force. It is the mission of Dairakuda Kan to obliterate all our hopes about subsequent generations, and for a three-hour period it succeeds in this grim task. But it pays an aesthetic price, and even its relentless purpose is eventually controverted by the balmy atmosphere of southern France. One must respect these images of the Hiroshima trauma, but it is impossible not to acknowledge also the pure starry vault under which this vision is enacted—the sweet air, the grace of the architecture, the happy crowds, the bustling streets, the whole intoxicating world of Avignon that offers such rich pleasures to the senses and the imagination.

THE QUEST OF PETER BROOK

(L'Os; Ubu Roi; The Ik)

Let me preface my sense of disappointment over Peter Brook's recent forays at La Mama E.T.C. with an expression of admiration for the way this man of the theatre has conducted his career. No one associated with the British or American stage has proved as daring or original—or so restlessly dissatisfied with his own achievements. Brook staged plays with the Royal Shakespeare Company that are still considered models of classical reinterpretation (just consider how conventional the RSC became after his departure). Brook could have remained with this company for the rest of his life, turning out productions of great distinction. There are some (and I'm among them) who wish he had. But something in this man is continually goading him into new departures. And *Le Centre International de Créations Théâtrales*, the international company he has been developing in Paris, represents Brook's attempt to evolve a whole new form of theatre, as radical a break with his RSC productions as *Marat/Sade* was with his Broadway production of *The Little Hut*. To turn away from successful patterns requires singular courage and vision. Brook has them both in abundance.

Having said this, I am also obliged to say that, in my opinion, Brook's quest for new adventures has not yet been followed by very interesting discoveries. Of the three Brook offerings at La Mama, I caught all but the most acclaimed, *The Conference of Birds*, though I managed to see an earlier version of this work some years ago at the Brooklyn Academy of Music. By reason of that omission, and because nobody has the right to make fundamental judgements on the work of many years, perhaps it is not appropriate for me to generalize about the work of the *Centre*. Nevertheless, *L'Os*, *Ubu Roi*, and especially *The Ik* struck me as sufficiently similar in conception and confused in direction to justify reflections about what might be wrong with the basic assumptions of the group.

I have two major quarrels, one philosophical, the other aesthetic. First of all, Brook, gifted as he is, is not essentially a creative artist—his strength is as a supreme interpreter. I don't mean to suggest that interpretation cannot be a creative act. I simply mean that Brook's greatest achievements have always been inspired by important texts. Of the current repertory, none of the plays, with the qualified exception of *Ubu*, is distinguished by very strong writing, and the result is that the company lacks a generating or transcendent vision. What Brook needs, in short, is a playwright. Like the Living Theatre, the Performance Group, and (on occasion) the Open Theatre—the ensembles of the sixties that apparently inspired Brook's current work—*Le Centre International* suffers occasionally from its own sultry, self-enclosed atmosphere, where precious theatrical resources are occasionally squandered in the service of a certain social or religious evangelism.

Brook's passion for developing an international community through the unifying means of theatre sometimes makes him seem a little like the Gary Davis of the modern stage—proselytizing for an ideal of world federalism. His disdain for what he calls the "deadly theatre"— meaning the shallow Western pieties of modern bourgeois theatregoing—has encouraged him to concentrate on theatrical transactions that transcend class, race, or national origin. He *has* created with his actors a simulated world community, successfully absorbing Orientals, French, Americans, Africans, and his English wife, Natasha Parry, into a single unit. But international audiences can be unified only by a very basic language with a very limited vocabulary. The farce vocabulary of *Ubu* being relatively universal, this play communicates fairly well (though I've seen *Ubu* better performed by the kind of Western actors for whom it was written). But when Brook gets into African ritual and primitive anecdotes, a faint touch of condescension begins to taint the edges of his theatrical egalitarianism.

The worst offender of this kind is *The Ik*, a dramatic piece based on *The Mountain People* by the anthropologist Colin Turnbull. Turnbull went to northern Kenya to investigate a tribe that, denied the right to hunt, had been reduced to starvation. Their condition was appalling; they felt nothing for the dead or dying; they were plunged into a deep anomie relieved only by the presence of food. Some of them ate stones; others simply rolled over and died. After observing the tribe for three years, Turnbull reached the conclusion that "those values [love, compassion, unselfishness, loyalty, etc.] which we cherish so highly, indispensable for both survival and sanity . . . are not inherent in humanity at all. They are not a necessary part of human nature."

This observation, though hardly remarkable, is quite moving in the context of the book. In Brook's production, it seems to be turned back on Westerners, many of whom leave the theatre feeling not sympathy over the plight of the Ik so much as guilt over their own full bellies. Turnbull himself is represented as a rather cold-blooded observer who shows little interest in the objects of his scrutiny except as clinical material for his camera or notebook. The only time he intervenes is when he sees a child stealing food out of the mouths of his weakened parents. And when he journeys to the Sudan, he goes there in order to observe what the Ik are like "when they have plenty of food." "Turnbull left in 1966," the narrative concludes. "In 1971, another anthropologist visited the Ik." So much for Western charity, so much for Western compassion.

I found something a bit troubling about this parade of human misery before an audience helpless to do anything about it. And I was disturbed in another way by Brook's production of *L'Os*—a piece based on a story by the North African writer Birago Diop. Played by the company in broad vaudeville style, *L'Os* is a simple tale about what the hero is willing to do for a marrowbone. Like most of Brook's settings, this one consists of a few plain objects, used in a sophisticated manner. And it carries the same implicit message of how privileged we are to witness the simple wisdom of the "little people." Was it possible that with these pieces Brook has created his own form of deadly theatre, which audiences now attended out of social rather than cultural piety?

Alfred Jarry's *Ubu Roi*, on the other hand, has some fine things in it, including a minimal setting composed of two huge storage wheels that work as thrones, chairs, chariots, juggernauts, and the like. It is played mostly in French, with occasional English phrases added ("Who will sew up the seat of your knickers?") to reinforce the absurdity. Only in this piece is Brook's company permitted to show whether they can act or not—a few of them can. I particularly liked Miriam Goldschmidt as Mere Ubu, cross-eyed and rubber faced, and Bruce Myers as Capitaine Bordure, played as an awkward, hump-backed clown. Andreas Katsulas, the only American in the troupe, plays Ubu with a protruding stomach and a rasping voice, providing in energy what he lacks in range. The goofiness occasionally descends into silliness, and the spirit of adolescent clowning occasionally palls. But there are some very funny images in the production—Ubu holding court with a toilet brush, the courtiers being executed by squashing themselves against a wall like flies—which are in happy contrast to the faint liberal condescension of the other plays.

It is easy to understand why Brook was attracted to this early Dadaist romp—it represents a total assault on Western literature, particularly the Shakespeare canon on which Brook cut his director's teeth. Ubu is a kind of monstrous Macbeth, persuaded by his wife to knock off the Polish king, Venceslas, before annihilating everyone else. And there are enough ghost scenes, battle scenes, oath scenes, man-eating bears, and ancestors screaming for revenge to satisfy a dozen productions of *Hamlet* or *A Winter's Tale*. But for all its primitiveness, *Ubu Roi* is the product of a highly sophisticated sensibility, and for all its rejection of European culture, it could only have been produced by the West. The same might be said of its director.

For, ultimately, Brook cannot shake off his inheritance, no matter how much he may despise it. Even his belief that he can is a Western idea, dating from Rousseau. Still, it is not my place to tell him to stop trying. He is in the grip of a powerful Romantic delusion now, but any idea one holds obsessively and long enough takes on its own validity. I don't think Brook has proved his point about the international roots of primitive theatre. But the effort, if not the result, compels respect, for it brings the theatre just a little closer to the serious purpose for which it was first conceived.

COMING AT HISTORY FROM TWO SIDES

(Master Harold . . . and the Boys; Wielpole-Wielpole)

I have often complained that the contemporary stage neglects contemporary history, that it is out of time. But in the course of a single day, it was my privilege to see two inspired theatrical responses to modern circumstances. Coming at history from opposite directions, both of these efforts reveal how provisional is the relationship between the dramatist and contemporary events, especially if the events are to be treated with honesty. Yet, both are signal triumphs, the one as an act of decency, the other as a work of art.

Athol Fugard's *Master Harold . . . and the Boys*, like this South African playwright's other works, is distinguished more by his majestic spirit than by his artistic gifts. Fugard is not a dramatist of the first rank in a class with Beckett, Brecht, or even the late O'Neill—he makes no deep metaphysical probes, he fashions no striking poetic images, he doesn't change our way of looking at the world. His theatrical impulses are similar to those of Jean-Paul Sartre, Arthur Miller, Arnold Wesker—writers who put their craft at the service of an idea. Like them, Fugard is more interested in identifying social injustices and inequities than with transforming consciousness, which is to say that he is less a visionary poet than a man of great liberal conscience. Fugard's conscience, however, is a judicious instrument—scrupulous without being paralyzed, partial without being simplified. He avoids self-righteousness—the customary pitfall of such writing—by acknowledging that he may be implicated in his own indictments. If not the most inspired of contemporary playwrights, he certainly has the greatest heart, which makes him the most attractive character in his plays.

Fugard's compelling subject is the corrosive effect of apartheid on the spirit of South Africa; in *Master Harold*, he may have found his quintessential racial anecdote. The play takes place in a grubby tearoom in Port Elizabeth, tended by two black men, the sedate, dignified Sam and the more slow-witted Willie. After a desultory opening during which Sam advises Willie about a dancing contest, they are joined by Hally, the schoolboy son of the white woman who owns the tearoom. Hally is obviously very fond of Sam, who was a surrogate father to him during his childhood. He just as obviously detests his own father, a crippled, insensate barfly, now preparing to return home after an extended hospitalization. Although Hally believes in social progress and admires humanitarian reformers, the prospect of his father's return triggers extraordinary aggression in him. In the scorching concluding moments of the play, he insists that "the boys" call him "Master Harold," then tells a brutal racist joke and spits in Sam's face.

Though sorely tempted, Sam does not strike Hally. Instead, he exposes him as a coward and a weakling, a creature riddled with self-hatred: "You've hurt yourself, I saw it coming. . . . You've just hurt yourself bad and you're a coward." Sam tries to turn the occasion into a positive learning experience about how one becomes a man; Hally is too ashamed to accept instruction. Sam offers reconciliation; Hally equivocates. The two part with a shared sense of failure and a shared conviction that the dream of racial brotherhood has suffered a damaging, perhaps irreparable blow. The play ends with the two black men locked in each other's arms, inconsolable, dancing to a jukebox tune.

Fugard arranges his anecdote as if he were placing tiles in a mosaic. This sometimes creates an impression of contrivance—twice the phone rings, for example, with information that turns Hally vicious right after he has made fervent humanitarian affirmations. Then, perhaps because Sam's insights into the self-hatred motivating Hally's behavior are so cogent, you are left with a sense that everything has been said, that there is nothing more to be revealed, which robs the evening of ambiguity and suggestiveness. Still, there is no denying the explosive impact of that ending, and Fugard has directed performances from the three players that are muscular and powerful. Casting Lonny Price as Hally may have exposed the author's hand a little prematurely. Price acts the role with sniveling authority, but if he didn't look and behave so much like a weasel from the beginning the shock of the ending might be even greater. As it is, there is no contest, especially when Danny Glover plays Willie with such tender simplicity and Zakes Mokae brings such extraordinary grandeur to the part of Sam.

But the real spiritual beauty of the play comes from Fugard. *Master Harold* seems to be a much more personal statement than his other works. It also suggests that his obsession with the theme of racial injustice may be an expression of his own guilt, an act of expiation. Whatever the case, his writing continues to exude a sweetness and sanctity that more than compensates for what might be prosaic, rhetorical, or contrived about it. At this rate, Athol Fugard may become the first playwright in history to be a candidate for canonization.

Tadeusz Kantor's newest creation with his Cricot 2 group, *Wielpole-Wielpole*, is also an attempt to distill history into dramatic form. Whereas Fugard deals with the African experience, Kantor's world is that of a small town in Poland during World War II. While Fugard writes in conventional realistic style, Kantor pursues radically avant-garde forms, somewhat influenced by Grotowski but nevertheless strikingly original in image and practice. Like the Jacobean John Webster, Kantor has an obsession with death that fixes his eyes on the skull beneath the skin. A companion to his great theatre piece *Dead Class*, *Wielpole-Wielpole* is a savage elegy for an entire race, a dazzling rumination on extinction and destruction in the chaotic nightmare world of modern Europe.

The very simple stage consists of crated wooden flats, a few wooden crosses staked in dirt, and a wooden closet against which Kantor—hollow eyed, ascetic, mournful, looking like a hybrid of Jan Kott crossed with a bloodhound—has draped himself, watching the audience enter. Throughout the performance, he is a conspicuous witness, sometimes entering the action to arrange an actor's hands, or to bring in furniture, or to pick up a fallen prop. Kantor's motives are clearly proprietary; this is his creation and the company has been rigorously trained and rehearsed to embody it. The result is something that not only changes your mind about the capacities of the theatre, but also alters your feelings about the state of being human— a vision so powerful that it competes successfully with what we normally think of as reality.

The inhabitants of Wielpole include nine soldiers, their faces and uniforms putty colored as if they had just been dragged up from their graves; a host of townspeople; and a pair of twins or, more accurately, clones, since they are not only identically dressed in bowler hats and long frock coats, but have identical frontier moustaches, identical gaps in their teeth, identical furrows in their brows. Kantor also makes generous use of dummies, one of them a priest who looks remarkably like Ernest Borgnine. It lies on a bed at the beginning of the play— soon the bed is cranked, revealing a living priest (also a Borgnine double) on the underside. What follows—performed in a spastic, mannequin-like acting style—are episodes from Kantor's remembered life of the town, each culminating in a grotesque parade around the stage to the accompaniment of a rousing two-hundred-year-old Polish marching song.

As in *Dead Class* where the parade of the dead was started up by a haunting waltz called "La Françoise," *Wielpole-Wielpole* uses music as a means of creating excitement, inducing nostalgia, dramatizing historical repetition. Kantor also makes striking use of symbolic props—not only that grim revolving bed, which looks like a torture instrument, but also an ancient metal camera that, when operated by a photographer's widow wearing a ghastly grin, transforms into a lethal machine gun. The most important artifact, however, is a large wooden cross on which the priest is crucified by the soldiers—perpetually, as if an eternal recurrence. Kantor's imagery throughout is essentially religious—the rituals of Christians and Jews alike being annihilated by the atrocities of war. In the climax of the piece, a rabbi in a yarmulke wearing a wooden Hebrew symbol is repeatedly mowed down by machine-gun fire, after which the dead come on stage to enact a sardonic parody of da Vinci's *Last Supper*, complete with naked dummies and the crucified priest.

Kantor folds up the cloth from this supper table and departs, leaving a skeleton in uniform as the final subject of the audience's contemplation. It is a fitting image for the fate of Eastern Europe in modern times—like the entire work, a superb distillation of history, from the hand of a master, in a strikingly original style. To Kantor and his company—and to La Mama's Ellen Stewart, who was instrumental in making the visit possible—we owe an immense debt of gratitude. They have proved that the ancient form called theatre is still capable of generating powerful perceptions and thrilling new styles.

THE TRAGEDIES OF APARTHEID

(Born in the RSA)

On tour myself with a theatre company, I missed *Woza Africa!*, the series of South African productions invited to play at Lincoln Center this fall. Having returned to Boston, I did manage to catch up with one of these presentations, perhaps the most celebrated, *Born in the RSA*. It was playing at the Strand Theatre, a palatial auditorium in poverty-stricken Dorchester, on the night the Red Sox were at Fenway taking their third game. Maybe that's why the theatre was so empty. Where were all those politically engaged students who, protesting university divestment policies, were creating shantytown theatre just last spring on the grounds of their own campus? No doubt back in the dorms with a keg of beer, watching Bruce Hurst put away the Mets.

The Strand is an ornate old house adorned with classical pilasters, Wedgewood ovals, a gilt proscenium, a sculptured circular ceiling— the kind they used to build in the thirties. *Born in the RSA* brought me back to the thirties too. A product of Barney Simon's Market Theatre Company of South Africa, an interracial group that has been working together since 1974, the show revealed seven remarkable acting talents at work, all of them motivated by a profound commitment to social change. I doubt that Americans have seen such indignation on stage since the days of the Theatre Union. What local causes in recent times have ignited theatrical fires of equal intensity? Vietnam? Desegregation? Feminism? Nuclear disarmament? Our social issues may be deeply felt but they rarely inspire similarly impassioned dramatic works.

RSA stands for Republic of South Africa, which makes the title slyly ironic. Whatever the government of South Africa pretends to be these days, it can hardly be called a republic, when the vast majority of black people is being systematically stripped not only of voting rights but of the right to live and work. To be born in such a "republic," the play implies, is to inhabit only three possible roles: oppressor, revolutionary, or passive witness. The play further suggests that to remain neutral in the face of the unspeakable actions of the Botha regime may be the most despicable act of all.

The word "play" is probably inappropriate here. *Born in the RSA* is more like a Living Newspaper, a series of testimonials delivered directly to the audience from a bare stage furnished only with a projection screen and some headline-covered platforms. Created in a collaboration between Barney Simon and the cast of three blacks and four whites, the piece proceeds through a sequence of declarative speeches about what it's like to live out a political nightmare. One by one, the characters introduce themselves: Mia, a middle-aged Jewish lawyer defending the rights of the oppressed ("We all have one thing in common—a desperate need to change the world we live in"); Glen, a white student at Witwatersrand University, recruited by security police to spy on his fellow students; his wife, Nicky, whom he betrays and abandons; Susan, an art teacher "with a fetish for men over six foot one" who becomes the mistress of lanky Glen; Thenjiwe, a female trade union leader running a small activist cell; her sister, a vigorous black woman with a ten-year-old child; and Zach, an unemployed black double-bass player and innocent bystander, transformed into a revolutionary in spite of himself.

The piece has a kind of story, a remorseless one, about the impact of Glen, the apolitical informer, on the lives of the other characters. A tall, weak man with Boer charm and a weakness for rawboned women, Glen advances from turning in his Marxist professor to informing on his own mistress when he finds a pamphlet in her bedroom entitled *Armed Struggle*. This action, pleasing to his superiors, gives him the ultimate high. For him, informing is less a patriotic duty than a personal drug of choice. When Susan leads him directly to Thenjiwe ("the Kaffir girl we've been waiting for"), Glen has them both detained and arrested.

From this point on, much of the play focuses on prison conditions—interrogations, tortures, warden brutality including attempted rape—a catalogue of indignities and injustices that inspire murderous reactions in the characters, not to mention the audience. Nicky attends Susan's trial, only to hear her husband, brought in to testify, identified as "lover Donahue." Her reaction lies somewhere between paralysis and catatonia—she leans against her kitchen stove and consumes a box of Smarties. But the ultimate crime for which the South African government is indicted here is a crime against children. The police have begun arresting black preteens for stoning cars, among them the son of Thenjiwe's sister. They make the children lie under oath, then jail them (Glen defends this with glib asides about American use of napalm). It is the kids who frighten the regime for it is they who will eventually bring it down ("the kids in Soweto stink, man, they stink of victory"). Thenjiwe's nephew is finally released from jail, with Mia's legal help, but not before he has been buggered and brutally beaten. Mia turns on Glen: "All I can see is a nice Kentucky necklace—a huge burning tire around your neck." Susan, spitting in his face, tells him he's not worth the match.

The final scene features Zach, the musician, observing white children at play—a group of little girls in crisp uniforms cavorting in a playground. "Do you know who is watching you?" he asks. "Be careful. They told you to be frightened of me. They were right. Beware of your black nannies too." He moves to the center of the playground and begins cracking skulls with a baseball bat. "I splintered arms and legs and spines. . . . I was everything they wanted me to be." But it is a fantasy. The bell rings to call the children into class, and Zach, watching them depart, hears himself yelling: "Fuck you for what you're doing to our children and fuck you for what you're doing to me." The play ends with the cast singing a half-ecstatic, half-threatening revolutionary song.

The small engaged audience with whom I sat gave the cast numerous curtain calls and a standing ovation. There was no denying the incendiary power of the evening or the accomplishments of the actors. This, with a vengeance, is what Eric Bentley once called "Theatre of Commitment," and it brings us something we haven't seen demonstrated in a long while, how commonly held belief in a cause can fuse individual actors into a close collective. Each performer has gifts of a very high order, along with the capacity to tell a well-rehearsed story as if for the first time, and each is joined in something larger that makes the parts inseparable from the whole. To preserve this collective identity, the actors are not identified by roles in the program. I think it only proper to cite them together in this review without singling any out for individual praise: Vanessa Cooke, Timmy Kwebutana, Neil McCarthy, Geina Mhlophe, Fiona Ramsay, Thoko Ntshinga, Terry Norton.

Yet, I must confess that I did not join the standing ovation and that I left the theatre feeling—despite my admiration for the performers—vaguely manipulated. It is a problem I usually have with the "Theatre of Commitment," no matter how estimable the cause—I recoil from its aura of exclusiveness, its odor of sanctity, its easy flow of self-righteous indignation. Anything that tries to unite people, paradoxically, runs the risk of also dividing them. Performed in a police state like South Africa, I can imagine *Born in the RSA* being received as an act of extraordinary courage as well as a strong insurrectionary instrument—preparation for the uprising that will inevitably come. Performed here, in the United States, it seems to be asking its audiences either to endorse violence or be condemned as inglorious sponges, mute and impassive in the face of evil.

I'm reluctant to accept such a narrow choice of roles, either in life or in the theatre. Also, I share Ivan Karamazov's conviction that there is no greater evil—no greater argument for the absence of God—than inflicting pain on innocent children. The treatment of black children by South African police makes us hate the Botha government. But to retaliate against white children, even in fantasy as Zach does, is to become indistinguishable from the other side. *Born in the RSA* builds a strong case for revenge, for outrage, for bloody reprisals. It assumes that those who favor apartheid or work on behalf of the regime are totally without redeeming features. It suggests that those who do not join the resistance, and even those who leave the country, are somehow identified with the oppressors. These assumptions may be necessary to a revolution, since like all wars, revolutions are built on the patterns of melodrama, conflicts between the forces of good and evil. But they subvert the very function of art, which is committed to a deeper understanding of the human experience. By accumulating injustices and stimulating resentment, *Born in the RSA* serves its activist cause well. But it sacrifices the varieties of art and the complexities of life to the obligatory simplicities of well-intentioned propaganda. Among the manifold tragedies of apartheid, indeed of any totalitarian system, is the way it tends to turn people of good will into victims of restricted vision. But surely there must be other emotional options, even in conditions of extreme circumstances, to those of guilt or rage.

THE STRATFORD DILEMMA

(Waiting for Godot; A Midsummer Night's Dream; Love's Labour's Lost)

To get to the Stratford Festival in Canada you must drive an hour and a half down the highway west from Toronto, past martial-sounding towns named Kitchener and Waterloo and Wellington. It is a little like traveling the M-1 from London, a landscape of graceful hills and proud farms, nodding corn and rolling terrain. When you arrive in the Canadian Stratford, however, you find it considerably more isolated than Stratford-on-Avon and nowhere near as lovely. It's rather stolid, in fact, even a little grubby, despite the presence of an artificial·lake adjacent to the theatre (no swans) and townspeople in white flannels and white dresses bowling on the green nearby. One assumes the festival chose this site because of its name—the same reason the American Shakespeare Festival built a theatre in the industrial area of Stratford, Connecticut. But although audiences continue to flock to this simulated English environment, and the level of the work remains relatively high, the theatre is essentially a tourist attraction with all that implies in regard to cautious play choices and transient audiences.

The festival, moreoever, carries on its back the burden of sustaining the Shakespeare inheritance in a North American culture suspended somewhere between England and the United States (the influence of the French Quebecois is generally ignored). Tyrone Guthrie, who founded this theatre, ducked the problem by importing English stars. But latterly the various Stratford regimes have been seeking solutions that would satisfy the demands of Canadian nationalism without violating artistic imperatives. The results are mixed, in many senses of the word. Under the artistic direction of the Hungarian-born John Hirsch, such expatriated English actors as Brian Bedford and John Neville and Edward Atienza perform side by side with a bevy of actors from Canada and the United States, providing an uncertain range of accents, approaches, styles.

This was most damaging in *Waiting for Godot*, a production in the smaller theatre begun under the direction of the American artist Joseph Chaikin. Dissatisfied with a member of the cast, and perhaps in the initial phase of his recent tragic illness, Chaikin left the show early in rehcarsal. Another director's name appeared in the program, but the production seemed to be rudderless. Playing Estragon and Vladimir were the British-trained actors Edward Atienza and Brian Bedford; two Performance-Group Americans, Paul Zimet and Andreas Katsulas, played Lucky and Pozzo. I was interested to see how the representatives of these different schools of acting would behave without a ship's captain. The English managed to survive by hugging available life rafts. The Americans went to the bottom.

Bedford and Atienza did a good-natured, technically adroit music-hall number that removed the incisors from the play, Didi coming on like Stan Laurel and Gogo like a cuddly pink-eyed Disney animal, possibly a mouse. Katsulas's crude speech and limited emotional range, on the other hand, turned Pozzo into an incomprehensible lout, while Lucky, looking like a fallen Southern aristocrat, seemed inexplicably well scrubbed. The stage was decorated with an elaborate piece of forest sculpture in a design that scrupulously specifies only a single tree. We managed, along with Didi and Gogo, to pass the time, but the production lacked depth, and totally ignored the extremes of Beckett's humor and desperation.

John Hirsch's *Midsummer Night's Dream* was more in control, though the director brought few new ideas to the play aside from a new bag of polyglot costumes. To the accompaniment of string music and twittering birds (for a moment I thought I was listening to the beginning of *Morning Pro Musica*), a boy resembling Huck Finn walked onto Desmond Healey's fake greensward and artificial mossy banks and started to read a book, joined later by an old gardener carrying a cart and a broom. This pastoral American mood was soon broken by a massive battle between Hippolyta's Amazons and Theseus's Athenians in glistening armor, Elizabethan ruffs, and Spanish helmets. Later, Theseus and Hippolyta reappeared as Oberon and Titania—a doubling that is now almost conventional though its purpose, apart from economizing on actors' salaries, has always eluded me. All the fairies were endowed with Mr. Spock's Vulcan ears, but Titania's troupe was clean and fair, while Oberon's was dark and simian in the manner of *Planet of the Apes*.

The rustics were led by the ubiquitous Brian Bedford as Bottom the Weaver, using his personal charm as compensation for any effort at characterization (the festival's star, he gets a lot of plum roles under directors who don't push him hard enough). The Pyramus and Thisbe scenes were consequently a medley of mixed opportunities. Aside from Bedford's desultory performing, the play-within-the-play was too well orchestrated (the tag lines were even punctuated by drumrolls) to capture its crude improvisatory comedy. The lion's costume was obviously conceived and executed by a designer. And all the mechanics employed those condescending Yorkshire accents that pass for English laboring-class dialect. I liked the energy of the lovers, though; the forest scenes still worked their magic; and Bottom's ass's head was the first I've seen that didn't muffle the actor's voice.

Michael Langham's production of *Love's Labour's Lost*, also fairly conventional, was nevertheless an exquisitely detailed and lucid reading of the play. Instead of tying to create an illusionist setting on Tania Moiseiwitsch's handsome thrust stage, John Pennoyer simply furbished it with a few vines and tree trunks, adding a statue of Father Time, and using charming Edwardian costumes to establish mood. "Our court shall be a little Academe," says the King of Navarre, doffing his academic gown and picking up a diploma from some bearded dons, before trying with his three young companions to maintain some scholarly resolve in the face of a visitation by the

Princess of France and her ladies in waiting. Meanwhile, Jaquenetta wanders through the action with her milk pails, being pursued by Costard and Don Armado and goosed by Holofernes with a bamboo cane. Installed in the fields by their monastic hosts, the ladies are equipped with tents and given archery lessons, while Nathaniel, a hip Anglican curate in sandals, tries to hold a conversation with Holofernes, who is snoring away his meal under a napkin ("Magisterial," says the schoolmaster, waking from his snooze and waving away a fart). This fragile difficult play is a delicate story of postponed gratification, of the unnatural suppression of the natural appetites, and I've never seen it better performed or more artfully contrived.

The marvel of the show is John Neville as an antique, foolish, yet oddly affecting Don Armado. Neville enters slowly as if walking on painful bunions, arm held aloft, hair wispy and gray, moustaches curled, wearing an old tattered naval uniform, fingerless gloves, and a cape that seems to be decaying on his body. Neville's model for the role is Don Quixote, and Jaquenetta is his Dulcinea. His Sancho Panza is the precocious Moth, played with sassy grace by Torquil Campbell (the boy's grandfather, Douglas, and father, Benedict, are also in the cast). Armado dips his pen in an inkpot attached to Moth's hat to write a love letter, and Moth begins to sing to him—youth lyricizing old age—moving Armado to tears. It is a remarkable performance, retaining all the qualities of the doltish silly lecher, along with something that is touchingly melancholy and transcendent.

The rest of the cast is very adroit—Benedict Campbell's elegant King, Joseph Ziegler's ironic Berowne, Douglas Campbell's country squire Costard, Nicholas Pennell's pompous Holofernes, Jan Wood's handsome Princess, Rosemary Dunsmore's witty Rosaline, Mary Haney's generous Jaquenetta. Michael Langham has squeezed every possible nuance out of the text, even managing to make the normally gnomic and tiresome scene between Boyet, Costard, and the ladies relatively coherent. For once, I felt that the updating of a Shakespeare play had a motive other than novelty. This was the one production I saw that demonstrated the strengths of the company as an ensemble.

Still, neither this nor any other festival play this season is very ambitious or original, and the problem of evolving a unified vision and clear identity for the company remains unresolved. John Hirsch, entering his final year as artistic director, has managed to stabilize this unwieldy operation—no easy task. His successor will have to decide its future purpose. Equipped with a large and gifted ensemble, a second company from Juilliard, an acting school, a huge support staff, and generous funding, the resources of Stratford are apparently limitless. The question now is whether these resources will be used to help develop an indigenous classical theatre for North America, or simply to continue serving as a semi-British cultural outpost for an indifferent tourist trade.

THE CLASSICAL AVANT-GARDE

(Clytemnestra; The Seven Deadly Sins)

As one of the events of the 1985 Venice Biennale Festival, the Rumanian-American director Andrei Serban and the Italian farceur Dario Fo discussed their differing approaches to the apparatus of *commedia dell'arte*, the first arguing for Gozzi's extravagant fantasies and magical transformations, the other for Goldoni's rougher-hewn, more socially engaged realism. It was a debate over the form and purpose of art that has been going on at least since Plato, but it nonetheless continues to have far-reaching political, social, and aesthetic implications. Should the theatre artist, whether for purposes of celebrating or criticizing reality, present life as it really is? Or should he show us life as it should be, an alternative world as imagined by a unique, sometimes visionary mind.

This argument reflects the irreconcilable conflict between realism and antirealism, between mainstream culture and avant-garde experimentation. Living playwrights being understandably sensitive regarding liberties taken with their works by self-proclaimed auteurs, the experimental director has usually found more scope and independence working with the classics. Although invariably controversial, the approach of what we might call the classical avant-garde is effectively challenging the established style of English classical production so beloved by mainstream audiences and critics. Often trained in Performance-Group techniques, these interpreters are creating what Cocteau called "poetry of the theatre" as distinguished from "poetry *in* the theatre" (e.g., the English verbal emphasis), subordinating language to visual imagery, metaphorical shocks, puppetry, movement, music, sound, and magic. They are also part of a genuinely international movement—developed to a large degree through the interaction of the European and Oriental theatre with the touring (or exiled) American avant-garde—which links artists as diverse in origin as Robert Wilson, Ariane Mnouchkine, Giorgio Strehler, Patrice Chereau, and Tadashi Suzuki.

Two recent contributions to the growing canon of avant-garde classics display these artistic and generic roots: Suzuki's *Clytemnestra* (performed at the Biennale in repertory with his Toga company's version of Chekhov's *Three Sisters*) and Pina Bausch's *Seven Deadly Sins* (performed by her Tanztheater Wuppertal as part of BAM's Next Wave Festival). The Suzuki piece is the last in a trilogy of Greek plays interpreted by this unusual Japanese artist, and it is a remarkable blending of past and present, tradition and experiment, as well as Oriental and Occidental culture. Performed on a bare stage adorned only by five chairs and three cylindrical urns decorated with the logo of Marlboro cigarettes, this piece is Suzuki's own compound of the Aeschylus, Sophocles, and Euripides variants of the Orestes myth, transformed into a cruel dream of family anguish.

Trained in Suzuki's rigorous, highly disciplined physical system, five actors sit impassively in black fedoras and kimonos, staring into space as the audience enters. Orestes appears—an American actor, speaking in English, though dressed in traditional Japanese robes— soon to be joined by three Japanese actors in magnificent Kabuki costumes and wigs, clicking their haunting glottal phrases to the accompaniment of wind sounds and percussion. Joined by Electra and later by Clytemnestra (ferociously portrayed by the majestic Kayoko Shiraishi), they perform a series of mysterious symbolic acts, signals of violence and disruption, transmitted through images of family disintegration. Electra carries an effigy of Aegisthus, which she emasculates with spite and loathing; Clytemnestra carries puppets of dead children, their mouths agape in pain. Orestes agonizes over Apollo's fearful matricidal command ("I walk a cliff edge in a sea of evil, but evil I will do"), then caught in the web of implacable fate stabs his mother in the chest and vagina. Staggering like a surprised bull at the death thrust of the matador, she falls slowly onto Electra and, when pushed roughly away, writhes on the floor, in an extraordinary display of realistic acting, for the long minutes it takes to die.

Later, Clytemnestra reenters as a baleful, hateful ghost, her eyeballs glowing red in her white face, to demand vengeance of the Furies. And despite Apollo's pleas, Orestes must suffer a sequence of punishments, including a beating administered by an old man in a Scottish cape using a club that transforms into an umbrella. Traditional Japanese music turns to modern kitsch played by a salon orchestra, as Orestes holds his sister in a loveless embrace for an incestuous act. Clytemnestra's ghost sinks a knife into Orestes, then covers him with her kimono; all exit, holding their Marlboro urns, as in a marriage procession. The tale has been told, through time warps and space leaps, frozen tableaux and naturalistic actions, in a remarkable merging of Eastern and Western tradition.

"The fundamental drama of our time," says Suzuki, "is anxiety in the face of impending disaster," and the Hiroshima trauma clearly informs the work of most advanced Japanese theatre, including Sanko Jukkai and Dairakuda Kan. The sense of disaster informing Pina Bausch's free rendering of the Brecht-Weill *Seven Deadly Sins* is of a more traditional German kind, with roots in the sadomasochistic fantasies of Fritz Lang, G.W. Pabst, and Frank Wedekind. The piece, originally conceived as a ballet, was choreographed by George Balanchine, first in Europe in the thirties and then (with Allegra Kent and Lotte Lenya playing the twin Annas) at the City Center in New York in 1958. Dance plays a part in the Bausch version, too, but it is a radical departure from the tone and intention of the original.

It's hard for me to judge this presentation. Musically, it's surprisingly weak, with Michael Tilson Thomas conducting Weill's exquisite melancholy music with an amplified orchestra heavy on gongs and cymbals, and Anna I being sung poorly by an actress faltering in pitch and tempo—her radio mike kept failing in crucial passages. (By contrast, Michael Feldman's conducting of the companion piece, *Don't Be Afraid*, as well as the singing in the Brecht-Weill song-collage, were exemplary.) Then, Brecht's sardonic vision of an imaginary America, where to commit "sins" such as Anger (against injustice) or Lust (selfless romantic love) is to risk falling off the economic ladder, has been totally abandoned in favor of relentless variations on the way men force their sexual attentions on women. There's only one sin in

Bausch's *Seven Deadly Sins*, and that's male lust. Hapless Anna II is mauled, manhandled, slapped, felt up, and abused in every conceivable way, becoming a jibbering wreck not just at the end, but after experiences in the very first city she visits. Even her exploiting family is entirely composed of coarse males, though Weill strictly specified the presence of a moustached mother (played by a bass in a wig and dress).

There is, besides, such an age difference between the two Annas that their relationship is no longer a conflict between the practical and emotional sides of a split character, but an association between a demimondaine and her patroness—Catherine Deneuve educating Susan Sarandon in *The Hunger*, with similar lesbian overtones. In short, the Marxist ironies of Brecht's morality play have been buried under monolithic sexual-existential themes.

And yet, while regretting the loss of substance in the original, one cannot help but be dazzled by Bausch's theatricalist imagination. Performed on a bare stage, with a floor designed like a concrete sidewalk (including sewer drains) decorated only with four Biedermeier chairs on which the family sits, the piece is full of physical invention and imagistic surprise. Anna I—signifying her loss of innocence by changing from a simple print dress and Minnie Mouse shoes to a series of suggestive gowns—is always being hounded by a single Leko light on a stand. Men wearing ghoulish makeup and plastered hair wander among the women, suggesting unspeakable acts. A bevy of girls in their underwear, some dazed and drugged, others with sappy smiles, still others defiant, travesty a Michael Bennett chorus line. Men and women identically dressed in black double-breasted suits do a jerky diagonal cross over the stage like robots in Lang's *Metropolis*. A sinister male in a goatee weighs and measures Anna, including her pubic area, as if she were a slab of meat, chalking results on the floor, before grabbing her buttocks and grinding her like a mortar. Spasmodic movements of love and jealousy, grotesque erotic fox-trots out of the drawings of Tomi Ungerer, drag acts, and gross scenes of eating—all help to convey the peculiarly German perception that society is indistinguishable from a butcher shop, where human flesh takes on the quality of pork and beef, and all human instincts are gruesome, vile, and ugly.

Bausch, in short, displays that imagination of disaster which is the hallmark of so much postmodernist art, and with it, the postmodernist insouciance in regard to the integrity of established works. Brecht, though he also expropriated a lot of authorial material for his own purposes (refusing to recognize the value of private property either in literature or life), would probably not have appreciated Bausch's indifference to his thematic intentions, but he might very well have recognized her affinity for his unacknowledged sense of existential horror. It is to the spirit, then, rather than the letter of the text that the classical avant-garde pays allegiance, and a continuing question in the controversy over its productions is whether that spirit is being rejuvenated or defiled.

PRIVATE VIEWS, PUBLIC VISTAS

(A Private View)

I am reluctant to write about Vaclav Havel's *A Private View* at the Public Theatre for reasons that suggest how political considerations can inhibit one's critical judgments. I have not greatly admired Havel's dramatic writings in the past (I found *The Memorandum*, for example, a post-Absurdist contrivance hamstrung by crude linear plotting). But in view of the courageous public actions of this Czech dissident, it somehow seems insensitive to be making aesthetic judgments on his technique. How does one criticize the art of a man exemplary enough to draw tributes from Samuel Beckett and Tom Stoppard without seeming to mitigate one's admiration for his personal heroism? Still, Havel is not just a symbol of political persecution, he is also a serious writer who both seeks and deserves an honest assessment. The problem is that Havel's new play is compromised by the very virtues that make him a hero to the West.

A Private View consists of three short playlets unified by its central figure, Ferdinand Vanek. When we first see Vanek, he has arrived, cap in hand, for an interview with his bibulous boss, the Head Malter in a brewery. An intellectual and a playwright, Vanek has taken this job for reasons partly economic (he needs money), partly political (a troublemaker banned from editorial jobs, he must identify himself with working people). But his beer-soaked interrogator, alternately menacing and friendly in the manner of a Kafka bureaucrat, views him as a condescending creature from another class whose friendship with such dissidents as Pavel Kohout is compromising his credibility with the authorities. Guzzling bottles of brew and interrupting their conversation for frequent piss calls, the boss holds out promise of a better-paying job if Vanek will fix him up with an actress and admit his dissident sympathies. Always humble and agreeable, Vanek will arrange the assignation, but stoutly refuses to inform on himself. The boss grows more sloshed, Vanek makes another entrance to start the interview again, this time assuming the coarse macho manners appropriate to his environment.

"I am a swine and the swine go home," says Brecht's Kragler in *Drums in the Night*, another character who learns that the best defense against authority is pliancy. The second playlet, however, suggests that Vanek's self-denigration is more a modest authorial pose than a strategy for political adaptation. Here Vanek visits two friends from his past, a swinging middle-class couple in a trendy apartment festooned with vulgar objects purchased abroad. "We're having our own little private view here this evening," they tell him. And as he drinks their whiskey from the "States," munches their gourmet "grundles," and tries to admire their conversation-piece confessional and Beidermeier clock, Vanek is unwillingly drawn into the experimental lives of this advanced couple. The wife puts her hand on Vanek's crotch and exposes her breasts while extolling the sexual prowess of her husband. Before long, the couple is making love in front of him—forcing the uneasy Vanek to avert his eyes ("Won't my being around make you nervous?").

Soon they get down to the real subject of the visit, which is to rebuke him for his unorthodox politics and his dissident associates (Kohout is again mentioned as a dangerous influence). If Vanek would only conform he could be enjoying similar luxuries and privileges. Throughout this colloquy, Vanek remains silent, unprotesting, a figure whose very impassivity seems to make his critics furious. Finally, Vanek expresses regret over having caused his friends so much trouble and anguish. And just as he adapted earlier to the proletarian camaraderie demanded by the Head Malter, he now sits contentedly listening to the burgeois friends' rock records and drinking their bourbon.

The plays, apparently, are based on real incidents (also, according to the translator, Vera Blackwell, "real people"). But although Vanek is undoubtedly an autobiographical figure, there are significant differences between the dissident Havel and his unprotesting hero. These are even more evident in the third and final playlet of the evening, *Protest*, which takes place four years later, in 1979. Here Vanek—just released from a year in prison for his political activities—visits a successful writer, Stanek. In the security of his studio, Stanek is able to profess deep contempt for the authorities—"this nation is governed by scum." But publicly, he has been enriching himself by writing for TV and film. Like any other media artist, he displays both guilt and defiance regarding the moral compromises necessary to prosper in such a job, but Stanek greatly admires Vanek's integrity in regard to art and human rights, even though, having read his play about the brewery, he disapproves of the "unrealistic" ending. Now a young friend of Stanek's daughter (she is pregnant by him) has been arrested for political reasons, and Stanek wants Vanek to submit a petition for his release.

Vanek has already written such a petition and collected some signatures, including that of Pavel Kohout. It never occurs to Stanek to sign it himself. Instead, he makes suggestions about how to make the document milder, less provocative, then offers Vanek some money for his persecuted comrades (naturally he doesn't want this known). Still preternaturally mild mannered, Vanek finally asks Stanek to become a signatory to his own petition. The panicked Stanek responds with an outpouring of shame and remorse. He has always assumed that only dissidents made protests, that if you wanted something dangerous done you turned to agents—"Can everybody become a fighter for human rights?" Filled with self-loathing, he determines to regain his lost honor and self-respect, and sign—then rehearses all the reasons why he shouldn't. He will lose his job, his son will be unable to continue with his studies, he will no longer be able to do any "backstage maneuvering." Inevitably, Stanek decides to withhold his name, and when he asks Vanek, "Are you angry?" receives the reply, "I respect your reasoning."

This Christ-like response enrages Stanek. He accuses Vanek of "benevolent hypocrisy," of "moral superiority," of hiding his contempt behind a mask of reasonableness. Still impassive, Vanek refuses to defend himself against these charges. But the issue resolves itself at the end of the play when news comes that the young man has already been released and the petition is unnecessary. Vanek assures the relieved Stanek it was his "backstage maneuvering" that produced the happy results, and, considering for a moment whether to return Stanek's donation, decides to keep the money and leave.

Clearly, Havel has created for himself an insoluble problem: how to dramatize the cowardice of others, by contrast with your own heroism, without appearing impossibly self-righteous. The playwright's strategy is to make Vanek at times a "swine who goes home," scraping before authority and conforming to whatever is demanded, at other times a model of compliant sweetness. Still, the savagery of Havel's satire on the moral dilemmas of those who lack his courage raises doubts about whether he shares his hero's charitable nature. And the difficult sacrifices he has made on behalf of human rights suggest that whatever his faults, conformity is not among them. Vanek, the character, is exonerated from Stanek's accusation of "moral superiority" by the uncritical way he behaves toward others. But the man who invented him cannot entirely escape the same charges.

It is a problem compounded by a conflict between the public and private aspects of Havel's character, between the hero who acts and the playwright who creates. I can't begin to suggest how it could be avoided, except to avoid writing from personal experience. But since political protest is at the very epicenter of Havel's obsessions, this alternative would rob him of his subject. Brecht escaped the problem because he had a much less exalted view of human character ("Unhappy is the land that needs a hero"), including his own. But without personal heroism, a once proud, progressive nation would be doomed eternally to slavish servility.

At the Public, Lee Grant's production strives bravely though not always successfully to disguise the contradictions in Havel's style and tone. Marjorie Bradley Kellogg's set is a garish false proscenium decorated with Communist worker symbols, tanks and hammers, providing an ominous reminder of the totalitarian context of the plays. And Stephen Keep, looking like a latter-day Leslie Howard, manages to keep the character of Vanek modest and charming in the face of the most irritating provocations. But it is these provocations, and Vanek's gentle response to them, that ultimately undermine one's faith in the veracity of the proceedings. They leave one wishing Havel could find a more direct expression of outrage, a better way to contrast his own behavior with that of his craven friends.

A POLISH POLITICAL FABLE

(Cinders)

Janusz Glowacki's *Cinders* is another interesting but flawed entry in the mini-festival of Eastern European plays being presented by Joe Papp at the Public Theatre. Like *A Private View* by the dissident Czech Vaclav Havel, this allegory by a defecting Polish dramatist is deeply engaged and passionately felt—a rebuke to the political insularity, moral limpness, and careerist motives of much American theatre writing. But also like Havel, Glowacki has not proved able to square his ideological designs with his dramaturgical procedures. I am again uncomfortable being obliged to apply aesthetic judgments to a work that took courage to publish. But *Cinders* is further proof that those who write under totalitarianism often have difficulty developing a convincing anecdote and an appropriate style.

Cinders takes place in a reformatory for girls near Warsaw, presided over by a weak humanitarian Principal about to be replaced by an ambitious and ruthless Deputy. The girls are in the process of rehearsing a school play, a dramatization of *Cinderella*, and a professional Film Maker has come to shoot a documentary of the rehearsal process while interviewing the inmates about their personal histories. The film, intended for wide distribution, is meant to "shake up those bleeding hearts in the West," though it is not specified how the true confessions of female thieves and hookers, intercut with scenes from a poorly dramatized fairy story, might influence the thinking of large Western audiences or make its director famous. Nevertheless, the Film Maker proceeds with his heartless on-camera interviews with the girls, recording squalid stories of incestuous relationships, robbery, rape, and violence. All in turn affirm that while Hitler is the man who hurt them most, the man who helped them most is the Deputy.

The girl playing the part of Cinderella, however, refuses to be interviewed or participate, aside from performing her role. Rather like Garga in Brecht's *In the Jungle of Cities*, she will use silence as an expression of her individual freedom and personal autonomy. Naturally, such dissent must be snuffed out, and virtually everyone in the institution—including some of the girls, though not the Principal—conspires to force her into confession. It is to the Principal alone, however, that she tells her true story during a quiet moment of mutual self-exposure: she struck her stepfather when he tried to force himself on her. She, in turn, advises the Principal to become reconciled with his estranged and erring wife, and the two of them, slowly, wanly, back into the only truly human relationship in the entire play.

But it is the Deputy who has the real authority in this institution, and he is determined that Cinderella will either cooperate with the Film Maker or be smashed by the system. When she continues to show passive resistance, the Deputy plants the Film Maker's watch under her pillow and, when this effort to discredit her fails, spreads the rumor that she is a "squealer," thus contriving to have her dealt with harshly by her own fellow inmates.

While engineering this plan, the Deputy listens admiringly to a melancholy song by the inmates about their lonely life in the reformatory, then proceeds to introduce revisions that totally alter the mood and content of the music and lyrics. "Just because it's a cell, why does it immediately have to be dark? . . . The cell should be bright . . . because this kind of pessimism is really uncalled for—it stems from an ignorance of our ever-improving prison system." Before long, such phrases as "shed my tears for wasted years" have been changed into "shed my *fears* for future *years*," and a gloomy lament has evolved into a cheerful, affirmative, hand-clapping anthem. The girls respond to these suggestions like malleable lumps of dough, and they are equally unresistant when the Deputy insinuates suspicions about Cinderella's treachery. In a climactic scene, they fall upon her and beat her savagely. The Principal, pinned to the ground, helplessly witnesses the mayhem. As the camera grinds away remorselessly, Cinderella cuts her wrists and expires on the floor.

It is a heavy-handed conclusion to a generally leaden story, where the pressures of allegory sometimes force the dramatist into unconvincing strategies. I may be missing something, but I don't understand the relationship of the Cinderella fable to the theatrical story. I also find it highly improbable that a group of hard-bitten reformatory inmates would consent to enact a fairy tale as a school play—a piece by Genet would be more likely. But Glowacki apparently chose this device because of its (rather obscure) parallels to his political allegory. Then again, certain key scenes—Cinderella's conversation with the Principal, the Deputy's reworking of the song, a nocturnal abduction for sexual purposes of two girls by the Deputy and the Film Maker—are either not credible in the context of the action or go on long after their ironies have been exhausted by the playwright. And the Film Maker's cold, detached recording of Cinderella's deterioration and death—so reminiscent of Robert Newton in *Odd Man Out* trying to catch on canvas the dying look in the eyes of the wounded James Mason—is too sketchily rendered to have much impact.

A different directorial approach might have illuminated the more enigmatic areas of the play or enhanced its sketchily written values. But John Madden's production, though generally well acted and designed, often compounds instead of solving the dramaturgical problems. Madden is capable of sensitive and meticulous staging, particularly with contemporary plays, but here he seems to sacrifice thematic clarity to theatrical pacing. The evening seems slick from the opening song—a well-rehearsed piece sung by the girls in three-part harmony—and it doesn't improve through the whizbang interlapping of dialogue and scenes. What emerges is a glossy professionalism apparently intended to varnish over the untidiness of the writing. But if *Cinders* had been left a little rougher, and considerably more edged, its meaning might have emerged more convincingly.

Madden, on the other hand, has cast and rehearsed the actors very well, particularly the men. Christopher Walken, his hooded eyes obscured behind dark glasses, feinting and dodging around his equipment like a boxer in leather jacket and black turtleneck sweater, is alternately cocky and bewildered as the intrusive Film Maker. Nothing this dangerous actor does is ever without interest. Robin Gammell as the Deputy provides a fine sneaky characterization of an invidious functionary on a cheerful ascent to power, rotating his head like a swivel as he makes a self-serving speech into an ambulatory camera.

And George Guidall as the Principal gives moral strength to a sacrificial character, the man of conscience trying to preserve a bit of justice in a society of wolves.

Among the women, Lucinda Jenney, who looks a lot like Lindsay Crouse, does presentable work in a role that could use a little more of Crouse's grit. And Dori Hartley, alternating as Prince Charming in the fairy story and the bull dyke who terrorizes the girls, is the one actress in the company who behaves as if she might have done some time in a reformatory. Andrew Jackness's setting—a green and white linoleum floor with institutional furniture—is appropriately bare, and Jane Greenwood's costumes—gray smocks for the girls, limp bureaucratic suits for the men—demonstrate how even contemporary clothes can aid character when created by a gifted designer.

But the play remains dense, opaque, strategic, overly contrived. Philip Roth has said, in a now celebrated statement, that in the West everything goes and nothing matters, while in the East nothing goes and everything matters. That the issues of *Cinders* matter is beyond dispute, but finding a way to express them under conditions of repression requires herculean gifts. Glowacki's style should become either more surreal or more credible, and he needs to trust his audience to recognize irony more quickly. Perhaps now that he has defected to the West, he will be able to put our underused theatrical freedom in the service of a more cogent purpose: the forceful presentation of a powerful political protest.

AN EXISTENTIAL BALLET

(Crime and Punishment)

This summer, Pepsico Summerfare in Purchase—also producing a rich variety of dance, opera, concert, and film offerings—has had the good sense, in theatre, to bring Liviu Ciulei's striking *Midsummer Night's Dream* from Minneapolis, and to invite the Cracow Stary Theatre production of Dostoyevski's *Crime and Punishment*.

The Stary Theatre arrived late when it couldn't obtain the required visas in time for the scheduled opening. The Department of Immigration had determined that this distinguished Polish company was not of sufficient importance to enter our shores. (Another Polish group was denied entrance to Cambridge when the same department concluded that, because the company wanted to play in a church, it couldn't possibly be a serious theatrical enterprise.) Well, one is loath to discourage government bureaucrats from trying their hand at drama criticism. But before expressing their aesthetic judgments they might do well to take a short course in theatre history. They might learn there that Western theatre *began* in a church, and that the Stary Theatre is one of the finest theatre ensembles in the world.

All ended well, after a vigorous letter campaign helped open our golden doors to both these alien companies, and we had the privilege of seeing Andrjez Wajda stage another production in the United States. Wajda had previously directed two plays with my own company—*The Possessed* in 1974 and Tadeusz Rozewicz's *White Marriage* in 1977—after I had had the opportunity to see his *Possessed* during a visit by the Stary Theatre to the London World Theatre Festival in 1973. At that time, Wajda had demonstrated an unusual feeling for Dostoyevski, a remarkable capacity to condense and compress his narrative for the stage. Wajda is one of those directors who move easily between film and theatre, often using the same actors in both media. He is, in fact, presently preparing a movie version of his *Possessed* for Gaumont Pictures.

In between films, Wajda has been developing his Dostoyevski cycle, first with a two-character version of *The Idiot* (not yet seen in this country) and now with *Crime and Punishment*. *Crime and Punishment* is experiencing something of a vogue in theatre these days. The dissident Russian director Yuri Lyubimov did a celebrated production at the Taganka Theatre in Moscow and then, after defecting to the West, staged it again two years ago in London (he is coming to the Arena Stage to direct the play in Washington). Wajda's version has been stripped down to its essential elements—skeletal, pointed, concise. It employs about nine actors playing a variety of parts, but it seems to focus in on only three characters: Raskolnikov, Porfiry, and Sonia.

Even Sonia could be expendable. The production is actually a mating dance between an investigator and his quarry, between pursuer and pursued. Structured in fourteen scenes, all of which take place after the axe murder of the two women, the play subordinates external events and physical action to concentrate on the religious-psychological agony of people in extreme circumstances. As played by Jerry Radziwilowicz, Raskolnikov, from the first moment we see him, is in a state of what the author calls "brain fever." Sporting a two-day beard and steel glasses, dressed in clothes that seem to be peeling off his body, legs bent, hands gnarled, the actor is sometimes hysterical, more often wired. He walks, toes first, as if on cotton, moving in circles and figure eights, or along the wall, his body shaped into a question mark of pain. In *The Possessed*, Wajda began with Stavrogin rattling off his confession at a breakneck pace, with the mud floor of the set caking on his trousers, as if the earth were preparing to swallow him up. In *Crime and Punishment*, Raskolnikov wanders through the action on the edge of madness, wearing a smile that is all teeth and no joy, his mouth moving in silent speech.

From the very beginning, he is presumed to be guilty. Wajda is more interested in the moral crisis of the character than in his narrative, or even in his motives. Porfiry knows about Raskolnikov's article in the *Periodical Review*, where he argued for the rights of extraordinary men to commit crimes and breaches of the law. These Nietzschean impulses are fully explored in the play. "I wanted to be Napoleon, that is why I killed her," Raskolnikov tells Sonia. "I simply did it. I did the murder for myself. . . . I wanted to find out whether I was a louse like everybody else—or a man. Whether I could step over moral barriers or not." And later, referring to the unnamed bureaucracy that could be the Nazi or Soviet extermination machine: "Where is my guilt compared to them? For they themselves kill millions, without any repercussions."

Still, Wajda remains less interested in the intellectual or historical implications of the gratuitous act than in its moral configurations—in how people behave in moments of crisis. In the first of his two scenes with Sonia, Raskolnikov begs her to tell him the story of Lazarus, desperately seeking the possibility of resurrection for himself. After he confesses his crime to her, she—her face shining, clear, enameled, almost transparent—hugs him, kisses his hand, and begs him to stand at the crossroads, kiss the earth, proclaim his guilt, adding, "I will follow you everywhere." Shuddering with self-hatred, unable to understand her love for him, Raskolnikov climbs on top of her with the mordant rejoinder: "Welcome your guest."

But the real love affair is between the murderer and his hunter, Porfiry Petrovich. Brilliantly played by Jerzy Stuhr as a mournful, thoughtful humanist, slightly humped, continually bemused, he is a chain smoker who builds up ash on the end of his (filter!) cigarette at such length that it reinforces suspense over when that other ash will fall. Porfiry moves in lovingly on Raskolnikov as if wooing him for a marriage. He is at once investigator, confessor, and moral conscience to an errant, recalcitrant friend. "Could you bring yourself to rob and murder?" he asks him at the first interview. "If I did," replies Raskolnikov, brushing his hand across Porfiry's vest, "I would certainly not tell you." Later, they have a moment of laughter together, Raskolnikov merely showing his teeth, Porfiry exploding in a hysterical fit that exposes his very glottis and ends in a fit of coughing. Striking Napoleonic poses, exercising his arms and shoulders, Porfiry circles his prey, mouthing affectionate phrases—"My dear Rodion Romanovich, my golden one"—while Raskolnikov squirms in his seat like a man whose insides are bursting out. He tells Raskolnikov how "attracted" he was to him when they first met, how "my heart was throbbing" when he decided to come. With Raskolnikov smiling in silence, Porfiry pokes him with his elbow, strokes his face, holds his hand, pats him, hugs him, exalts him, flatters him, even gets on his knees to plead for his confession.

But Porfiry is not entirely a man of compassion. When the demented prisoner Mikolka, abstractedly touching the floor with his fingers, admits falsely to the murder, he falls into a rage and brutally kicks him. And he goads Raskolnikov into telling the truth not by wheedling or cajoling but with disdainful gibes: "You made up a theory and were ashamed when it broke down," Porfiry jeers, warning him not to commit suicide without leaving behind a "brief but precise note." At the end, he disappears altogether. Raskolnikov confesses tonelessly to Porfiry's clerk, "It was I who killed the old pawnbroker and her sister Lisaveta with an axe and robbed them," while the clerk shows the material evidence to the audience (sitting on wooden benches), as if they were members of a jury.

Krystyna Zachwatowicz's design for *Crime and Punishment* is as fragmentary and as powerful as the production, a series of blistered wooden slats and moldings, cobbled together to form a skeleton of shattered rooms and windows. The design features a pretense of decoration—a photograph of the tsar, framed like a legal document, an odd piece of lace in one of the windows, a flowerpot, a desk covered in green pool-table felt, a bruised tin cylinder for a lamp. We look through doors as if to eavesdrop on the action, or watch the slats change for another perspective on a room. It is a complete world, parallel with our own, yet minimal, bare, and demented. And it collapses entirely when this existential ballet comes to an end, with a clerk presenting evidence, and the murderer washing his hands and the axe with soap: "No trace of blood on it. No trace. No trace."

JAN KOTT, SUPER DRAMATURG

(The Theatre of Essence)

In his introduction to Jan Kott's new collection of essays, *The Theatre of Essence*, Martin Esslin calls him a vestige of a vanishing intellectual class: the guardian of culture and *homme de lettres*. It is a surprising way to characterize the maverick who challenged critical orthodoxy by turning Shakespeare into an anti-Stalinist and reading Greek tragedy through the bifocals of Bertolt Brecht, but I think he is essentially correct. A literary humanist infatuated with the art of the living theatre, a classicist absorbed with the most advanced dramatic forms, an ex-Marxist still dreaming revolutionary fantasies, Kott is something of an anomaly among contemporary scholars—aloof yet engaged, ironic and passionate, a neutral in the battle of the Ancients and the Moderns. Kott is capable of employing the most arcane structuralist and semantic instruments to unearth the radical implications of a text—all the while affirming that a play has no real life until it is staged. This suggests a certain indifference to our literary and political wars. But it is precisely because he is more interested in performance than argumentation that Kott has had so powerful an influence on modern theatre. As the intellectual inspiration for Peter Brook's influential production of *King Lear*, Kott's most famous essay,

"*King Lear* or *Endgame*" (included in his celebrated twenty-year-old book *Shakespeare Our Contemporary*), had a continuing impact on conceptual Shakespeare production comparable only to that of Granville-Barker's Shakespeare essays in the early part of the century. But I suspect that all of Kott's writings have such seminal ambitions— seeds scattered in the rehearsal room as well as the classroom, later to bloom in the form of directorial ideas.

Much of Kott's appeal stems from his irrepressible enthusiasm, an energy at the root of the man's nature, indeed in the very quality of his speech, an often incomprehensible compound of squeaks and shrieks in an often incoherent brand of English that Esslin calls "Kottish." In his new book, this enthusiasm is largely stimulated by the artistic products of his native Poland—the "nowhere" of Alfred Jarry when he made it the mythical setting of his *Ubu Roi*. Eight of the sixteen essays in the volume (nine if you count the Rumanian Ionesco) are about Slavic writers or stage directors, six of them Polish. Yet, even those who do not share Kott's fascination with Witkiewicz or Gombrowicz or Borowski will be interested in the links he establishes between what is usually considered an isolated Middle European literature and the more familiar avant-garde movements of the West. Actually, modern Polish dramatists—who have never really enjoyed the acclaim in this country extended to such innovative Polish directors as Jerzy Grotowski and Tadeusz Kantor—have excited interest among recent critics largely as signposts toward the theatre of the absurd. Even Kott is inclined to read them as road maps. His essay on Stanislaw Witkiewicz (or Witkacy as he called himself), for example, is an intriguing analysis of "a man who came too late"—a precursor of Existentialism who painted and wrote under the influence of narcotics, a prophet of the university revolts of the sixties, an ancestor of Artaud in his approach to the theatre as a sacred place of myths and dreams. Yet, Kott seems reluctant or unable to inspire interest in Witkacy for the quality of his own work rather than for his resemblance to other interesting writers and thinkers.

The significance of Witold Gombrowicz for Kott, on the other hand, is in the way he faced him toward the drama of the past. With *Ivona*, Kott discovered Shakespeare; with *The Marriage*, he found Molière and Rabelais; with *Operetta*, he was in the grip of Aristophanes. In Kott's tendency to establish relationships between the material he examines and similar works of literature, he might strike a casual reader as somewhat academic, except that at the root of these correspondences there is always a profound metaphysical or social or political response as well. It may indeed be that in studying these Polish writers, particularly the Auschwitz novelist Tadeusz Borowski, a suicide at thirty, he is attracted to them precisely for the existential quality of their lives, as desperate men living in extremis under various forms of totalitarianism.

Kott's essays on such experimental directors as Grotowski and Kantor—and his favorite, Peter Brook—have more significance because of the greater impact these figures have had on our own theatre. His appreciations of Kantor's harrowing *Dead Class* and *Wielpole-Wielpole*, not to mention Peter Brook's *Carmen* (though Kott values this production considerably more than I do), are splendid demonstrations of his capacity to surrender himself to what he considers "perfect" theatre experiences: "Perfection signifies only itself and its own possibility. Like a beautiful nude girl. Like a beautiful nude boy. Perfection signifies nothing more than its own existence." Kott's identification of perfection with the human form suggests why he values the theatre so highly—he loves its traffic with the flesh, and, particularly, its nubile actresses.

But Kott's admiration for the fleshly creatures who walk the stage has always been inseparable from his sense of destiny and fatality. It is life and death that inform his concept of the "theatre of essence"— "the human drama freed of accident and of the illusion that there are choices. Essence is a trace, like the still undissolved imprint of a crustacean on a stone." It is what follows an existence created with a sense of free choices, and cancels it, "what remains of us" when everything else has gone, full of doom and finality like death or the Last Judgment.

How wonderful that Kott finds this in the theatre, Sir Philip Sidney's "poor stepsister of the arts," so long disdained by literary humanists. Like most complicated passions, however, Kott's love of essential theatre is easily converted into rage over failed promises. But his examples of meretricious examples of the art are not, as you'd expect, drawn from the commercial stage but, surprisingly, from among the more celebrated avant-garde creations. Two of his key essays are fierce attacks on Grotowski—a director whose influence on our own performance-oriented theatre groups in the late sixties and seventies was without precedent or equal. Significantly, Kott condemns Grotowski not for artistic failures but rather for his remorseless aestheticism and monasticism, and particularly for his religiosity. "After Grotowski's appearances in England and in the United States," he writes, "a couple of nimble-witted critics noted with a certain astonishment that the greatest artistic success of a country which considered itself 'socialistic' was the mystic theatre of obscure religious experiences." Kott is able to admire the heroic discipline of Grotowski—and particularly of his leading artist, Ryszard Cieslak, whom Kott calls one of the great actors of the world—without abandoning himself to the uncritical awe that possessed countercultural and aesthetic critics in the seventies. Kott's objection to Grotowski's theatre, quite simply, is that it is totally apolitical, infatuated with torture, humiliation, and death—a theatre, as it were, for sadomasochistic monks. "I am not sure," he concludes, "whether to accept Grotowski's metaphysics one must believe there is a God. But I am certain that one must give up hope and renounce the possibility of revolt."

This was written before Grotowski abandoned directing for a while to become a guru encouraging followers to hug trees and chase the vernal equinox, but it was the first salvo in Kott's war on the whole phenomenon of "Impossible Theatre," as Herbert Blau called it in a book of the same name. Grotowski, the Living Theatre, Schechner's Performance Group, even his beloved Peter Brook at the time of *Orghast at Persepolis*, were all improvising a sterile aesthetic, where actors learned to scream before they learned to talk, and the window connecting spectators to the stage was shut down by self-reflecting performers engaged in endless rehearsals. Kott saw the clearest reflection of Impossible Theatre in the Haight-Ashbury scene, where flower children turned into pimps and hookers and pot-inspired Bacchic revels were replaced by heroin-influenced violence, just as he saw its consummation in the Kool-Aid killings ordered by Jim Jones in Guyana.

These passages suggest a deep conservative impulse underlying Kott's avant-garde sympathies; often Kott reflects the awesome difficulty of integrating a radical aesthetic with a radical politics. Nevertheless, his obituary for the avant-garde (*"post-modern . . . sounds like post-mortem"*) is premature. I am not certain what he would say about the phoenix that has risen from the ashes of the movement he once declared moribund—the mesmerizing images of *Einstein on the Beach*, the savage ironies of Mabou Mines' *Dead End Kids*, the powerful postlapsarian visions of Martha Clarke's *Garden of Earthly Delights*. But I suspect he might find his demand for a social-metaphysical "theatre of essence" entirely satisfied by these recent triumphs of postmodernism, for they represent a significant theatrical flowering that future historians, perhaps Kott himself, may one day characterize as virtually unprecedented in our culture.

If Kott is sometimes a poor prophet, he is still unequaled in his capacity to draw the parameters that define theatrical achievement. Two of the essays in this book are appreciations of Japanese theatre, coincidentally one of the strongest influences on current postmodern theatrical expression. His description of Noh drama ("surrender to the art of Noh begins in fatigue"), of Bunraku ("in which the mechanism is completely bared"), and of Kabuki ("sex and cruelty in this theatre are signs") could be appropriately applied not only to contemporary productions of Brecht and Genet but also to some of the recent explorations of Robert Wilson, JoAnne Akalaitis, Andrei Serban and Patrice Chereau. Indeed, Oriental influences have now reached down even to Broadway musicals such as Sondheim's *Pacific Overtures*, though not exactly in the form Kott would praise.

The two essays in this volume that show Kott's virtuosity at its most dazzling, however, are not about performance at all, and one of them is not even about the theatre. "The Serpent's Sting," which he calls an introduction to his autobiography, is a fascinating exercise in etymology as a pathway into religion and history, where Kott follows the evolution of the word *sting* from its association with the serpent in the Garden of Eden to its development into the "Hegelian sting" which turns history itself into a form of poison—all as a way of explaining the author's early relationship to the Communist party.

And his essay on Gogol's *The Inspector General*, the crowning glory of the entire book, ranks with Nabokov's as a source of insight into the bottomless wonders of this strange work. Nabokov interpreted the play as a nightmare; Kott reads it as a tragic farce providing links between *commedia dell'arte* and the Marx Brothers and Chaplin, and later Beckett, Ionesco, and Kafka. For Kott, Gogol has created a funny-dreadful world that could only be illustrated by Daumier, where food and eating are the animating images of the comedy, and the nose is the most important organ. By identifying Khlestakov with Harlequin and by analyzing the action as a conflict between a House of Virtue and a House of Deceit, Kott manages to explore the classical roots of the play and its place in theatrical history while also examining its significance in the history of totalitarianism—not to mention his own history at the hands of the Secret Police.

The remaining essays in *The Theatre of Essence* are of varying quality. A piece on Las Vegas as a gigantic setting for the theatre of the absurd ("At five in the morning Las Vegas offers one of the most perfect visions of hell") strikes me as somewhat rambling and forced. His essay on Ionesco, properly admiring of the early short farces, fails to notice a serious deterioration of focus in Ionesco's bloated later plays. And his effort to read Ibsen "anew," while crammed with Kott's customary historical insights (he associates the liberated Hilda Wangel in *Master Builder* with the first woman to cast off corsets, and observes that the play, which culminates in Solness's fatal fall from a tower, was completed in the same year as the construction of the Eiffel Tower), strikes me as occasionally shaky in its judgments. I can't agree that the problematical *John Gabriel Borkman* is Ibsen's finest work ("the only one without a fracture and the only one in which Ibsen is not self-indulgent"), especially when Kott seems to admire it largely because it reminds him of *Endgame*.

While I'm quibbling with these masterly essays, let me mention that Kott's tendency to use different translators (twelve in all) for different essays results in a rather uneven English style, and that the book is indifferently edited. There are occasional variations in the names of characters and playwrights—Beckett's *Hamm* is misspelled as *Ham* (though the clove in this gammon is accurately rendered as *Clov*)—with other errors due to Kott's sometimes mistranslated prose. The famous wails of the Living Theatre in *Paradise Now* ("I'm not allowed to travel without a passport," "I'm not allowed to take my clothes off," "I'm not allowed to smoke marijuana," etc.), for example, come out this way: "We are not allowed to walk around naked, undress, and share grass with each other," which sounds like a passage from the original Polish. (Also, Kott, describing the first performance of the work at Yale, speaks of students "mating in a difficult, uncomfortable, and elaborate lotus position," whereas what I remember is a lot of groping with no sexual consummation whatever).

Still, the importance of this essay lies not in its minor details but in its moral context, which is also true of most of the essays in the book. In *The Theatre of Essence*, Kott is attempting to do for modern theatre what he previously did for Shakespeare and the Greeks, namely to provide a new way of seeing and staging plays in the hope of changing the way we think about our lives. As such, he continues to be a pivotal figure among theatre commentators—generous, dedicated, original, profound. He is another Vergil reincarnated in the form of Super Dramaturg, leading the benighted practitioners of the stage through the bosky thickets of theatrical possibility. I value this man for his intellect and his character. I admire his new book. I am honored to be his colleague and friend.

Part III

Positions

OPINIONS AND CONVICTIONS

Today's text is provided by the poet Heinrich Heine as quoted in a letter to Harold Clurman by Clifford Odets: "Heine said originally that the reason we could no longer build Gothic structures was because they were built from convictions, and we had only opinions. Lacking today the communal life (culture?) that breeds convictions— no longer desirous of abstaining and abnegating self for the greater glory of . . . God, the Christian era is now dying and nothing is yet here to replace it." What a potent distinction!—between an age informed by passionate beliefs and one characterized by purely personal views—and what a devastating charge to make within earshot of a professional opinionator hired to pass judgment regularly on the state of the theatre.

Nobody seriously believes that critics ever helped to build cathedrals. But the notion is disturbing that we might be among those actually blocking their construction. Now I think I know why my obligation to pass judgment has always been a little embarrassing. Oh, I have strong views all right, and it's no secret I can be as arrogant and opinionated as any of my brethren. But the question I have never been satisfactorily able to answer is why my opinions should be considered any more accurate than those of the average theatregoer. It's not enough to produce advanced degrees or even testimonies of practical experience in the profession; so could hundreds of other theatre Ph.D.'s and aging theatre veterans. Credentials can help to inform one's opinions, but they can't guarantee their accuracy. What will then? Posterity perhaps, assuming anyone cares to remember what we once thought. Still, even history is less concerned with a critic's opinions than with his style and ideas. Bernard Shaw was very frequently wrong in his theatrical judgments. To the end of his days, he disliked Oscar Wilde's masterpiece *The Importance of Being Earnest*, much preferring Wilde's trashy melodrama, *An Ideal Husband*, and he praised Ibsen's plays in the wrong order and for all the wrong reasons. Yet, despite his prejudices and errors of judgment, Shaw remains our one example of an ideal drama critic.

We prefer Shaw to a critic with a better box score not just because of his prose style but because he wrote out of conviction. He had a vision of theatre larger than his estimate of individual plays. He had a sense of culture that transcended his personal vanity. Compare our un-Gothic times where merely to be appointed drama critic for a newspaper or magazine is to assume delusions of authority. Even the most inexperienced scrivener, seeing himself in print, is possessed by an impulse to make *ex cathedra* pronouncements. How easy it is to let the criticizing self usurp the criticized object. This behavior is urged on us by the position; it is also demanded by the reader. Of immediate interest in a theatrical notice is not the critic's sense of life, ideas, or vision, but whether or not we liked the damned thing—ironically, since our opinion is the most perishable thing we produce.

Positive and negative judgments are rarely of practical use to theatre people; their only value is to the audience. Once responsible both to his readers and to the stage, the reviewer today feels accountable primarily to the theatregoer, for whom he prepares a form of consumer's report, a guide to comparative shopping. This is understandable, considering the astronomical cost of tickets, but it engages even the more reflective critics in the economics of theatre, not its art. It also encourages hasty, superficial judgments. Consider, for example, the following sentence from my recent review of *The Dresser*: "It has a strong performance from Paul Rogers as Sir; it has a weak one from Tom Courtenay as Norman." Today I feel sheepish about such adjectives, not just because they are blunt and lacking in reinforcement but because my impressions might have been different on another occasion. Performances change from night to night; so, by the way, do a reviewer's moods. Under pressure to publish an opinion, I recorded a fixed perfunctory judgment on a mutable spontaneous process.

I'm not suggesting that theatre critics should abandon judgments but simply that we wed them, whenever possible, to a passionate conviction. It would help, also, if we could temper our declarations with a little self-doubt, remembering that we are fallible too. "I have come to believe," I wrote some years ago, "that the least valuable criticism is that composed of naked assertions of taste (the kind Danny Kaye parodied when, being asked how he liked the Himalayas, replied, 'Loved him, hated her!'). And that is why critics with an ambition to be remembered have poured so much energy into analysis and commentary in the hope that their perceptions might somehow outlive their opinions." If we cannot avoid making judgments, then at least we can try to give those judgments meaning by investing our criticism with reference and learning and a transcendent view of the art we have elected to serve.

Will this help to build cathedrals? I think so, if we can ever be persuaded that a cathedral exists for something other than weddings and confirmations and the comfort of its parishioners. I think a similar thing might be learned about the nature of permanent theatres. Recently, a drama critic for another periodical wrote these words about the failure of the acting company at the Brooklyn Academy of Music: "As soon as the BAM demise was announced, out came the predictable bitter protests from the high-minded apostles of repertory. New York/America demands instant success, they told us yet again; the public and the critics want stars, want glitz, want smart new scripts, won't judge an allegedly growing ensemble by standards different from those used on Broadway. All the usual moans were moaned again about American philistinism in the face of an attempt to build a repertory theatre. To those high-minded people, it is apparently irrelevant that the plays of the second season, like most of the first season, were intolerably performed. The apostles apparently feel—and the theatre is the only art where such a feeling exists—that we ought to go regularly to a company's bad productions just to keep the company alive, so that they can grow to give good performances for the next generation or perhaps the one after."

The only one of these "high-minded apostles" I could identify was myself—there was no mistaking the references to one of my recent articles. Since my colleague left me unnamed, I'll leave him anonymous too, but I believe he offers a good example of what Heine meant by the difference between opinions and convictions. It is not just that he is dazzled by his own "standards" ("It was dreadful. . . . I've rarely seen five productions I could more easily have done without"), but that these opinions seem so much more important to him than the survival of a struggling young company. It is possible to make such judgments, no matter how bald and unqualified, and still recognize that something was lost.

I don't think anybody defended the BAM company's quality in its second season or suggested that people go to see bad productions. I certainly didn't. In fact, I emphasized that "the artistic loss was minimal." To me, the failure was significant in the context of other, more adventurous nonprofit theatres closing down, especially since these losses went largely unrecorded in the press (the *New York Times*, for example, which carried the original announcement of the company on its front page, never reported on the demise of BAM, though it was the only repertory theatre in town). I interpreted this to mean that reviewers like our irritable friend were rating each new BAM production on the same consumer graph as the offerings of the commercial theatre, treating its demise like the closing of a Broadway show that had failed to meet the competition of the marketplace.

I see nothing in his recent statements to change my impression. It is one of the failings of those accustomed to sitting and judging results to be ignorant of the process that achieves those results. But one way to create theatrical works of art is through the slow, organic evolution of developing theatre companies. One does not ask a critic to suspend his standards when evaluating such work, only to recognize as well that a permanent theatre will never have the opportunity to improve enough to meet his "standards" if it ceases to exist. To endorse the destruction of the BAM company because this critic found the second season "dreadful" (even though he expressed "qualified hope" for the first) is not very different in kind from calling for the extinction of the United States because our recent policies have failed and our last five presidents have been lemons. Would he approve the loss of a noncommercial publishing house because of a run of bad books or the end of public radio because of a series of boring programs? Isn't it possible that the preservation of a potentially useful though imperfect institution is at least as important as one's opinion of its quality at any given moment in time?

We who stand in judgment of the theatre have been so busy arbitrating hits and flops that we have failed to provide a context for our criticism, or a consistent point of view, or any salient purpose other than a reputation for good taste. Thus, we have been inexorably absorbed into the commodity culture, left to traffic insolently between the manufacturer and the consumer. At the risk of sounding "high-minded" again, I propose we take a careful look at Heine's distinction, and try to base our standards of value on something deeper than a self-infatuated love of our own personal impressions. Without softening our opinions, we might (how hard it is to say this!) invest them with a little humility.

Humility should come easily enough once we remember how often critics have been wrong in the past. A majority of our tribe initially failed to see the quality of *Ghosts*, of *The Seagull* and *Three Sisters*, of *Heartbreak House*, of *Playboy of the Western World*, of *The Iceman Cometh*, of *Waiting for Godot*, and dozens of other works now recognized as masterpieces. We also allowed one of the few theatrical cathedrals ever built in this country, the Group Theatre, to expire of critical indifference and neglect, because we were too busy savaging the productions to see the value of the company. "This is murder, to be exact," wrote Odets on the occasion of just such a critical reception with the Group, "the murder of talent, of aspiration, of sincerity, the brutal imperception and indifference to one of the few projects that promised to keep the theatre alive. . . . Something will have to be done about these 'critics,' these lean dry men who know little or nothing about the theatre, despite their praise of the actors and production. How can it happen that this small handful of men can do such murderous mischief in a few hours? How can it be that we must all depend on them for our progress and growth . . . they who are not critics, who are insensitive, who understand only the most literal realism. . . . How can the audience be reached directly without the middleman intervention of these fools?"

It is a plaint we hear often in the theatre from those whose backs have felt the critical lash, and for that reason it is easy to dismiss. But if there is just a gram of truth in the charge, do we not stand condemned in the court of history as enemies of the imagination? And is this the epitaph by which we would hope to be remembered?

VARIETIES OF THEATRICAL EXPERIENCE

Recently a theatre management requested that I not review a certain production because the only time I could see it, close to opening, was on a date one night before the critics were officially invited. I did not consider this prohibition unreasonable—theatres have the right to determine when, or even if, a play is ready for critical evaluation. But since the production had been running in previews for over a week, I found it odd that anyone could imagine profound changes happening between one performance and another taking place the very next night.

It then occurred to me (with a start) that I probably would have assumed much the same thing and acted in much the same way regarding one of my own productions. As a theatre director, I share the view that any set of circumstances can have a radical effect on performance, even on succeeding nights. As a critic, I tend to think these variations exist more in the minds of theatre professionals than in the consciousness of those who sit in the audience. Which of me is correct? And what peculiarities of the theatre can explain my split attitudes, my polarized beliefs?

Practitioners are involved with process, observers with results. Since critics form opinions on the basis of a single viewing, we have to assume that the performance we see is fairly representative of those seen by all other audiences. How else are we to commit ourselves with confidence to the relatively permanent state of print? If conditions alter judgment, then there is no stable basis for critical evaluation. Our function is in doubt. It is largely to protect the mystery of our guild that we shrug off apologetic theatre people who greet us saying, "The opening was nervous," or "The energy was low because of a two-day layoff," or "Maude was having trouble with her shoes," or "The overfed Saturday night audience always slows down the show." We know it is a natural impulse to make excuses for inferior work, and actors, playwrights, directors, and producers are as human as the rest of us about rationalizing failure.

Still, anyone who watches the same production in a succession of performances does have to admit that a show can change drastically between the matinee and the evening. Such changes occur often enough in the rehearsal process—a process critics, unfortunately, are rarely in a position to observe. They happen particularly in the final week of technical rehearsals when the introduction of sets, costumes, props, and lights first eclipses the acting, then lifts it into new dimensions. But even after a production has opened and is presumably "fixed," the nightly performance variations have the potential to bring joy or despair into the heart of anyone monitoring the show.

Then there is the audience itself, an element whose influence on performance can never be fully measured. Spectators at a play are not passive witnesses. They are, in a profound sense, additional members of the cast. An audience that rustles programs or coughs or displays other forms of restlessness can throw actors as much as a late entrance or a misplaced prop. Similarly, the audience's healthy laughter or rapt attention can charge a performance with electrical energy. For these reasons, actors speak of audiences as if they had collective personalities or a single identity—friendly or hostile, young or old, bored or attentive, intelligent or dumb. That's why someone visiting an actor's dressing room with praise on his lips will commonly hear his compliment returned: "But you were a wonderful audience." Unlike movie stars, who are unconscious of how the audience is responding, or even if it is there, stage actors consider the audience as collaborators in the process, responsible in no small part for the quality of the performance.

It is true that critics, in their effort to render an objective judgment, usually ignore the audience response—though many of them profess to represent the taste of the average theatregoer. The opening-night audience of the musical *Nine*, for example, carried on in such a tumultous fashion that for a while I feared that the 46th Street Theatre was in danger of demolition, going the way of the Morosco and the Helen Hayes; I hadn't witnessed such riotous behavior since VJ Day in San Francisco during the summer of 1945. Yet, the reviews the next morning neither echoed nor even mentioned the previous night's enthusiasm. This is understandable given the bizarre nature of New York theatre, where standing ovations greet the most dismal displays, and opening nights usually resemble the storming of the Bastille. But even in the theatres of more sedate American cities, an audience's reactions are rarely reflected in reviews.

We critics pride ourselves not only on our detachment but on our steadiness. Once having delivered a judgment, we rarely change our minds. I suspect we are less frightened of being caught in error than of being forced to admit that the whole process of criticism is considerably less than scientific. For this reason, it is probably necessary to believe that the objects we judge are equally steadfast. Imagine our discomfort at discovering that the same play that thrilled or bored us early in the run is capable later of creating an entirely contrary impression. Still, it's a fact that our initial judgment is based on extremely shaky grounds. Myself, I identify brilliance by a tingling sensation that begins around the area of my lower back and then crawls up my spine. I like to think that tingle has brains, though it can be induced by things that are fake or manipulative (Spielberg's *E.T.*, for example, with its Disneyland treatment of children and alien beings), but I know it's not constant. I have felt it often—and lost it often—watching a single production over a period of months.

Since I'm in a confessional mood, let me admit something else. We critics are not impervious to the influences of the moment. I suspect we are more successful at shielding ourselves from the audience than overcoming the frustrations of getting to the theatre, of the hurried meal in an inferior restaurant, of the rudeness of the box office. And what about the companions we bring? Since press agents are kind enough to provide us with two theatre tickets, whoever fills that other seat—be it wife or parent or friend—is bound to be an influence. I once invited a particularly opinionated acquaintance to join me at a play, asking only that he try not to prejudice me by expressing his feelings. He agreed, and twenty minutes later fell fast asleep. This represented a conspicuous, and contagious, form of prejudice, so I rudely nudged him awake.

The presence of a critic can also affect a performance, especially if the critic is powerful. Some actors rise to these occasions, others withdraw, which in turn creates a difficulty for producers regarding whether the critic's presence should be announced. (It's usually better to ignore it, though actors have a way of knowing.) But contrary to common opinion, reviews don't have a lasting influence on performance except insofar as they affect the size of audiences. A bad notice can temporarily demoralize a sensitive actor (sometimes it has a galvanizing effect). But a small house will almost invariably create a pall in the dressing room unless, of course, the company has such a powerful conviction about the play that it would perform it on the Arctic tundra.

This uneasy alliance between those on opposite sides of the footlights creates a permanent state of tension that, in turn, is responsible for a great variety of theatrical experience. That is what both fascinated and frustrated the playwright Pirandello about the theatre process. Part of it is fixed and immutable, part is unpredictable, in flux. Pirandello, who resented the way actors changed his words, also recognized that spontaneity was necessary to life. To ask an actor to refrain from improvising was to freeze a work of art in a permanent state of paralysis. Critics, like all those who deal with words, must assume that what they see is stable and fixed. But a production that remains the same from night to night is a dead thing that narcotizes the audience and fails the playwright.

So what is the actor's function in this paradoxical, enigmatic equation? To inhabit a role so completely that each performance will be a vital, immediate, fresh creation. And what is the critic's role? To sustain the pretense that what he is witnessing on one overwrought, unnatural occasion is pretty much what people will be seeing for the rest of the run. And what is the function of the audience? To judge for themselves in this conflict of fixed opinions and provisional events.

BOARDS VERSUS ARTISTS

At this writing, many cultural institutions are engaged in ongoing internal disputes, which in some cases are endangering their continuing existence. Tensions are often present in collective creative enterprises—people of temperament don't always work easily together.

But it's hard to recall a time when the quarrels have been so numerous or so well publicized. Usually content to record the malpractices of politicians and corporate executives, investigative journalism is now eavesdropping on the boardrooms and rehearsal halls of opera companies, theatres, symphony orchestras, dance groups, and foundations, making the normally sequestered issues dividing professionals, trustees, and management an occasion for an orgy of press exposures.

The *New York Times* alone, in recent weeks, has featured articles on the donnybrook in progress between the board of Lincoln Center and the board of the Vivian Beaumont, the endless saga of the musicians' strike against the New York City Opera Company and the backstage bickering among its trustees, the fiscal and artistic problems of the Stratford Shakespeare Festival in Canada, the nonmusical discord being recorded between symphony orchestra conductors and their players, the prospects of the Bliss regime at the Met, the spiritual malaise afflicting resident theatres throughout the country, even the disputes over grants occurring among the officers of the MacArthur Foundation. This makes for fascinating reading, but in the aggregate it also suggests that something has soured inside our cultural institutions, which cannot be accounted for entirely by the straitened economic condition of the arts at the present time.

The case of the Beaumont is representative. Always the problem child of the Lincoln Center family, it is now being told it will be kicked out of the house altogether if it doesn't straighten up its room. Previous regimes at the Beaumont (there have been five in twenty years) were criticized for their programs; the current leadership is being faulted for its lack of program. The Beaumont has now been dark for five of the last six years, and if Richmond Crinkley, the current director, has his way, renovations will keep it dark indefinitely. Crinkley's preference for reading blueprints instead of developing artistic policy, for collecting building funds instead of raising production money, is the major issue dividing the board of Lincoln Center and the board of the Beaumont, which recently voted (in the absence of its president and chairman) to extend Mr. Crinkley's contract another two years.

In retaliation, the Lincoln Center board voted to deny the Vivian Beaumont the name of Lincoln Center, and to cut off all income from the garage and the corporate drive. It charged that the Beaumont had failed to fulfill the central condition of its lease, namely to produce plays. This function Mr. Crinkley still stoutly refuses to perform—very shrewd of him considering that the one season he managed to throw together was singularly lacking in ambition, artistry, or taste. Thus far, in fact, Mr. Crinkley has failed to display any credentials for his job whatever, apart from an extraordinary capacity, through politicking and lobbying his handpicked trustees, to hold on to it. And while he keeps the Beaumont boarded up, along with the smaller, more experimental Mitzi Newhouse, he spends his leisure time producing on Broadway and trying to auction off the name of the Beaumont auditorium to the highest bidder. Meanwhile, he continues to draw a substantial salary plus fringe benefits and expenses—handsomely rewarded, like farmers paid for not growing alfalfa, for not producing plays.

This backstage drama has limited entertainment possibilities that will have to serve until the time when some genuine theatre is staged at the Beaumont. But it begins to suggest a fundamental reason why the Beaumont, along with so many other artistic institutions, is experiencing such traumas these days. The problem is a vacuum of leadership. Given the circumstances, one cannot question the appropriateness of the actions taken against the Beaumont, though there is a question whether Lincoln Center is legally empowered to influence the independence of one of its resident members. On the other hand, a board will seldom dare to question the conduct of a creative organization, or make a grab for power, unless there is a leadership failure. Lacking a strong director, the trustees will move in like sharks the moment they sense a loss of energy or commitment.

And this has been the case increasingly with the arts as the first generation of America's cultural leaders has begun to die off or retire. The founder of a theatre, a dance company, an orchestra, or an opera is the person who determines its vision and direction. It is this individual who defines the identity of the institution, who informs and articulates its goals and direction. Boards are then formed, to help with fund-raising and to establish links with the community. And as long as the leader remains firm in his conviction, these boards are content with their limited roles. If not, they are replaced. When the trustees of Trinity Repertory in Providence, for example, tried to fire its founding artistic director, Adrian Hall, following a controversial season, he responded by disbanding the board and starting a new one composed of more loyal supporters. And when Joseph Papp took over the Beaumont, he insisted on a board that accepted the limits of its powers—contributing to the fiscal strength of the theatre rather than trying to influence its policy.

Nobody at the Guthrie Theatre in Minneapolis would have dared to tell its founder what to produce or how to produce it, any more than people would have told Balanchine how to choreograph or Picasso how to paint. But the directors who succeeded Tyrone Guthrie have all been under managerial constraints to keep subscriptions stabilized and budgets in balance, to the point where the current artistic head—a world-famous European experimental director—has been charged with producing a summer season composed entirely of musicals, sequentially scheduled since the theatre no longer performs in rotating repertory.

After the first generation of founding artists, in other words, the director tends to become an employee rather than a leader—hand-picked by a board that thereafter controls his destiny. The obsessional quality of the enterprise gives way to more cautious and careful management, while the director spends his time not just planning a season and producing plays but winning the confidence of his board, a process that Peter Zeisler of TCG (Theatre Communication Group) calls "interaction, mutual respect, communications and concern—a commitment to partnership [that] makes new demands on everyone." Zeisler goes on to argue the need for more education of trustees so they will realize that success does not mean momentary popularity or box-office appeal or even critical acclaim. It means rather the "less visible development that insures long-term artistic achievement." Nevertheless, he is responding to a condition in which trustees have gained considerable power over the running of theatres, and where weakened artistic leaders, instead of exercising the authority originally invested in their positions, are now behaving in recognition of the fact they serve at the discretion of their boards.

The analogy with our cherished electoral institutions makes it difficult to criticize a procedure so consensual in its design. But the most adventurous art is not democratic, it is meritocratic, even autocratic, and little of consequence has ever come out of "interaction" with partners who need to be educated into a passion for the creative process (the true supporter, who already feels this passion, doesn't need "interaction"). I fear Zeisler's cordial appeal is a prescription less for positive collaboration than for consensus mediocrity, less a basis for mutual understanding than an invitation into the turmoil we now see afflicting many nonprofit institutions. It is a well-known fact of American culture, reflecting the values of a materialist society, that we have always been more comfortable with management structures and architectural plans than with the troublesome intangibles of the creative imagination. It is not just Richmond Crinkley who knows that money is more easily raised for a renovated theatre with some-body's name on it than for an actor's salary or a playwright's fee. But if we don't want all our cultural institutions to turn into Stonehenge—abandoned artifacts visited by tourists who no longer know their function—then the new generation of artistic leaders had better regain control of their companies, fill the leadership vacuum, and fire their institutions with some of their original conviction.

THE ANT AND THE GRASSHOPPER

The Broadway theatre season, an arthritic grasshopper, has not yet begun to rub its wings; off Broadway is in a cocoon; the Beaumont butterfly remains in chrysalis; the insect kingdom is quiet. Consider-ing the consequent inactivity of culture journalists and the unex-pected availability of feature pages, it is not surprising to see another fantastical stage creature crawling from its heap, the ANT (American National Theatre). In the same week, Roger Stevens and Donald Seawell unveiled a five-million-dollar plan for creating the ANT in Washington and Joseph Papp outlined a ten-million-dollar plan for founding it in New York. Although Papp's money has yet to be raised, Stevens and Seawell have managed to accumulate some of theirs through the sale of the ANTA Theatre on Fifty-second Street. An early version of the ANT, ANTA is an acronym for American National Theatre and Academy, a now moribund institution that, though created with federal approval in the thirties, never amounted to much more than a letterhead and a building. The fate of ANTA, and the origin of its would-be successor, raise suspicions that the idea of an American National Theatre is intimately linked, if not totally identified, with the history of American real estate.

Mr. Stevens, who began his career as a real estate tycoon before becoming a Broadway producer and proprietor of the Kennedy Center, announces the formation of an American National Theatre periodically (most recently, in January 1979). Mr. Papp outlines his plans for an all-star resident theatre company whenever business is slow at the Public. The timing of these dispatches, and the unskeptical way they continue to be reported in the press without mention of the fate or frequency of previous such announcements, suggests that, in addition to belonging to the history of real estate, the American National Theatre is rapidly becoming a chapter in the history of publicity. Perhaps it is time to examine the whole overpublicized, underinvestigated concept.

It is typical of our nation, and its passion for instant culture, to assume that a National Theatre will come into being through a press conference. If we take a moment to look at countries that support such exalted institutions, it is obvious that they have not developed overnight. The Comédie Française, for example, began life as a seventeenth-century acting company touring the provinces under the leadership of Molière. It later played Paris alongside rival companies, and did not achieve national-theatre status until the twentieth century, after it had already become fossilized. As for the British National Theatre, it is a very recent outgrowth of a company formed in the early part of the century that took its name from a delapidated theatre called the Old Vic, first built in 1818. This company was granted neither national status nor state architecture until it had established a glorious record of achievement under Olivier and Richardson, linked to a rigorous training program under Michel Saint-Denis. Like their gardens, European national theatres usually took centuries to grow.

It is debatable, moreover, whether national theatres are possible or even desirable in countries of great size and diversity. Where is China's National Theatre, or those of India, Australia, or Canada? The Soviet Union supports theatre companies in virtually all of its major population centers, but not even such cherished institutions as the Moscow Art or Leningrad Gorki theatres could claim national status without insulting the culture of other cities and disenfranchising other ethnic groups. The United States is even more diverse in its ethnic and racial makeup than the USSR. How could a single

American theatre hope to speak for audiences that include blacks, Hispanics, Jews, WASPs, Irish, Italians, Poles, Hungarians, Orientals, women, and gays, to name but a few of our countless special-interest enclaves, and still maintain an artistic identity of its own? I have often deplored the balkanization of American culture, its failure to develop a unified heritage in the face of so many fragmented, conflicting demands. Because of its community nature, theatre has an important role to play in any process of unification. But it is foolish to think we can have a single National Theatre until we have become a homogeneous nation.

As a matter of fact, the United States does have a National Theatre at present, but it exists in no one institution. It is a compound of the numerous nonprofit resident theatres scattered throughout the land which, over the past two decades (at least), have been offering a great variety of theatrical fare to a great variety of audiences. The press often calls these theatres "regional." It is an unfortunate, vaguely condescending misnomer resented by members of the movement since it suggests that these highly sophisticated institutions are provincial. The same press, paradoxically, praises these theatres for producing risky new works that New York's (nonregional?) theatres are often afraid to touch. But there is one sense in which resident theatres *are* "regional." In addition to their national responsibility to develop new plays and production techniques for the American theatre at large, they also discharge a local obligation, in addressing, both through season programs and affiliate activities, the problems of the surrounding community. In trying to identify the nature and needs of their audiences, such theatres recognize that the stage is not simply an isolated activity self-enclosed within a proscenium and a curtain, but also a continuing dialogue between artists and their neighbors. The content of this dialogue is not always congenial conversation, nor does it usually generate consoling, reinforcing dramatic material. Rather, it has been the responsibility of these institutions to stretch, challenge, even provoke their audiences out of a conviction that, aside from providing art and entertainment, theatre in a community has a dynamic social, educational, even evangelical role.

At least one such theatre, the Arena Stage, already exists in Mr. Stevens's hometown, where for over three decades Zelda Fichandler has been offering new and classical plays to a faithful and appreciative audience. Unlike the Kennedy Center, which houses in its sumptuous halls productions on their way to or from New York, the Arena has tried to be a theatre for the city of Washington, assuming that what's good for the capital can sometimes also be good for the nation. I find it ironic that the Kennedy Center, a well-endowed building with no history whatsoever of originating work with a company, has declared itself *the* National Theatre, while the Arena, a permanent institution with a considerably more distinguished and adventurous record, continues to be considered "regional."

Mr. Stevens is a shrewd and effective Broadway producer with better than average taste, a good reputation among his colleagues, influence in Congress, and access to wealth. If he wants to start a repertory company and hire a competent artistic director to run it, more power to him. It would be a better use of the Kennedy Center than its customary showcase glitter. On the other hand, to call this phantom company the American National Theatre is to confer upon it premature status and prestige before anyone has staged a play or even signed a contract. As for Mr. Papp, he at least has past experience with resident companies (he formed one every summer during the early years of Shakespeare in the Park). And he has the confidence of some of the best actors, directors, and playwrights in the profession. A major repertory company under his direction could be a genuine contribution to the culture of a city that for years has failed to support one; it would certainly be more of an artistic challenge for Papp than running around trying to put together another *Chorus Line*. Still, few know better than the pragmatic Joseph Papp how difficult it is to build such a company in New York, and how much concentration, persistence, and selflessness it takes to get such a difficult project under way.

At all events, if such a company ever materializes, and he has been promising us one for years, I hope Mr. Papp will have the good sense not to nationalize it until he has established its stability and clarified its function. This will take at least a decade. Perhaps we should call a moratorium on all discussions of an American National Theatre, even at the risk of leaving our theatre leaders speechless and our reporters without copy. It is a media illusion with no basis in reality aside from money and real estate, and we have the Beaumont as proof that these materials alone do not produce ANTs. The ANT usually starts to crawl when the grasshopper is lying helpless on the ground. But the two creatures are more alike in nature than would first appear, and equally distant from the process of organic dramatic art.

MUSICAL CHAIRS

Every few years or so around this time, nonprofit theatres begin to shuffle their leadership, which sometimes says more about the state of these institutions than the plays they produce or their annual reports. Roger Stevens—having conjured a poltergeist called the "American National Theatre" at the Kennedy Center—recently appointed Peter Sellars to be its medium, luring this young man away from the Boston Shakespeare Company he had led for less than a year. Whatever its impact on the quality of Washington culture or the future of the abandoned Boston company (now in limbo), the move was shrewdly calculated to score powerfully with the media, without whose collective breath no air would lift (or fill) this South Sea Bubble. Now it is rumored that the board of the Guthrie Theatre—uneasy with the defection of subscribers every time Liviu Ciulei stages something out of the ordinary—has been talking about dropping this gifted classical interpreter in favor of a more conventional artistic director. If this occurs, it would be a kind of Vietnam raid, destroying a valuable theatre in order to save it.

In perhaps the most portentous raid now contemplated, the board of the Vivian Beaumont, represented by former Mayor John Lindsay, has been negotiating with Gregory Mosher, artistic director of the Goodman Theatre, to become the leader of a Lincoln Center house embarrassingly dark for the past six seasons. This is a significant choice for many reasons, not least of them because it suggests that New York may finally be abandoning its fitful efforts to support a major classical repertory company. In the years following the sole Crinkley season at the Beaumont, another vacuum appeared in the city's shrinking theatrical life—the loss of a major showcase for serious new American plays. Broadway's doors are closed to such risky ventures unless they first demonstrate box-office appeal elsewhere. Joseph Papp (who staged only American plays his very first season at the Beaumont) has lately been concentrating on works by European dissidents or the British imports now in vogue. Playwrights Horizons seems to favor screwball comedies and witty satires. Where do heavy hitters go when they want to swing for the bleachers?

To the resident theatres, obviously, and particularly to Chicago, where Mosher has established the Goodman's reputation as a center for new American playwriting. At the root of this development is Mosher's long-standing friendship with the dramatic laureate of Chicago, David Mamet. But the Goodman is now becoming a home for disenfranchised playwrights from all over the country. (In approaching Mosher, the Beaumont board undoubtedly noticed that the only significant American plays of the last Broadway season—Mamet's Pulitzer Prize winning *Glengarry Glen Ross* and David Rabe's *Hurlyburly*—originated at the Goodman in appealing productions.) Mosher is not a flashy director in the Meyerhold tradition. But perhaps for that very reason he inspires extraordinary confidence in the writers he lovingly nurtures. This year, he decided to make these writers the nucleus of a resident company (it is called the New Theatre Company), supplemented by a cadre of actors performing at the small second stage of the Goodman while the main stage is occupied with visiting shows from other theatres and large-scale works such as *Huck Finn* and *A Christmas Carol*.

On a recent trip to Chicago, I saw the group's first production, Chekhov's *The Cherry Orchard* directed by Mosher in a new adaptation by David Mamet. (After this comes a new play by John Guare and an eerie Mamet exploration of psychic swindles called *The Shawl*.) The Chekhov is a risky, perhaps foolhardy choice with which to launch a new company. It requires ensemble playing of the highest quality and experience, and these actors are just beginning to get to know each other. Nevertheless, the production represents a deliberate effort to establish the company's identity swiftly, along with an obvious determination to discover an appropriate American style for modern European classics.

Mosher is a minimalist director who believes a play should be uncluttered by visual metaphors or elaborate designs. Like his production of Mamet's *Edmond*, some seasons back, this *Cherry Orchard* is played on a bare stage adorned by only a few sticks of furniture. The most startling thing about it is Mamet's adaptation, which is bound to be a source of considerable controversy. Working from a literal translation by Peter Nelles, Mamet is clearly determined to excise anything unnatural or literary from the play's language. His version is an act of deconstruction designed to exhume the living energies of Chekhov's writing from under the heavy weight of "masterpiece" topsoil. As a result, the dialogue is a series of interrupted sentences, random hesitations, odd emphases, overlapping lines, simultaneous speeches, and, above all, a colloquial, almost Chicagoized idiom. Mamet the adaptor has turned Chekhov's *Cherry Orchard* into a Mamet play.

Since Mamet has perfect pitch, his dialogue is always authentic and persuasive. Here is a random sample, take from the first act:

GAEV: What a bore. Ah. Ah . . . I bite my tongue. I beg your *pardon*. *Varya*, speaking of your fiancé. In . . .

VARYA: . . . Uncle, . . . let's just . . .

LYUBOV: There's no need to be—we're all glad for you. *Varya*. We are. He's a good *man*, he's . . .

This halting speech with its hints of crudeness and inarticulacy will undoubtedly prove a happy hunting ground for American actors trained in Studio methods. But where Mamet might be faulted is in the way he makes everybody sound alike. His adaptation enjoys a unified style at the cost of Chekhov's theme and character intentions. This is, after all, a play about a change in the social order, and if Ranevskaya stammers as much as Lopakhin or Yasha, then all the semantic differences separating the educated aristrocracy from the servant and middle classes begin to break down—which is to introduce prematurely the democratic leveling process Chekhov (not altogether blissfully) predicted in the play.

The acting reinforces one's sense that class distinctions are being ignored. Mike Nussbaum (of *Glengarry Glen Ross*) is an excellent Semyonov-Pishchik, an exhausted Jew with drooping eyes and knees that seem to sag to the floor. W. H. Macy plays Trofimov with just the right note of intellectual goofiness. And Lindsay Crouse, perhaps a touch too young and not quite volatile enough for Ranevskaya's mercurial moods, nevertheless proves herself a strong mature actress with a rich, supported voice. But there is little to distinguish

Lyubov's daughter Anya from her adopted sister, Varya, or for that matter from the governess Charlotta or the servant Dunyasha, except for slight variations in the timbre of American ingenues. Most disconcerting of all is the Lopakhin of Peter Riegert. Aside from barking his lines at a pitch out of sync with the intimate playing of the other actors in this small house, Riegert transforms this warmhearted vulgarian into a villain out of the mortgage melodramas Chekhov was satirizing. He also appears to be motivated in his vengeful behavior (and his inability to connect with Varya) by a secret passion for Ranevskaya.

I am arguing with this production, but I mean this as a tribute to its strong point of view and clear point of departure. If nothing else, it will help to undermine our silly critical notions of "definitive" Chekhov. Mosher's minimalist approach (like Peter Brook's chairless *Cherry Orchard* in Paris) has his characters sitting on the floor, and omits that ominous harp-string sound, while virtually abandoning any attempt to establish environment, including the cherry orchard outside. Still, he and Mamet make one rethink the play, and that is no small virtue. I'd like to see this company in another *Cherry Orchard* after a few seasons of playing together in a succession of other works.

That opportunity may arise if Mosher agrees to take over the Beaumont, though it is likely that what he would establish there is a playwrights' company doing mainly American plays. Most of the discussions thus far have focused on the Mitzi Newhouse Theatre at the Beaumont, an intimate auditorium similar to the Goodman's second stage. It is reasonable to expect that Mosher would charge it with the same policy. He would like to preserve his attachment to the Goodman, perhaps using the second stage as a preparation area for production at the Newhouse. This is causing some resistance among members of the Goodman board, who understandably object to the theatre Mosher brought to such prominence being used primarily for New York tryouts. What still seems unformulated is a policy for the main stage of the Beaumont. Mosher, who has shown little recent interest in the Goodman's main stage, does not seem temperamentally equipped to mount the kind of lavish classical productions demanded by that formal proscenium house. It may be that some other director will be hired, under Mosher's supervision, to satisfy the theatregoing appetites of a large subscription audience. Another possibility might be for Mosher to import significant classical productions from other resident theatres—as the Arena Stage recently borrowed Lucian Pintilie's brilliant *Tartuffe* from the Guthrie. This would at last give New York the opportunity to see what they've been missing all these years, in residencies short enough to preserve the identity of the visiting companies.

But now a warning. Before settling into darkness under Richmond Crinkley, the troubled Beaumont first took its leadership from Broadway under Kazan and Whitehead, then from the resident theatre ranks under Herbert Blau and Jules Irving of San Francisco's resident Actors Workshop, and then from the adventurous off-Broadway showcases of Joseph Papp. In each case, it reached out to success and turned it into failure. Now the Beaumont is reaching toward a Chicago theatre with a record of developing new American plays that occasionally end up in the market—attracted, as usual, to the commercial result rather than the artistic process. This approach fills a New York vacuum and it may work. But it is bound to put a new kind of pressure on Mosher unlike anything he experienced in Chicago—a pressure to deliver marketable goods. The career of this valuable man could be at a dangerous turn. It would be tragic if the pressures of his new position damaged his capacity to work quietly with gifted American writers, if we were obliged to witness two theatres being destroyed in order to save one.

MOONLIGHTING

Two prestigious British artistic directors got in Dutch recently as a result of moonlighting: Peter Hall, who heads the National Theatre, and Trevor Nunn, who runs the Royal Shakespeare Company. Both were publicly rebuked by the London *Times* for enriching themselves at the expense of their respective institutions. It was an inflammatory charge, particularly at a time when government subsidies for British theatre are dwindling, and some suspected that Rupert Murdoch and his newspaper might be retaliating against the National Theatre's bilious portrait of them in the David Hare/Howard Brenton play

Pravda. Whatever the case, both men responded by filing court actions against the *Times* for punitive damages in order to clear away the taint on their reputations.

One must be careful not to prejudge the outcome of a pending suit (in England, one wouldn't even be allowed to write about it). But this flap raises some interesting issues which may help to clarify what has become an alarmingly murky area of ethical behavior for serious theatre artists. The allegation by the *Times* is that Hall and Nunn have become multimillionaires through commercial enterprises, some involving their subsidized theatres, some not. Hall has been receiving royalties from productions on Broadway and the West End—*Equus* and *Amadeus* among them—while Nunn has punched musical cash registers with *Cats*, *Starlight Express*, *Les Miserables*, and other tuneful windfalls. Neither man denies that he has profited from these theatrical properties. They argue rather that their profits have been exaggerated, and their companies have profited more.

The extent of their income from these extracurricular activities has not been disclosed. But for Nunn at least it is questionably high. To take the most conspicuous example, *Cats* has been playing on Broadway to 101 percent capacity for almost four years. Its weekly take is in the neighborhood of $470,000; directors normally get between 1 percent and 10 percent of the gross, depending on their box-office power. Assuming Mr. Nunn receives a modest 5 percent, he is drawing royalties of over $23,000 a week, or over a million dollars a year in New York alone, not counting the movie sale, the subsidiary rights, or the touring company (which can bring in more than $300,000 a week on the road).

It is considered bad form in democratic countries to criticize an artist's prerogative to command high fees (Communist stage directors are actually just as demanding when weighing offers from theatres in the free world). Many would argue that people such as Hall and Nunn have the right to get as rich as anyone else in our culture, especially since the salaries of artistic directors are not very high. Compared with the art market—where a single painting can fetch a million dollars or more—or with the fees commanded by superstars in opera and classical music, the subsidized theatre is small potatoes. Defending his habit of supplementing his National Theatre income with commercial ventures, Peter Hall, in his *Diaries*, wrote poignantly of the financial troubles he incurred as a result of a number of failed marriages and of his inability to concentrate on work when the bill collector was continually pounding on the door. Aren't an artist's needs as pressing as those of a real estate developer? Indeed they are, but an artist also has some obligation to his calling. The theatre is the only one of the performing arts where people are able to traffic freely between commercial and serious forms. Hence, it is virtually unique in having the potential to implicate its more accomplished talents in specious activities.

Painters, opera singers, and conductors have the capacity to earn a lot of money in our culture, but they are normally paid for doing work they were trained for. In the theatre, the most whopping salaries are reserved for kitsch like *Cats*, not for collective pieces like *Nicholas Nickleby*. Trevor Nunn directed them both; only the second stretched his talents. Collecting his Tony for *Cats*, Nunn remarked: "All I can do is purr," and added, "in England we dream of New York . . . the place where we learn how to do musicals." But it is not unreasonable to ask how much dreaming about New York has affected his dreams of running a classical company, how much "learning how to do musicals" transformed his approach to Shakespeare or influenced his choice of new works at the RSC.

The real issue of moonlighting, in other words, is not the way it inflates the director's money market portfolio but how it affects his talent and, by extension, his involvement with the theatre he leads. It was recently revealed that Nunn had agreed to stage the musical *Chess* on Broadway with the proviso that the Shuberts agree to produce another version of *Nicholas Nickleby*. This somewhat Faustian contract at least involved the RSC—but in an act of commerce, not of art. Compare the negotiations of these establishment directors with such committed artists as Peter Brook or Jerzy Grotowski or Giorgio Strehler or Ariane Mnouchkine or Peter Stein, none of whom (Brook excepted in early career) ever even contemplated working on the commercial stage or long abandoned their companies unless (like Grotowski) to abandon the theatre. The result of their exemplary fidelity was a series of works uncompromising in their vision, unsparing in their purpose, created by artists indifferent to wide audiences or culinary spectacles.

I'm suggesting that a serious consequence of excessive moonlighting is the damage to the company's sense of loyalty insofar as the director's truancy inevitably communicates itself to other members of the group. When Laurence Olivier, still director of the National, accepted some TV commercials, he stipulated that these be shown only in the United States, lest he compromise his reputation among his English acting peers. No such provisos appear in the contracts of his successors in the British theatre establishment. Nunn accepts tasteless musical assignments on the West End as well as Broadway, while Hall seems to spend more time each year away from his theatre than with it. Partly for this reason, the great days of English acting companies, the days when Olivier, Scofield, Finney, Richardson, and Gielgud could occupy the same stage, are over. No sooner does a gifted actor appear on the scene than he is whipped off to movies, television, or the commercial stage, contributing only minimal service to the classical company that brought him prominence.

Of equal seriousness is the influence of moonlighting on a company's choice of plays. It is hardly accidental that the commercial preoccupations of Hall and Nunn have coincided with a significant falling-off in the adventurousness of their theatres. In a sense, the RSC and National are moonlighting whenever they transfer a production to the West End because the actors are then working under different contracts in plays designed for popular audiences. Although not without danger, it is one thing to move a show to a commercial venue for the sake of reaching more spectators or even bringing additional income to a sorely undersubsidized theatre. It is quite another to organize a season in the hope that a percentage of the choices will prove to be commercial hits. Such decisions may well be unconscious; they are certainly subtle and hard to establish. But they are nonetheless insidious, and they are proving significant enough to stimulate talk now in London arts circles of limiting the number of products a subsidized theatre can transfer to the West End.

No such talk is heard in our own country where moonlighting and commercial transfers—often under the auspices of the non-profit institution—are not only approved but encouraged. The artistic director of one large theatrical institution is currently on an indeterminate leave of absence to direct movies, plays, and operas throughout the world. Another—having declared Broadway the "Mecca" toward which everyone aspires—is remounting two works from his repertoire in several cities of the country, New York being their final destination. One does not wish to suggest limits on the possibilities of talented directors in a culture of opportunity. But to accept the leadership of a theatre is to assume certain obligations and responsibilities. For years, I have annoyed theatre people with moralistic sermons on the way we exalt careers and celebrity at the expense of growth and development. I have worried particularly about the corruption of the non-profit theatre movement by commercial opportunism. Now the situation seems to be reaching a head and at last the consequences are being seen. The crises at the RSC and the National, and the stir over Trevor Nunn and Peter Hall, are object lessons in what happens to a theatre when private ambition displaces institutional loyalties, when personal needs overshadow the good of the whole.

MOONLIGHTING II

To judge from newspapers and news magazines, Broadway is healthy again, thanks to a pair of blockbuster musicals from Britain. Critical opinion is divided over which of these extravaganzas is more sublime (British critics prefer *Starlight Express*, American critics like *Les Miserables*). Who cares anyway? Both of these monumental money machines were guaranteed hits long before they even opened, with advance sales in the millions. Where critics *have* been developing a consensus (Frank Rich's article "The Empire Strikes Back" is the required reading here) is over how Britain has managed to conquer Broadway in its last remaining stronghold. Traditionally the proud possession of Americans, the musical is now entirely dominated by composers, lyricists, designers, and directors from the other side of the ocean.

The explanations offered for this are interesting: the English have learned how to substitute spectacle for story; they know how to exploit rock conventions on the stage; they understand the secret of substituting trance-inducing rhythms for a lyrical score. Since theatregoers are happy again and theatre owners are back in business, it's probably pettish of me to raise objections. But my own conclusion in reading about these developments is not that the British have conquered Broadway. It is that Broadway has totally debauched the British. If anyone had prophesied, twenty years ago, that the man responsible for staging the top four West End and Broadway musicals of the eighties was going to be the artistic leader of the Royal Shakespeare Company, he would have been pilloried for impugning the integrity of British culture. Yet, the theatre wonder who brings us *Cats*, *Les Miserables*, *Starlight Express*, *Chess*, and who knows what everlasting triumphs to come, is none other than Mr. Trevor Nunn of the RSC. I know it's considered tasteless to begrudge artists the kind of earnings commanded by chief executive officers of the *Fortune* Five Hundred. Still, Mr. Nunn's income and stock participation are such that might even bring a glint of envy to the eyes of Ivan Boesky. The trade magazine *Variety*—calling Nunn "the new Midas of Legit"— estimates that at a bare minimum he is pulling down $100,000 a week (or over five million a year) in fees and royalties alone.

It was for such activities that both Nunn and Peter Hall of the National Theatre were assailed last spring in the British press for enriching themselves at the expense of their companies. Now Mr. Nunn has virtually abandoned serious company work in order to manufacture musical epics, putting his considerable staging prowess at the service of emotional manipulation—as if Meyerhold had formed an alliance with Victor Herbert. In retrospect, even *Nicholas Nickleby* begins to look like a rehearsal for such epics as *Les Miserables*—if produced today you could bet it would have an Andrew Lloyd Webber score. It was in *Nicholas Nickleby* that we first encountered Mr. Nunn's indignation against an abstraction he calls "social injustice" (remember Roger Rees trying to stimulate our guilt glands as we filed into Shubert Alley?). This, we are told, is also the chief theme of *Les Miserables*. Now that Nunn has garnered so many financial prizes, the only thing left for him, apparently, is the Jean Hersholt Humanitarian Award (perhaps he'll consider tithing his royalties).

As a critic for a London paper in 1972–73, during Trevor Nunn's early years at the RSC, I first noticed how a theatre the once idealistic Peter Hall had built into a powerful and simple Brechtian mechanism had turned into an instrument for showy theatre machinery, stage design, and massive crowd scenes. With hindsight, Nunn's Stratford production of *Titus Andronicus*, with its ostentatious engineering and Cecil B. DeMille battle paraphernalia, seems like a dry run for *Cats*, with its Steven Spielberg space ships and epic junkpiles. But nothing in those early days suggested that the RSC would eventually develop a partnership with the West End, producing musicals and plays as auditions for Broadway. Nor does the RSC seem in any way reformed by Nunn's departure. At this very moment, the company is touring *Kiss Me Kate* in the provinces, while its rival, the National Theatre—inspired by what already appears to be the triumphantly mediocre vision of Peter Hall's successor, Richard Eyre—is preparing a series of American musical comedy revivals for the fall.

Under Laurence Olivier, the National Theatre occasionally produced musical froth, too. But in those days this sort of thing was a holiday for a company devoted to Shakespeare, Ibsen, and new British drama. Today, the state-supported companies are taking holidays most of the year, expending their energies in developing produce for commercial markets. Reading Joe Orton's fascinating diaries (newly edited by John Lahr), and hearing him bitch about the British theatre of the mid-sixties, I was nevertheless struck again by how committed were its playwrights, directors, designers, and actors, how ambitious its goals and aspirations. Although subsidized plays and productions sometimes found their way onto the West End stage, British companies of the time felt no compulsion to design their wares for commercial consumption, and as a matter of fact few were ever successful on the commercial stage. Pinter's *The Homecoming*, in its brilliant RSC production, for example, was stopped in its tracks on Broadway by Walter Kerr, while Orton's own *Entertaining Mr. Sloane* enjoyed a run of only thirteen performances, like all of his New York productions a dismal failure.

By contrast, what passes today for "serious drama" on the Broadway stage are the brittle comedies of Tom Stoppard that come to us courtesy of the National Theatre, along with the middlebrow pretensions of Peter Shaffer and the domestic farces of Michael Frayn, while the Royal Shakespeare Company is busy sending us musicals. American producers (not to mention American critics) visit London regularly to shop for potential Broadway hits; and the British theatre, both commercial and subsidized, responds by trying to manufacture a potentially satisfying product. Under these circumstances, I don't think it is churlish to ask: Who has conquered whom? Has the Empire struck back—or struck out?

The question is important because the conduct of the English theatre has always had an important ripple effect on our own. The

state-subsidized British repertory system, with its devotion to classical plays and new works normally scorned by commercial producers,
was one of the chief models for the budding American resident theatre
movement. Now the majority of non-profit theatres both in England
and the United States have abandoned their original goals to become
launching pads for marketable commodities and partners in commercial production. Without models, aspiration crumbles and definitions
become cloudy; and with the disintegration of the British repertory
model, there are precious few theatres left in the English-speaking
world where artists can feel valued for themselves and not for their
capacity to generate profits, publicity, and royalties. Admittedly,
there are persuasive economic reasons for this deterioration in the
original purpose and ideals of the art theatre movement—principally
the drastic cuts in theatre subsidies under Thatcher and Reagan, and
the selfish atmosphere of entrepreneurism and careerism encouraged
by conservative governments. It is tough enough to live with the
greed, blunders, insensitivity, mean-spiritedness, opportunism, stupidity, and corruption of a bad time. But when our traditional
defenses—the consolations of art and the perceptions of artists who
might analyze and challenge these conditions honestly—are neutral-
ized, then patience and hope begins to fade.

LIBERTY AND LIBERTIES

July has been a month for reflecting on American freedom. The
Statue of Liberty was rededicated by President Reagan a few days
after the Supreme Court ruled that homosexuals have no rights, at
least in Georgia, to make love behind closed doors. At the moment
Reagan was conducting his patriotic orgy on Governor's Island,
pinning a medal on Henry Kissinger and celebrating Frank Sinatra's
moral purity, a mass migration may have been in progress to those
states on the East and West coasts that still have statutes protecting
homosexual rights (once again the cry is: "Wagons ho!"). As for the

newly refurbished Statue of Liberty, she is being elevated less into a symbol of freedom—or even of the open door since we are tightening immigration policy at the same time we are exalting immigrant traditions—than of religious iconography: a homegrown American Madonna with a four-and-a-half-foot nose. Soon the crippled and the infirm will be rushing to touch her copper hide in search of some miraculous cure.

The theatre, being a public art, has always been precariously poised regarding its intrinsic freedoms. Until quite recently, there were moral and sexual constraints; in the thirties and forties, the constraints were political; from the sixties on, constraints have come from a variety of pressure points. Muzzling theatrical expression has always been a sport for groups across the whole ideological spectrum, from extreme right to extreme left. In the most recent flap, a production was excluded from an international festival in Baltimore because of protests from another country. The Theatre of Nations, sponsored by the International Theatre Institute under the presidency of the Nigerian playwright Wole Soyinka, decided to ask Peter Hall to stage his National Theatre production of George Orwell's *Animal Farm* under private auspices at Baltimore's Mechanic Theatre, after representatives of the USSR objected that the work was anti-Soviet.

The fallout from this decision was highly contaminated. Peter Hall cried censorship while Soyinka, having conceded the justice of the Soviet complaints, asserted that his compromise had saved the festival. The resulting acrimony between these two men of the theatre was delicious. Hall accused Soyinka of "Orwellian double-think," while Soyinka countered that Hall "has behaved so badly . . . he should jump in the lake." But it had a positive result in forcing a reexamination, and new appreciation, of Orwell's prophetic novel. The other positive result was the debate it stimulated over the question of censorship in the theatre in response to real or imagined insult.

Soyinka's position, and that of Martha Coigney, vice president of ITI, is that dropping Hall's production from the festival was necessary for the sake of international amity. Mrs. Coigney affirmed that her organization is "guided by the principle of mutual respect of the national traditions of each country." Soyinka insisted that "compromises are made to save a gathering of different cultures." The fact that the Soviet Union was not represented in this festival was ironic but not considered relevant, since its satellites would have protested too, and boycotted the affair. Hall's position was that contact and understanding between nations is important, "but not at any price." Naturally, everybody in the theatre world, including me, had a few words to say to the *Times* correspondents who reported the flap, not once but on three separate occasions.

My own position was that nations, like people, communicate with each other best not by suppressing ideas but rather by exchanging them. Civil libertarians know that freedom of expression cannot be limited to those who share your opinions. If not available to all, it is available to none. Soyinka's decision set a dangerous precedent for the future. It made it infinitely harder, for example, to defend a controversial Soviet play—one perhaps with anti-American content—from suppression by elements of the right. Hall was correct to characterize the "solution" proposed by the festival as a benevolent form of censorship. If a professor, dropped from his own university for "dangerous thoughts," is helped to find a post in a college nearby, he is nonetheless a victim of suppression. Hall was enunciating a crucial principle of free expression, while ITI was acting on an idea of consensual amity and good fellowship—at the expense of artistic freedom.

The puzzling thing to me was how many American theatre people, most of them of liberal beliefs, could ignore this principle in the name of international harmony. But this is a good deal less puzzling when one remembers how vulnerable dramatic art has always been to external pressures from special-interest groups. Unlike the press, where the First Amendment is jealously guarded as a fundamental right, the American theatre has seldom put up a particularly determined fight in defense of its own freedoms. It is virtually impossible to produce Marlowe's *Jew of Malta* these days because of the protest of Jewish groups; Strindberg is rarely staged lest he arouse the ire of feminists; *Huckleberry Finn*, in its various stage adaptations, is still attacked in the mistaken belief that it libels the blacks; Durang's *Sister Mary Ignatius Explains It All For You* has fallen victim to conservative Catholic pressures. Almost any powerful dramatic work can be construed—whether correctly or not—as an insult to some sensitive group or individual; but while the rights of peaceful protest must be staunchly protected, so must the rights of the thing being challenged.

Theatre history is a chronicle of riots against plays, the most celebrated being the fracas at the opening of *Playboy of the Western World*. At that time, audiences interrupted the Abbey Theatre performance of Synge's great play, shrewdly perceiving it to be a slander on Ireland, while Yeats stood alone on stage, screaming at the protesters, "You have disgraced yourselves again." Can anyone imagine an American producer today addressing an audience in that manner? Theatre people have a notorious need to be liked and a notorious fear of giving offense. They can tolerate, without comment, the most outrageous assaults on their calling—and the most ignorant interpretations of their work—if these come from ethnic, sexual, religious, or racial groups who imagine they've been insulted. But the price we pay for our timidity is a growing fear of risk, if not a growing fear of truth. And in the theatre, as elsewhere, only the truth will set us free—"the truth," as Hannah Arendt ruefully added, "which is always awful."

I'm not suggesting that the theatre should be deliberately provocative, but if it's not provoking someone, then it's probably not doing its job, which is to rearrange consciousness. Constitutional safeguards still allow the arts a wide latitude of expression. What's sometimes missing is the courage to employ those freedoms. The rise of ethnic, sexual, and racial awareness—and the invention of such carelessly strewn epithets as *racist* or *sexist* or *homophobe*—has had the effect of thinning the once-tough American skin almost to the point of invisibility. Obviously, it is necessary to be alert to prejudice, but the result of oversensitivity is that many artists find it virtually impossible to create a work of the imagination without imposing some form of self-censorship. Perhaps that is why contemporary American playwrights prefer to write about family conflict and personal relationships rather than extend into public and potentially controversial subjects. Perhaps that is why, when they touch on social themes, they generally limit themselves to such community-endorsed evils as the villainy of the CIA or the scourge of AIDS, while approaching the touchier subjects of race and sex in a consensually approved manner. And perhaps that is why we find the demythologizing satire of Richard Pryor and Howie Mandel so refreshing. Only stand-up comedy today seems brave enough to open up forbidden subjects and expose them to the air through irreverent, uninhibited comment.

As Lenny Bruce once reminded us in a priceless skit, everyone is prejudiced against somebody, but the consequence of denying these feelings publicly is only to send them underground, where they fester and sicken. Genuine racism didn't disappear in America because of legislation or interdiction any more than genuine anti-Semitism disappeared in Germany or Austria after the fall of Hitler. Kurt Waldheim was always there waiting, like a wart, to rise through the transparent skin of religious tolerance. If you push a virulent enemy underground, you can't see him to fight him. And the means you use to suppress your enemy may also be used to suppress a friend.

The Bill of Rights, which incorporates the First Amendment, was an afterthought to the Constitution, largely designed to protect minority rights. Americans are very pious regarding freedom of speech as an abstraction, but its specific advantages are enjoyed primarily by writers, journalists, radicals, and artists. Freedom of speech often collides with the will of the majority, which is why it is protected in courts. It is why the theatre must protect it as well. Henrik Ibsen, who also faced suppression and censorship, knew that freedom was not just a question of voting rights, religious tolerance, or international brotherhood, but something larger and more metaphysical: "As to liberty," he wrote to George Brandes, "I shall never agree to making liberty synonymous with political liberty. What you call liberty, I call liberties; and what I call the struggle for liberty is nothing but the steady, vital growth and pursuit of the very conception of liberty. He who possesses liberty as something already achieved possesses it dead and soulless; for the essence of the idea of liberty is that it continue to develop steadily as men pursue it and make it part of their being." It is these words, and not Emma Lazarus's condescending tribute to "wretched refuse," that should be engraved on the base of the Statue of Liberty, for it is these words that remind us how threats to liberty can lie dormant even in the most benevolent hearts.

THE POST-MODERN BLUES

(The Post-Modern Aura)

Critics have been so busy lamenting the decline of the arts they may not have noticed their own discipline is languishing too. No great authoritative mind is thinking freshly, clearly, and generously about literature or society. The golden age of Trilling, Wilson, Howe, Kazin, Macdonald, Rahv, and others characterized by their broad view of culture has been eclipsed by the leaden climate of a dry narrow decade, with its arcane structuralist pyrotechnics and Neo-Conservative ideological purifying rites. Recognizing this, Charles Newman, in his book *The Post-Modern Aura* (Northwestern University Press), has attempted to restore cultural criticism and history of ideas to their former primacy as intellectual disciplines—a brave, necessary, only marginally successful effort.

Newman's prose reflects the extremity of the problem he is trying to solve. It is often unreadable, dense and oblique, shrouded in technical philosophical terms or graceless colloquialisms. Ironically, Gerald Graff's brief preface to the book is a much more coherent statement of its argument—a critique, in Graff's words, "of the pretensions of the literary-cultural Avant-Garde in the United States today . . . [and] also a critique of the current opposition to the Avant-Garde—neo-realists, academic humanists, and political conservatives." Newman thus casts his net wide enough to include not only American Post-Modernism (contemporary *literature* only), but also all the forces currently arrayed against the Post-Modern sensibility, not excluding public indifference.

What Newman means by "Post-Modern" is never very clear. He is usually more eager to discharge his quasi-conservative fusillades than to bother defining his target. One notes that the "Post-Modern aura" was developed in opposition to the reigning Modernist movement initiated by Flaubert and extended by Joyce, Eliot, and Hemingway, and their effort to link classical traditions to modern perceptions. But Newman identifies precious few Post-Modern writers to illustrate his thesis, which may be why his book has no index. William Gass, John Barth, and Donald Barthelme appear from time to time to represent the Formalist position, while Saul Bellows stands in for Realism. But although the book is studded with scores of philosophers, economists, intellectuals, and structuralists, it offers only niggardly references to the specific artists who constitute its main subject, raising suspicions that Newman, though a novelist himself, is considerably more interested in his ideas than in his examples. Unfortunately, the ideas—as even the titles of his terse chapters ("The Threnody of Solipsism," "The Sublation of the Avant-Garde") sometimes indicate—suffer from a kind of terminal opacity.

Despite all this, I found the book refreshing. Without being a Marxist himself, Newman looks at literature and society through a Marxist prism, and perhaps his most original and controversial assertion is that inflation has affected not only our economics, but also the very way we perceive and propagate our art: "Inflation is reflected in late capitalism not as political havoc but as cultural anomie." Since advanced capitalism, in order to stimulate demand for goods, must needs destroy all vestiges of tradition, it is a perfect breeding grounds for a literature that denies any parenthood, with each writer posing as the last novelist writing the last novel. Newman goes so far as to correlate the consumer price index from 1930 to the present with a graph of literary fashions, in order to demonstrate how fluctuations in the value of money were paralleled by an enormous expansion of the intellectual class. Newman thus sees Post-Modernism as the culminating point of two related inflationary revolutions—an explosion of talent and scepticism following World War II and a revolution in criticism and pedagogy, particularly in journalism and the university.

It is the second revolution that evokes Newman's deepest scorn and generates his most negative energies. Identifying the intellectual liberal classes as publicists for a Modernism stripped of its terror and adversary role, Newman charges these critics with making all art potentially respectable and accessible and thereby bringing about the anti-intellectual reaction of Post-Modernism, a movement impatient with mind and, in the words of Robert Alter, "often tinged with the exhilaration of hysteria about the validity of language and the very enterprise of fiction." But, according to Newman, the second revolution makes the whole idea of an Avant-Garde a sham, since it cannot exist when the Establishment is not coherent enough to attack. This is not a new idea—it was first formulated by Trilling—but it is used to reject both the Post-Modernists and their enemies.

Chief among the latter are the Neo-Conservatives, many of whom have turned into enemies of literature itself in the belief that it can be replaced with their own essays. Newman correctly perceives that if the Avant-Garde is still twitting the bourgeoisie of the fifties, the Neo-Cons are still obsessed with the Avant-Garde of the sixties: "The myth of the doomed creative artist fighting the smug philistine has been replaced by the myth of the parasitical artist living off the public trust." Still posing as Modernists, these critics are continuing to attack mass culture while defending the very social system that insures its hegemony, thus creating "a new 'Adversary' style as shrill and ideological as that of the Anarcho-Leftism it has replaced . . . [offering] no new new standards but only a stingy pathos, that minor tonality which only echoes a dispirited Avant-Garde."

Newman is equally acute about modern literary criticism, which he calls socially useless, a "tyranny of methods," incorporating the artistic prerogatives of self-glorification and megalomania. He is particularly stern toward Harold Bloom, whom he accuses of reducing literature to an Oedipal fantasy (thus validating the generational aggression of graduate students), of confusing art and criticism, and (a fault the author shares) of unclear thought: "Criticism is artistic in that it ought to intensify and clarify perception—not make it impossible."

By the end of the book, Newman has settled down to some serious business—not just the individuals and movements that vitiate culture but the institutions that are helping to destroy it, particularly television and publishing. He sees perniciousness in the way TV treats all events as pure "story," ignoring the complexity of language and the plasticity of life (thus generating in Post-Modernism an unnatural hatred of narrative), and he attacks conglomerate publishing, itself enslaved by bookseller chains, for reducing literature to packaging, for flooding the market with "issue" books (blacks, women, youth), and for creating its own kind of artistic suppression: "A classic totalitarian society censors at the production point. An oligopolistic democracy censors at the distribution point. . . . If a book deserves to be printed and is refused because it won't sell 10,000, that is censorship."

Finally, Newman examines the antinomy between Formalism and Realism, between a literature no longer concerned with the way we live but rather with an endless "interrogation of its own artifice" versus the more accessible, more popular writers who refuse poetical effects and critical theorizing, who dismiss even the Modernist tradition as irrelevant or obscurantist. The conflict is meaningless, Newman writes, when the real enemies are the concentration of economic and political power, careerism, boredom, the cynicism of cultural producers, and the sheer bewilderment of the public. Our literary crisis, in short, is largely institutional, so when Newman, in a hortatory passage, calls for a literature that will help us "unlearn" the traditional oppositions by once again resonating with experience, he seems to be ignoring the very obstacles he has just described. Still, the capacity of this man to contemplate the central questions, no matter how crabbed his diction or gnarled his thought, is itself an encouraging sign in a culture that otherwise seems so bleak and narrow.

I am myself not as despairing as Newman about the future of Post-Modernism, though the institutional environment is much as he depicts it. I speak of course from the perspective of theatre, which Newman fails to consider, but I persist in a belief that there has been an extraordinary outburst of Post-Modernist energy lately, not entirely divorced from experience or moral passion, still groping toward tradition, and that there is a considerable-sized audience poised to receive it. Newman asks, in a typically negative passage, "What happened to that newly sophisticated and enthusiastic literate public created within distinct memory by the explosion of higher education, the new pedagogy, and the enthusiastic assimilation of foreign cultures?" I would answer that it is still visible, and surprisingly hospitable, to compelling works of art, particularly in music, dance, and theatre. The audience for Philip Glass, Laurie Anderson, Steve Reich, and Jean-Michel Jarre—all of whom combine popular styles, classical modes, and Avant-Garde forms—is huge and growing, while the experimental dance and theatre explorations of Mabou Mines, the Wooster Group, Meredith Monk, Paul Taylor, Twyla Tharp, Ping Chong, Martha Clarke, and, preeminently, Robert Wilson, while reflecting the anomie and irony of the age, are also attempting to investigate traditional moral, social, even political subjects, though with new technical and experimental equipment.

It is not hard to produce examples of Post-Modernist music, dance, and theatre that are as self-reflective, solipsistic, alienated, and addicted to "endless, unnerving change" as Newman's Post-Modernist literature. But being involved with a public, the performing arts are always more obliged to discharge a public function. Perhaps because sophisticated critics have largely ignored the performing arts recently, the "second revolution" has not yet absorbed or rationalized their accomplishment. Still, the accomplishment exists and grows, validated by an increasingly receptive audience. It may be, as Newman says, that the Avant-Garde, political and cultural in Europe, is merely aesthetic in America, but there is more to advanced art than just attacking a real or putative Establishment: artistic change may also be measured by revolutionary changes in perception. This is another way of saying that while the institutional environment for culture may be more rigid and venal than ever, and while much of what currently passes for Post-Modern art is fake or corrupted, this country is crazy enough, sufficiently diverse and unpredictable, perhaps even confused enough, to accommodate any inspired figure with the inner resources to break through our baffled sensibilities and transcend our institutional boundaries.

SNARLS FROM THE BEDCLOTHES

Confined to bed with a pneumonia caused by one of those stubborn viral imports from Taiwan, I was permitted to contemplate only theatrical events that came via television, radio, and the newspapers. A high fever always puts you in a state of conflict with your bedclothes. But if I thrashed about enough to leave my Simmons looking like the Meuse-Argonne, this was partly a result of how I reacted to these media irritants. Here follows a short list of what has been raising my temperature lately, which you are perfectly free to dismiss as proceeding from a heat-oppressed brain.

Reagan's acting: I resent hearing Ronald Reagan described as a "former actor." What he has always been—even as a leading man in Hollywood—is an Announcer. That he is one of the most persuasive the entertainment industry has ever produced makes this distinction no less important. Good announcers—Jack Benny's Don Wilson and Johnny Carson's Ed McMahon are examples—often join the banter, but they are basically middlemen between the sponsors and the show. Reagan doesn't act a role. He sells a product—or at best he acts the role of someone selling a product. Reagan first hit his stride as front man for *General Electric Theatre*, not only introducing (and sometimes performing in) the homogenized playlets that followed the commercials, but touring us around the whole General Electric inventory: refrigerators, radios, lamps, toasters, etc. Anyone who remembers him from those days recognizes where he first developed what has since become known as the presidential style. When he proudly displayed the freezer compartment, his baritone rumbling over the new automatic icemaker, Reagan had already assumed all the skills and talents of the Super TV Salesman. The crinkled smiling eyes and waggish shake of the head before a self-mocking anecdote; the sententious crooning delivery, spoken with just enough hesitation to make each phrase seem invented; the emphatic cadences closing in on the low low price of the product; even his walk and his wave—a muscle-bound amble, the arm lifted above bulging pectorals that appear to have been just released from a session with the barbells—all date from the fifties and his marketing of G.E. household wares.

That walk, by the way, suggests the one real role with which Reagan identifies, other than weekend cowboy: Commander-in-Chief. I bet he would have killed to take George C. Scott's place in the movie of *Patton*. Military bands, especially playing "Hail to the Chief," seem to start his glands secreting. What a delicious opportunity to march, strut, wave, smile, stand stiffly erect with hand over heart and eyes directed Godward, and best of all, administer a snappy salute to the flag, a visiting dignitary, or a Boy Scout leader.

The question then arises: Is Reagan formulating policy or only announcing it? Yes, one knows how fiercely he feels about Nicaragua and Star Wars, how devoted he is to scrapping federally funded social programs, how much he supports the idea of a balanced budget and a revised tax code, how committed he is to fighting terrorists everywhere, except where they originate. But what is his responsibility—to devise such plans or to study the script he's handed and then deliver it to the public? I rather doubt, for example, that Reagan could have framed his celebrated characterization of the Contras as "the moral equivalent of the Founding Fathers"—a status to which he has now elevated the "national hero" Colonel North. That literary gem must have been invented by someone else (possibly Criminal Division Chief Stephen Trott, who recently declared in his own voice that "Ed Meese deserves a medal"). This habit of conferring historical immortality on anyone who kills, steals, rapes, cheats, lies, or breaks the law in the interests of the administration is perhaps its most cheeky innovation. But such things continue to be said in violent contradiction of moral reality only because our Amiable Announcer knows precisely how to say them, with just the right unctuous sincerity, with just enough throaty sentiment and conviction.

So I believe Nancy Reagan when she says her husband knew nothing about the covert transfer of funds to the Contras—nothing there to announce. The primary reason he was told about the plan to liberate hostages in return for arms was so that he could broadcast it, if not by the election than by Christmas time—the season when all his equally likable colleagues in advertising, public relations, and the media were also announcing yuletide greetings, gifts, and bargains, while secretly trying to sell us something we didn't want and didn't need.

the CIVIL warS: When I heard that the *New York Times* had sent Donal Henahan to cover the opening night of the Rome section of *the CIVIL warS* at the Brooklyn Academy of Music, I could have written his review for him. Henahan's contempt for the director, Robert Wilson, and composer, Philip Glass, is already on record. What then could have possessed the *Times* to dispatch such a declared enemy of advanced art to such an important postmodernist occasion when there were critics on the staff—John Rockwell and Frank Rich are examples—perfectly capable of understanding and appreciating its intentions. Predictably, Henahan treated the work as some kind of pernicious acid poured on the holy shroud of Western artistic traditions. But as Matthew Epstein argues in the current issue of *Daedalus*, it is precisely this kind of blinkered (and powerful) criticism that has made New York look so provincial as an opera capital by contrast with most German cities, Wales, Scotland, or even Santa Fe and Chicago.

My illness prevented me from seeing the Rome *CIVIL warS* during its run. But we staged a piece of it (the Epilogue) in Cambridge, along with the Cologne section and the "Knee Plays" from the same monumental work. I've also heard portions of Glass's score on tape.

For Henahan to call this music "numbingly primitive . . . incidental and trivial"—or to say the "work . . . makes as little sense as its name"— is virtually to abdicate the obligations of critical perception for the luxury of discharging profuse amounts of bile and spleen. I happen to believe that Glass is the finest American composer after Gershwin, one who, under Indian influences, has restored an ecstatic lyricism and passionate rhythm to advanced music without losing its experimental thrust (my high estimate of Robert Wilson's work is also on record). I know this opinion is not shared by many music critics. But the issue is not whether we opinionators agree on individual theatrical or musical tastes, or even whether the Rome *CIVIL warS* is equal in quality to the other sections of this twelve-hour work. Rather, it is whether contemporary criticism is proving itself equal to what is happening in contemporary culture. Following twenty-five years of severe drought between 1950 and 1975, when it sometimes looked as if the performing arts (dance excepted) were going under, its great figures yielding to death or old age and no significant heirs in sight, we are now experiencing a great outpouring of talent in music, opera, theatre, and performance art, right here in these United States. That this talent still has to go to Europe to achieve recognition suggests that American criticism has not kept pace with its achievements—worse, that criticism has fallen into the conservative slough of our politics, hunkering down on what is safe and secure, putting up barricades before the temples of established values. The paradox is that while the critics remain hostile to this artistry, the audiences are beginning to respond, so that perhaps for the first time in history the avant-garde is proving a popular rather than a coterie phenomenon. As for those who scandalously continue to pour such scorn and derision on the heads of modern artists, I advise them to reread Yeats's "On Those Who Hated *The Playboy of the Western World*." What they are exposing is a strain of fratricidal hatred—an extension, in short, of *CIVIL warS*, as denoted in that bizarre typography Donal Henahan made so little effort to understand.

Simon and Frayn: When the critics trash the genuine artists in our midst, they have to find some substitutes. In the theatre, the current heroes are Neil Simon and Michael Frayn! *Time* magazine recently devoted eight pages and a cover to Simon's new play, *Broadway Bound*, while recommending it for a Pulitzer Prize—who says the news magazines don't pay enough attention to the arts! Loath to sound like all those people who know they hate Robert Wilson's work even when they haven't seen it, I'll try to avoid comment on *Broadway Bound*. I certainly noticed Simon's determination to deepen the sitcom in his last piece, *Biloxi Blues*, and I expect to find the same commendable effort here. But is Neil Simon worthy of being elevated into the pantheon of the blessed just because he is now trying to leaven his one-liners with good honest sentiment? Tom Stoppard was afforded the same awestruck deferential treatment after a few of his characters were seen to weep in *The Real Thing*. Who says a critic's heart is made of stone?

Michael Frayn is being praised again, this time for having taken an unfinished and presumably expendable piece of Chekhov juvenilia and transformed it into a usable theatrical vehicle called *Wild Honey*. I can speak with a little more familiarity about this production since I actually *saw* it in Los Angeles before the New York opening, and I can say without hesitation it's unbearable. The play already enjoys a number of perfectly decent adaptations under such titles as *Platonov* and *Don Juan in the Russian Manner*, the most effective being Alec Szogyi's *A Country Scandal*. This one—having excised what its star, Ian McKellen (in a radio interview), called all the "philosophical, pedantic stuff"—turns the play into an artificial sex comedy, a bubbleheaded Feydeau farce.

I don't want to sound too custodial here; the play is hardly a neglected masterpiece. Chekhov destroyed the original manuscript when it was rejected by a Russian actress; what we have is a voluminous early draft, more valuable to scholars than to spectators. Still, one has to watch the damned thing on stage, with everyone circling each other like windup china figures and Ian McKellen preening about like a self-infatuated dandy. One can only attribute his success as a philanderer to the fact that his women like to be barked at; his Platonov is an exercise not in acting but in voice placement. A lot of perfectly competent American actors have been stranded by this concept of Russian aristocrats as exiles from English playing fields, and by Christopher Morahan's persistently mechanical direction. Recognizing the power of old Pearl White thrillers, Mr. Frayn puts a choo-choo train on stage, and makes Platonov commit suicide by throwing himself, smiling, onto the tracks. For all I cared about any of these artificial people, they could all have been run over by a train.

310 / *Robert Brustein*

THE HUMANIST AND THE ARTIST

In *Theatre Notebook*, the celebrated theatre critic Jan Kott confesses to an attraction to actresses. He was still a schoolboy, he tells us, when he found himself backstage for the first time in his life, clutching a bunch of flowers at the dressing room door of the beautiful Polish actress Lena Zelochowska. Her invitation to enter the room so terrified him that he threw the bouquet on the floor by her feet, and fled.

I am persuaded that, in the intervening years, Professor Kott somehow managed to overcome his terror of the histrionic female animal. But what I find most telling about this story is not his early shyness around women, but rather that his first experience of theatre was of flesh, not language, not scholarship. Looking at Lena Zelochowska with his young, amorous, awestruck eyes, he knew from the beginning that the theatre was something tangible, material, alive.

That is the infinite sadness of the theatre—that it is written in flesh and the flesh is mortal. The actresses who so enchanted the young schoolboy Kott are now all either dead or very ancient. And while the plays in which they performed may have survived in published texts, the performances themselves are now only a fading memory in the minds of the surviving spectators. We in the theatre work always in the knowledge that our work is transient. The months of preparation, the weeks of rehearsal, the days or weeks or months or (if the play is successful) even years of performance—intense as they may have been at the time—lose their physical life the moment the show closes. And that is why a disbanded company of actors, meeting in reunion after many years of separation, find themselves left with nothing to talk about, except to retell anecdotes about performances past. They are trying to stop time, to reconstitute a lost reality, to give some value to a transparent, abandoned episode. "*Ephemera, ephemera,*" says the old actor in David Mamet's play about the stage, *A Life in the Theatre*, as he looks over the vast, empty expanse of empty theatre seats. For ephemeral is precisely what a life in the theatre is doomed to be.

We have methods, in our technological society, with which to preserve the memory of performance—film and videotape, photographs and audiocassettes—none of them very satisfactory. The essence of theatre, which is its presence and immediacy, is invariably lost on celluloid or tape, and in some ways this is a blessing. Styles of theatre change so rapidly that records of performances often seem embarrassing. Marlon Brando is said to have revolutionized naturalistic acting when he first appeared on stage as Stanley Kowalski in *A Streetcar Named Desire*. Looking at the filmed version of that performance today, admirable as it is, makes us conscious not of a new naturalism, but of a stylization so special it attracted dozens of imitators. In the same way, the voice on record of Forbes-Robertson reading Hamlet or John Barrymore acting Richard III now sounds surprisingly cracked and hammy, though both were considered models of "natural" acting in their time. And that has been the awful fate of the theatre—to claim to be providing a model of truthfulness and reality for one age that invariably strikes the next generation as stilted and stuffy. Actors are, in a very real sense, what Hamlet called them—"the abstracts and brief chronicles of the time." Abstract and brief they are indeed. It is immediate time, in all its fleeting, changing evanescence, that they are doomed to chronicle.

So we should be grateful that the theatre leaves no adequate permanent record of itself. We are spared the embarrassment—an embarrassment often expressed by filmmakers—of encountering a work we once were proud of now looking yellow and crumpled, like a piece of fading parchment. It remains true, of course, that the literary side of production is more likely to withstand the ravages of time than the acting or production. The text is often still readable after the performance has died. It is a paradox of the theatre that a text has no real life until it is acted, yet the text is the one thing about the performance that manages to survive.

This is one of those paradoxes that obsessed the Italian dramatist Luigi Pirandello, a paradox that both attracted him to and repelled him from the stage. Only in the spoken performing arts could something fluid and spontaneous have a formal impact on something fixed and immutable. Only in the theatre could we simultaneously satisfy our hunger both for permanence and for change. The words a dramatist wrote were etched in stone, but the actor's art had the capacity to change these words through an improvised action, an extemporized speech, an accident of memory, perhaps even in a catastrophe in the physical theatre itself. "We are not free," wrote the French theatre theorist Antonin Artaud. "And the sky can still fall on our heads. And the theatre has been created to teach us that first of all."

This distressed Pirandello as a writer who valued his own words; it also fascinated him as a philosophical animal playing with ideas. So much so that, in his three plays about the theatre—*Six Characters in Search of an Author, Tonight We Improvise, Each in His Own Way*—he experimented with the conflict between his written language and the actors who, though pledged to speak it, sometimes preferred to substitute their own words, their own lives, expressions, gestures.

The actors' resistance to the playwright is traditional—perhaps it is influenced by a residual memory of early forms of theatre, when performers not playwrights dominated the attention of the audience, when what held the stage were not plays but mimes, interpolations, scenarios, improvisations. Perhaps this resistance reflects the feelings all of us have about hardening into a fixed character determined by others, which others are then in position to analyze and catalogue, perhaps dismiss. It is a resistance to cause-and-effect thinking, to predestination, to determinism, to the sense that we are not free. In a late play, *When One Is a Somebody*, Pirandello dramatizes the sadness of an aging, famous writer (very probably himself), whose every work is acclaimed the same way, no matter how original or innovative it is. He therefore feels trapped inside a persona or mask he finds false to his authentic self. His solution is to publish his next volume of poetry under a pseudonym, and to pretend it has been written by a young man. For a while, the subterfuge succeeds, and the author is hailed, by critics and readers alike, as a new, vital source of youthful energy whose poems vibrate with life. Eventually, of course, the poet is found out, and treated exactly as before—as a distinguished, venerable man of letters with absolutely nothing new to say. In the final scene, he gives a formal speech at a solemn ceremonial occasion; his words are chiseled in marble behind him as he speaks.

So the theatre's greatest failing is also its most triumphant quality—its vulnerability to Time. Like all living flesh, it yields, but also like flesh, it is pulsing and alive. It is this bridge of flesh that has the capacity to span the wide gulf that has traditionally existed between humanism and art, between what is completed and enshrined, and what is ongoing, developing, in process. It is the capacity to be in time and of time that gives the theatre the potential to unite two species—the humanist and the artist—who normally behave toward each other like two mutually hostile and antagonistic carnivores.

In stating this, perhaps I am suggesting something that is not generally acknowledged or openly admitted—namely, that the humanist and the artist, whom one would expect to be natural allies, often tend to ignore each other, when they are not sending off hostile signals. This surprising chasm between two professionals, whose interests overlap, worries me more about the future of American art, particularly its future in the university, than almost any other problem. And if the chasm is not soon bridged, then neither will be able to function in our society with the fullness and amplitude and intelligence that each profession needs in order to flourish.

One thing I have learned over the years is that the ultimate division in this nation is not between conservative and radical, or Democrat and Republican, or elitist and populist, or middle class and working class, or technologist and primitive, or black and white. It is rather a split between those who love the imagination and wish to advance its potential, and those who scorn and fear it. This may sound as if I am pitting artists against the rest of humankind. Quite the contrary, there are a large number of people currently practicing theatre, music, literature, painting, and—need I say?—criticism whom I think of as chief among its enemies. Where you stand in this adversary relationship is determined not by what you do, but by how you respond, by the nature and quality of your spirit. It is determined by how you appreciate the talents and capabilities of others, by whether you are open or closed to what at first seems strange and unfamiliar. And I'm not speaking of a fixed condition, either. I know many people who began with a tendency to close themselves off from imaginative experience, but who later developed extraordinary capacities of response.

So it is possible to be a carpenter or an insurance agent and love the creative imagination, just as it is possible to be a university professor and despise it. I have known a number of distinguished faculty members, many of them in English departments teaching the imaginative literature of the past—Blake and Yeats, Dostoyevski and Tolstoi, Dante and Machiavelli, Proust and Joyce—who have maintained a curious indifference toward modern artists. Yet, these artists had the same adventurousness and quality as those they were teaching

314 / *Robert Brustein*

and studying. If they went to the theatre, they usually chose escapist Broadway commodities, and if they attended classical plays, they invariably preferred conventional revivals. When I was at Yale, running a theatre predominantly designed for a university audience, our most alert, demanding spectators, oddly enough, came not from the English department but from the School of Medicine: epidemiologists, pharmacologists, psychiatrists, internists, doctors, and nurses.

I can only guess at an explanation for this curious situation. One is that those who consider themselves custodians of the past sometimes have an impulse to preserve the past in formaldehyde. In their role as trustees of literature, some scholars seem to feel at ease only with what is authorized and established, which means they are generally conservative in their theories of art, and particularly suspicious of modernist heresies. Classics are regarded with awe and reverence, and new interpretations are often a source of unease and disquiet. I suspect the relationship between the teacher of literature and the practitioner is not so different from that of the art historian and the painter, or the musicologist and the composer. Those engaged in practice seem to constitute a threat to those engaged in curatorial, pedagogical tasks.

I am generalizing wildly, and all generalizations admit of exceptions. But I hope I am describing something you recognize. In the university, there are no wars more savagely fought than those between the literature and theatre departments, and no appointment more fiercely resisted than that of a creative writer or a practicing artist. And the resistance I am describing comes not only from the cloistered academic but from some of the most adventurous literary minds of the age. My old teacher, the great critic of literature and society, Lionel Trilling, once astonished me, after hearing of my interest in the theatre, by wrinkling up his nose and expressing disapproval. It was an inferior art (he informed me), slightly vulgar, not worthy of a serious person's attention. I assumed that he, as an expert in nineteenth-century English literature, was referring to the admittedly inferior dramas of his own period. But no, his disdain was more far ranging than that. He considered the whole of drama to be an orphan of literature. I reminded him, feeling very impertinent, that the greatest writers of all time—the Greek dramatists, the Elizabethans, Molière, Racine, Ibsen, Chekhov, Beckett, Brecht, Shakespeare himself—had all written for the theatre; so, though obviously with considerably less success, had most of the English authors he admired. It was astonishing to me that this brilliant teacher—and I revered him above all living critics—could exclude from his consideration a form of literature so preeminently creative and imaginative.

Only later did I learn that Trilling's disdain masked an early passion that he now considered somewhat shameful. He had hung around theatres as a young man, perhaps admiring actresses as Jan Kott did, and he had even written an approving essay about the early works of Eugene O'Neill. When he began doing textbook anthologies toward the end of his life, Trilling included a fair share of plays in his table of contents, and wrote some brilliant introductory essays about them. I took this to mean that his adversary feelings toward theatre were over. Still, what Trilling was expressing in his earlier remarks to me was the suspiciousness felt by the literary profession in general toward the products of the stage. It was first articulated by Plato in *The Republic*; it was spread throughout Sir Philip Sidney's *Defense of Poesy*; it animated the Puritan hostility that closed down the English theatres for eighteen years following the Cromwellian Revolution. The only way one could put on a play during the Puritan Interregnum was to call it an opera, which perhaps explains why the theatres built in this country in the nineteenth century were usually called opera houses, even though the works done there were spoken not sung. It may even explain why the most popular offering in the third season of the American Repertory Theatre season near Puritan Boston was not a play at all, but an opera, *Orlando*, and why the space where it was staged is called the Loeb Drama Center, not Loeb Theatre.

This Puritan hostility toward stage presentation, recently documented by Jonas Barish in a perceptive study called *Anti-theatrical Prejudice*, has left residual effects up to the present time, especially in the academy. In many English departments, there remains a deep distaste for that which has been "staled" on the stage or "clapper-clawed" by the general public. To many literary academics, even Shakespeare and Sophocles are considered private writers whose poetry is best scanned in the contemplative quiet of the study—writers who would probably have composed prose narratives if the form had been invented in their time.

Now I am a professor of literature myself. But first as an actor, and later in a double role as director of a theatre and head of a conservatory of training, I developed the same conviction as Jan Kott did at that moment he dropped his flowers at the feet of Lena Zelochowska—that the great works of dramatic literature have no reality whatever until they have found their life on the stage. Although the performing arts are still unwelcome at many major American and English universities—it was a professor at Harvard who declared a course in acting to be equivalent to a course in butchering meat—I believe that without the performing arts no university can be complete. If a library is a quintessential research facility, where students of Hellenistic poetry or Idealistic philosophy can investigate the primary and secondary sources of their disciplines, then surely a theatre or concert hall is a living library, where the works of drama or music are in a position to find their true, significant form. It is true that many of these performances are of poor quality; so are many works of scholarship. The important thing is that both scholar and artist should be striving to achieve the highest standards of excellence.

On the other hand, it is a curious aspect of university life that the same people who value professionalism in the humanities often tend to prefer amateurism in the arts. A distinguished professor of philosophy, who takes a stern attitude toward the research papers of his students, recently announced publicly that the best Shakespeare production he had ever seen was one done by an ad hoc student group in a residential house. Now we have all enjoyed extracurricular student productions, just as we have often appreciated student recitals and concerts. But the difference between music and theatre is that while most undergraduate pianists are trained, most undergraduate actors are not. The vitality and imagination and energy of student performance do not sufficiently compensate for an incapacity to speak verse, interpret, characterize, or move gracefully on stage. To say that amateur theatre production is preferable to that done by people with training is really to express contempt for the stage. It is another way of saying that the closet is the most congenial place to examine a play.

So a drama, like a musical composition, really has no ultimate meaning until it has found some embodiment in the fleshly corporality of gifted, trained performers, and this may explain why women and physicians generally constitute the largest audiences for serious theatre. In addition to their intellectual and emotional capacities, both groups stand in a special relationship to the human body. The one by nature, the other by profession, the one through childbearing and nurture, the other through healing and care, have managed to develop a special sensitivity to the kind of natural shocks that flesh is heir to. It is true that one of these shocks can be the size of the doctor's bill. I don't mean to idealize a profession that has often been an appropriate subject for anger and satire, both in the past and the present. But perhaps in recognition of the special nature of women and doctors in regard to physical matters, the modern theatre, at least, has tended to treat both groups as the true humanists of modern times.

It is not Serebryakov, the overindulged professor in Chekhov's *Uncle Vanya*, who understands the misery of the household or protests the plunder of the forests. He is too busy plagiarizing his books, when not exploiting his brother-in-law's free labor. No, the sympathetic humanist in that play is the humane doctor, Astrov. It is not the intellectuals, in the plays of Ibsen, who represent the vanguard of thought and action. It is his female characters, Nora Helmer in *A Doll's House*, Mrs. Alving in *Ghosts*, and Hilda Wangel in *The Master Builder*, just as it is his doctors—Rank, Relling, Stockmann—who are the first to identify the rotten foundations of the social order. Shaw had no use for doctors—he believed, like his predecessors Ben Jonson and Molière, that they are paid to flay a man before they kill him. But he had no patience with orators or liberal intellectuals either. The soft spot in his heart was reserved for what he called the "unwomanly woman"—Candida, Major Barbara, Ann Whitefield in *Man and Superman*—who he believed to be most closely in touch with the life force.

Still, as I cautioned earlier, art is not happy with rigid classifications, and ultimately even this generalization will not hold. A love for the creative imagination is no more a matter of sex or profession than it is of class or educational level or economic status or color. It is rather a gift enjoyed by anyone with psychic generosity, with spiritual expansiveness, with the capacity to face and accept the unknown. Those who reject the imagination are really afraid of life, in all its unkempt, untidy, unpredictable disorder. They resent what cannot be categorized or pigeonholed, what cannot be organized into principles, frozen into theories. And this may help to explain why the university it still likely to be somewhat hostile to the performing arts. Like most institutions, it tends to attract those who want security and order, to whom the unconditioned nature of a living art can sometimes constitute a threat.

318 / *Robert Brustein*

And what about artistic institutions? Are they not subject to the same kind of dangers? Of course they are, and they frequently attract the same kind of security-minded people. The pressures in our culture are simply enormous to channel the rough, ruffled waters of art into navigable streams and smooth, sheltered harbors. These are pressures that come from without; they are also pressures that come from within. How tempting it is to yield to them when they promise peace and tidiness and serenity and approval. And how dangerous, too, for yielding can only lead to a rigidified, conventionalized, safety-conscious art.

The professional theatre today, like all professional organizations, is peopled with fanatics of precision, both in the artistic and managerial areas, spawned by the incredibly complicated procedures of bookkeeping and fund-raising, and by the compulsion of institutions to bureaucratize themselves. As a result of the severe economic problems afflicting the performing arts, such people have begun to dominate the profession, for they sing a siren song of stability and salvation, perhaps even solvency. Such people are important and valuable, but only as long as they serve in a subordinate rather than a ruling function. They are dangerous when they rise to the surface and dominate the arts because they are willing to perform tasks others find onerous.

Because these onerous tasks have multiplied recently, performing-arts groups are currently dominated by these people and their procedures. Some theatres now determine their season choices by sending questionnaires to their subscribers, inquiring after their favorite plays; others base their programs on the kind of fare likely to find favor with the current fashions in public and private funding; one theatre I know, a large, prestigious institution, once considered replacing its current artistic director with a computer—programmed to measure, on the basis of what proved successful with audiences in the past, what combination of plays and players would work in the future. These are theatres run by human calculators, practical, hard-headed people who can justify their procedures by reference to ledgers and balance sheets. But if the management of an artistic institution does not love the imagination, first and foremost, if it does not dedicate itself to the growth of its artists and the development of its public, if it prides itself only on being a self-perpetuating machine, then it might as well be running a processing plant or a fast-food chain.

For the primary function of a theatre is not to please itself, or even to please its audience. It is to serve talent, even when that talent is unruly and disorderly (not, however, when it is destructive, for that ruins the work of the whole). Why this emphasis on the individual talent at the expense of the institution? Because the institution was originally founded—though it sometimes forgets this—for the sake of that talent. It is the destiny of institutions to become routinized, just as it is the fate of successful revolutionaries to turn conservative, authoritarian. As the French philosopher Charles Péguy phrased it: *Tout commence en mystique et finit en politique.* But what use is the practical expertise, the *politique*, unless the institution preserves its *mystique*, its animating idea? And what keeps the fleshly theatre alive but a passionate idea, which is its very mystical breath of creation.

I do not mean to sound disrespectful of all the important administrative functions required for the survival of a collective artistic enterprise. I believe these must be performed, and performed well—but only for the sake of the *mystique*. There is no question whatever in my mind that an arts group that clings stubbornly to its original purpose will eventually triumph, just as I have come to believe that there are forms of survival that almost make failure and defeat seem preferable. I am saying nothing new in suggesting that it is the process of struggle, not the result of success or victory, that is most ennobling. Sophocles understood this, and so did Shakespeare and Ibsen. And Chekhov knew that the creative example, even if momentarily snuffed out by the forces of darkness, would eventually seed itself and multiply. These playwrights are not only our material in the theatre, they have become our mentors and guides. We must be nourished by their example—and multiply.

Let me mention another philosopher-guide, a man not normally associated either with the theatre or the flesh—the Greek philosopher Plato. He disdained all "imitations," especially plays; he believed that artists should be excluded from his ideal Republic. But he was an artist himself, and not a bad dramatist either, to judge by his account of Socrates' trial and death. Plato understood that the ultimate reality was not to be found in material things or institutions, but rather in the Idea, the *mystique*. This Platonic Idea is hard for us to swallow today because it is a spiritual concept, immaterial, as vaporous as thoughts. It is something independent of the physical life; yet it gives our physical life its meaning. It is the spirit that transforms and animates, that pushes us forward, that yields no rest. The institution without an Idea is a decaying institution, no matter how prosperous or popular it may seem at the moment. For it is flesh without spirit, body without soul, an organism with dead cells that prevent its vital growth.

To speak personally for a moment, there were years when I was at Yale—dark and difficult years—when we had an Idea all right, but it sometimes seemed as if we had very little else. We were not a popular theatre, we were failing to communicate our purpose to the public or the company or the students, and as a result our own convictions were getting a little shaky, too. In a moment of despair, my wife turned to me and asked, "What are we doing it for?" And I, not certain what I meant, replied: "We're doing it for Plato." For thirteen years in New Haven, and then for succeeding years in Cambridge, we tried to do it for Plato, and it was not long before we discovered that Plato was not a phantom, that his Idea was composed of flesh and blood, that it was in a lot more people than we ever dreamed. And it was in that Idea that spirit and flesh were unified, and the humanist and the artist held out their hands to each other and were one.